Dénes Bernád

Bulgarian Fighter Colours 1919–1948

Vol. 1

Published in Poland in 2018
by STRATUS s.j.
Po. Box 123,
27-600 Sandomierz 1, Poland
e-mail: office@mmpbooks.biz
as
MMPBooks,
e-mail: rogerw@mmpbooks.biz
© 2018 MMPBooks.
http://www.mmpbooks.biz

ISBN
978-83-65958-18-1

Editor in chief
Roger Wallsgrove

Editorial Team
Bartłomiej Belcarz
Robert Pęczkowski
Artur Juszczak

*Research and text
(in English)*
Dénes Bernád

Colour profiles
Jesters-Ink
Pannon Pixels
Simon Schatz
Balázs Kakuk

Proofreading
Roger Wallsgrove

DTP
Stratus sp. j.

Printed by
Drukarnia Diecezjalna,
ul. Żeromskiego 4,
27-600 Sandomierz
www.wds.pl
marketing@wds.pl

PRINTED IN POLAND

Table of Contents

Acknowledgements

Michael Balss, Dobrinka Boneva, Ivan Borislavov, Sven Carlsen, Ventsislav Chakov, Boris Ciglić, Hans-Georg Dachner, Gencho Dimitrov, Ivan Drenikov, Ventsislav Gramatski, Tony Jones, Nikolay Katsarov, Jaroslav Kreč, Boris Kodikov, Dimităr Lazarov (deceased), Petăr Manolev (deceased), Petko Mandzhukov, Wojciech Mazur, Mitko Mitkov, Teodor Muhovski, Peter Neuwerth, Kamen Nevenkin, Nikola Nikolov, Günther Ott, Penyo Penev, Jiří Rajlich, Stanimir Stanev, Gerhard Stemmer, Vesselin Stoyanov, Rémi Tracanelli, Todor Vălkov, Pavlin Vitanov, Josif Zagorski (deceased).

Photo Credits

Nikolay Bakalov, Ivan Borislavov, Stephan Boshniakov (principal contributor), Nikolay Bratoev-Krizhitski, Bulgarian Aviation Museum (Krumovo), Ventsislav Chakov, Boris Ciglić, DVIA (Veliko Tărnovo), Toshko Dragiev, Ivan Donchev, Saúl Garcia, Thomas Genth, Nikolay Gichev, Iliya Hadzhiliev, Nikolay Katsarov, Peyo Kolev, Tomasz J. Kopański, Jaroslav Kreč, Laslo, Nikolay Lazarov, Manyo Manev, Petăr Manolev (deceased), Mitko Mitkov, Erik Mombeeck, Teodor Muhovski (principal contributor), Peter Neuwerth, Eddie Nielinger, Aleksandar Ognjević, Michal Ovčáčík, pan.bg, Ministry of Defence Photo Archive (Sofia), Preslav Panchaliev, Valentin Petrov, Petko Popganchev, Todor Popov, Jiří Rajlich, Philippe Saintes, Dragan Savić, Nikolai Stanchev, Vesselin Stoyanov, Todor Vălkov, Martin Vyroubal.

Foreword

Bulgaria is arguably historically the most underrated Axis ally that actually fought the Allies during World War II. However, since the Bulgarian Army did not participate in the epic anti-Soviet war, it largely avoided the attention of historians focused on the Eastern Front. Despite remaining outside the main battlefronts of World War II, this Balkan country endure its fair share of warfare, particularly due to the combat activity of its small fighter air force against the armada of US bombers and their fighter escorts, in 1943 and 1944. By the time the last American warplanes vacated Bulgarian airspace in late August 1944, about one hundred of them were left behind, crashed on the territory of wartime 'Greater Bulgaria' (less than half due to Bulgarian interference, though). This notable air activity is largely unknown outside Bulgaria, and is not very much popularised even within the country, despite fully deserving attention.

Very few books have been published about this topic in the past 70 years, in general, let alone in English. Except for the works of the most proficient Bulgarian aviation author, Col. Dimitar Nedialkov, who authored the most detailed account of the topic so far, called 'The History of Bulgarian Air Power', published by Albatros MDV, Sofia, in 2012, and a series of bilingual booklets titled 'Air Power of the Kingdom of Bulgaria' and 'Bulgarian Fighters', only a duo of Bulgarian authors endeavoured to touch this topic in English. They are Stephan Boshniakov and Petko Mandzhukov – whom the Author met for a couple of beers in Sofia, in May 2004 – who devoted a mere 20 pages to the top Bulgarian fighter pilots in 'Slovakian and Bulgarian Aces of World War 2', published by Osprey, UK, in 2004. The only non-Bulgarian author thus far who summarised the main events related to the activity of the Bulgarian aviation during World War II, first in German, then in English, is Hans Werner Neulen. He penned a 22-page chapter in his 'In the Skies of Europe', book published by The Crowood Press in 2000. Beside these aforementioned orks, not much of substance has been published so far in English, or as a matter of fact in any other international language, about the rich history of the Bulgarian aviation in World War 2.

As for books in the Bulgarian language on the activity of the air force, they are surprisingly few. Most notable is the series of three small format books, written by ret. Gen. Maj. Dr. Yordan S. Milanov, which deserves mention. These three booklets (vol. 1, 1995; vol. 2, 1997 and vol. 3, 1999) cover the history of Bulgarian military aviation from 1912 to 1945. They were of great help to me, particularly the information contained in tabular form, easier to digest. Later, the manuscript was published in a single volume, called 'Bulgarian Air Force at War (1912–1945)', by 'Eăr Grup 2000', Sofia, in 2008. The two-volume book by Ivan Borislavov

Monument to Bulgarian aviators, located in Crystal Park, near the University of Sofia. It was erected in 1941 and unveiled the next year. The words under the pilot's figure say: "Higher and higher... to Bulgarian aviators from Bulgarian students". During Communist times, it was relocated to a largely deserted park, and was reinstated only after the regime change in 1989. This statue represents all Bulgarian airmen, and it is a fitting opening illustration to this book dedicated to them. To the memory of all airmen fallen on Bulgarian soil, regardless the flag they fought under, I respectfully express поклон, poklon (bow).

Veteran fighter pilot and instructor with an illustrious, 16-year career, Petăr Manolev (89 years old at that time), along with the Author in Sofia, on 21 May 2004. "Our fighter aviation washed the smeared face of Bulgaria", he said looking straight into my eyes. Those profound words still ring in my ears 13 years later.

and Rumen Kirilov, 'Airplanes of Bulgaria', is also worth mentioning, particularly vol. I (Litera Prima ed., Sofia, 1996), dealing with the period up to the end of WW 2. Finally, a small book by Rumen Rumenin, awkwardly called 'American Terrorism Against the Bulgarians' (Zhar Pticha, i.e. Phoenix, Sofia, 2004), provided some useful data on bombing events, as well as US and Bulgarian airmen.

These few titles only skimmed this complex topic, however. They generally lack the amount of precise details one would expect from a scholarly historical book. Even when such particulars (e.g., aircraft serial numbers, airmen's names, locations, dates, statistics, etc.) are given, they are often erroneous, or misleading. The breakthrough in a 'deep dive' approach into a specific aspect of Bulgarian aviation, in English, is expected to appear very soon, in form of a book dedicated to the Avia B.534 'Dogan' biplane fighter in Bulgarian service. This exemplary work, authored by the Prague-based Jaroslav Kreč – a sample of the manuscript has been reviewed by the Author – to be published by JaPo Books in the Czech Republic, will reveal the precise and detailed history of this nimble pre-war Czechoslovak fighter biplane that even most Bulgarian historians are unaware of.

Ret. Polkovnik (Colonel) Manolev, dean of veteran Bulgarian airmen, passed away on 19 March 2013, at the age of 97. (via Aepo/ Aero)

When my interest about Bulgarian aviation was raised at the end of the 1990s, none of the aforementioned English language books had yet been published. Therefore, lacking any substantial printed sources in an accessible language, I decided to 'dig in' deeper, directly at the source. This niche theme nicely fitted my general interest in the history of Central and East European aviation that I pursue. Obviously, my biggest hindrance was, and still is, the lack of any command of the Bulgarian language. However, I did manage to become skilled in reading Cyrillic characters, and to learn the few basic Bulgarian words crucial to studying any text about aviation.

With the help of a couple of Bulgarian friends – I would highlight primarily Teodor Muhovski, Nikolay Katsarov and Kamen Nevenkin – as well as the aforementioned Czech historian Jaroslav Kreč, I managed to grasp the content of primary documents found during my week-long research trip to the Bulgarian Military Archives (DVIA), located at Veliko Tărnovo, in 2004. Later on, a virtual friend performed 'proxy' research at DVIA on my behalf, in 2014-2015. The many documents unearthed at the archives – some of them reviewed for the first time since they were created in the 1940s – form the backbone of my knowledge about Bulgarian aviation history and the narrative of this very book.

During my research trip to Bulgaria, in May 2004, besides working for a week at the Military Archives, I also had a chance to meet personally a couple of prominent veteran airmen, most notably Petăr Manolev and Dimităr Lazarov, both living in Sofia. I also met the son of the most prolific Bulgarian fighter 'ace' of WW 2, Veselin 'Vesko' Stoyanov, who kindly allowed me to look into the archive and photo albums of his late

Ret. Polkovnik (Col.) Dimităr Lazarov (90 years old at that time), former instructor, then commanding officer of the Messerschmitt Bf 109G-equipped 692. Yato, in his Sofia home, in the company of the Author, on 22 May 2004. "The German pilots were very good to us, we highly respected them. After we turned against them [on 9 September 1944], we were reluctant to fight them, had hard feelings, but had to follow the orders". He passed away in July 2010, at the ago of 96.

father, Stoyan. These fine people, witnesses of an era gone by, gave me unforgettable moments that I cherish even now.

Co-operation with various Bulgarian historians and enthusiasts wasn't always straightforward, and often hit roadblocks. I tried to approach several people I knew were interested in our common topic. Many replied only once or twice, without offering any substantial assistance. Others did not reply at all. Contact with Bulgarian specialised authorities and institutions was also difficult, often cumbersome. Nevertheless, with the help of a few truly caring and enthusiastic Bulgarian (and Czech) friends, mentioned above, I managed to 'squeeze' out important information and a number of astonishing photos from these institutions. Many thanks for their sustained effort. I am also in debt to Stephan Boshniakov for the many photos he kindly sent me throughout the past two and a half decades. Besides them, a number of people, listed in the Acknowledgment section, assisted my work, in some way or other.

My special thanks go to the four graphic artists, 'Jester's Ink', Balázs Kakuk, Simon Schatz and Viktor Szalai, who have created marvellous artwork that greatly enhance this book. We have worked together for many hours in clarifying the most minute details of the aircraft, as well as the camouflage and markings they wore, so we could illustrate the Bulgarian fighters of WW 2 as accurately as possible, based on the limited amount of information and black & white photos available. I truly hope they will continue to fare along with me in the upcoming journeys I already dream about.

One of finest Bulgarian pilots featured in this book is Poruchik (1ˢᵗ Lt.) Nedělcho D. Bonchev, commanding officer of the Bf 109G-equipped 652. Yato, 2/6. Orlyak. He ended up the sixth most successful Bulgarian fighter pilot, with eight victory points on his tally, earned for destroying two 'Flying Fortresses' (one by ramming!), as well as damaging a 'Liberator'. He had to bail out twice during combat. Bonchev died in German captivity, at 26, after being shot down by light anti-aircraft artillery fire on 5 October 1944. Post mortem he was elevated in rank to Kapitan, as of 1 January 1945, and decorated. For the fallen, death was always instant; official rewards arrived only later, if ever. I firmly believe the so far untold story of such brave airmen must be shared with a wider audience. This two-volume book is their story, the Bulgarian airmen's, and the fighter aircraft they flew, in peace and in war.

To these fine people, few and far between, 'A Few Good Men' (Jack Nicholson, I salute you!), I address simply, but straight out of my heart, by saying благодаря, i.e., blagodarya, thank you, in Bulgarian.

Following an unrealised book project with Squadron/Signal Publications (Texas, USA), in 1997, the first concrete result of my research activity related to the history of Bulgarian aviation was the two-part series of articles about the first 35 years of Bulgarian aircraft production. This study, titled 'Balkan Birds', was published in the UK in 2001, in the issues No. 94 and 96 of AIR Enthusiast Quarterly. However, the pinnacle of my research, spanning more than two and a half decades, is represented by this two-volume book on Bulgarian fighter and fighter-trainer aircraft. I have worked on the manuscript for over ten years, vacation after vacation, week-end by week-end. I spent uncounted number of days (and nights) in attempting to decipher the actual story of the Bulgarian fighter force, the aircraft types employed and the people who flew them. When I asked a prominent Bulgarian aviation historian, otherwise not overly friendly and helpful (his name is included in the Acknowledgments) about a specific detail regarding a particular aircraft, he replied the following: "Не знам. Никой не се задълбочава в темата, както Вас!" ("I don't know. No one gets deeper into the subject than you do!")

A final thought. Some are proud of climbing a high mountain, others for running the marathon. I take pride not in my physical strength, but in my mental stamina. I am satisfied that I managed to compile a 250,000-word text, illustrated with over 700 photos and almost 100 high quality colour profiles, about an obscure topic related to the history of a country whose language I don't speak, over 1,000 km from my home, thus making personal research very difficult. But eventually I made it! I reached the peak, I crossed the finish line. A true mental marathon it was! Honestly, I have never thought I would reach this far. Therefore, I consider this two-volume work the pinnacle of my career of aviation historian and author – so far.

I trust I managed to put together the mosaic properly, and illustrate it accurately, to the delight of the ultimate audience. You, the Reader.

Dénes Bernád
Christmas Eve, 2017

The Author can be contacted directly, at the following e-mail address: denesbernad@hotmail.com

Camouflage Paints and Colours
of Bulgarian Aircraft (1937–1945)

It was during the research and writing phase of the Camouflage and Colours chapter of the Hungarian Fighter Colours book[1], when the Author realised that the topic of paints and lacquers used on aircraft exported to Germany's allies is much more complicated than thus far described in various specialised literature, if mentioned at all. It turned out that this topic has been little researched. Usually, the very simplistic view of "standard German RLM camouflage colours were used" is prevailing. In fact, this brief and simplistic statement cannot be farther from the truth! It is now obvious that this topic needs a fresh look, research has to start from scratch, all preconceptions have to be set aside. This new vision and in-depth research led the Author and his colleague, György Punka, to discover the Hungarian-produced aircraft paints and lacquers, primarily by Krayer E. & Co in Budapest (the Cellaetern brand of nitrocellulose paints), their unique colour shades (similar, but not identical to the German RLM camouflage colours), the original paint and lacquer recipes of Krayer, and the wide range of specialised chemical products manufactured in Hungary prior to and during the war. All these details were totally unknown until the aforementioned book was published in 2013[2].

1. This beautiful silhouette study of an Arado Ar 65F fighter, taken in 1938, is a fine example of a German aircraft delivered to Bulgaria in an overall Light Grey livery. Additional ornaments were Red wraparound engine cowling and rearward tapering flash, tricolour rudder, as well as the typical colourful Bulgarian markings.

---

1   Dénes Bernád, György Punka: *Hungarian Fighter Colours*, vols. 1 and 2, published by MMP Books/Stratus, Sandomierz, Poland, in 2013 and 2014, respectively.

2   For details, please see the chapter titled 'Camouflage and Colours of Hungarian Fighter Aircraft (1930-1945)', particularly the sub-chapter called 'The Aircraft Paints and Lacquers of Krayer & Co.' (pages 39-44).

The Author attempted a similarly thorough approach to the hypothetical Bulgarian aircraft paint and lacquers production. However, during the study phase of the topic – done primarily through proxy research in Bulgarian archives – we found no trace of indigenously produced Bulgarian paints and lacquers suitable for aircraft of wooden, metal, or mixed construction. On the bright side, while scrolling through a multitude of documents looking for details of various imported aircraft, a number of invoices were found, issued by German paint and lacquer suppliers. These invoices reveal a large variety of specialised aircraft finish chemicals being imported, some surprising brands and types, which will be discussed later on. Therefore, it can be safely stated that there was no aircraft paint and lacquer production in Bulgaria prior to and during the war. All such specialised paints and other materials were imported, primarily from Germany. Following Bulgaria's unilateral exit from the Axis camp and joining the Allies (i.e., the Soviets) in early September 1944, after the German matériel stocks had been exhausted, Soviet origin paints were most probably used on all aircraft types, including German ones, which still soldiered on.

The first fighter aircraft types impressed in the Bulgarian Air Force (VNVV) in 1937 were German and Polish ones (Heinkel He 51C and Arado Ar 65F, as well as the PZL P.24B). [Photo 1] The Fo-cke-Wulf Fw 56A fighter trainer also came from Germany, in 1937. Obviously, these aircraft arrived finished with paints and lacquers available in their countries, but considering their export status, which will be detailed later on.

With the arrival, or expected arrival, of a large number of aircraft, and taking into consideration the existing mixed aircraft park, VNVV HQ issued an order on 14 April 1938, in an effort to standardise the identification colours used on aircraft, based on their role. Here is the transcript, edited by the Author:

V. PAINTING THE AIRCRAFT
For better recognition of aircraft based on their role, they will be painted as follows:
- School aircraft – entirely yellow (a little bit orange hue).
- Trainer and Reconnaissance – basecoat paint entirely olive green, nose [and so-called 'cheatline' along the fuselage] blue.
- Fighter trainers – basecoat paint entirely olive green, nose [and so-called 'cheatline' along the fuselage] red.
- Bomber trainers – basecoat paint entirely olive green, nose [and so-called 'cheatline' along the fuselage] dove grey.
- Passenger, sports and others – [various] keeping account of aesthetics and after approval from the control service.
- Reconnaissance – looking from above, all [visible] parts to be in camouflage (protective) paint, while at the lower side all [visible] parts in light blue, nose [and so-called 'cheatline' along the fuselage] blue.
- Fighters – like reconnaissance [aircraft], nose [and so-called 'cheatline' along the fuselage] red.
- Bombers – like reconnaissance [aircraft], nose [and so-called 'cheatline' along the fuselage] dove grey.
- *Lineyni* [close support/ground attack] aircraft – like reconnaissance [aircraft], nose [and so-called 'cheatline' along the fuselage] orange (…)

Note: based on available information and photos, this order was applied only partially. [Additions in square brackets are the Author's]

Unfortunately, no precise description of the camouflage colours is given. However, one could attempt to make the link between the general colour description and the list of imported German aviation paints.

German Aviation Paints and Lacquers

Let us now analyse the most interesting topic, the German aviation paints and lacquers used on export aircraft.

Based on available photographs, the first imported fighter and fighter trainer aircraft types may have arrived in Bulgaria in two distinctive paint schemes: one consisted of Dark Green upper surfaces over Light Blue, or Silver [Photo 2]; while the other one, less common, of overall Light Grey [Photo 1]. The first instinct of the Author, before finding the aforementioned German invoices in the Bulgarian archives, was to select the matching aircraft paints available at that time to *Luftwaffe* aircraft, namely RLM 62 *grün* for Green (the often quoted RLM 71 *dunkelgrün* is out of the question, as it appeared only later on) and RLM 65 *hellblau* for Light Blue. As for the Light Grey, the obvious choice would be RLM 63 *hellgrau*, or RLM 02 *RLM-Grau*. However, based on the research done on the painting standards of

2. This photo of a Focke-Wulf Fw 56A fighter trainer, taken in 1937, is an example of the alternative paint scheme of German aircraft delivered to Bulgaria, consisting of Dark Green upper surfaces over Light Blue. The typical Bulgarian ornaments and markings are present here as well.

Luftwaffe aircraft and the usage of aircraft paints and lacquers in Germany and abroad, it's now clear that official German standards (like the RLM' L.Dv. 521 and its predecessors) did *not* necessarily apply to aircraft exported abroad! This makes sense, as those aircraft – even if the type was also employed by the *Luftwaffe* – were being used in different circumstances, in separate jurisdiction, not subject to German laws. The most advanced paints produced in the IIIrd Reich, according to the latest technology and standards, were badly needed for the *Luftwaffe* itself, and represented top technological achievements, thus trade secrets, not to be exported abroad. The following quote is from the L.Dv. 521/1[3] revised standard, issued on 22 March 1938: *"The present instruction for treatment and usage of aircraft paints is only to be used in its own business section. The colour shades 70 and 71 which are specified on the colour shade card are not allowed in any case to be produced, or exported to foreign countries (...)"* One direct consequence of this quote is that in reality there were no German warplanes exported prior to, and in the early phase of WW 2, to friendly and neutral states in the well-known RLM 70/71 black green/dark green upper camouflage scheme, despite the plethora of colour drawings of various quality and reliability, published in specialised aviation literature. This clause had a direct influence on the Bf 109Es sold to Bulgaria, as detailed in the respective chapter.

Consequently, individual German aircraft manufacturing companies *could* and occasionally *did* use on aircraft slated for export older paint stocks they had available in their warehouses. These paints and lacquers could not be used any more on aircraft to be delivered to the *Luftwaffe*, as they had become obsolete from the point of the latest RLM regulations and their structure and pigmentation was by then considered outdated. The manufacturers *could* also use other aviation paints from the specialised market, which were not necessarily fitting any more the latest RLM standards, thus were cheaper and readily available. It's worth noting, however, that the quality of those paints and lacquers was adequate for the purpose, as they had been used on *Luftwaffe* aircraft just recently; only they did not represent the latest technology advancements (i.e., the obsolescent multi-layer paint system, e.g. the products of company Dr. Kurt Herberts (DKH), in comparison to the modern single-layer one, i.e. Ikarol-style, produced by Warnecke& Böhm), thus did not necessarily fit all current RLM regulations, or the technique of applying them on airframes. These differences had a visible effect, too, important for the topic of this book, as *the colour shades of paints used on exported aircraft were not necessarily identical to the well-known RLM shades!* Therefore, using the familiar RLM codes and paint chips in identifying the precise hues of these paints used on exported aircraft could be misleading.

It also has to be stated that the above assertions are valid *only* for aircraft originally directly exported by aircraft manufacturers, or the specialised German military technology exporting companies, primarily prior to and in the first phase of the war. Combat aircraft handed over to Germany's Axis allies exclusively for frontline use, mostly from 1942 on, wore standard *Luftwaffe* paints and camouflage schemes, as they were serviced alongside *Luftwaffe* warplanes by the same repair workshops and by the original factories as well. These warplanes lent to the Axis allies remained German property. Finally, from about 1943 on, the newer warplane types exported to the Axis countries, or built in licence abroad, all wore standard *Luftwaffe* camouflage schemes.

---

3   Title of the standard: 'Draft Specification of Handling and Application Instructions for Aircraft Paints (1938)'.

3. Case study of the airframe finish of German aircraft exported abroad in the 1930s [in this case, the first Dornier Do 24K flying boat – actually the Do 24V3 prototype, registered X-1 – delivered to the Netherlands, in July 1937]. See main text for details of the specific aviation paints used on the airframe.

4. Advertisement of aircraft paints made by Dr. Kurt Herberts & Co. Lackfabrik (DKH), supplier of aviation specific chemicals to Bulgaria, also through Messerschmitt AG.

5. Advertisement of the Ikarol series of aviation lacquers (paints) made by Warnecke & Böhm, supplier of aviation lacquers, paints and other specific chemicals to the Bulgarian air force.

Another important point to be made is that – based on the Author's research – there were *no* specific 'export paints and colours' used on aircraft sold abroad. All aviation paints and lacquers were produced by German companies originally intended for domestic use. Some were included in the RLM standards, others were not. Therefore, the quality of the paints could vary, as could their colour shades[4].

One documented early case of 'export' livery concerns the Dornier Do 24K flying boat sold to the Netherlands in 1937 [Photo 3]. The documents referring to the airframe's surface protection list the following: 'Ikarol light metal primer *grün* (green) 201' as primer, while 'Ikarol topcoat I *grau* (grey) 103/1' and 'Ikarol topcoat II *Hollandgrau* (Holland grey) 103/2' for the exterior. For another batch of Do 24Ks, also sold to the Netherlands in the same timeframe, 'DKH oil primer *grün* (green) L 40/41' as primer, while 'DKH nitro topcoat *grau* (grey) L 50/51' and 'DKH nitro enamel *Hollandgrau* L 40/52' for the exterior are given. If we take note of the customer's nationality being mentioned (i.e., *Holland*), the striking differences are the different suppliers and dissimilar identification of the grey paints used on the same aircraft type to be exported to the same customer in a similar timeframe! Apparently, basic market laws (i.e. cost and delivery time) prevailed in selecting the product to be used on export aircraft, not intended for *Luftwaffe* use, where sticking to RLM standards was a must.

In the first case, the number '103' refers to a Warnecke & Böhm product, i.e., a two-layer surface protection paint type. The numeral 1 after the slash indicates the first layer, while 2 denotes the second layer. Contrary to the similarity, number 2 does *not* indicate the shade of grey, it's not a reference to the RLM-*Grau* 02 (which is shade number 02 in the RLM chart). The actual colour is given by the description, namely *grau*, or grey (we can ignore here the name Holland, which in this case refers to the end customer).

In the second case, interestingly, a different paint company's product is given, namely DKH[5]. [Photo 4] The procedure described above was identical to the DKH product as well. The colour shade is also given separately, in the description, not in the products' codes.

Another example, taken from a later date, concerns the all-metal Heinkel He 112E (E for export) fighters sold to Rumania in August 1939. They were painted with 'Ikarol 133 RLM-*Grau* (02)' – a Warnecke & Böhm product [Photo 5] – as described in the technical handbook's maintenance chapter issued in the Rumanian language (available in the Author's private collection). This time, the finish was identical to the *Luftwaffe* warplanes that were painted in RLM-*Grau* (*Farbton* 02), hence the reference to the RLM standard.

---

4 Even standardised (so-called 'RLM standard') paints were not always the same shade, due to differences in raw materials a particular chemical company used, their recipes, the manufacturing technology, etc. Differences in shade were minor, though.

5 DKH is short for Dr. Kurt Herberts & Co. *Lackfabrik*, located in Wuppertal-Barmen.

The Case of the Bulgarian Bf 109E's Colours

Returning to the Bulgarian topic, it's impossible to pinpoint the precise paints and lacquers (and the producing companies) – most importantly, the camouflage colours' shades – without the relevant documentation being available that would make a direct link between a particular aircraft type and the paints imported. A primary source would be the Bulgarian edition of a particular aircraft type's technical handbook, none of which is available to the Author, however. Only a single case linking certain German paints to a particular aircraft type in Bulgarian service could be established by the Author. It concerns the Messerschmitt Bf 108B and Bf 109E, supplied to Bulgaria in April 1940 (see appropriate chapter for details).

Offer No. 601/29.01.1941 by Messerschmitt AG, listing the spare parts and accessories for the batch of Bf 108Bs and Bf 109Es delivered the previous year, includes the following paints and lacquers: 84 kg aircraft paint L 40/62 DKH, 84 kg aircraft paint L 40/65 DKH and 84 kg aircraft paint L 40/70 DKH, all delivered in 28 kg cans, a barrel of 100 kg paint thinner, and 2 kg black insignia/markings paint. Contrary to some sources, the L40/xx coding (generally used *before* the Handling and Application Instruction for Aircraft Paints LDv. 521/1 came into effect officially on 22.03.1938) was *not* a specific colour paint, but rather a category of paint, and usually was completed with the colour description. However, in the aforementioned offer no specific colour shades were given; therefore, no particular colours can be identified.

The link between the Messerschmitt factory's early Bf 109E models and the paints and lacquers of Company Dr. Kurt Herberts (DKH) is actually of no surprise. The maintenance manual of the *Luftwaffe*-bound Bf 109C/D[6] mentions on page 135 the following paints: '*DKH-Sichtschutzfarbe grün* (green) L 40/71', '*dkl. grün* (dark green) L 40/70' and '*blau* (blue) L 40/65' as camouflage colours. These were to be applied by spraying on the all-metal airframe after the surface had been primed with '*DKH-Ölgrund* L 40/41*' (no colour is given), while '*DKH-Nitrodecklack grau* (grey) L 40/51' is recommended for the cockpit's interior surfaces, as well as on certain exterior panels (*Verkleidung, ausen*). Interestingly, the colour shades are again given as descriptions, not in the paints' codes, as already highlighted above.

It is imperative to notice that the two greens' hues are described differently than by the eventual RLM colour standard that came in effect later on! Here, L 40/71 is described as *grün* (green) – a description fitting RLM 62 – while the later RLM 71 is darker, i.e., *dunkelgrün* (dark green); L 40/70 is described as *dkl. grün* (dark green), while the later RLM 70 is even darker (*schwarzgrün*, or black green)! Apparently, a certain DKH material number (e.g., L 40/52) was *not* referring to a particular colour, as so far was assumed by various authors and sources (in this case, 'RLM 52' did not exist). Since there are various colour descriptions to L 40/52, ranging from Grey to Black[7], one could speculate that L 40/52 was most probably a general base lacquer formula to which a number of different pigments could be added to make various colour coatings. In other words, L 40/52 was the product name, while the descriptive name behind that product (i.e. *grau*, or grey) defined what the final lacquer product generally looked like. Therefore, for example, L 40/70 *dunkelgrün* was *not* necessarily equivalent to RLM 70 *schwarzgrün*.

One can only speculate that following a new edition of the RLM aircraft finishing standard coming into effect, Messerschmitt AG sold abroad (in this case to Bulgaria) its extant stock of by then obsolete (otherwise reliable and quality) DKH-made paints, whose colour shades were not corresponding any more to the newly introduced RLM standards...

German Aircraft Lacquer and Paint Export to Bulgaria

All German aviation lacquers and paints imported by Bulgaria in the ten years discussed in this chapter are given in Annexe 1, listed in chronological order[8]. These special chemicals were used on both imported German aircraft as well as domestically manufactured ones[9]. Based on the order and arrival dates it can be guessed, but not proven, which paints may have been used for certain aircraft types.

---

6 *Anlage 35 – Farbanstrichliste, Bf 109C und D. Entwurf eines Flugzeughandbuches*, L.Dv. 556/2, *Ausgabe* 1938.

7 Another example of the DKH paints of the L 40/xx family can be found in the Dornier Do 17E *Handbuch* (manual), published in 1937 by Dornier *Werke* and approved by the RLM. Annex 18 covers the paint finishes. The following paints are mentioned, including the method they should be applied on the airframe: two coats of DKH-*Nitrodecklack* L 40/51 *silbergrau* (Silver Grey) and one coat of DKH-*Nitroemaille* L 40/52 *silber* (Silver)!

8 Not only paints and lacquers were imported from Germany, but other aviation specific materials as well. For example, a contract signed on 12.04.1940 with Company Georg Schwarz in Berlin calls for the delivery of 6.900 m² of veneer for aircraft production. '*Abnahme-Prüfung von Webwaren*' (Acceptance protocol of woven fabrics), dated 16.04.1943, lists 27.000 m² of *Leinenbespannstoff* (linen fabric) for aircraft, type 60L *Qualität* II K, purchased from Company Carl Weber & Co., Germany.

9 For a detailed study in English of Bulgaria's indigenous aircraft production, please consult '*Balkan Birds: Thirty Five Years of Bulgarian Aircraft Production*', written by this book's Author, published in AIR Enthusiast magazine, by Key Publishing (UK), issue No. 94, July/August 2001, and No. 96, November/December 2001.

If we extract only the paints used to camouflage aircraft – the 'hot' topic of this chapter – the following short list of camouflage paint types emerges: DKH-made L 40/xx paint and lacquer family, as well as BC.6954 (or BC.6954/6663)[10] and BC.12431 top cover paint of the Herboloid brand, offered in large variety of colours and shades, supplied by Herbig-Haarhaus Lacquer Factory. [Photo 6]

The first identified document is an offer by Herbig-Haarhaus for its Herboloid brand of *Flugzeugelacke* (aircraft lacquers, i.e., paints), dated 25.01.1940. The Herboloid BC.6954/6663 type of aircraft

6. Header of a business letter sent by Herbig-Haarhaus AG, the main supplier of aviation lacquers, paints and other specific chemicals to the Bulgarian air force.

7. Typical repair paint and oil toolbox, supplied with every German aircraft. This particular box contains the following paints (as per the original manual's description): F): Flieglack Fl 7122.02, Fl 7122.76, Fl 7122.075, Fl 7122.74, Fl 7160.22, Fl 7160.21, Fl 7130, Fl 7135.02 (each sample stored in 2 kg tins). Along with paints, diluents (thinners) were also supplied, as follows: Verdünnung Fl 7200.00 and Fl 7230.00, the former in 5 kg, the latter in 1 kg amounts. It is not known which aircraft type this toolkit was supplied with; however, judging by the camouflage colours Farbtöne (colour shades) 74/75/76, most probably it was a day fighter aircraft.

top cover paint was offered in great variety of colours and shades: Gold, Olive Green, Silver, Blue, Yellow (Light Orange shade), Pigeon Grey, Crimson Red, Black, Insignia Green, Insignia White, Green (for camouflage), Yellowish Brown (for camouflage) and Brown (for camouflage). Of these colours, Green, Yellowish Brown (Khaki? Sand Yellow?)[11] and Brown are specifically mentioned by the German supplier as typical camouflage colours (for upper surfaces). However, the Bulgarians may have used other colours as well for camouflaging their aircraft (like Olive Green, or Pigeon Grey). For the lower surfaces the Blue, Pigeon Grey, or Silver[12] could be equally used. Most interesting is the 'Yellowish Brown' camouflage paint, which could mean a Khaki, Drab, or Sand Yellow shade. No use of such yellowish brown camouflage colour is known on early *Luftwaffe* aircraft. This colour shade may have represented the Polish or the Czechoslovak khaki camouflage paints, but this theory is unconfirmed.

Following the offer from January 1940, there was a contract signed with Herbig-Haarhaus in May for 21 tons (!) of aircraft lacquers, varnishes and paints. Unfortunately, only the material codes are given (surface covering paint type BC 6954/6663 is included), but one can safely assume the contract was for the aviation specific chemicals mentioned previously in the January offer.

The offer by Messerschmitt AG to the Royal Bulgarian Ministry of War of spare parts and other matériel for Bf 108 and Bf 109, dated 29 January 1941, includes aircraft lacquers and paints as well. The offer lists *Flieglacke* (aviation lacquers, i.e., paints) L 40/62, L 40/65 and L 40/70 (without giving the colour shades), as well as a small dose of Black marker paint (no code is given), along with the matching diluent (thinner), manufactured by DKH. The text clearly refers to "the 10 *Jagdeinsitzer* [single-seat fighter aircraft] Me 109E delivered by us in 1940." This is the single direct link between a particular aircraft type and the camouflage paints used, mentioned previously. [Photo 7]

Another contract was signed with Herbig-Haarhaus two years later. The contract, dated 24 April 1942, did not include the aforementioned BC.6954/6663 paint family; instead, the modern single layer paint type BC.12431 was offered, in the following colours: Olive Green, Silver, Orange Yellow, Insignia White, Insignia Green, Insignia Crimson, Red and Black. Of these, the following shades could have been used for camouflaging aircraft: Olive Green (for upper surfaces) and Silver (for lower surfaces and certain metal

Abb. 60 Kiste Farben, Öle, Fette

---

10 In L.DV. 521/1, *Ausgabe* B from 1938, page 9, *Flieglackkette* 22, BC.6954 is listed as a former code of Herbig-Haarhaus for *Flieglack* 7115.

11 For example, as distant comparison, 'light yellowish brown' is the shade of the A-21 type upper camouflage colour used on Ilyushin Il-2 assault aircraft, or Petlyakov Pe-2 bombers of the Soviet Air Force. The Federal Standard equivalent of this *light* Soviet camouflage colour shade is identified as FS 34201, which appears to be a light khaki. If darker, it was comparable to Polish khaki (approx. FS 34088) and Czechoslovak khaki (approx. FS 34097).

12 Silver paint, as such, is not necessarily a 'camouflage' paint *per se*, as it's shiny, thus highly visible; therefore, contrary to the very purpose of such 'hiding' colours. Its primary function was corrosion protection, or a top dope meant to chemically and mechanically unify the mixed layers applied under it to the airframe. Sometimes silver colour lacquer is merely a covering/closing 'unilacquer' with metal-oxide, i.e., silver, pigments. Nevertheless, it was sometimes used as covering, or finishing lacquer, replacing standard camouflage paints of light grey, or blue. This was the case of the under surfaces of certain Avia B.534s, or Heinkel He 51s, for example.

panels, or auxiliary tanks, e.g. of the He 51). This theory is strengthened by the next protocol with Herbig-Haarhaus, dated 11.08.1942, which called for the delivery of only these two colours.

The 'insignia' type of paints were obviously needed for the Bulgarian tricolour to be applied on the rudder, as well as for the bright engine wraparound painting and rearward tapering fuselage flash. The black and white colours were intended for the new 'St. Andrew' cross style Bulgarian military marking and the aircraft's serial number displayed in white on the fuselage and (occasionally) on the lower wing surface (in black). The light orange hue yellow was needed for the Axis style identification (yellow rudder and elevators; occasionally, narrow mid-fuselage stripe, as well as upper and lower wingtips). Obviously, the insignia type paints were not needed any longer, as they are missing from the August order.

A new protocol was signed in October 1942, calling for aircraft lacquers (BC.12431) in the following colours and shades: Olive Green, Silver (the two probable camouflage colours), as well as Insignia White, Insignia Red, Yellow (light Orange shade) and Black. In the same month, detailed tests of various Herbig-Haarhaus aircraft lacquers, wooden mastic fillers and thinners, imported by the company of Dr. B. Dzhabarov in Sofia, were performed. All materials passed the tests; they met the prescribed technical conditions/requirements (see Annex 2). [Photo 8]

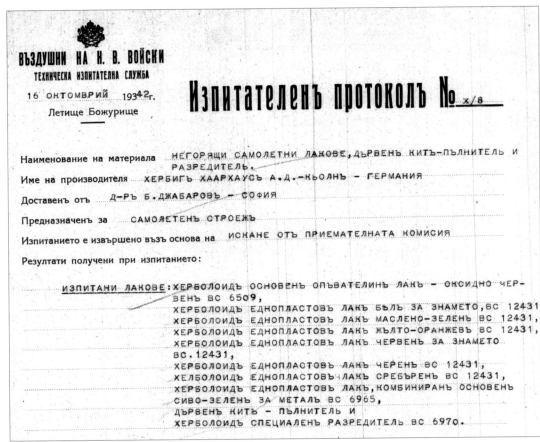

8. Detailed tests of various Herbig-Haarhaus aircraft lacquers, mastic fillers for wood and thinners were performed in Bulgaria in October 1942. All materials passed the tests with flying colours. Complete translation of the full document can be found in Annex 2.

Interestingly, the annex dated 30 March 1943 to an unidentified contract with Herbig-Haarhaus lists *both* the older style two-layer (BC.6954/6663) and the newer, single-layer paint family (BC.12431). The latter paints are additionally labelled by a two-digit number (16, 29, 30, 34, 32, 31, 35, 36), which identifies the colour and hue of the paint, as follows: 16=Orange Yellow, 29=Olive Green, 30=Silver, 34=Insignia White, 32=Black, 31=Insignia Red, 35=Dove Grey, 36=Blue. One can assume that the earlier delivered aircraft were painted with the former, older technology paint family, while the newly delivered ones with the latter, newer paint family, so both stocks had to be replenished.

On 8 April 1943, yet another new contract was signed with Herbig-Haarhaus for the delivery of another larger quantity of aircraft finishing chemicals and pastes, including lacquers and paints, this time all of the new BC.12431 family. This contract called for three different specifications (identified as I, II and III). The paints ordered were of the following colours and shades: Yellow (Light Orange shade No. 16), White (34), Insignia Green (33), Insignia Red (31), Black (32), Silver (30), Olive Green (29), Blue (36) and Dove Grey (35).

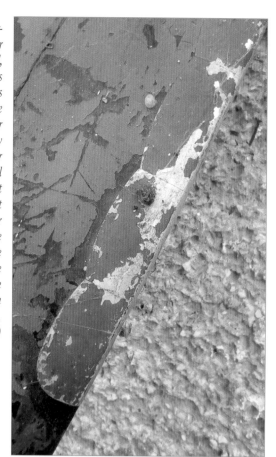

These photos of a surviving wartime propeller were sent from Razgrad, in the 11ᵗʰ hour (just days before the manuscript was closed). Reportedly, the German-made propeller was removed from an early DAR-3 Garvan I trainer aircraft, although several other aircraft types would fit as well. Of utmost interest is the mid-Green colour that survived on parts of the propeller. This is an ultra-rare occasion to see a genuine camouflage colour shade used during the war, even if it was faded by the sun. (Photos G. Dimitrov)

At the end of the same year, the first lacquers and paints identified by the standard 4+2 digits, showed up in an invoice issued by a new supplier, Bachmann, von Blumental & Co. *Flugzeugbau* (BBF)[13], located in Fürth, Germany, to the Aviation Repair Shop of Skopie[14]. The invoice, dated 24 November 1943, lists the following *Flieglacke*: 7122.70, 7122.71, 7161.27, 7122.02, 7122.65. The first four digits describe the lacquer material (e.g., No. 7122 *Flieglack*, to be used on metal surfaces for land based aircraft used in European climate[15]), while the last two digits following the dot correspond to the colour shades of

---

13 The same company supplied to the Skopie Repair Shop not only aircraft finishing chemicals (like lacquers, or paint stripping agents), but aircraft strap (girth) as well.

14 Today known as Skopje, capital of Republic of Macedonia (FYROM).

15 Another variant to be used for seaplanes (in permanent contact with seawater) was 7102, while for aircraft used in the tropics was 7109.

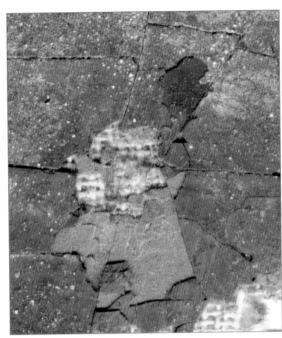

This small piece of fabric originates from an unidentified Bulgarian aircraft, which reportedly flew during wartime. It is the only such genuine piece the Author has come across and owns. Unfortunately, 99% of the original dark green paint chipped away, only a tiny dot remained. The Author placed the fabric onto an RLM 62 Green paint chip attached to the book 'Luftwaffe Colours, 1935–1945', by Michael Ullmann (Hikoki, 2002). Obviously, no exact match can be ascertained of this small sample (see lower right area); however, the similarity of the colour shades is apparent. RLM 71 Dark Green and RLM 70 Black Green were all visibly darker than the mid-green dot on the fabric. If anyone has genuine parts, or wrecks of Bulgarian aircraft used during the war, with even small amount of camouflage paint preserved on them, the Author would be delighted if he was contacted through the e-mail address given on bottom of page 6. The information could be used in future books related to Bulgarian aviation.

the official RLM paint chips, namely: 70=Black Green (RLM 70), 71=Dark Green (RLM 71), 27=Yellow (RLM 27), 02=RLM Grey (RLM 02) and 65=Light Blue (RLM 65). These colours refer to the earlier *Luftwaffe* camouflage scheme of 70/71/65, introduced in 1938 and used on fighters officially until mid-1940 (when it was replaced by the 74/75/76 combination, which officially lasted until July 1944), while on bombers and other aircraft until around mid-1944 (often, until the end of the war).

A seemingly unrelated piece of information, originating from a US military intelligence report compiled by the assistant military attaché of the US Embassy in Turkey, Maj. Cedric H. Seager, dated 9 February 1944, summing up the effects of the recent allied bombing of Sofia, contains the following paragraph: "*The principal Bulgarian warehouse of the German* I.G. Farben Industrie, *situated in the* Ulitsa Ierish, Sofia, *is reported to have been completely gutted during the raid of 10 January 1944.The warehouse was full of chemicals, chemical products and dyes* [i.e., paints] *when destroyed.*" This loss may have greatly affected the supply of aviation paints and lacquers to the Bulgarian air force for a while.

It has to be noted that both VNVV and *Luftwaffe* aircraft were repaired at the Skopie Repair Shop; therefore, it's no surprise that standard German paints and lacquers were used, which were complying with the RLM standards. The absence from the list of the newer paint shades used on fighters (74=Greenish Dark Grey, 75=Mid-Grey and 76=Light Blue) is conspicuous, however. One plausible explanation could be that the first-line fighters were repaired in German-controlled workshops, where they received standard *Luftwaffe* camouflage schemes. Indeed, it's known that most (all?) Bulgarian Bf 109Es and Gs that needed major repair and overhaul were sent to the ASAM Works at Pipera, Rumania, which specialised in Messerschmitt aircraft.

Deliveries of the top quality Herboloid paints by Herbig-Haarhaus continued in 1944 as well. On 30 March, 101,000 kg (!) aircraft finishing chemicals were ordered. Another order has been identified in the archives, dated 04.07.1944. Of the BC.12431 family, the following colours were listed: 35=Dove Grey, 31=Insignia Red, 32=Black, 33=Insignia Green, 30=Silver and 16=Orange Yellow. Interestingly, no (olive) green camouflage colour (No. 29) can be found in the list any more.

The last document linked to Herbig-Haarhaus Lacquer Factory – the main supplier of aviation finishing chemicals to Bulgaria – is an invoice dated 8 July 1944. It does not contain any specific paints or lacquers, only paint diluent (thinner). However, imports were carried out right until Sofia unilaterally severed its alliance with Berlin in early September 1944 (see Annex 3).

After the last stocks of German aviation lacquers, paints and other specific chemicals were exhausted, the Bulgarians turned to the Soviets, their new ally. However, the author could not find any reference to Soviet paints being used by the VNVV, but the choice seems obvious.

One final document related to aircraft lacquers and paints identified is a request from the Bulgarian company 'Chimimport', addressed to the Czechoslovak company *Spojené Tovarny na Barvy a Laky – Národní Podnik, Praha* [United Paint and Varnish Factory – National Corporation, Prague], in November 1948. This inquiry referred to samples of aerosol paints for wood, metal, fabric, signs, cleaners, wash-off fluid, thinners and enamel lacquers, with their corresponding numbers for each colour. There is no confirmation of any deal having been made, however.

Conclusion

All airworthy aircraft had to be repainted after a certain time spent in service. Generally, aircraft paint warranty was given for one year by the manufacturer. However, this does not necessarily mean that every aircraft was repainted after one year, as aviation paint protection usually lasted longer. However, after 2-3 years, the paint layer decayed to a certain extent, chipped away, thus had to be replaced, or at least repaired. Aircraft that suffered an accident had to be partially or completely repainted. Thus every aircraft was repainted once or twice, sometimes even more during its lifetime. Accordingly, camouflage colour shades – the main topic of this chapter – changed slightly, or more prominently over time. Pinpointing the precise shade worn by a particular aircraft based on black and white photos is nearly impossible. Nevertheless, the author attempted to get as close as possible – within the obvious range of error – to the actually colour shades Bulgarian fighter aircraft wore prior to, during, and shortly after the war, often by using the 'educated guess' approach. The Reader will eventually decide if he has succeeded to an acceptable degree, or not.

As a side note, if a modeller ponders which colour shades, available on the market, should he/she use on his/her scale model of the early Bulgarian fighters and fighter trainers of German origin, the Author recommends RLM 62 (Green) and RLM 65 (Light Blue), without being able to positively prove the veracity of these hues being the actually used ones, however. The ex-Polish and ex-Czechoslovak aircraft retained, at least initially, their respective original camouflage colours, as described in the individual chapters.

Wrapping up the topic, this is how close this book's Author could get to the Bulgarian camouflage colours and paints – a topic debated in print for the first time – with the limited research possibilities and resources available to him. It is now the task of Bulgarian historians to 'deep dive' into this highly interesting, but so far totally neglected, subject and dig out the missing direct links, as suggested above. Hopefully, one day wrecks of Bulgarian wartime aircraft will also emerge – the Author could not locate a single such piece, despite intensive inquiry in many directions, except for the small piece of fabric depicted here – which would help pinpoint the actual colours, and perhaps the camouflage paints as well.

Annex 1 (compiled by Dénes Bernád)

Type of document	Date	Original text	Translated text [notes in straight brackets]

Angebot (Offer)	25.01.1940	Auf unbrennbare Herboloid-Flugzeugelacke
		a) Grundlack oxydrot BC.6509
		b) C.1213 neu
		   – graugrün BC.6965
		   – silber BC.6966
		c) farblos BC.6952
		   – Füller BC.9002
		   – aluminium BC.6953
		   – grün lasierend BC.6929
		   – gold BC.6954
		Flugzeugelacke:
		1. grau BC.9022
		2. Verdünnung BC.2787
		3. olivgrün BC.6954/6663
		4. silber BC.6954/6663
		5. blau BC.6954/6663
		6. gelb-schwach-orange BC.6954/6663
		7. taubengrau BC.6954/6663
		8. carminrot BC.6954/6663
		9. schwarz BC.6954/6663
		10. fahnengrün BC.6954/6663
		11. fahnenweiss BC.6954/6663
		12. grün für camouflage BC.6954/6663
		13. gelb-braun für camouflage BC.6954/6663
		14. braun für camouflage BC.6954/6663
		15. spezial BC.6970
		16. Verteiler BC.9017
			[Offer] for non-flammable Herboloid aircraft paints
			a) Primer, Oxide Red BC.6509
			b) [Nitro cleaning liquid] C.1213 new
			   – Grey Green BC.6965
			   – Silver BC.6966
			c) [Pore Filler] Colourless BC.6952
			   – Filler (putty) BC.9002
			   – Aluminium BC.6953
			   – Green, shiny BC.6929
			   – Gold BC.6954
			Aircraft lacquers:
			1. Grey BC.9022
			2. Diluent [thinner] BC.2787
			3. Olive Green BC.6954/6663
			4. Silver BC.6954/6663
			5. Blue BC.6954/6663
			6. Yellow Light Orange BC.6954/6663
			7. Pigeon Grey BC.6954/6663
			8. Crimson Red BC.6954/6663
			9. Black BC.6954 / 6663
			10. Insignia (for flag) Green BC.6954/6663
			11. Insignia (for flag) White BC.6954/6663
			12. Green for camouflage BC.6954/6663
			13. Yellowish Brown [Khaki? Drab?] for camouflage BC.6954/6663
			14. Brown for camouflage BC.6954/6663
			15. Special BC.6970
			16. Spread [?] BC.9017

Договор (Contract)	08.05.1940	С Хербиг Хархаус за доставка на 21 000 кгр негорими самолетни лакове	[Contract] with 'Herbig Harhaus' [i.e., Herbig-Haarhaus Lacquer Factory, Köln-Bickendorf] for the delivery of 21.000 kg of non-flammable aviation lacquers [see below]
Приложение (Annex)	08.05.1940	BC.6059 C.1213 BC.6965 BC.6966 BC.6952 BC.9002 BC.6953 Комбиниран N.11 BC.6954 BC.9022 BC.2787 BC.6954/6663 BC.6970 BC.9017	BC.6059 C.1213 BC.6965 BC.6966 BC.6952 BC.9002 BC.6953 Composite No. 11 BC.6954 BC.9022 BC.2787 BC.6954/6663 BC.6970 BC.9017
Приложение (Annex)	29.01.1941	Към оферта N. 601 за части Ме 108 и Ме 109 (...) 84 кг Самолетен лак L 40-62, 84 кг самолетен лак L 40-65, 84 кг Самолетен лак L 40-70, 100 кг Разредител във варел, 2 кг Черна боя за знаци	[Annex] to offer [by Messerschmitt AG] No. 601 of spare parts for Me 108 and Me 109. (...) 84 kg aircraft lacquer L 40/62, 84 kg aircraft lacquer L 40/65, 84 kg aircraft lacquer L 40/70, 100 kg diluent [thinner] in barrel, 2 kg black insignia paint

Договор (Contract)	24.04.1942	С Хербиг-Хаархаус лакова фабрика Кьолн-Бикендорф за: Оксидно-червен опъвателен лак ВС 6509 (1) Специален разредител ВС.6970 (28) Еднопластов лак ВС.12431: масленозелен (29) сребърен (30) жълто-оранжев (16) бял за знамето (34) зелен за знамето (33) червен за знамето (31) черен (32) Дървен кит пълнител ВС.9002 (8) Сиво-зелен грунд ВС.6965 [6595] (3)	[Contract] with Herbig-Haarhaus Lacquer Factory, Köln-Bickendorf, for: [Fabric] stretching lacquer, Oxide Red BC.6509 (1) Special diluent [thinner] BC.6970 (28) Single layer lacquer BC.12431: Olive Green (29), Silver (30), Orange Yellow (16), Insignia (for flag) White (34), Insignia (for flag) Green (33), Insignia (for flag) Crimson Red (31), Black (32) Filler (putty for wood) BC.9002 (B) Primer, Grey Green BC.6965 [or 6595] (3)
Протокол (Protocol)	11.08.1942	За приемане на лакове Оксидно-червен опъвателен ВС 6509 (1) Разредител ВС.6970 (28) ВС.12431 зелен (33), сребърен (30) Сиво-зелен ВС.6965 (3)	[Protocol] to accept lacquers [Fabric] stretching [lacquer], Oxide Red BC.6509 (1) Diluent (thinner) BC.6970 (28) [Lacquer] Green (33), Silver (30) BC.12431 [Primer] Grey Green BC.6965 (3)
Изпитателен протокол (Test Protocol)	28.08.1942	(...) Оксидно-червен ВС.6509 Разредител ВС.6970 Сребърен ВС.12431 зелен ВС.12431	(...) [Fabric stretching lacquer] Oxide Red BC.6509 Diluent (thinner) BC.6970 Silver BC.12431 Green BC.12431
Протокол (Protocol)	05.10.1942	фактура от 25.08 и 01.09.1943 Оксидно-червен основен ВС 6509 (1) Разредител ВС 6970 (28) ВС12431 масленозелен (29), сребърен (30), жълто-оранжев (16), бял за знамето (34), червен за знамето (31), черен (32) ВС 6965 сиво-зелен (3) Кит ВС 9002 (8)	Invoice from 25.08 and 1.09.1943 Primer, Oxide Red BC.6509 (1) Diluent (thinner) BC.6970 (28) BC.12431 Olive Green (29), Silver (30), Orange-yellow (16), Insignia (for flag) White (34) Insignia (for flag) Red (31), Black (32) [Primer] Grey Green BC.6965 (3) Kit [Putty] BC.9002 (8)
Изпитателен протокол (Test Protocol)	10.10.1942	Лакове: Оксидно червен ВС 6509 Бял за знамето ВС12431 Маслено-зелен ВС12431 Жълто-оранжев ВС12431 Червен за знамето ВС12431 Черен ВС12431 Сребърен ВС12431 Сиво-зелен за метал ВС 6965 Разредител ВС 6970	Lacquers: Oxide Red BC.6509 Insignia (for flag) White BC.12431 Olive Green BC.12431 Yellow Orange BC.12431 Insignia (for flag) Red BC.12431 Black BC.12431 Silver BC.12431 Grey Green for metal [surfaces] BC.6965 Thinner BC.6970
Приложение (Annex)	30.03.1943	Лакове: ВС 6952 (7) ВС 9002 (8) ВС 6929 (11) ВС 7000 (40) С 1213 (2) VL 7826 (6) ВС 6509 (1) ВС 12431 (16, 29, 30, 34, 32, 31, 36) ВС 6954/6663 ВС 6970 (28)	Lacquers: BC.6952 (7) BC.9002 (8) BC.6929 (11) BC.7000 (40) C.1213 (2) VL.826 (6) BC.6509 (1) BC.12431 (16, 29, 30, 34, 32, 31, 36) BC.6954/6663 BC.6970 (28)
Договор (Contract)	08.04.1943	За доставка от Хербиг Хаархаусна негорими самолетни лакове по спецификации	Delivery of Herbig-Haarhaus non-flammable aircraft lacquers to specifications.

		Herbig Haarhaus Spezifikation I, II, III	Herbig-Haarhaus Specification I, II, III [see below]
Vertrag (Contract)	08.04.1943		
Спецификация I (Specification I)	08.04.1943	За лакове: Оксидно червен ВС 6509 ВС12431 Жълт слабооранжев (16) Бял (34) Зелен за знамето (33) Червен за знамето (31) Черен (32) Сребърен (30) Масленозелен (29) Син (36) Гълъбовосив (35) Разредител ВС 6970 (28) Уравнител ВС 9017 (41) Поропълнител ВС 6952 (7) Кит за дърво ВС 9002 (8) Лак зеленикав ВС 6929 (11) Разредител ВС 7000 (40) Обезмаслител С 1213 (2)	[Specification] for lacquers: Oxide Red BC.6509 BC.12431 Yellow Light Orange (16) White (34) Insignia (for flag) Green (33) Insignia (for flag) Red (31) Black (32) Silver (30) Olive Green (29) Blue (36) Dove Grey (35) Diluent (thinner) BC.6970 (28) Leveller [?] BC.9017 (41) Porosity Filler [Putty?] BC.6952 (7) Putty for wood BC.9002 (8) Greenish Lacquer BC.6929 (11) Diluent (thinner) BC.7000 (40) Degreaser C.1213 (2)
Спецификация II (Specification II)	08.04.1943	Самолетни лакове: Безветен ВС 6952 (7) Обезмаслител С 1213 (2) Лак за лепене на плат оксидно жълт VV L 7826 (6) Еднопластов лак ВС 12431 зелен за знамето (33) бял за знамето (34) масленозелен (29) карминовочевен (31) черен (32) жълт-слабооранжев (16) гълъбовосив (35) син (36) грунд Е 1 кафяво-червен кит сив покривна боя синьо-сива разредител	Aircraft lacquers: Colourless BC.6952 (7) Degreaser C.1213 (2) Fabric gluing lacquer, Oxide Yellow VV L 7826 (6) Single coat lacquer BC.12431: Insignia (for flag) Green (33) Insignia (for flag) White (34) Olive Green (29) Crimson Red (31) Black (32) Yellow Light Orange (16) Dove Grey (35) Blue (36) Primer E 1, Brownish Red Putty, Grey Roof paint, Blue-Grey Diluent (thinner)
Спецификация III (Specification III)	08.04.1943	Разредител Кит сив Лак за лепене оксидно жълт VV L 7826	Diluent (thinner) Putty, Grey Bonding lacquer, Oxide Yellow VV L 7826
Spezifikation I (Specification I)	08.04.1943	ВС 12431 (16) (34) (33) (31) (30) (29) (32) (36) (35) ВС 6970 (28) ВС 9017 (41) ВС 6952 (7) ВС 9002 (8) ВС 6929 (11) ВС 7000 (40) С 1213 (2)	BC.12431 (16) (34) (33) (31) (30) (29) (32) (36) (35) BC.6970 (28) BC.9017 (41) BC.6952 (7) BC.9002 (8) BC 6929 (11) BC.7000 (40) C.1213 (2)
Spezifikation II (Specification II)	08.04.1943	ВС 6952 (7) С 1213 (2) VL 7826 (6) ВС 12431 (33) (31) (29) (31) (32) (16) (35) (36) Grund E 1 Grau Blaugrau Verdünnung	BC.6952 (7) C.1213 (2) VL.7826 (6) BC.12431 (33) (31) (29) (31) (32) (16) (35) (36) Primer E1 [Putty] Grey [Roof paint] Blue Grey Diluent (thinner)

Spezifikation III (Specification III)	08.04.1943	Verdünnung Grau VL 7826	Diluent (thinner) [Putty] Grey VL.7826 [bonding lacquer Oxide Yellow]
Ursprungs-Zeugnis (Certificate of Origin)	09.04.1943	Lacke HH 055564 1-242 Lacke 058435 1-71	Paints 055564 1-242 [by] HH [Herbig-Haarhaus] Paints 058435 1-71 [by Herbig-Haarhaus]
Rechnung (Invoice)	23.10.1943	За ремонт на самолети в работилница Скопие от фирма Бахман (Bachmann, von Blumental & Co. Flugzeugbau). Rechnung N.43438 от 23.10.1943 за доставка на 100 meter Gurtband 20x2,5 , 50 kg Abbeizmittel N.7209.99, 50 kg Abbeizmittel N.155	Company Bachmann, von Blumental & Co. *Flugzeugbau* shipped the following to repair aircraft at Skopie Workshop: Invoice No. 43438 of 23.10.1943 to supply 100 meter strap (girth) 20x2.5, 50 kg paint stripping agent No. 7209.99, 50 kg paint stripping agent No.155.
Rechnung (Invoice)	24.11.1943	За ремонт на самолети в работилница Скопие от фирма Бахман (Bachman von Blumental & Co Flugzeugbau). Rechnung N.43746 от 24.11.1943 за доставка на Flieglack 7122.70, 7122.71, 7161.27, 7122.02, 7122.65.	Company Bachmann von Blumental & Co. *Flugzeugbau* shipped the following to repair aircraft at Skopie Workshop: Invoice No. 43746 of 24.11.1943 to supply aviation lacquers 7122.70, 7122.71, 7161.27, 7122.02, 7122.65.
Протокол (Protocol)	03.12.1943	За доставка на лакове от Хербиг Хаархаус ВС 6929 (11) зеленикав ВС 6509 (1) червен Разредител No. 45 Очистител С 1213	Delivery of lacquers by Herbig-Haarhaus BC.6929 (11) Greenish BC.6509 (1) Red Thinner [diluent] No. 45 Cleaner C.1213
Протокол (Protocol)	20.12.1943	За доставка на лакове от Хербиг Хархаус безцветен ВС 6952 (7) Поропълнител ВС 9002 (8) Ботслак зеленикав ВС 6929 (11) Покривен синкаво-сив No. 44	Delivery of lacquers by Herbig-Haarhaus Colourless BC.6952 (7) Pore filler [putty] BC.9002 (8) Boat [?] lacquer, Greenish BC.6929 (11) Roof [paint], Blueish-Grey No. 44
Rechnung (Invoice)	19.02.1944	Rechnung N.734 WL 42785 (Nr. 47) WL 42784 (Nr. 46)	Invoice No. 734 [by Herbig-Haarhaus] WL 42785 (Nr. 47) WL 42784 (Nr. 46)
Поръчка (Order)	30.03.1944	За херболоид самолетни лакове 101 000 кг	Order for Herboloid aircraft lacquers, 101.000 kg
Протокол (Protocol)	19.06.1944	За доставка на разредител N.42785 (47) и опъвателен лак безветен N.42784 (46)	Delivery of diluent No. 42785 (47) and a tension lacquer, colourless No.42784 (46)
Изпитателен протокол (Test Report)	20.06.1944	Опъвателен лак WL 42784 /46/ Специален разредител WL 42785 /47/	Tensioning lacquer WL 42784 (46) Special [lacquer] diluent (thinner) WL 42785 (47)
Доставка (Delivery)	24.06.1944	Лак опъвателен безцветен 42784 (вътр. 46) Лак специален разредител 42785 (вътр. 47)	Colourless [fabric] tensioning lacquer 42784 (int. 46) Special lacquer diluent (thinner) 42785 (int. 47)
Ursprungs-Zeugnis (Certificate of origin)	?	Herbig Haarhaus Lack und Verdünnung 060801/1-26	Herbig-Haarhaus Lacquer and diluent (thinner) 060801/1-26
Протокол (Protocol)	26.06.1944	Прием на материали от Германия за летище Варна (...) 15. FIVV 3305.2 7262 Паста – боя 15 кг. (...)	About acceptance of material from Germany at Varna airfield (...) 15. FIVV 3305.2 7262 Paste–paint 15 kg. (...)
Rechnung (Invoice)	04.07.1944	Herbig Haarhaus Lackfabrik Lacke: BC 12431 (35) (31) (32) (33) (30) (16) VL 7826 (7) BC 6952 (7) BC 6509 (1) C 1213 (2) E 1 (42)	Herbig-Haarhaus Lacquer Factory Lacquers: BC.12431 (35) (31) (32) (33) (30) (16) VL.7826 (7) BC.6952 (7) BC.6509 (1) C.1213 (2) E.1 (42)
Rechnung (Invoice)	08.07.1944	Herbig Haarhaus Lackfabrik Verdünnung: BC 6970 (28)	Herbig-Haarhaus Lacquer Factory Diluent (thinner): BC.6970 (28)

Писмо (Letter)	11.1948	От „Химипорт" до фирма Spojene Tovarny na barvy a laky – Narodni podnik, Praha искане за мостри от аеро-лакове за дърво, за метал, за плат, боя за надписи, очистители, измиватели, разредители и емайл-лакове със съответните им номера за всеки цвят	From "Chimimport" to company *Spojené Tovarny na Barvy a Laky – Národní Podnik, Praha* [United Paint and Varnish Factory – National Corporation, Prague, Czechoslovakia] Request for samples of aerosol paints for wood, metal, fabric, signs, cleaners, wash-off fluid, thinners and enamel lacquers, with their corresponding numbers for each colour.

Annex 2

His Majesty's Air Force (VNVV)
Technical Testing Service
16 October 1942
Bozhurishte Airfield

Test Protocol No. X/8 [H/8]

Name of the [tested] material: non-flammable aircraft lacquer, wooden mastic filler and thinner.
Name of the manufacturer: Herbig-Haarhaus AG, Cologne, Germany.
Imported by: Dr. B. Dzhabarov – Sofia
Intended for: aircraft construction

The tests were carried out based on request from [VNVV] acceptance committee.

Tested lacquers:
Herboloid main stretching lacquer – oxide red, BC.6509
Herboloid single-layer lacquer – insignia (for flag) white, BC.12431
Herboloid single-layer lacquer – olive green, BC.12431
Herboloid single-layer lacquer – yellow-orange, BC.12431
Herboloid single-layer lacquer – insignia (for flag) red, BC.12431
Herboloid single-layer lacquer – black, BC.12431
Herboloid single-layer lacquer – silver, BC.12431
Herboloid single-layer lacquer – combined grey-green, for metal, BC.6965
Herboloid mastic filler for wood and Herboloid special thinner, BC.6970

The lacquers have to be veneered well with a brush and spray gun. The airplane fabric is covered very well with five brush-strokes, while the metal covers with main grey-green (colour?) with one brush-stroke. The wooden mastic filler fills up very well the pores of the wood.

The painted surface is proper, the film is smooth and flexible, homogeneous and firm.
Painting and polishing is completed in 24 hours, including the drying of the last layer, and is ready for use and assembling.

The polished film is resistant against moisture, gasoline, benzene and gasoline-benzene mix.
The fabric painted/polished with non-flammable aircraft lacquer is fireproof, i.e., when set on fire it begins to burn; however, when the flame is removed it quickly extinguishes and carbonization occurs.

The lacquers fill up very well the fabric.

Upon the complete painting/polishing of the aircraft fabric with four layers of main lacquer and one layer of covering lacquer, the weight of the lacquer increases with 197 grams per square meter, while the strength of the fabric increases by about 50%.

The special thinner dilutes the lacquers very well in every respect.

Conclusion: the lacquers, the wooden mastic and the special thinner meet the technical conditions/requirements.

[Signatures]

Annex 3

Directorate of Foreign Trade
Sofia (...)
No. 17803-9-16.08.1944
Reply to telegram of Exportin-Sofia, No. 6055/12.8.1944
To: Ministry of War
Supply Department
Topic: Import of aircraft pastes from Germany
(...) we announce that aircraft pastes ordered in Germany will be delivered by the following companies:
100 kg *Flugzeugfugenpaste* No.7267, and
100 kg VDM 20 *Grafit Schpindelölpaste* [?]
.... by company Warnecke and Böhm, Berlin-Weissensee, Gotestrasse 15
1000 kg *Enteizungspaste* G2 [?]
... by company Gustav Ruth [Lackfabrik, Wandsbeck], Temperol Werke, Hamburg-Blankenese, Hamisoweg 8.
200 kg *Kremzerweiss*
.... by company Bleiberger Bergwerks Union [BBU], Klagenfurt.
Please send your representative to Berlin to contact these companies to buy these aircraft pastes.
Director (...)

Annex 4

(Receipt of German aviation paints, lacqueurs and thinners)

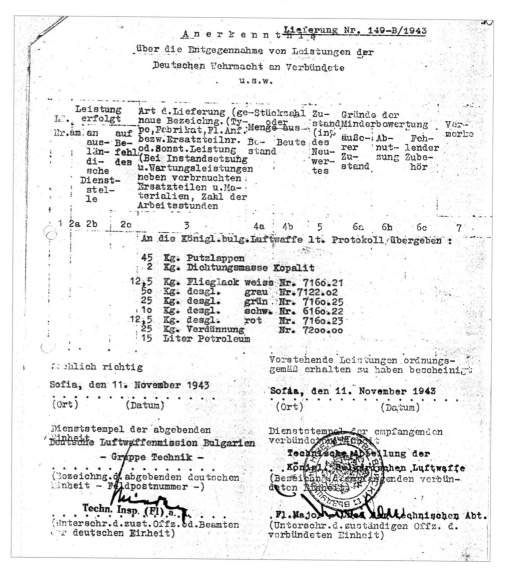

Markings and Codes
of Bulgarian Aircraft (1919–1949)

The Kingdom of Bulgaria ended World War 1 on the defeated side. As a consequence of the harsh peace treaty signed at Neuilly-sur-Seine, France, on 27 November 1919[1], all surviving aircraft and aero engines that could be located by members of the Inter-Allied Aeronautical Commission of Control (IAACC) for Bulgaria were scrapped.

Nevertheless, before the peace treaty was penned and its provisions officially took effect in mid-1921, there was a brief period when limited activity of Bulgarian aircraft was permitted under strict Allied supervision. By the time the first Allied aviation inspectors arrived in Bulgaria, in the last days of 1918, notably RAF Captain E. W. Chatterley of 16th Wing, who inspected the airfield at Bozhurishte – at that time occupied by French troops – from 31 December 1918 and 17 January 1919 and assessed his findings in a comprehensive report[2], all surviving military aircraft were assembled at Bozhurishte main military airfield [photo 1]. Instead of the military markings of the defeated Central Powers – either the newer straight-arm white bordered black 'beam' cross, or the older white bordered black 'Maltese Cross' – some of them sported coloured cockades (roundels), resembling those used by the Allied Powers [photo 2A]. Based on the detailed report compiled by RAF Captain F. Wells at the Salonika Aircraft Park on 2 February 1919[3], this new type of military marking was identified as "bull's eye" style, consisting of a 9" (228.6 mm) diameter red dot in centre, surrounded by two 5" (127 mm) thick rings, the middle one being green, while the outer one white – consistent with Bulgaria's national colours [photo 2B]. The roundels were placed on either side of the mid-fuselage. Based on photographic evidence he submitted with his report; these new roundels and the obsolete crosses were simultaneously worn by a few aircraft.

1. At least sixteen warplanes of various types and in various conditions (some without tyres or propellers) line up on Bozhurishte main air base of the Bulgarian air force at the end of World War I. With a very few exceptions, all of them would fall to the axe, according to the harsh post-war peace treaty signed at Neuilly-sur-Seine, France, on 27 November 1919. All of them display the 'Maltese Cross' type marking also used by German and Austro-Hungarian aircraft.

---

1   For details of the Peace Treaty's Air Clauses, see Fokker D.VII chapter's initial footnotes.

2   „*Report on the Armament of Bulgarian Aeroplanes & Seaplanes from Information Obtained During a Visit to Bojouristi Aerodrome, Sofia, and the Seaplane Station at Varna by Capt. E. W. Chatterley, O. i/c Gunnery, 16th Wing, R.A.F. (31.12.1918-17.1.1919)*" A.I.(T.) Folder No. 51 (Air Historical Branch of the Air Ministry, UK). For further details of Cpt. Chatterley's findings, see Fokker D.VII chapter.

3   „*Report on Aeroplanes, Seaplanes, Engines, Buildings, Equipment, etc. Inspected in Bulgaria in Accordance with Instructions Contained in Air Ministry Letter A.I.2 (G) of 26/11/1918 with Photographs (Enclosed) by Capt. F. Wells, O. i/c Workshops, Salonika Aircraft Park, R.A.F. 3/2/1919*" A.I.(T.) Folder No. 52 (Air Historical Branch of the Air Ministry, UK). For further details of Cpt. Wells' findings, see Fokker D.VII chapter.

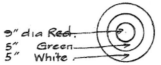

Bulls eye on either side of fuselage at rear of observers cockpit.

Upper surface of top planes two maltese crosses 5' 6" square, with 2½" white edge. Crosses on undersurface of lower planes and rudder obliterated with white paint. No camouflage scheme.

On other aircraft, the old cross-type marking was simply overpainted in white, also in cross shape, or square. [photo 3]

Additionally to the roundel type marking, several aircraft assembled at Bozhurishte also wore on the fuselage, in front of the roundel, a white square of 2'-8" (812.8 mm) sides, with a large, black Cyrillic letter 'B' in the centre, probably denoting 'Boris'. [photo 4A and 4B] The rudder – where the Maltese Cross-style marking used to be – was completely overpainted in light grey, or white.

As noted, these markings were observed on land-based aircraft collected at Bozhurishte airfield during the winter of 1918/1919. The seaplanes assembled at the main seaport of Varna, on the shores of the Black Sea, around the same time, also wore makeshift roundel type marking. This was applied over the obsolete cross-type marking. However, this time, the colours and their arrangements were identical to those of the French marking, namely blue dot in the centre, surrounded by two rings, the middle one being white, the outer one red. The tricolour roundel was applied on the mid-fuselage (over a white square), while the rudder was divided vertically in three equal areas, the inner one being painted blue, the centre one white, and the outer one red, consistent with the French national colours. [photo 5A and 5B]

There was a notably different type of marking, observed on a Friedrichshafen FF.33L type seaplane (No. 1271) by the same Capt. Wells. The marking consisted of a multi-coloured triangle, with white, green and red borders, each 2' (609.6 mm) long, with a yellow rampant lion in the centre, on a crimson background. This marking was applied on both fuselage sides, on the rudder, as well as on the upper surface of the upper wing and the lower surface of the lower wing, in a larger version, with the sides of the equilateral triangle being 5' (1524 mm) long each. [photos 6A and 6B]

Unbeknownst until now, this colourful triangular insignia was introduced *prior to* the war's end, sometime in 1918, as proven by a photograph depicting the *Văzduhoplavatelna Stantsia* (Air Navigation Station) on 16 July 1918. [photo 6C] The precise date of the marking's introduction is unknown, as is the date when it was abolished. It is also unclear if this marking was applied solely on seaplanes, or on landplanes as well (less likely). By contrast, the white-green-red roundel was certainly in use on Bozhurishte-based demilitarised warplanes until the aforementioned peace treaty forbade any sort of flying in Bulgaria in 1921.

The Secret Years

Once the strict clauses of the Neuilly Peace Treaty came in effect, all domestic airplanes disappeared from Bulgarian skies – but not for too long. Even before the IAACC inspectors left Bulgaria in the last days of 1922, a couple of aircraft, hidden in barns and cellars, had been brought to light and secretly restored to flying condition. When these 'clandestine' aircraft eventually took off, they did not wear any markings or codes, and were painted in neutral colours, usually light grey, or cream. [photo 7] This covert, intermediary situation changed after Bulgaria ratified the International Civil Aviation Treaty on 5 July 1923. From that moment on, its air vehicles could officially carry civilian registrations sanctioned by the international community.

Bulgaria had originally been assigned by the International Commission for Air Navigation (ICAN, or CINA, as per the French language acronyms) the letters 'Z-B' on 28 February 1923. However, this was

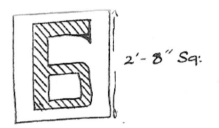

2'- 8" Sq.

This device on either side
of fuselage under observers cockpit
black letters on white ground.

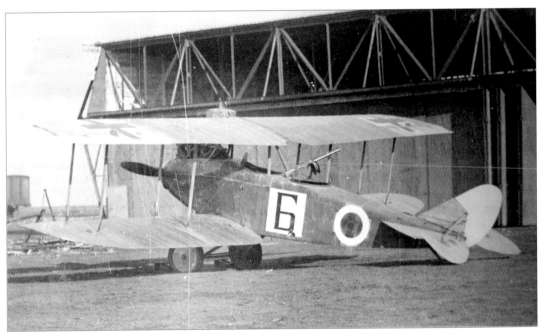

3. This photo of a rubber tyre-less Albatros C.III general purpose biplane was taken from the final report compiled by RAF Captain F. Wells. Notice the previous Central Powers marking on the fuselage and tail had been overpainted in white.

4A. Sketch of the special marking, consisting of a large, black Cyrillic letter 'B' (denoting "Boris'), made by RAF Captain F. Wells, as observed on the fuselage of a DFW C.V multi-role combat biplane.

4B. The DFW C.V showing the large, black Cyrillic letter 'B' applied in a white square, photographed on Bozhurishte airfield, during the winter of 1918/1919. The biplane also sports on its fuselage a makeshift Bulgarian cockade over the original cross. However, the wing crosses were left uncovered. Note the rudder was painted over with some sort of light grey, or perhaps yellow, as there is a visible contrast between the recently applied white paint on the fuselage and the rudder hue. The ailerons are also a bit lighter than the rest of the upper wing's colour, and could be the same colour used on rudder.

5A. A Bulgarian manned Friedrichshafen F.F.33E (1916, Naval No. 862) type seaplane photographed at Varna seaport by RAF Captain F. Wells in early 1919. The aircraft displays French cockades on fuselage and wing surfaces, applied right over the obsolete Central Powers marking (covered with white squares), as well as vertical red-white-blue tricolour bands on the rudder.

valid briefly and only on paper, as domestic flying was still officially forbidden at that time. The country registration was changed to 'B-B' on 26 June 1923, at a subsequent meeting of ICAN. Thus, the official civilian air registration of Bulgarian aircraft became B-Bxxx (the latter three signs being a combination of capital letters, denoting a particular aircraft). [photo 8] However and quite ironically, despite the rule, officially there were no airplanes in Bulgaria these civilian registrations could be applied to.

The first aircraft – ironically ordered and delivered by Bulgaria's First World War enemy, France – arrived in Bulgaria only in late 1923. Curiously and quite inexplicably, some of these French aircraft (four Potez VIIIs and four Hanriot HD-14s, followed shortly by five Caudron C.59s), purportedly imported to equip the fledgling Bulgarian air club, based at Bozhurishte airfield, were delivered in military markings! [photo 9] These consisted of a cockade type insignia, red dot in centre, surrounded by two circles, green in the middle and white outside, identical to the roundels worn briefly in 1919/1920. The roundels were applied over a black square, placed on the outer surface of the upper wing and the under surface of the lower wing. [photo 10] The difference from that early post-war period was that this time the rudder was painted in Bulgarian national colours of white, green and red, applied in vertical stripes. However, as shown by photographic evidence, the order these colours were applied on the rudder differed not only by aircraft type, but by individual aircraft as well. On Potez VIIs and Caudron C.59s it was the red stripe which was inside [photos 11 and 12], close to the fin, while on all Potez XVIIs it was exactly the opposite, the white stripe was inside, close to the fin. [photo 13] On the Hanriot HD-14s, both colour sequences can be observed. Later on, apparently the latter version, with the white stripe inside, became the standard on both imported and domestically made aircraft. Instead of civilian registration letters, these early French imports were identified with Arabic numerals applied on the mid-fuselage, also in military style. [photo 14] From mid-1924, the military style numbers on the fuselage were replaced on all French aircraft with regular civilian registrations, but the rudder stayed tricolour – a feature peculiar

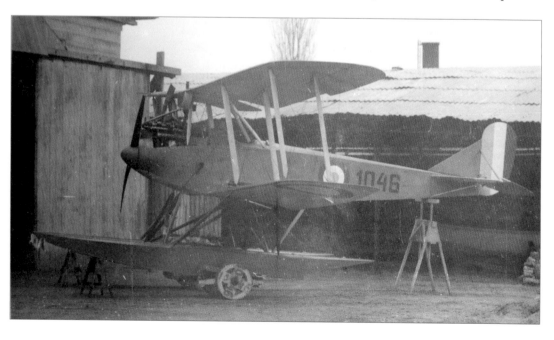

5B. Rumpler 1916 seaplane (No. 1046), also photographed at Varna seaport in early 1919. This one also displays French cockades on fuselage and wing surfaces, and blue-white-red tricolour stripes on rudder.

Identification features consist of multi coloured triangles, with the device of a Lion in the centre, painted as shown in sketch.

White
Green
Yellow Lion
Crimson
Red.

Those on top planes have sides measuring 5' 0". Those on bottom planes are similar. Those on either side of fuselage and rudder have sides measuring 2' 0".

6A. *A markedly different style of military marking was observed on a Friedrichshafen FF.33L (No. 1271) type seaplane, also anchored at Peynerdzhik seaplane station, located south of Varna. Capt. Wells' sketch details this rare gaudy marking (and thanks to it, the proper colours are described for the first time).*

6B. *Original photo of the aforementioned seaplane, No. 1271. This marking was used only briefly, probably between 1918-1920.*

6C. **Below:** *Still of the Văzduhoplavatelna Stantsia (Air Navigation Station), taken on 16 July 1918, as described on the original print's reverse. This photo depicts all three identification versions Bulgarian-manned seaplanes wore. One wears the well-known black Maltese-cross style marking and serial number on fuselage (at left). The centre one has the colourful triangle, described earlier. The all-silver (or light blue) painted third one, at right, bears black crosses on the wings, but only the name LYAPCHEV on the fuselage side, in memory of the first lost Bulgarian seaplane pilot, Lt. Preslav G. Lyapchev, who died in the North Sea together with his German instructor, in a flight accident, on 10 June 1916.*

7. A sole Fokker D.VII had escaped the unwanted attention of the vigilant members of the Inter-Allied Aeronautical Commission of Control (IAACC), thus survived until better times for Bulgarian aviation arrived. When it eventually took off again after several years in hiding, it wore neither markings, nor codes, except for a four-leaf clover on the wheel hub, which also was soon deleted.

8. Bulgaria was assigned by the International Commission for Air Navigation (ICAN, or CINA, as per the French language acronym) 'B-B' as civilian aviation registration, on 26 June 1923. Ironically, officially, there were no aircraft in Bulgaria at that time this register could be applied on. One of the first domestically built aircraft to bear civilian registration (from 1926) was B-BAPA, the second-built U-1 (DAR c/n 2) trainer. Seven copies of the venerable W.W. 1-era DFW C.Va multi-role combat biplane were built by DAR (State Aircraft Workshops), Bozhurishte, in 1925 as the Uzunov-1 (or DAR U-1). The "U" prefix honoured the memory of Ivan Uzunov, a well-known Bulgarian pilot, who lost his life on 14 April 1925 while performing aerobatics aboard an Austrian-made Avis B.S. II (coded A-16). The first Bulgarian-made series production aircraft type was used as a trainer for Bulgaria's secret air force.

to military aircraft. This latter detail was clearly against the rules, which required the civilian aircraft of the defeated nations to be devoid of any display of the national colours[4].

By contrast, the aircraft imported from Great Britain – namely three Bristol 88 'Bulgarian Tourers' and two Avro 522 floatplanes – arrived in full civilian registrations, with the rudder devoid of Bulgarian colours, a large letter B being applied instead, as per the regulations. [photo 15] The same letter was applied on both sides of the horizontal stabilisers (tailplanes) as well. Later on, the rudders of these British aircraft were retrofitted with the Bulgarian colours. The initial trio of Bristols (four more followed later on), registered B-BECA, B-BEHA and B-BEPA[5], became the first Bulgarian aircraft to officially wear civilian registrations, in effect from April 1924.

The style the civilian registrations were applied on Bulgarian aircraft varied greatly. The simplest case was when the black registration letters were applied directly on the fuselage sides and wings, right over

---

4   Hungary, who was in the same situation like Bulgaria, was not allowed to show the national colours on its aircraft until early 1937. For details on the markings and codes of Hungarian aircraft (1919-1945), please consult Dénes Bernád, György Punka 'Hungarian Fighter Colours', vol. 1, published by MMP/Stratus in 2013, pages 10-33.

5   Apparently, the Bulgarian official who assigned the civilian registrations to the early aircraft attempted to use Latin letters that could also be read by Cyrillic alphabet (in this particular case, B-BECA=V-VESA, B-BEHA=V-VENA and B-BEPA=V-VERA).

Аеродромъ Божурище: новитѣ аероплани　　　　　фот. А. Б.

1923.

9. *The Bulgarian national aviation magazine Летецъ (Letets), or Airman, published the first photo of the "new aeroplanes" lined up at Bozhurishte main air base in late 1923. These French aircraft (Potez VIIIs, closest to the camera, at left, Hanriot HD-14s, farthest from camera, at left, as well as Caudron C.59s, at right) – purportedly imported to equip the fledgling Bulgarian air club – were delivered with military markings! Notice the order the Bulgarian national colours were painted on the rudder (the white vertical stripe is best visible) differed from airplane to airplane.*

НАШИТѢ НОВИ АЕРОПЛАНИ: „ПОТЕЗЪ"

НАЙ-МАЛКИЯТЪ отъ всички наши аероплани е „Анри Потезъ", типъ 8. Той е бипланъ съ двойни команди; снабденъ е съ моторъ „Анзани", 60 К С. Устройството му е едновременно и просто и здраво. Скелетътъ на крилетѣ и стабилизиращитѣ плоскости сж отъ дуралуминий. Тѣлото му е направено отъ фурниръ безъ болтове и желѣзни схватки. Колесницата му е съ колела и съ олео-пневматични ударосмекчители. Чрезъ изолиране на една отъ командитѣ за управление, той се превръща въ аеропланъ за усъвършенствуване. Малкитѣ му размери го правятъ чувствителенъ и повратливъ въ въздуха, а значителния коефициентъ на сигурность го прави годенъ за всички въздушни акробации. Въ състезанията

презъ 1921 год., устроени отъ фирмата „Зенитъ", между Парижъ и Лионъ, той е билъ класиранъ втори — за най-малъкъ разходъ на горивни материали.

Характеристикитѣ на „Потезъ" сж:

Разпереность	. . . .	8　м.
дължина	. . . .	5·70　„
височина	. . . .	2·50　„
носяща площь	. . .	20.20 кв. м.
тегло празенъ	. . . .	250 клг.
полезенъ товарь	. . .	230 кгр.
общо тегло	. . . .	480 кгр.
натоварване на кв м.	. .	24 кгр.
„　„　К. С.	. .	8 кгр.
скорость при земята	. .	142 клм.
скорость при кацане	. .	40 клм.
максимална височина	.	4000 м.
изкачва 2000 м. за 11 м.		

Нашитѣ нови аероплани: „Потезъ"　　　　　фот. аер. Божурище

10. *The same aviation magazine Letets published a photo as illustration to the technical characteristics of the Potez VIII where the military marking applied to the wing upper surface is clearly seen. The cockade type insignia, applied over a black square, consisted of a red dot in centre, surrounded by two circles, green in the middle and white outside – identical to the roundels worn briefly in 1919/1920.*

29

11, 12, 13. As noted earlier, the order the Bulgarian national colours were applied on the rudder varied. E.g., on the depicted Potez VII (B-BILO) and Caudron C.59 (B-BETA) it was the red stripe that was inside, close to the fin, while on all Potez XVIIs (B-BPEK) it was exactly the opposite, the white stripe was inside. Later on, apparently the latter version, with the white stripe inside, became standard.

Пропаганда на Българския Аероклубъ: една нова членка на клуба, въ аероплана
„Потезъ" (аеродромъ Божурище)

14. Instead of civilian registration letters, these early French aircraft were identified with Arabic numerals applied on the mid-fuselage, consistent to military style. Potez VIII, No. 4, is depicted on this photo taken from Letets magazine, issued in early 1924.

the natural coloured skin (fabric or plywood). [photo 16] There were cases, however, when the registration was surrounded by a white or black rectangle. On other occasions, the black letters were applied over a white rectangle, bordered in black. [photo 11 and 12] Although in most situations the registration letters were plain black, in certain instances the black letters were outlined in white. In many cases the last four letters of the registration were underlined with a black horizontal line. [photo 17] This practice purportedly denoted private aircraft, although all Bulgarian air vehicles – with the exception of the two Junkers F13 transports, which belonged to the short-lived BUNAVAD domestic airline – were owned by the state. In other cases, the registration letters were not underlined. Curiously, even within the same aircraft type, both versions could be observed (for example, the Potez XVIIs). The letter B, officially to be applied on the rudder, was either omitted (as the rudder was painted in Bulgarian colours), or applied on the fin instead. Also, the same letter B which was supposed to be applied on both sides of the horizontal stabilisers (tailplanes), was either present or not. In rare cases, the civilian registration was followed by a dot (as was the case with the Avro 552s). This great variation of civilian registration styles prompts the would-be modeller of inter-war Bulgarian aircraft to use solely period photographs in order to build his/her scale model as accurately as possible.

At one point, most probably in 1930, the direction the Bulgarian national colours were painted on the rudder changed from vertical to horizontal. [photo 18 and 18A] Shortly after this, but independent-

15. By contrast to the early French types, the aircraft imported from Great Britain arrived in full and properly applied civilian registrations. Depicted is B-BECA, a Bristol 88 'Bulgarian Tourer', which officially was the first civilian aircraft registered in Bulgaria, in April 1924. Notice the rudder devoid of the military-style Bulgarian national colours, instead a large letter B being applied on it (as well on the horizontal tailplanes), as per regulations.

31

ly, the Bulgarian civilian registration changed, too. This was in accordance with the resolution of the International Radio Telegraph Conference held in Washington, D.C., on 25 November 1927, which took effect on 1 January 1929. According to the resolution, the civilian registration of Bulgarian aircraft changed from B-Bxxx to LZ-xxx. However, a couple of years passed before all aircraft in Bulgaria actually changed their registrations. This was officially due by the end of 1931; however, for a period after the deadline, both the old and new registrations were visible on aircraft, until the B-B registration was finally phased out sometime in 1932. An original photograph of a DAR-1 *Peperuda* (Butterfly) light trainer, taken at Bozhurishte main air base on 25 August 1932, shows the aircraft still wearing the old-style B-BIKA registration, but with a horizontally divided tricolour rudder. For a short time period, one could see Bulgarian aircraft wearing either the new or the old civilian registration. [photo 19] This transition period lasted until repainting was concluded on all aircraft.

Theoretically, the old 'B-B' country code gave way to the new 'LZ' code, while the last three letters, identifying a particular aircraft, remained unchanged. However, there were odd situations, when the registration was altered erroneously. This was the case of the second prototype of the indigenously designed DAR-3 of 1929, which was initially registered as B-BDIA, then changed to the erroneous LZ-BDIA for a short time, until it became LZ-DIA. Letov Š-18, B-BIBO, became for a short period in 1932 L-ZIBO [photo 20], before switching to the regular LZ-IBO. Gliders were not subject to any of these regulations, they were usually identified only by a name, completed by the country's civilian registration 'LZ' when flying abroad. [photo 21]

Based on photographic evidence, the military style roundels did not fully disappear in the mid-1920s, occasionally springing up alongside the regular civilian registration, possibly during covert war exercises. On one such photograph, a couple of locally-built DAR-1 basic trainers are seen with large Green-White-Red (centre dot) roundels applied on the bottom wing's lower outer surface, at the extremity of the civilian registrations, lined up on the secondary airfield of Vratsa, in 1931 (still wearing the B-Bxxx type registration, but the rudder colours are divided horizontally). [photo 22]

Rebirth of the Air Force

The formal (re)birth of the *Văzdushni na Negovo Velichestvo Voyski* (VNVV, or His Majesty's Air Army) happened on 27 June 1937, when Tsar Boris III handed over the combat flags to the four newly formed *orlyatsi* (air groups) at Bozhurishte main air base. Prior to this official event, a new military marking had been designed and applied to all newly-delivered German combat aircraft lined up on Bozhurishte's grass. This new military marking was based on the Bulgarian tsarist coat of arms, and resembled closely the Bulgarian Order of Bravery, 4th Class. It consisted of a forward-facing rampant yellow (or golden) crowned lion over a red (crimson) dot, in centre, surrounded by a yellow (or golden) bordered white circle. This arrangement was placed over a yellow (or golden) bordered red (crimson) Maltese-style cross, with two yellow (or golden) crossed swords. This rather complicated heraldic design

17. Although in most situations the registration letters were plain black, in certain instances the black letters were outlined in white, as was the case of B-BISA, a Letov Š-18 (Šmolík), registered in 1926. In many cases, including this particular one, the last four letters of the registration were underlined with a black horizontal line, which purportedly denoted private aircraft (although all aircraft were property of the Bulgarian State).

18. At one point, the direction the Bulgarian national colours were painted on the rudder changed from vertical to horizontal. This must have happened before 1932, as the depicted DAR-1 'Peperuda' (Butterfly) trainers still wear the B-B style register. Notice how B-BIKD, at left, has the colours aligned on the rudder vertically, while B-BIKE, at right, has the same colours applied horizontally. DAR-1 was the first truly indigenously designed airplane, by a team headed by German professor Dipl.-Eng. Hermann Winter.

18A. Modern full-scale replica of the DAR-1, photographed in May 2009, showing all the markings and codes, as well as livery, Bulgarian civilian aircraft wore after the standards were regulated in 1931. (I. Donchev)

19. In accordance with the resolution of the International Radio Telegraph Conference held in Washington, D.C., on 25 November 1927, the civilian registration for Bulgarian aircraft changed from B-Bxxx to LZ-xxx. However, a couple of years had passed until all aircraft in Bulgaria actually changed their registration. This was officially due by the end of 1931; however, for a period after the deadline, both the old and new registration versions were visible on aircraft, until the B-B registration was finally phased out in 1932. This was the case with this pair of DAR-1s (B-BIKD, at left, and LZ-IKH, at right).

20. Theoretically, the old B-B country code gave way to the new LZ code, while the last three letters, identifying a particular aircraft, remained unchanged. However, there were odd situations, when the register was altered erroneously. This was the case of the depicted Letov Š-18, ex-B-BIBO, which became, for a short period in 1932, L-ZIBO, before switching to the regular LZ-IBO.

21. In 1935, DAR-Bozhurishte built three 'Komar' type gliders under Polish licence [called 'Albatros', 'Rilski Orel', or 'The Eagle of Rila (Mountain)', and 'Polska Chuchuliga', or 'Field Lark']. The first one participated at the Berlin Olympics in 1936, where reportedly it won a gold medal. 'Albatros' is depicted with the Olympic circles on its nose, followed by Bulgaria's civilian registration code LZ, in a form used by gliders when flying abroad.

was superimposed over a large diameter white circle[6]. [photo 23A] The diameter of the marking, based on calculations done by the Author using various photos with valid reference dimensions (e.g. tyre size), varied between 900 mm, 800 mm, or 600 mm, depending of the aircraft type and the location on the airframe it was applied to. For example, on the PZL P.24s, the largest size roundel (around 900 mm) was applied on the wings, while on the fuselage the smallest size (around 600 mm) was used. The 'tsarist roundel' type military marking – unofficially referred to as знак "кръст за храброст", or 'Bravery Cross' Sign – was applied in six positions: on either fuselage sides and on the upper and lower surfaces of the wing(s). [photo 24] The rudder continued to be painted in three identically wide horizontal stripes in Bulgaria's national colours – white, green and red (from top to bottom).

The domestically built military trainers (of DAR and KB design) kept their civilian registrations for a while. These Bulgarian trainers switched to military markings and codes only gradually, in the late 1930s, or early 1940s [photo 25]; and not all of them, some flying with pseudo-civilian markings until the end of their service life. Similarly, imported German basic trainers kept their civilian registrations until they were written off and scrapped. For a short while, those indigenous trainers – most notably the DAR-3 'Garvan I' – flew with dual markings, featuring military roundels on the fuselage and civilian registrations on the wing surfaces.

On two early German aircraft types – the Arado Ar 65 fighter and the Dornier Do 11 bomber – an elaborate 'Royal Cipher' was also applied on the airframe. This emblem symbolised the generosity of Tsar Boris III, who reportedly paid for these aircraft with his own money and donated them to the air force[7]. This 'Royal Cipher' of about 1000 mm height and 600 mm width consisted of a yellow (or golden) Cyrillic letter 'B' (B for Boris) with the identically coloured royal crown over it, superimposed over a red (crimson) shield, which was outlined with thick green and white borders – symbolising Bulgaria's national colours. [photo 23B]

With the introduction of military markings, a numbering system was also established to identify individual aircraft. It consisted of two groups of numbers, one applied on the fin, the other one on the rear fuselage. [photo 26] On bomber aircraft (e.g. Dornier Do 11), the first group of numbers was applied in front of the fuselage marking, while the second one was aft. The meaning of these two groups of numbers is not fully understood; however, the Author believes the two-digit numbers (for fighters and fighter trainers consisting of 11, 22, or 33, for bombers of 55), applied on the fuselage, represented the *yato* (squadron), i.e. 11 was the 1st *Yato*, 22 the 2nd *Yato*, and so on. The single-digit number on the tail surface may have referred to the place the machine had in a particular two-aircraft *dvoyka* (pair), or four-aircraft *krilo* (flight/squad) of a particular *yato* (squadron) of a particular mixed *orlyak* (group). For example, aircraft No. 11-1 was the first aircraft of the P.24 flight/squad of the first squadron of a certain group, while aircraft No. 33-8 was the last aircraft of the He 51 flight/squad in the third squadron of the same group. In respect of fighters and fighter trainers, subject of this book, the dozen PZL P.24s wore the following number sequences: 11-1 to 11-4, 22-1 to 22-4, 33-1 to 33-4, while the dozen He 51s wore 11-5 to 11-8, 22-5 to 22-8 and 33-5 to 33-8. Finally, the half-dozen Fw 56s wore 11-9 to 11-10, 22-9 to 22-10 and 33-9 to 33-10. The only straightforward situation was with the dozen Do 11 bombers, which

22. Apparently, coloured roundels were occasionally used alongside regular civilian registrations, possibly during covert war exercises (only on the wings, probably on the lower surfaces only). In this particular photograph, a couple of locally built DAR-1 basic trainers are seen with large Green-White-Red (centre dot) roundels applied on the bottom wing's lower outer surface, outside the civilian registrations (still wearing the B-Bxxx type register, but the rudder colours are divided horizontally). Curiously, the few Potez XVIIs – a clearly military aircraft type – visible on the photo, at right, do not wear this roundel. Photo taken at the secondary airfield of Vratsa, in 1931.

---

6   Bulgarian and foreign printed sources mention that occasionally a red border was applied around the roundel. However, the Author found no photographic proof of this occurrence.

7   Other, mostly non-Bulgarian, sources mention that these two-dozen aircraft were actually a gift by Hermann Göring to Tsar Boris, who then handed them over ceremoniously to his air force.

23A. The formal (re)birth of the Văzdushni na Negovo Velichestvo Voyski (VNVV, or His Majesty's Air Army) happened on 27 June 1937. Prior to this official event, a new military marking had been designed and applied to all newly-delivered German combat aircraft. This new military marking, depicted on the fuselage of an Arado Ar 65F fighter, was based on the Bulgarian royal coat of arms and resembled closely the Bulgarian Order of Bravery, 4th Class.

23B. The new, so-called 'Tsarist Roundel' type marking (at right), along with the Royal Cipher of Tsar Boris III (at left), as worn on the side of an Arado Ar 65F.

wore codes from 55-1 to 55-12 applied on the fuselage (the fin was already 'taken' by the so-called royal cypher), on either side of the military marking. [photo 27]

The two-number system, although widely used, was not the only one introduced when the Bulgarian air force was officially unveiled in mid-1937. The dozen Arado Ar 65 fighters were identified by a small white text on the fin top, which included the aircraft type, in Cyrillic (i.e. 'Ap.65'), followed by a serial number starting with 101, linked to the aircraft type with a dash. [photo 28] Later, a large black number was written on the tail surface, which repeated the last number of the serial (1 to 12). Other military aircraft types – e.g. Avia B.122 fighter trainers – were also identified with large black numbers written across the tail surface, without displaying a small size complete identification as was the case with the Ar 65, however. This 'large black number on tail' style numbering system was applied on civilian-registered basic trainer types as well, as noted later.

Along with identifying its airplanes with military marking and numbers, the VNVV also introduced a policy in assigning a code name to each aircraft type in service. These code names were overwhelmingly birds and other small animals names – e.g. 'Yastreb', or Hawk, identifying the P.24 fighter, or 'Prilep', or Bat, assigned to the Do 11 bombers – and their usage became the norm in both official and unofficial paperwork[8]. One of the rare deviations to this naming standard happened with the imminent arrival of the 'top notch' German fighter, the Messerschmitt Bf 109E, which was assigned the name 'Strela', or Arrow, by an air force decree dated 15 May 1940. Later on, such departure from the classical birds' names became more frequent.

With the arrival, or expected arrival of a large number of aircraft, and taking into consideration the existing mixed aircraft park, VNVV HQ issued Order No. 53, on 14 April 1938, in an effort to standardise the identification colours used on aircraft, based on their role. Here is the translated document[9], edited by the Author[10]:

COMMANDER OF THE AIR FORCE Nr. 53 14 April 1938 Sofia	O R D E R Technical	Strongly confidential

For greater expeditiousness in issuing air navigation certificates, as well as for easier bookkeeping of the new registration assigned to aircraft and control of their status, the registration and issuing of certificates will be performed in the future by the control department. Thus, a special card-index will be created and maintained for all aircraft of the Air Force, according to order Nr. 399 from 30 December 1937.

---

8 For a comprehensive, but still incomplete, list of all code names identified by the Author, see the Appendices.

9 Many thanks to Teodor Muhovski for translating the document.

10 Many thanks to Ventsislav Chakov for submitting the document.

I. REGISTRATION SIGN

School, trainer and all other aircraft, which do not have armament and have no intended location for such, will bear registration marking according to the convention. It consists of the letters LZ, plus combination of 3 Latin letters, located on both sides of the fuselage, as well as on the top wing surface and on the lower wing surface, according to appendix Nr. 1 [not available]

Combat and all training aircraft, which have armament, or have location intended for such, will wear the military badge (red Bravery Cross over a white circle) on both sides of the fuselage and on both the upper and lower wing surfaces, according to appendix Nr. 2 [not available]

II. REGISTRATION NUMBER

For easy and comfortable entry of the aircraft in corresponding books, they will bear a given registration number, which is applied with white paint on both sides of the vertical stabilizer (fin), in the shape of a fraction (there is no mention of the triangle!). For example, 18/7112, in which the divisor means the aircraft type and the numerator the aircraft number of the given type (see appendix Nr. 1 and Nr. 2) [not available]

The [lower] number represents the purpose (role) of the aircraft, as follows:

School aircraft for primary training – all numbers from 7001 to 8000 ending in number 1. For example: 7001, 7021, 7031, 7041, 7121, 7931.

Reconnaissance trainers – all numbers from 7001 to 8000 ending in number 2. For example: 7002, 7012, 7022, 7532, 7992.

Fighter trainers – all numbers from 7001 to 8000 ending in number 3. For example: 7003, 7013, 7643, 7893.

Bomber trainers – all numbers from 7001 to 8000 ending in number 4. For example: 7004, 7014, 7544, 78......... [last characters missing, but something ending in 4].

Passenger, sports, sanitary, test and other aircraft – all numbers from 7001 to 8000 ending in number 5, for instance: 7005, 7015, 7345, 7895.

Reconnaissance (combat) – all numbers from 7001 to 8000 ending in number 6. For instance: 7006, 7026, 7996.

Fighters (combat) – all numbers from 7000 to 8001 ending in number 7. For instance: 7007, 7017, 7027, 7897.

Bombers (combat) – all numbers from 7001 to 8000 ending in number 8. For instance: 7008, 7018, 7028, 7568.

'Lineen' (i.e., ground attack, close support) aircraft – all numbers from 7001 to 8000 ending in number 9. For instance: 7009, 7019, 7569.

Remark: The category number 10 is currently reserved in case a new type of aircraft is introduced in service, which would not fit the already listed types [to the Author's knowledge, this never happened].

IV[1]. IDENTIFICATION OF THE AIRCRAFT IN SQUADRON (*YATO*)

The allocation of the number of the aircraft in a particular *yato* will be done by writing the number on the white field of the national flag on both sides of the rudder. For example, number 5 means the fifth plane in the *yato*.

V. PAINTING THE AIRCRAFT

For better recognition of aircraft based on their role, they will be painted as follows:

School aircraft – entirely yellow (a little bit orange hue).

Reconnaissance trainers – basecoat paint entirely olive green, nose [and so-called 'cheatline' along the fuselage] blue.

Fighter trainers – basecoat paint entirely olive green, nose [and so-called 'cheatline' along the fuselage] red.

Bomber trainers – basecoat paint entirely olive green, nose [and so-called 'cheatline' along the fuselage] dove grey.

Passenger, sports and others – [various] keeping account of aesthetics and after approval from the control service.

Reconnaissance – looking from above, all [visible] parts to be in camouflage (protective) paint, while at the lower side all [visible] parts in light blue, nose [and so-called 'cheatline' along the fuselage] blue.

Fighters – like reconnaissance [aircraft], nose [and so-called 'cheatline' along the fuselage] red.

Bombers – like reconnaissance [aircraft], nose [and so-called 'cheatline' along the fuselage] dove grey.

---

1   For some reason, point No. III is missing from the document (it must have been a clerical error)

'Lineyni' [i.e., ground attack/close support] aircraft – like reconnaissance [aircraft], nose [and so-called 'cheatline' along the fuselage] orange (...).

VI. NATIONAL FLAG

For recognition of our aircraft by the population, the colours of the national flag – white at the top, green in the middle and red at the bottom – will be painted on the rudder.

By the given instructions, the control department must determine the new recognition signs, registration numbers, designation of the units the aircraft is attached to, etc. Also, it must give directions for gradually replacing the old registrations with the new ones. The registrations that remain the same will not have to be changed. The ones that must be changed will be done at the proper moment – overhauling, repair, repainting, etc.

No later than the end of the year, all aircraft must be already painted with the new recognition signs and registrations.

The aircraft that will take part in the summer training must be painted with the new recognition signs before the event.

APPENDIX: two examples with the signs and designations of the training and the combat aircraft. [not available]

REMARK: Send examples to: Intendant, the Airfield unit and the Accountant.

Signed: Colonel Boydev

Note by the Author: based on available information and photos, this order was applied only partially. Bombers and bomber trainers did not have any 'cheatline' applied along the fuselage. The nose and 'cheatline' of 'lineyni' aircraft were actually red, not orange. It is also highly questionable if all school aircraft were actually painted wraparound yellow/orange, as stipulated by this order. Probably there was an additional order issued later, correcting these details. [Additions in square brackets are the Author's]

The aforementioned document stipulates that trainers must be painted completely yellow. Certainly, imported aircraft wore their original factory livery, not yellow, at least on their arrival in Bulgaria, and most probably until the end of their service life. However, Bulgarian-made trainers may have been painted yellow at the factory, as per local standard[11]. It's extremely hard to differentiate yellow from light grey on period black/white photos. However, the Author believes this line-up of DAR-9 trainers, freshly rolled off the assembly line (and paint shop) of the DSF Plant in Lovech, may have indeed been painted overall yellow. [Photo 28A]

Occasionally, Bulgarian military aircraft were applied with special markings, in honour of a certain person or event. During WW 1, Bulgarian-manned warplanes occasionally bore specific names, distinguishing them from their German ally wearing the same military marking. [photos 29A and 38] A couple of Heinkel He 51 fighter aircraft sported a large text applied in black capital letters on their lower wing undersurface in mid-1937. One of these spelled: СИМЕОНЪ, or Simeon – the name of Tsar Boris' new-born son – while the other carried миньорЪ, or Miner, in honour of the coal miners of the town of Pernik, who reportedly paid for that particular aircraft. A PZL P.24 fighter aircraft bore a white Cyrillic text on both sides of the fuselage, which spelled: *Симеонъ Князъ Търновски* ("Simeon Knyaz Tărnovski"), also referring to the new-born son of the Tsar, Crown Prince Simeon Tărnovski (born on 16 June 1937). [photo 29B]

---

11   Stoyan Stoyanow in his memoirs recalls: „*In the Summer of 1937 (...) at Kazanlak (...) in June (...) the airfield was like a natural green carpet, on which the yellow painted training aircraft lined up, delightning the eye.*" Unfortunately, he doesn't give the aircraft type, only that it was a two-seater.

24. The 'Tsarist Roundel' type of military marking was applied in six positions: on both sides of the fuselage, as well as on the upper and lower surfaces of the wing, as depicted on this freshly delivered Focke-Wulf Fw 58KB-1. The Bulgarian national colours are yet to be applied on the rudder.

A few Bulgarian aircraft types (most notable the Heinkel He 45, but proof exists where it can be seen on at least one He 72, No. 2), which wore the new military marking, also displayed for a short while a new version of the roundel on their underwing surfaces (and possibly on the upper one, too). The roundel appears to have consisted of rings of red-green-white (inside dot) colour, superimposed over a white square background. This marking was probably used during wargames, and was of temporary and limited use only. [photo 30]. Interestingly, a photo published in a periodical, depicting a couple of Dornier Do 11 bombers in flight, shows a different roundel painted over a white square on the wing undersurface. This time, the roundel did not have a white dot in the centre, meaning that these temporary identification markings, used during wargames, were not identical.

The Peculiar Bulgarian Triangle

The IInd part of the aforementioned Order No. 53 of 14 April 1938 called for the introduction of an individual *nomenklaturen nomer* (NN, or registration number) for all Bulgarian aircraft, military and civilian registration alike. Indeed, as described, this NN was a combination of two numbers: the bottom one (the denominator of the fraction), made of four digits, identified the aircraft type by its category, while the top one (the numerator of the fraction), made of one to three digits, represented the individual aircraft's serial number within that particular category[12]. The four-digit number always started with 7, which denoted powered aircraft[13]. The last digit, spanning from 1 to 9, represented the military category the particular aircraft was part of. The two digits in the centre of the four-digit NN, from 00 onwards, represented the serial number of the aircraft type, in loose chronological order, based on its planned date to enter service with the VNVV. For example, sticking to the topic of this book, the first fighter aircraft type introduced in Bulgarian service, the Heinkel He 51, was identified with the aircraft type category number 7007, while the last one introduced during the war, the Dewoitine D.520, became 7077 (namely the eighth fighter type in VNVV service – actually the seventh, as one was left unassigned, see the list of fighter aircraft types, on page 42).

As mentioned above, a particular aircraft in its category was identified with an increasing sequential serial number, starting with 1. In writing, this individual aircraft number was separated from the cate-

---

12 Usually, but not always (notable exceptions being the Messerschmitt Bf 109G and Dewoitine D.520 fighters), the individual aircraft serial number shown in the NN was identical to the number written first on the rudder top, then later, on the fuselage side (and often on the wings) of military aircraft.

13 The issue of the usage of the NN on gliders (if it was the case at all) is still not clarified. In official VNVV aircraft write-off documents, where all aircraft are identified by their NN, the few gliders that are mentioned (three Komar and four Zögling, written off on 1 June 1943) are identified by their construction numbers. However, on a rare period photo showing a finless UP-1 glider (licence made Grunau 9) being towed by youngsters in the early post-war period, a pentagon-like form can be observed under the horizontal stabiliser (tailplane), consistent with the location of the NN triangle on powered aircraft, without any numbers being visible in it, however [photo 33].

25. Document dated 25 April 1940, detailing the change from civilian registration letters to military-style registration numbers of five 'DAR Z-Yu' (sic! also known as DAR-3) "Garvan II" following remotorisation at the DSF Works (where the Siemens "Jupiter" engines of 480 hp were replaced with Alfa-Romeo 126 RC-34 types of 750 hp output). After this process, the aircraft type changed to DAR-3-b "Garvan II", and the aircraft received instead of the civilian registrations (in the LZ-DI_ row) individual registration numbers (Nomenklaturen Nomer), identifying individual aircraft of a certain type (2/7046, etc.), as well as military markings (not explicitly mentioned in the document).

26. With the introduction of military markings, a numbering system was also established to identify individual aircraft of the VNVV. It consisted of two groups of numbers, one applied on the fin, the other one on the rear fuselage, as shown on the Fw 58KB-1 krilo of the 5. Bombardirovachen Orlyak (Bomber Group). The meaning of this numbering system is not fully understood; however, a theory drawn up by the Author can be read in the main text of this chapter.

gory number by a slash, which together gave the aircraft's individual *nomenklaturen nomer*, e.g. 3/7096 (which thus identified the third Ar 196 floatplane placed in VNVV service). [photo 31]

On aircraft, this *nomenklaturen nomer* was applied within an equilateral triangle of 300-mm-long sides, which was divided in two by a horizontal line. The two sets of numbers detailed above were written in the two separated areas of the triangle, as a fraction, as follows: the aircraft's individual serial number was written in the numerator (at the top), while the four-digit category number was written in the denominator (at the bottom). [photo 32]

An order of the VNVV Command, issued on 27 October 1939, which describes the categorisations and classification of various equipment and spare parts used by the air force, lists the following 'flying equipment' categories:

Group 1, Летателни уреди (Flying equipment)
A, Aircraft: 1. School
               2. Training – reconnaissance
               3. Training – fighter
               4. Training – bomber
               5. Travel [i.e., courier, liaison], sports, medical, test aircraft
               6. Combat – reconnaissance
               7. Combat – fighter
               8. Combat – bomber
               9. линейни ('lineyni'), i.e., battle/combat, or ground attack
B, Seaplanes
C, Gliders
D, Balloons

Both official lists closely resemble the NN categories empirically reconstructed much earlier by the author based on photographic evidence, as follows[14]:
1=basic trainer
2=advanced trainer
3=fighter trainer
4=bomber trainer
5=miscellaneous (transport/courier/liaison/specialised trainer/test aircraft)
6=reconnaissance
7=fighter
8=bomber
9= assault/ground attack/dive bomber

14 Note: In the late 1950s, about when the MiG-19 entered service, the category definitions must have changed, or abolished, as the MiG-19 fighter received the category number 7201, which originally would mean basic trainer. It is possible that the entire category system was reset and started anew, with all newly introduced aircraft types being assigned subsequently increasing numbers: 7201=MiG-19P jet fighter, 7202=Mil Mi-4 helicopter, etc. However, the clarification of this issue is beyond the scope of this book.

27. The dozen Dornier Do 11 bombers of the 5th Bomber Group wore numbers from 55-1 to 55-12 applied on the fuselage, on either side of the military marking (as the fin was already covered by the so-called "royal cipher").

28. The dozen Arado Ar 65 fighters that entered service in early 1937 – thus after the first wave of warplanes had arrived from Germany – were identified by a small white text on the fin top, which included the aircraft type, in Cyrillic (i.e., 'Ap.65'), followed by a serial number starting with 101, linked to the aircraft type with a dash

28A. Based on the order issued on 14 April 1938, all trainers must be painted completely yellow. Certainly, imported aircraft wore their original factory livery, which was usually light grey. However, Bulgarian-made trainers may have been painted yellow at the factory, as per local standards. It's extremely hard to differentiate yellow from light grey on period black/white photos. However, the Author believes this line-up of DAR-9 trainers, freshly rolled off the assembly line (and paint shop) of DSF Plant in Lovech, may have indeed been painted yellow overall. LZ-BCD was the 10th DAR-9 (2/1 series), NN 10/7051.

41

29A. During World War 1, Bulgarian-manned warplanes occasionally bore specific names, distinguishing them from their German ally wearing the same military marking. In this particular case, the name written in Cyrillic letters, ТУТРАКАН (TUTRAKAN), painted on the fuselage of an Albatros C.III, refers to a Bulgarian city located in north-east Bulgaria, on the right bank of the River Danube. After the short Second Balkan War of 1913, it was incorporated, along with all of Southern Dobrudzha (also known as Quadrilateral), in the Kingdom of Rumania. During World War 1, the town was the location of the important 'Battle of Tutrakan (Turtucaia, in Rumanian)', during which Bulgarian and German Central Powers forces defeated the Rumanian forces. At rear, in the observer's location, Lieutenant Colonel Vasil Zlatarov, commanding officer of the Bulgarian Aviation during World War 1, is seated.

Here is a list of the fighter aircraft types in Bulgarian service, followed by their Bulgarian code names (where the NN was identified):

7007 = Heinkel He 51C 'Sokol'
7017 = PZL P.24b 'Yastreb'
7027 = Arado Ar 65F 'Orel'
7037 = Avia B.534 'Dogan'
7047 = Messerschmitt Bf 109E 'Strela'
7057 (1st) = Avia B.135 (No codename)
7057 (2nd) = Messerschmitt Bf 109G 'Strela'
7067 = not assigned (theoretically reassigned to the latecomer Avia B.135, not implemented)
7077 = Dewoitine D.520C1 'Devoitin'
7087 = Yakovlev Yak-9D/M
7097 = Yakovlev Yak-9P/U/T
7107 = Yakovlev Yak-23 'Strela-1'
7117 = Mikoyan &Gurevich MiG-15/15bis 'Strela-2'

It has to be noted that the peculiar triangle most probably started to be applied on aircraft not at the moment the aforementioned order was issued on 14 April 1938, but later, probably sometime in

29B. Occasionally, Bulgarian military aircraft were applied with special writings, in honour of a certain person or event. This practice was used from the WW 1-era. The depicted PZL P.24 fighter aircraft bore white Cyrillic text o on both sides of the fuselage, which spelled: Симеонъ Князъ Търновски ("Simeon Knyaz Tărnovski"), referring to the new-born son of the Tsar, Crown Prince Simeon Tărnovski (born on 16 June 1937).

30. A few Bulgarian warplanes wore, for a short while, alongside the regular military marking also roundels on their under-wing surfaces (it is unlikely that they were applied on the upper wing as well), superimposed over a white square background. One description mentions this symbol as black circle, with white dot in centre, applied over a white square. These markings were probably used only during wargames, and were of temporary use only. One such rare occurrence is documented by the enclosed indifferent quality photo, which depicts a couple of Heinkel He 45s, lined up for inspection.

mid-1939[15]. The first documented occurrence of the usage of the NN (except for the 'Chayka' photos mentioned in footnote 15) – as found by the Author – is dated 16 November 1939, when DAR-3-Yu, LZ-DIN, was upgraded and refitted with a 750 HP Alfa-Romeo 126 RC34 radial engine at the DSF Workshop, being henceforth officially referred to as DAR-3-b, *Garvan* II, NN 1/7046.

Up to late 1945, the triangle was applied on the fin of the aircraft, at about 100 mm from the rudder hinge, usually in white on dark surfaces, or in black on light surfaces, but exceptions did happen. From October 1945 on, with the introduction of the so-called 'Home Front' (OF) type marking, flash lines in Bulgarian national colours were applied horizontally across the entire tail surface, thus covering the area where the NN triangle was supposed to be applied. Therefore, the triangle was moved under the horizontal stabiliser (tailplane). [photo 34]

The use of the *nomenklaturen nomer* along with the aircraft type's typical Bulgarian code name was the norm. Only exceptionally and very seldom was the aircraft's original construction number mentioned in official Bulgarian documents. Even components were inscribed with this identification triangle, along with that particular aircraft's type code and serial number. [photo 35] This NN was used up until the 1970s, or even later, including on the early MiG jets, as shown in the sample illustrations. [photos 36 and 37]

For a comprehensive, but still incomplete, list of all NNs identified by the Author and unveiled in printing for the first time, see the Appendix.

It has to be noted that without this triangle being displayed, typical to all Bulgarian military aircraft[16] in the aforementioned time period, any aircraft artwork or scale model cannot be considered as accurate and complete.

Pro-Axis Style Marking

As Bulgaria firmly entrenched itself into the Axis camp, the issue of introducing a pro-Axis style military marking became imminent. This change was needed, as the roundel worn by Bulgarian aircraft resembled the markings generally used by the Allies, while the East European Axis allies generally opted, or would opt, for cross-like markings.

---

15   Fact is, the official accident report of a He 45 "Shtärkel" of 1 May 1939, the one involving a He 51 "Sokol" of 8 May 1939, and a DAR-3 "Garvan" of 31 May 1939 all refer to the aircraft by their serial number written on the fuselage, without identi-fying them by the NN, as was customary in all official documents dated from late 1939 on. By contrast, the photo of a factory fresh PZL.43 "Chayka", NN 10/7139, made at Warsaw airfield in Poland certainly earlier than 30 June 1939, clearly displays the triangle on the fin (curiously without the horizontal line inside the triangle). A post-accident photo taken in Bulgaria, at Kazanlăk airfield, of another PZL.43 "Chayka", NN 4/7139, on 20 September 1939, also shows the aircraft wearing the white triangle on its fin. The aircraft wears no visible serial number on its airframe, as usually was the case of aircraft in service with VNVV, thus is must have been a freshly delivered aircraft.

16   The sole exception encountered by the Author, presented in this book, is the Focke-Wulf Fw 56 trainer, which did not have a fin, thus there was no area to place this triangle on, as per the regulation.

31. In April 1938, a universal coding system, called nomenklaturen nomer *(NN, registration number), was introduced to identify all Bulgarian aircraft – wearing military or civilian registration (however, this system was implemented on aircraft only a year later). In writing form, the individual aircraft number, placed first, was separated by the category number, identifying a particular aircraft type, which together gave the aircraft's individual* nomenklaturen nomer. *On this photo, the NN 3/7096, written on the protecting canvas, identifies the third Arado Ar 196 floatplane in VNVV service. This particular aircraft is currently displayed at the Aviation museum in Krumovo, near Plovdiv. It was recently restored in wartime livery, complete with St.Andrew's Cross-type military marking, as the only aircraft type used by the Bulgarian air force during the war and afterwards.*

32. On aircraft, the nomenklaturen nomer *(NN) was applied within an equilateral triangle, which was divided in two by a horizontal line. The two sets of numbers (detailed in the previous photo caption) were written in the two separated areas of the triangle, as a fraction, as follows: the aircraft's individual serial number was written in the numerator (at the top), while the four-digit aircraft type category number was written in the denominator (at the bottom). This peculiar Bulgarian triangle is illustrated as applied, in black, on the fin of a domestically built DAR-9 'Siniger' biplane (c/n 89), registered LZ-BPB, NN 2/7051. The trainer may have been painted yellow overall.*

Details of the initial versions of the proposed new marking are sketchy; the only available information is that three versions, based on the 'St. Andrew's Cross'[17] (i.e. an X shape), were tested on several aircraft of the 1st *Orlyak*, based at Bozhurishte, in March 1940. The purpose of these tests was to determine which one of the three versions was most visible (Order No. 14 of 1st *Orlyak*, 18.03.1940). There is no primary information available on the outcome, but it can be assumed that the well-known version applied later on was the winning design. It has to be noted that it was not a novelty for Bulgarian aircraft to wear military marking resembling the 'St. Andrew's Cross', applied in black (not green, as some artwork suggests). At the end of World War I, such a marking was occasionally worn on a variety of aircraft, including at least one Albatros C.III two-seater, although it was not officially sanctioned. [photo 38]

The final version of the new marking – unofficially referred to as знак Андреевски Кръст, or 'Andrew Cross' Sign – consisted of a large black X, applied over a black bordered white square. Officially, the square length had to be the 2/3rd of the fuselage height where the marking was to be applied, although this scale was not always kept. In reality, the length of the square side had to be big enough to cover the former roundel type marking in cases when it was applied directly over it. In other cases, when the location of the new marking was different to the previous roundel's location, the square's size could be smaller than the roundel's diameter. Therefore, the dimension of the square varied between 900 mm, 800 mm and 600 mm (as measured on various photos, where reference dimensions, like tyre size, were visible and measurable), also depending on the location on the airframe it was applied to (as was the case with the previous roundel).

The cross width was 1/5th of the square's length, while the width of the black border around the white square was 1/50th of the square length. The new marking was applied in six positions, often – but

---

17 Andrew the Apostle, also known as Saint Andrew, born in the early 1st century, was a Christian apostle and the brother of Saint Peter. He was the most prominent preacher of Christianity in the area on the shores of the Black Sea that would eventually become Bulgaria. Andrew was sentenced to death by crucifixion for his Christian preaching, and tied to a sideways lying cross-like structure, in the form of the letter X, hence the historic "St. Andrew's Cross" name.

33. It is unclear if the NN was also applied on gliders. This photo shows a UP-1 glider (licence made Grunau 9) being towed by youngsters in the early post-war period. A pentagon-like geometric form can be observed under the horizontal stabiliser (tailplane), to the left of the head of the man at left, consistent with the location of the NN triangle on powered aircraft, without any numbers being visible in it, however.

34. From October 1945 on, with the introduction of the so-called 'Home Front' (OF) type marking, the flash lines in Bulgarian national colours were applied horizontally, across the entire tail surface, thus covering the area where the NN triangle was supposed to be applied. Therefore, the triangle was moved under the horizontal stabiliser (tailplane), as depicted on this Yak-9M, NN 34/7087.

not always – in the same location where the previous roundels had been placed (frequently applied right over the roundels, as was the case with Messerschmitt Bf 109Es – see appropriate chapter). Officially, the marking had to be placed on the mid-fuselage (at two times the distance of the fuselage width, measured from the rudder hinge) and on both surfaces of wings. In case of biplanes, it was applied on the top surface of the upper wing and the bottom surface of the lower wing. The marking's location on the wings was officially set to ½ of the wing's chord width where the marking was applied. The rudder stayed in the national tricolour. [photos 39].

This new marking was officially introduced by the Ministry of Defence Order No. 243/26.06.1940[18], signed by Lt. Gen. Teodosi P. Daskalov, Minister of War. Based on period photographs and airmen's memoirs, the marking change started to be applied first on the recently arrived modern aircraft types (for example, the Bf 109E – see appropriate chapter). On secondary types (e.g. trainers), or older aircraft, the switch to the new marking happened only gradually, by the end of the summer of 1940. For example, the *Obraztsov Orlyak* (the so-called 'Model' Group), at that time under reorganization, included reference to this new marking only in its order dated 26 August 1940. There were even cases when some aircraft displayed, for a short while, both the obsolete and the newly introduced markings! [photo 40]

---

18 An otherwise well informed Polish book (*PZL.23 Karaś, PZL.42/43, PZL.46 Sum* by Tomasz J. Kopański, Stratus Publ., 2013) gives the date the new marking was introduced on as 15 July 1940. A Bulgarian author, Alexander Mladenov, identifies the date the new marking was introduced as 25 November 1940, based on a War Ministry order dated 20 June 1940. However, the Author sticks to 26 June 1940 as the date the new marking was officially introduced.

35. The only original aircraft component with the typical triangle on it found by the Author is tubing from a Yak-9P fighter, preserved at the Bulgarian aviation museum at Krumovo (see photos 52A and 52B). Interestingly, the sign is actually an equilateral (isosceles) trapezoid, not a triangle. The aircraft's individual serial number is written in the numerator (at the top), while the four-digit aircraft type category number in the denominator (at the bottom), resulting in the NN 27/7097. What is believed to be the aircraft's construction number, 0267, is also stencilled on the tube, also in red, over the truncated triangle.

The change of military marking aroused the interest of foreign states, and not only the neighbours. Traces of this event can be found in American diplomatic papers as well. Occasionally, crude hand sketches illustrate the topic [photos 41A and B].

As was the case when the previous military marking had been introduced three years earlier, non-combat aircraft types – mostly basic trainers, both domestic and foreign designs – were not applied with any military marking, rather they kept their previously used civilian registration until the end of their service life. Besides the civilian registration, they were identified by large size black numbers applied on the fin (e.g. Fw 44) [photo 42], or the entire tail surface (e.g. Bü 131), while in certain cases both occurrences happened (e.g. He 72).

Months before this new military marking was introduced[19], the serial number identifying a particular aircraft (identical to the number written in the top area of the triangle) moved from the fin to the top of the rudder, in the form of a small black number applied on the white section. Parallel to this, the so-called 'krilo number' disappeared from the fuselage. This style of identifying individual aircraft by a number on the top rudder was discontinued in 1941, at an unspecified date, being replaced with a larger number applied on the rear fuselage, aft of the national insignia. Relying again on scarce photo evidence, there are photos, albeit only a couple, where the so-called 'Tsarist roundel' type marking is sported on aircraft with the new style white serial number aft of it (e.g. a Letov Š.328 *krilo*, comprising of Nos. 23, 17, 21 and 25). By contrast, there also photos that show the new style military marking (St. Andrew's Cross) along with the serial number still on the rudder top well into 1941, more precisely in late April, early May, when the Yellow ID colour had already been introduced [photo 43]. This detail highlights once again just how difficult is to follow the changes in marking of Bulgarian aircraft and pinpoint their actual introduction in the field.

Returning to the case of the serial number on the fuselage, for the best contrast, the one or two-digit serial number was applied in white over dark (e.g. green) camouflage paint, or in black over a light-coloured surface (e.g. aluminium or grey). Usually, the same serial number was repeated on the under surface of the (lower) wing, in black, and occasionally – and only for a short time period – on the upper surface of the (top) wing, in white. Of course, as usual, there were exceptions to this rule, as proven by period photographs, so the location of the serial number on the lower wing varied. In a few cases, the aircraft did not wear any visible serial numbers, only the triangle on the fin (as was the case of PZL.43A, No. 4/7139, photographed at Kazanläk airfield on 20 September 1939, see earlier footnote). Most probably, these rare occurrences happened with training machines, and lasted for a short while only.

Officially, the height of the serial number applied on the fuselage and wings had to be 7/18th (or 39%) of the fuselage width where the marking was applied (reference dimension C), the width of the number ½ of reference (C), while the thickness of the digit 1/8th of reference (C). The distance between the numeral and the fuselage marking ought to be 7/72nd (or 10%) of the reference (C). [photo 39]. Of course, these ratios were only informative, as in reality the size and shape of the numerals depended on the available stencils, if any.

---

19 A photograph depicting a Fw 56 *Komar* in the hangar of the Karlovo repair shop, dated 12.03.1940, show the aircraft still wearing the early dual identification number, along with the roundel type marking.

36. *The* nomenklaturen nomer *(NN) was used up until the 1970s, including on MiG jets. This MiG-19P, No. 01 formerly No. 436 (c/n 620436), NN 13/7201 (triangle applied on the mid-fuselage, underneath the wing), is shown as sample illustration. The Author believes the entire aircraft type category system was reset sometime in the late 1950s and started anew, with all newly introduced aircraft types being assigned subsequently increasing numbers, regardless of their role, or category. Thus the MiG-19P, clearly a fighter type, was assigned with the aircraft type number 7201, which originally meant a basic trainer.*

37. *Photographic proof of the usage of the NN on more advanced jets includes this MiG-21 F13, No. 719, c/n 1019, NN 9/7274 (triangle applied on the mid-fuselage), For general description of the post-war aircraft registration systems, see note under the List of NNs (however, this topic falls out of the immediate scope of the Author's research).*

38. *At the end of World War I, the military marking resembling St. Andrew's Cross was rarely worn on a variety of aircraft, including at least an Albatros C.III two-seater (depicted), although it was not officially sanctioned. This particular biplane was named КРИВОЛАК (Krivolak) after the victorious battle of Krivolak (Macedonia), against the French, in November 1915.*

47

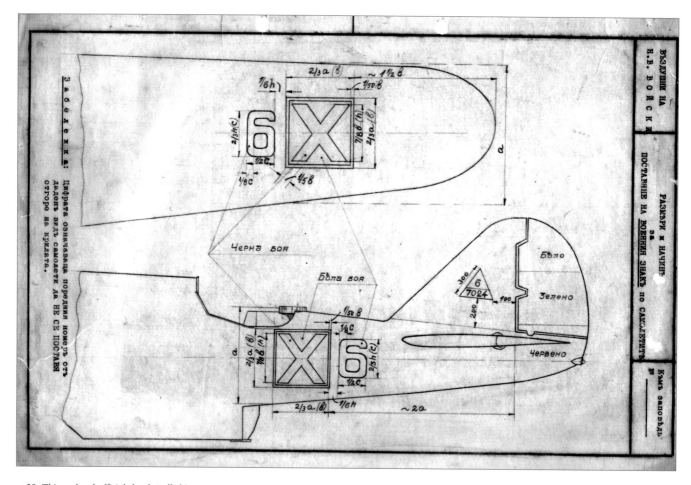

39. *This undated official sketch (called 'размери и начин за поставяне на военния знак по самолети', or, 'size and method of applying the marking of military aircraft') details how the new marking, known as the 'St. Andrew's Cross', had to be applied on aircraft and in what size. Interestingly and in contrast to the previous VNVV military marking, the size of this one depended on the fuselage height (identified with 'a' on the sketch) at the point the marking was applied on. The size of the square had to be identical on both the fuselage and wing; however, in practice this was not always observed. Interestingly, the aircraft outline in the sketch clearly represents the PZL.43 bomber; however, the aircraft category number of the NN, as written on the bottom of the triangle, 7024, was the one assigned to the domestically built KB-6/KB-309 Papagal (Parrot) two-engine trainer and light transport aircraft.*

40. *Curiously, this KB-4 Chuchuliga II, NN 16/7022, Bulgarian-made reconnaissance and trainer aircraft, sports both the obsolete roundel and the newly introduced square shape marking. The diameter of the roundel is identical to the length of the square, which appears to be around 600 mm.*

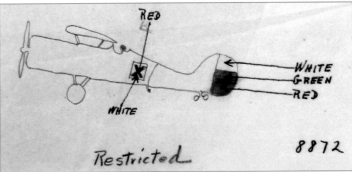

41A. Left: *An unlikely source detailing the new Bulgarian military marking are US diplomatic files. A 'note-verbale' issued by the Bulgarian Royal Ministry of Foreign Affairs and Cults in Sofia, on 13 August 1940, informs the US Legation in Sofia of "the new distinctive markings of recognization (sic!) of Bulgarian military airplanes," and encloses the following simple hand-drawn sketch.*

41B. Above: *Another US diplomatic document mentioning Bulgarian military marking was issued by the US Embassy in Istanbul, Turkey. Report No. 8872 of 3 February 1944 details "the markings on Bulgarian pursuit planes", based on verbal (i.e. spy) information, as well as the 15.12.1943 issue of the Bulgarian newspaper 'Trakiets'. The following primitive hand-drawn sketch was enclosed to the report, signed by the military attaché, Brig. Gen. Richard G. Tindall, as illustration. Noteworthy is the colour of the marking's centre cross, identified as red.*

Identification Colours and Codes

The Kingdom of Bulgaria joined the so-called 'Tripartite Pact' (also known as the 'Axis Pact'), led by Hitler's Third Reich, on 1 March 1941. Just days after, German warplanes appeared in the skies of Bulgaria and landed on various strategically located airfields throughout the country. Prior to the onslaught on Yugoslavia and 'Operation Marita' – the invasion of Greece by German and Italian troops – on 6 April, all Axis aircraft flying in the vicinity of the would-be battle zone had been identified with distinctive yellow markings (usually using RLM 04 paint), the so-called 'Axis Yellow' marking, albeit in slightly different ways. *Luftwaffe* aircraft had their engine cowlings and often their rudders painted in yellow, occasionally complemented by narrow mid-fuselage and mid-wing bands. [photo 44] Hungarian warplanes had their entire tail sections and engine cowlings covered in semi-transparent yellow, in rare cases complemented by a 500-mm wide mid-fuselage and mid-wing band, while Rumanian aircraft had similarly coloured, but narrower (about 200 mm) bands on their mid-fuselage and mid-wings, along with yellow cowlings.

Based on photographic evidence, starting from late March/early April 1941[20] Bulgarian aircraft had their rudders and engine cowlings painted yellow, except for those fighters which had already sported the typical Bulgarian 'flash' scheme comprising of an overall yellow engine cowling followed by a gradually tapering yellow 'flash'[21] along the fuselage. On these aircraft, only the national tricolour on the rudder gave way to yellow. On certain aircraft types – like the Arado Ar 65F – the red colour of the engine cowling and the rearward tapering fuselage stripe was replaced with yellow, to align it with the new 'Axis' colour coding [photo 45]. A few aircraft types, e.g. Avia B.534s, PZL.43s and Letov Š-328s, also featured a narrow (about 200 mm wide) yellow band around the mid-fuselage. [photo 46] Contrary to other sources, the wingtips were not painted yellow at this time, in April 1941. Yellow wingtips – initially on the lower surface only – appeared around the time the anti-Soviet war started on 22 June 1941. Later on, a few aircraft types – again the Avia B.534, the PZL.43 and the Letov Š-328, occasionally the early Bf 109G, even the DAR-10A prototype, can be mentioned – had their upper wingtips painted yellow as well, along with their elevators. [photo 47] This practice helped the biplane aircraft types flying over the Black Sea (part of the so-called *Galata Orlyak*) – just like the northern neighbour's I.A.R. 39s – to be positively differentiated from Soviet aircraft.

---

20 A photograph taken by a German *Luftwaffe* man at Sofia West airfield in March 1941 shows a PZL.43 'Chayka' bomber devoid of any yellow ID marking. The serial number, 'Black 5', was applied on the top of the rudder, which was still painted in the national colours.

21 Called in Bulgarian Шлейф, or 'shleyf'.

42. Non-combat aircraft types were not applied military markings, they were identified by civilian registrations until the end of their service life. Besides the civilian registration, they wore large size black numbers applied on the fin, as is the case of the depicted Fw 44J Vrabche, LZ-FOK (assigned with NN 10/7021), Werknummer 2297, 'Black 16'. This particular accident happened on the Asĕn landing ground, west of Kazanlăk, on 27 May 1938. Interestingly, this very aircraft was later on photographed wearing 'Black 10' on the rudder! Based on the directive on markings and colours, VNVV training shouldhave been painted yellow overall. It's unclear, however, if this directive was valid on imported aircraft as well, which usually wore factory applied paint schemes – until repainted during scheduled overhaul at a specialised workshop in Bulgaria.

A photograph of a freshly arrived Bf 109G-2, No. 36, which did not yet have the serial number applied on the fuselage, dated 19.07.1943, shows the engine cowling, the rudder, as well as the elevators being yellow. The colour of the upper wingtip is inconclusive [see 'master' photo in vol. 2]. On certain photos, depicting the first '*Strela*' Gs impressed into service, the upper wingtips are yellow. However, a very rare colourised photo, included in a wartime Messerschmitt calendar, shows a Bf 108B '*Taifun*', 'White 5', with yellow engine cowling, rudder and elevators, lower wingtips, but no yellow upper wingtips. This fact casts doubt upon this practice being common on *all* fighters and fighter trainers (as the '*Taifun*' was for Bf 109 pilots). This topic needs to be further researched, using good-quality photos.

Published artworks show, and erroneously labelled black/white photos describe, Bulgarian warplanes – especially the Messerschmitt Bf 109G and Dewoitine D.520 fighters, but occasionally also the Ju 87D *Stuka* dive-bomber, or the KB-11 '*Fazan*' army co-operation aircraft – as wearing a wide yellow rear (or mid-) fuselage band as per Axis standards, as seen on all *Luftwaffe* and other Easter European aircraft. This – with a very few exceptions – was *not* the case for Bulgaria, however. Modellers, authors and artists tend to confuse the post-September 1944 white pro-Allies identifications (rear fuselage band included) with the yellow pro-Axis marking – this is the source of the error. As hinted in the caveat, there were a few exceptions to this display of yellow rear fuselage marking. The author found only one such case displayed on VNVV fighter aircraft, namely a Bf 109G, where the rear fuselage band was undoubtedly yellow. The relevant photo depicts 'White 3' turned on its back after a taxiing accident on soft terrain. This doomed aircraft also has the rudder, lower wingtips and rear fuselage band in yellow. [photo 48]

On rare occasions, and for a short while only, German aircraft that were delivered to Bulgaria kept their original *Luftwaffe* marking and radio codes (the so-called *Stammkennzeichen*), as was the case with the Dewoitine D.520, or a few Bf 109G fighters [for sample photos, see appropriate chapters].

As mentioned earlier, the aircraft's serial number applied on the rear fuselage usually matched the serial number of the NN written on the top of the triangle, and was assigned to the particular aircraft in a growing sequence, based on the date they were impressed into service. Notable exceptions to this rule were the two 'top notch' fighter types the Bulgarians defended their airspace with, the Messerschmitt Bf 109G and the Dewoitine D.520. From about mid-1943 on[22], these two fighter types were identified according to *Jagdwaffe* style, by coloured numbers (known as Бордни номера, i.e. *bordni nomera*, or board numbers, in English).

Based on former Bulgarian fighter pilots' memoirs, paired with available photographs, the following numbering scheme of the two predominantly Bf 109G-equipped *orlyatsi* (groups) of the 6. *Iztrebitelen Polk* (Fighter Regiment) can be reconstructed (without confirmation by official documents, however):

Shtab na orlyaka (group staff): yellow numbers,
1st *Yato* (squadron): white numbers,
2nd *Yato* (squadron): green numbers,
3rd *Yato* (squadron): red numbers.

The memoirs of *Ppor.* Petăr K. Petrov, former Bf 109G fighter pilot in 2/6. *Orlyak*, 662. *Yato*, apparently back this colouring system theory: "*642. Yato had white fuselage numbers (C/O Por. Viktor Pavlov),*

---

22 The first Bf 109G-2s that arrived in early 1943 kept the existing practice of using individual serial numbers, identical to the number written in the triangle, number which was also applied on the bottom wing surface in black. They switched to the coloured number only later on, in the Summer of 1943 – see appropriate chapter.

43. *A KB-4 reconnaissance biplane, NN 18/7022, stands on the concrete runway of Balchik airfield, close to the shores of the Black Sea, sometime in late April/early May 1941. In the background, a Luftwaffe He 111P and a very rare Ju 88B long-range reconnaissance aircraft can be seen. Ju 88 V24 and V25 – the two Ju 88B prototypes that were used by V.f.H. of 1.(F)/Ob.d.L. for long-range recce missions over the Soviet Union – entered service on 14 and 30 April 1941, respectively. Notice the 'St. Andrew's Cross' style marking on the wing under surface and the black number 18 on the top of the yellow rudder.*

44. *Prior to the onslaught on Yugoslavia and 'Operation Marita' of 6 April 1941, Luftwaffe aircraft participating in these operations had their engine cowlings and rudders (often the nose section and the elevators as well) painted yellow, as seen on this bellied Bf 110C of LG 2, L2+NR, used as background for a souvenir shot by Bulgarian and German soldiers in April 1941.*

45. *From early April 1941 on, most Bulgarian warplanes had their rudders, elevators and the engine cowlings painted in yellow. On certain aircraft types – like the depicted Arado Ar 65F trainer – the red colour engine cowling and rearward tapering fuselage flash was replaced with yellow, to align it with the new 'Axis' colour coding. A few kept their red fuselage flash, and only the engine cowling and rudder were repainted in yellow. However, this was the exception rather than the norm.*

51

46. *Alongside Luftwaffe aircraft operating in the area, Bulgarian warplanes also had their rudders, elevators and the engine cowlings painted yellow from early April 1941 on. A few aircraft types, like the depicted PZL.43A, NN 23/7139, 'White 23', also featured a narrow (about 200 mm wide) yellow ring around the mid-fuselage, as additional recognition feature.*

47. *This Letov Š-328 reconnaissance biplane, caught by the lenses of the photo camera over the Black Sea, has its upper wingtips painted yellow (besides the bottom ones), along with the elevators – a detail unnoticed yet by published sources.*

48. *Although of indifferent quality, this photo is the only one seen by the Author where a Bulgarian fighter aircraft clearly wears a yellow rear fuselage band, as was the norm with* Luftwaffe *and other East European Axis aircraft flying on, or in the vicinity of, the Eastern Front. 'White 3', a Bf 109G, turned on its back after a faulty taxiing on soft terrain. Along with the rear fuselage band, this doomed aircraft also has the rudder and lower wingtips in yellow.*

652. Yato *had green fuselage numbers (C/O Por. Nedelcho Bonchev), while 662.* Yato *had red fuselage numbers (the squadron's C/O, Por. Asen Kovachev, flew on 'Red 1').*"

2/6. *Orlyak* had coloured serial numbers without outline, while 3/6. *Orlyak* had coloured serial numbers outlined [see numerous photos in the chapters dealing with the Bf 109G and D.520]. No information on the colour scheme applied to fighters of the 1/6. and 4/6. *Orlyatsi* is available, although most probably was similar to their sister *Orlyatsi* detailed above. Of course, as it is with other cases of the application of Bulgarian markings, there are exceptions to this reconstructed scheme[23], thus it should not be taken as 'written in stone'.

Numbering of the aircraft identified with coloured fuselage (board) numbers was from 1 to 16, and No. 1 was usually flown by the squadron's commanding officer.

Often wide white spirals can be observed on the black painted spinner of various Bulgarian warplanes. Based on *Luftwaffe* regulation, this distinctive Axis recognition marking was introduced on German (and presumably other Axis aircraft) subordinated to *Luftflotte* 4 fighting on the Eastern Front in late July 1944 (on the 'Invasionsfront' a month earlier). However, Bulgaria was most probably not considered as a combat area of this *Luftwaffe* high unit fighting on the East, as between February and September 1944, Bulgarian fighter units were subordinated to *Jagdabschnittsführer Bulgarien*, which was under direct command of *Jagdfliegerführer Balkan*.

A photo of a Bulgarian Bf 109G, dated on the rear 19 June 1944 (see photo in vol. 2), but showing snow on the ground, thus pointing to a much earlier date, also clearly displays this white spiral. This proof questions the actual timing this distinctive marking was applied on Bulgarian warplanes, and places this date earlier than *Luftflotte* 4 regulation stipulates (also valid for aircraft of Rumania and Hungary). A *Luftwaffe* order, dated 10 February 1944, stipulates the following: "*To avoid confusion with enemy aircraft, the C-in-C of the German air force has issued the following instructions to all fighter and heavy fighter units: (...) 4) All fighter aircraft of* Luftflotte *3 and Reich are to have a black and white spiral painted on the spinner. Size one and a half spirals turning in the same direction as the spinner. Width ⅛ of the diameter of the spinner.*"[24] As specified, this particular order was issued to *Luftflotte* 3 and the units defending Germany proper (the *Reich*); however, it may have been valid for other areas as well, like the Balkans where Bulgaria lies. At the last minute, one of the Author's friends drew his attention to a photo of a '*Strela*' in a hangar, No. 5 (as seen on the port wing lower surface). It clearly sports the wide, white spiral on the black spinner, pointing towards the usage of this Axis recognition and safety marking in Bulgaria as early as from September 1943 – in contradiction to what has been known until now.

In late August 1944, after Rumania had defected from the Axis camp and joined the Allies' camp, Soviet troops reached Bulgaria's borders. Bulgaria – the majority of its population being sympathetic to the big Slavic neighbour across the Black Sea – did not declare war on the Soviet Union despite pressure from Hitler, keeping neutrality in respect of the Axis-Soviet war. Nevertheless, the Soviet Union did declare war on 5 September, and invaded the country the very same day. On 9 September, the Bulgarians changed sides and joined the Allies (in practice, the Soviet Union) in their war against Nazi Germany. The Bulgarian Army, the air force included, was ordered to fight the retreating Germans, their erstwhile ally.

This radically new situation, when Bulgarian warplanes had to co-operate with the Soviet air force (VVS), required new identification for Bulgarian aircraft that would identify them as 'Allies' (to the So-

---

23 A photograph of a Bf 109G-6 identified with what appears to be 'Black 10' is such an exception (see colour profile in the appropriate chapter in vol. 2).

24 Many thanks to Nick Beale for this ULTRA capture of the original German order.

49. Following Bulgaria's about face of 9 September 1944, when it left the Axis camp and joined the Allies, Bulgarian warplanes had to co-operate with the Soviet air force (VVS). This change required new identification for Bulgarian aircraft, that would identify them as 'Allies' (to the Soviets, that is). Accordingly, white identification colour was applied on Bulgarian airplanes, starting on 20 September 1944. The white colour was applied on the tips of both the lower and upper wing, as well as in the form of a mid or rear fuselage band. The spinner should have been painted white as well (where it was the case). At the same time, all yellow paint had to be removed. This new identification colour is shown on the depicted Focke-Wulf Fw 44J, LZ-FEN, Werknummer 2743, NN 39/7021, photographed in mid-September 1944. This particular photo was chosen by the Author to also show a strangely painted Dewoitine D.520, seen in the background at left (which sports a wide, white mid-fuselage band just aft of the cockpit, under the antenna mast). That particular camouflage scheme was undoubtedly of Bulgarian origin.

viets, that is). For the 5th and 17th Air Armies of the VVS fighting on the southern (left) flank of the front (covering Rumania and Bulgaria), the white colour was generally used as identification. This colour was introduced on aircraft of the Rumanian air force as well, starting from early September. The same had to apply to now 'friendly' Bulgarian airplanes, too. [photo 49]

Therefore, by Decree No. I-1332/20.09.1944, the marking and identification colour worn by Bulgarian aircraft was modified, as follows:

1. *The wingtips, on both sides, have to be painted with a 1 m wide white area.*
2. *The spinners also have to be painted white.*
3. *A 0.5 m wide band has to be painted around the fuselage, aft of the national marking.*
4. *All yellow paint must be removed.*

As has been highlighted many times earlier, in practice there were many exceptions to the rule when it comes to Bulgarian markings and codes. Photographs taken post-September 1944 reveal yellow paint still occasionally being used in parallel to the white (e.g. on the rudder of at least one Fw 189) [photo 50], the 'white spiral on black spinner' type of Axis recognition feature left on the propeller hubs (e.g. on Bf 109Gs, Ju 87Ds and Do 17Ms), rear fuselage band applied in front of the fuselage marking, not aft (e.g. on Ju 87Ds), rear fuselage band much wider than the prescribed 0.5 m (e.g. on Bf 109Gs), etc. Despite the numerous exceptions, it can generally be stated that if the upper and lower wingtips, and especially the rear fuselage band – occasionally referred to as бял "пояс", or white "belt" – of a Bulgarian aircraft appear in very light colour, the photograph must have been taken after mid-September 1944 (up to the end of 1945, as noted later on).

The introduction of the white 'pro-Soviet' identification colour did not affect the usage of the existing military marking, i.e. the 'St. Andrew's Cross'. Contrary to what has been published so far, this cross-type, Axis-style identification marking was used for more than a year after Bulgaria left the Axis camp, well after the war's end.

Despite being informed about the new ally, Soviet pilots occasionally mistook the cross-shape marking for a 'fascist symbol' and fired upon Bulgarian aircraft. One such 'friendly fire' incident occurred on 9 March 1945, when a Do 17 'Uragan' bomber, used as long-range courier aircraft by the 73rd *Yato*, was shot at by a pair of Soviet Lavochkin La-5 fighters over southern Hungary. The Bulgarian pilot, *Podporuchik* Karaghiaurov, managed to crash-land his stricken mount 25 km from the Pécs main air base. Even after the belly landing, the trigger-happy Soviet fighters kept shooting at the doomed aircraft. Luckily for the crew, they escaped from the shot-up aircraft.

The subsequent investigation by the joint Bulgarian-Soviet committee following this grave incident revealed that the Soviet pilots fired upon the Bulgarian machine, identified with the 'St. Andrew's Cross', believing that a 'fascist' aircraft was in their gunsights, despite the clearly displayed white identification colour. Therefore, as an interim measure, the Bulgarian airmen suggested the aircraft flying on the Sofia (Bulgaria)-Zemun (Yugoslavia)-Pécs (Hungary) route and back be identified, instead of the black cross, with a large orange-red dot, surrounded by a 10-cm wide white ring. The air force headquarters in Sofia initially accepted the proposal. However, after this experimental marking was reportedly applied on a couple of aircraft in the rather primitive conditions existing on Pécs airfield [photo 51], came a new

order from Sofia prohibiting the usage of the red dot style symbol[25]. The reason was simple: it was identical to the Japanese marking, i.e. an Axis power still fighting the Allies!

Based on the memories of veteran airman Yordan Pelev, former pilot in the Do 17-equipped long-range reconnaissance 73rd *Yato*, which mostly covered the Sofia-Zemun (Yugoslavia)-Pécs (Hungary) route, the squadron's airmen suggested an additional 10-cm wide green ring to be added around the similarly thick white ring surrounding the red centre dot; however, there is no proof this marking was ever applied on aircraft. At the end, bureaucracy and indifference prevailed, thus everything stayed the same; the 'St. Andrew's Cross' style marking was kept in place up to the end of the war, and a while beyond.

As the war neared to its end, the influence of the Communist forces in Bulgaria – occupied by the Soviet Army – increased significantly. The so-called 'royalist' officers started to be purged from the ranks of the army, the air force included. Scores were put on trial in 'kangaroo courts' and executed for 'treason'. As a result of the so-called 'democratization' of the army and air force, the necessity to change the symbols connected to the 'Tsarist' period arose. One of these symbols was the 'St. Andrew's Cross' marking used by the army and air force, which – despite being an old Orthodox religious symbol – was associated with the 'fascist' era.

The starting point for the design of the new marking was the aforementioned proposal by Bulgarian airmen located at the airfield of Pécs, a red disk surrounded by a white circle. However, in order to complete the red and white colours with the third colour of the Bulgarian flag, a horizontal green line was added across the circle. When turned 90 degrees (as applied on the wings), the symbol could be also identified with the Cyrillic letters ОФ (i.e. OF), short for Отечествен фронт (i.e. *Otechestven Front*, or Fatherland Front) – a coalition of leftist powers, dominated by the Communist Party, that performed a coup d'état in early September 1944, and ruled the country since that turning point. This military symbol is sometimes called the 'Republican marking'. [photo 52A and B]

Despite different sources giving the date of the marking change at various times[26], it actually happened officially on 4 October 1945, by Decree No. 474, issued by the Commander of the People's Air Force[27], and signed by Maj. Gen. Gancho I. Manchev. Since this post-war insignia is less known, it's worth quoting the relevant parts of the original specification:

50. As noted in the previous photo legend, yellow 'Axis' recognition colour ought to be removed from Bulgarian aircraft following the 'about face' of September 1944. However, in practice there were many exceptions to the rule when it comes to Bulgarian markings and codes. One is the case of the depicted Fw 189A-2 Oko ('Eye'), NN 14/7106, 'White 14', where the yellow colour was overpainted on the lower wingtip and rear fuselage; however, strangely, it was left untouched on the rudder. The spinners were not painted white, either.

---

25 On a couple of photos depicting Petlyakov Pe-2 bombers, freshly delivered by the USSR, a large red dot surrounded by a thin white circle, without the horizontal green bar, is visible on the fuselage side. However, this is most probably due to the poor quality of the photos, where the colour shade difference between red and green are indiscernible.

26 Various published Bulgarian sources give the date as September 1944, March, April or May 1945, none of them is valid. A photo of a KB-4, No. 7, dated 16 July 1945, still shows the 'St.Andrew's Cross' marking and a mid-fuselage ring in white.

27 The royal appellation has largely disappeared from the name of the air force (originally VNVV, *Văzdushni na Negovo Velichestvo Voyski*, or His Majesty's Air Army) since the beginning of 1945, the air force being usually referred to in documents as simply VV (*Văzdushni Voyski*, or Air Army).

51. *Following a 'friendly fire' incident that occurred in March 1945, when Soviet fighters shot down a Bulgarian Do 17 bomber over Southern Hungary, Bulgarian airmen suggested the aircraft flying on the Sofia (Bulgaria)-Zemun (Yugoslavia)-Pécs (Hungary) route and back to be identified with a large orange-red dot, surrounded by a 10-cm wide white ring, instead of the Axis-style black cross. This experimental marking was applied only on a couple of aircraft. On this official photograph, taken at Pécs airfield on 1 June 1945, a Junkers Ju W34, captured from the Germans, can be seen in the background. What is most interesting is the Bulgarian tricolour, applied horizontally on the tail surface, as well as a roundel type marking barely visible on fuselage side and underwing surface. This could very well be the temporary marking introduced to avoid 'friendly fire' incidents with Soviet fighters. Curiously, the engine's NACA ring was not painted white, as was the Junkers Ju 52/3m's in the foreground. The wingtips don't appear to sport the white recognition colour, either. Loss lists mention a Ju W34 Dărvenitsa (Bedbug) crashed on Pécs airfield, on 1 July 1945, killing all aboard. Chances are, it was this particular aircraft that was subject of the described deadly accident.*

52A and B. *After the war's end, with the Communists gaining absolute power, the 'St. Andrew's Cross' marking – associated by them with the 'fascist' era – was replaced with a new military marking, reflecting the changed times. The new roundel could be also identified with the Cyrillic letters OF (ОФ), short for Отечествен фронт (i.e., Otechestven Front), or Fatherland Front – a coalition of leftist powers, dominated by the Communist Party. Despite different sources giving the date of the marking change at various times, it actually happened officially on 4 October 1945. Along with the roundels, the tail surface received a tricolour band spanning it horizontally. The 'OF' marking is nicely seen on this recently restored Yak-9P, prob. constr. no. 0267, NN 27/7097, 'White 27', exhibited at the Bulgarian aviation museum at Krumovo, near Plovdiv. (photos V. Petrov)*

53. *The OF-style roundel gave way sometime in 1951 to the red star type marking. It consisted of a white dot in centre, surrounded by green and red rings (Bulgaria's national colours). The Bulgarian cockade was edged by a thin white circle. This was inscribed into the centre of a five-point red star, edged in white. This style of pro-Soviet marking was typical of those Soviet satellite countries that were once part of the Axis allies (Rumania, Hungary, Bulgaria). The NN written in triangle remained unchanged. The depicted Yak-9M, NN 29/7087, shows this new marking. Notice the 'board number' on the fuselage (4, or ending in 4), is not identical any more with the aircraft's individual number of the NN (shown in the top area of the triangle).*

54. *The crashed aircraft is Yak-9, construction number 4415339, NN 101/7087, piloted by an aviatrix, лейтенант Мария Атанасова (Lieutenant Mariya Atanasova), who hit the ground at Polikraishte, near Gorna Oryahovitsa, on 22.08.1952. The aircraft broke in two, but luckily she escaped unhurt. The new, Communist inspired military marking is clearly seen on the airframe.*

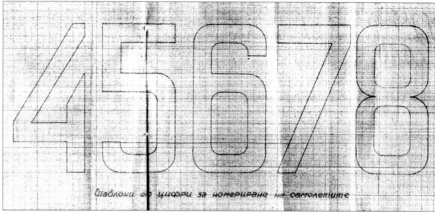

Шаблони от цифри за номериране на самолетите

55A and B. Photocopied annexes to the order referring to the new markings and codes to be used on aircraft, dated 4.10.1945, point #3: "Triangle with the nomenclature and the registration number". The hand-written sentence on the bottom reads: "Stencils/ patterns of numerals/cyphers for numbering of aircraft".

1, National marking (in original 'boen znak', or 'combat insignia')

The new marking consists of two concentric circles: a red [dot] of 50 cm diameter [centre] and a white [circle] of 80 cm diameter [around it]. These circles are crossed by a horizontal green stripe [bar] of 80x15 cm size. This green stripe [bar] has to have a 1 cm wide white border. The marking has to be located on both sides of the fuselage, in place of the old insignia of the "old material" [i.e., the older aircraft types, in service during wartime], or in place of the insignia of the "new material" [i.e., reference to the newly delivered Soviet aircraft types, where they should replace the Red Stars]. If it is impossible to apply the marking with the prescribed diameter, the white circle can have 75 cm diameter, while the red circle [dot] has to stay 50 cm diameter. The green stripe [bar] in this case can be 75x15 cm. When the "old material" [see note above] has to be repainted in the future, the marking should be relocated back, to the location [of the marking] on the "new material" [see note above]. The national marking has to be applied also on the [lower] surface of the wing, in the location of the old marking, with the diameter of 60 cm (red dot in centre) and 90 cm (white circle around it)[1]. The green stripe [bar] has to be 90x15 cm. The markings should not be applied on the upper surface of the wing.

2, National tricolour

The [stripes of] white, green and red colours [from top to bottom] have to be applied horizontally; all three stripes have to have 15 cm width. The tricolour has to be placed on both sides of the upper area of the vertical surface; the white stripe has to be located at about 22 cm from the fin tip. On the [larger] He 111 and Ju 52 aircraft, the width of the stripes should be 20 cm.

3, Triangle

It is made of white lines, each [side of the equilateral triangle] of 30 cm length. On smaller aircraft, it is possible to be applied in smaller size, each triangle side of 25 cm length. The triangle and the numbers [inside it] should be applied with the old, existing templates (8 mm thick line width/characters). The dimensions of the digits should be 55x30cm [actually mm], or in smaller size triangles the digits should be 50x25cm [again, mm].

4, Sequence of board numbers and colour marking in different air units

4a, At combat air units: the board numbers are white, of one or two digits, with the dimensions of 60x30 cm and line thickness of 8 cm. They are placed on both sides of the aircraft [fuselage], 20 cm in front of the national marking on the "new material" and 20 cm aft the national marking on the "old material", until the aircraft is repainted [during major repair and overhaul]. The centre of the digits is placed on the horizontal axis of the national marking. On [either side of] the wings, the numbers should not be applied. (...) In the future, while the "old material" is repainted, the marking and digits should be applied as on the "new material".

The sequence of board numbers should be from 1 to 40 [in the following units]: 1/6., 2/6. and 3/6. Fighter Orlyatsi, 1/2., 2/2. and 3/2. Ground Attack ("Shturmovi") Orlyatsi; while from 1 to 32 in the 1/5. and 2/5. Bomber Orlyatsi.

To identify the different aircraft with the same board numbers from various orlyaki, the propeller blades [sic! actually the spinners] have to be painted, as follows:
- in the first orlyatsi (1/6., 1/2., 1/5.) bright red,
- in the second orlyatsi (2/6., 2/2., 2/5.) light blue,
- in the third orlyatsi (3/6., 3/2.) yellow.

If any aircraft in an orlyak has to be written off, the replacement aircraft will receive the same board number and [spinner] colour.

In addition, a 15 cm wide stripe has to be applied on the vertical tail surface in the same colour as the propeller [spinner]. The stripe has to have an angle of 30 degrees from the vertical, and should start from

---

1 The specification fails to mention that the green bar should face the direction of flight, i.e. pointing forward.

the upper edge (front) downwards (back). This coloured stripe should not cross the tricolour [on the tail], should stop at the upper edge of the flash and should continue under it².

4b, At reconnaissance, school, training, transport and other [secondary] units: [markings and codes should be] identical to the combat units; however, the fuselage [board] numbers are not from 1 to 40, but according to the "registration numbers" (from the triangle). Also, the coloured propeller [spinners] and tail stripes should not be applied.

The present order complements the [previous] order No. 298 of 22 June 1945 and Order No. 90 of 21 September 1945.³

2   A photo depicting an Il-2 'Shturmovik' from 7 o'clock clearly depicts a light coloured diagonal line across the tail surface.

3   Original translation courtesy of Jaroslav Kreč, edited and annotated by the Author.

This order of marking change was applied on aircraft in the next several weeks, being largely completed by the end of the year. Indeed, the post-accident photograph of a DAR-9 trainer, taken on 19 October 1945, shows the white pro-Soviet identification colour being still carried on the rear fuselage and both wingtips. Despite the slow pace of the marking changes, from early 1946 on the new 'democratic' OF insignia identified Bulgarian military aircraft up to about mid-1951[28]. At that point, it gave place to the red star type marking outlined in white, with a white dot in centre, surrounded by a green and a red ring (Bulgaria's national colours), the latter ring outlined by a thin, white circle.

This red-star-type military marking was peculiar to those Soviet satellite countries of Central and Eastern Europe that were once part of the Axis (Rumania, Hungary, Bulgaria). [photos 53 and 54] This Communist-style marking stayed in place until September 1992, almost three years after the democratic changes had taken place in Bulgaria, being the Bulgarian military marking in effect for the longest period (41 years). After that point, the Bulgarian military reverted to red-green-white (inside) roundel, adopted first in late 1918 (but in reverse order of colours), which is still in effect today.

Along with the new identification markings, the style and shape of the serial (board) numbers and the ones written in the triangle were standardised[29] as well – at least theoretically. [photos 55A and B]

28   Arado Ar 96B, NN 21/7035, destroyed in accident on 26 May 1950, wore the OF-style marking. Post-accident investigation photos of Yak-9, NN 1/7087, happened on 14 September 1950, show the wreck still displaying the OF-style marking. Similar photos documenting the accident of another Yak-9, NN 101/7087, which happened on 22 August 1952, show the wreck already displaying the Red Star type marking. As comparison, the Hungarian military marking change to a very similar red-star layout happened on 16 June 1951, while the Rumanian one happened on 28 July 1950.

29   Excerpt from the following original document, dated 4.10.1945, called: Заповед относно знаците на самолетите (Order regarding signs on aircraft), Point No. 3: За триъгълника с номенклатурния и регистрационния номер (For the triangle with the nomenclature and the registration number).

56. Unlike other Axis (and Allies) aviation units, unit emblems were not of widespread usage in the Bulgarian air force. Only very few combat units had their own emblems. This included all aircraft of the seaplane Yato (squadron). Depicted is the top seaplane type employed by the Bulgarians, the Arado Ar 196A-3, with a squadron emblem consisting of a quacking duck wearing clogs (wooden shoes), with a bomb under its right wing (similar to the Luftwaffe's 3./SAGr. 125 emblem, based at Varna until mid-February 1944). Notice the yellow (?) service stencils on the fuselage and wing leading edge are in Bulgarian.

A few words about squadron and personal emblems. Unlike other Axis (and Allies) aviation units, unit markings/emblems were not in widespread usage in the Bulgarian air force. Only very few combat units had their own emblems. Identified unit emblems were worn by aircraft of the 1st, 2nd, 3rd (all Avia B.71) and 4th (Do 17M) Bomber *Yata* (of the 5th Bomber *Polk*), the 343rd Reconnaissance *Yato* (Fw 189), the Seaplane *Yato* (Ar 196, He 42, He 60) [photo 56], as well as the Bf 109Es of the so-called '*Galata*' *Orlyak* (see appropriate chapter). The topic of pilot's individual emblems is even less known. Some may have been inherited aircraft, featuring such emblems from the previous (German) owners, some others were clearly individual. [photo 57] It can be stated though that in the VNVV these cases were the exception, rather than the norm.

An occurrence unique to the Royal Bulgarian Air Force (VNVV) was the prominent presence of the Royal Cipher of Tsar Boris III on several early aircraft types, as noted earlier [photos 27 and 28]. The air force emblem was displayed only on official documents. [photo 58]

There are several other emblems seen on various combat aircraft, most notable Bf 109Es and Gs (see appropriate chapters); however, it's uncertain if these were unit markings, or personal emblems. [see photos in the Messerschmitt Bf 109E and G chapters] Occasionally, slogans could also be seen on individual aircraft (like "9th September" on a captured ex-Croatian Dornier Do 17Z bomber photographed well after the about-face of 9 September 1944). [photo 59]

Finally, an oddity. There were individual cases when a particular aircraft displayed the word BULGARIA; however, this had nothing to do with the Bulgarian aviation *per se*. [photo 60]

57. Bulgarian fighter aircraft displayed only very rarely personal insignias, which were often inspired by unit emblems seen on Luftwaffe warplanes. This was the case of the personal mount believed to be of Podporuchik Hristo I. Petrov of 2/6. Orlyak. It displays an artwork clearly inspired by the early emblem of I./JG 52 (later on, used by 2./JG 52), a black wild boar on a green shield, surrounded by a thick, white frame. The fuselage number of this particular Bf 109G-6 is believed to be 'Red 1'.

58. This diploma illustrates the official name and emblem of the Royal Bulgarian Air Force. It was awarded to Kandidat podofitser, or Candidate NCO Ivan Georgiev Proshopov, who graduated from the operator NCO school located at Sofia airfield. Interestingly, although the diploma was issued after the war, on 27 July 1945, the 'royal' appellation ('His Majesty's Air Forces'), on top, as well as the crown atop the stylized Cyrillic letter B, in centre, were left uncensored. Although Bulgaria was officially a kingom until 9 September 1946, when it became republic following a referedum, references to the monarchy were frowned upon by members of the new leftist government and state institutions.

59. *Rarely, slogans or other personal mottos could also be seen on individual aircraft. This particular photo shows a captured ex-Croatian Dornier Do 17Z bomber photographed after the Bulgarian about-face of 9 September 1944, with the word '9ᵗʰ September' (9ᵗⁱ септември) on its lower nose area. These inscriptions and slogans served as propaganda for the new leftist Government.*

60. *Finally, an oddity. The picture shows a Raab-Katzenstein (RaKa) RK IIa biplane, c/n 34, German civilian register D-1121, in the summer of 1930. The text BULGARIA displayed on the fuselage side has nothing to do with Bulgaria, as it's rather an advertisement for a cigarette factory, called Salomon Krenter Zigarettenfabrik 'BULGARIA', located in Dresden, Germany.*

ANNEX

Aircraft ID codes (Шифър за самолетите), in effect from 23.08.1945

School aircraft:	Учебни:
1. Vrabche-V	1. Врабче – В
2. Kanarche-K	2. Канарче – К
3. Lyastovitsa-L	3. Лястовица – Л
4. Siniger-S	4. Синигер – С
5. Patitsa-P	5. Патица – П
6. Byuker Bestman-BB	6. Бюкер Бестман – ББ
7. Chuchuliga I-Ch I	7. Чучулига I – ЧI
8. Chuchuliga II-Ch II	8. Чучулига II – ЧII
9. Chuchuliga III-Ch III	9. Чучулига III – ЧIII
10. Soyka-A	10. Сойка – А
11. Lebed-Le	11. Лебед – Ле
12. Tyulen-T	12. Тюлен – Т
13. Komar-Ko	13. Комар – Ко
14. Osa-O	14. Оса – О
15. Gălăb-G	15. Гълъб – Г
16. Papagal-Pa	16. Папагал – Па
17. Buhal-Bu	17. Бухал – Бу
Warplanes and Trainers:	**Бойни и тренировъчни:**
1. Sova-So	1. Сова – Со
2. Drozd-Dr	2. Дрозд – Др
3. Haynkel 111-Hl	3. Хайнкел 111 – Хл
4. Garvan III-G III	4. Гарван III – ГIII
5. Vrana-Vr	5. Врана – Вр
6. Fazan-F	6. Фазан – Ф
7. Akula-Ak	7. Акула – Ак
8. Tsiklop-Tsk	8. Циклоп – Цк
9. Dogan-Dg	9. Доган – Дг
10. Strela-St	10. Стрела – Ст
11. Mesershmid Gustav-Mg	11. Месершмид Густав – Мг
12. Avia 135-Av	12. Авиа 135 – Ав
13. Devoatin-Dv	13. Девоатин – Дв
14. Zherav-Zhr	14. Жерав – Жр
15. Uragan-Ur	15. Ураган – Ур
16. Petlyakov-Pe	16. Петляков – Пе
17. Shtuka-Shtk	17. Щука – Щк
18. Yak-9-Ya	18. Як-9 – Я
19. Ilyushin 2-I	19. Илюшин 2 - И

Fokker D.VII
Bulgaria's Sole Fighter Aircraft of the 1920s

On 4 October 1918, the very day Tsar Boris III signed the army demobilisation decree, seven Fokker D.VII fighters[1] arrived from Germany to Bozhurishte main military airfield, by train[2]. They were in transit from Germany for over two months, due to the hectic state of the railway traffic in Bulgaria. Obviously, the fighters arrived too late to actively take part in any military operations, which had already ceased.

The Neuilly-sur-Seine peace 'dictate' – as Bulgarian historiography labels the treaty – signed on 27 November 1919, contained an 'air clause', which forbade the existence of any air force.[3] Accordingly, it stipulated that all warplanes, as well as airframes, spare engines and parts and armament shall be handed over to the Allies [i.e., to be destroyed][4]. Accordingly, all warplanes Bulgaria still officially had – including all but one Fokker D.VII – were handed over to the victorious Allies, to be eventually scrapped.

The following series of photos were taken during the inspection of RAF Captain E. W. Chatterley of 16th Wing, at Bozhurishte airfield, from the 31st of December 1918 to the 17th of January 1919. The British officer found the air base "in disorganised condition", with "most of the personnel being absent". This first shot shows the general view of the main hangar, with a couple of D.VIIs visible, at right.

---

1 One of them was Serial No. 5322/18, another one was No. 5324/18, while a third one was No. 5355/18, all manufactured by *Albatros-Werke*, all fitted with a 160 HP Mercedes engine.

2 Another post-WW 1 source gives eight Fokker D.VIIs that arrived to Bozhurishte on 28 November 1918. The difference may explain the sole aircraft that could be hidden and thus spared from destruction.

3 SECTION III. AIR CLAUSES.
ARTICLE 89. *"The armed forces of Bulgaria must not include any military or naval air forces. No dirigible shall be kept."*
ARTICLE 90. *"Within two months from the coming into force of the present Treaty the personnel of the air forces on the rolls of the Bulgarian land and sea forces shall be demobilised."*

4 ARTICLE 93. *"On the coming into force of the present Treaty all military and naval aeronautical material must be delivered by Bulgaria and at her expense to the Principal Allied and Associated Powers. Delivery must be effected at such places as the Governments of the said Powers may select, and must be completed within three months. In particular, this material will include all items under the following heads which are or have been in use or were designed for warlike purposes. (...) Complete aeroplanes and seaplanes, as well as those being manufactured, repaired or assembled. (...) Engines (...). Nacelles and fuselages. Armament (...)"*

The object of inspection by Captain Chatterley was Fokker D.VII, 5355/18 – "the newest type of scout airplane", which "had been used very little, if at all" – and particularly its armament. This biplane is seen here parked in front of the main hangar. Notice the propeller-less Nieuport Nie.24C1, at right, and the Albatros C.III, sporting a white cross on its fuselage, in the hangar.

The armament of the Fokker D.VII consisted of a pair of Spandau fixed machine guns, firing through the propeller arc. 500 rounds were carried by each gun.

The destruction was supervised by members of the Aeronautical Inter-Allied Commission of Control[5], as part of Bulgaria's de-militarisation, stipulated by the aforementioned peace treaty.

RAF Captain E. W. [Ernest William] Chatterley of 16th Wing inspected the airfield at Bozhurishte, located on the outskirts of Sofia, and the seaplane station at Varna, on the shores of the Black Sea – at that time both strategic air bases being occupied by French troops – from 31 December 1918 to 17 January 1919. The freshly promoted captain found seven Fokker D.VIIs among the existing 36 aircraft (and 3 wrecks) – *"which had been used very little, if at all, in Bulgarian Service units, when hostilities ceased."* Interestingly, none of these advanced fighters were included in the two existing air protection flights[6], based at Bozhurishte air base. His main focus was Fokker D.VII, 5355/18, particularly its armament. RAF Capt. F. Wells (from Salonika Aircraft Park) also visited Bozhurishte airfield and Varna seaport, presumably in the same time span as his compatriot. He compiled a list of inspected aircraft, including Fokker D.VII, 5324/18, makers no. 5923, fitted with a 160 HP Mercedes engine, No. 42990 (see Annex).

Eventually, all but one Fokker fell to the wrecker's axe. The lone survivor was successfully hidden in a barn, and re-emerged after the inspectors (members of the Inter-Allied Commission

5 ARTICLE 100. *"It will be the special duty of the Aeronautical Inter-Allied Commission of Control to make an inventory of the aeronautical material which is actually in possession of the Bulgarian Government, to inspect aeroplane, balloon and motor manufactories and factories producing arms, munitions and explosives capable of being used by aircraft, to visit all aerodromes, sheds, landing grounds, parks and depots situated in Bulgarian territory, and to authorise where necessary the removal of material and to take delivery of such material."*
"The Bulgarian Government must furnish to the Aeronautical Inter-Allied Commission of Control all such information and legislative, administrative or other documents which the Commission may think necessary to ensure the complete execution of the air clauses, and in particular a list of the personnel belonging to all Bulgarian air services and of the existing material, as well as of that in process of manufacture, or on order, and a complete list of all establishments working for aviation, of their positions and of all sheds and landing grounds."

6 The first flight (squad) consisted of two D.F.W C.5s, one Roland [D.III] and one Nieuport [Nie.XXIV], while the second flight (squad) was made of three L.V.G. D.V's and two or three Roland [D.III]. Another Nieuport [Nie.XXI] used to belong to this squad as well; however, it had to be retired as it had become unserviceable.

Three views of one of the main protagonists of Captain Wells' inspection, Fokker D.VII, 5324/18. The detailed description of this particular aircraft, including camouflage and markings, can be read in the Annex.

of Control) had left the country in the mid-1920s[7]. That particular aircraft, now fitted with a 200 HP Mercedes engine, had its machine guns removed and was fitted with a decoy rear cockpit to make it look like a two-seat trainer. It was then used by Gendarmerie's Air *Otdelenie* (Department)[8] from 1923 on. Early next year, the biplane received civilian registration B-BIXP. In 1927, it was assigned to a secret fighter *yato* (squadron) – officially called '*sportno yato*' – along with a Bristol 'Tourer' and four indigenous DAR-1 trainers. This 'sports' squadron was placed under the Дирекция на въздухоплаването (i.e., *Direktsiya na văzduhoplavaneto*, or Aviation Directorate).

Reportedly, on 7 October 1925, Captain Marinov flew for two hours aboard the D.VII and reached a record height of 7,000 m. This was quite a significant achievement with the obsolescent biplane, with open cockpit, propelled by a fatigued WW 1-era engine of only 200 HP.

The biplane was fitted in secret with machine guns circa 1926, and then used by the clandestine Bulgarian air force's fighter *yato* as Bulgaria's *only* combat-ready fighter aircraft. Occasionally, the lone Fokker took

7 The Inter-Allied Commission of Control officially ceased to function in Bulgaria on 1 June 1927. In fact, its active role in policing the peace treaty in Bulgaria had ceased earlier.

8 A document that explicitly mentions the Air Gendarmerie is the Royal Decree No.16/10.04.1921, by which *Poruchik zapasniya* (1st Lt. in reserve) Nikolay Petrini was appointed as head of the Airplane Depot of the Air Force Gendarmerie (in original Въздухоплавателното жандармерийско, or *Văzduhoplavatelnoto zhandarmeriysko*).

off to intercept various foreign aircraft, which flew across the Bulgarian skies with impunity, at will. One such encounter was recorded, as follows: sometime in 1926, a Yugoslav military aircraft appeared over Sofia. The Serbian pilot was careless, as he knew that Bulgaria had no military aviation. Little did he know that at Bozhurishte airfield, a pair of 'Maxim-Spandau' machine guns was mounted, "occasionally", on the lone Fokker D.VII. Upon sighting the uninvited "guest", Todor Rogev, famous fighter pilot, war veteran and test pilot, promptly took off with the Fokker. Rogev, a Bulgarian ethnic native of Macedonia, by then under Yugoslav rule, thus with no particular reasons to like the Serbs, approached the casually flying Yugoslav warplane. The surprised pilot of the Bréguet Bre.14 quickly turned around and headed back to Yugoslav airspace. However, the faster Fokker D.VII soon caught the intruder and made a few buzzes at close range. Despite being known as a 'hot head', Rogev refrained from opening fire, knowing how negative for Bulgaria the result would have been. After all, his message came across clearly to the intruder, namely that Bulgarian airspace cannot be penetrated with impunity. Bulgaria was not *"a house without dog"* – as Rogev fittingly put it.

The repercussions did not wait for long, though. The Serbian pilot spotted the machine guns fitted to the Fokker. Based on his report, an Allied military delegation descended upon Bozhurishte air base three days later. They found the Fokker, however, without any trace of a machine gun ever being mounted on it. Reportedly, the Yugoslav member of this delegation, a certain Captain Ghyorghyovich, teased the Bulgarians: *"Gentlemen, why don't you mount machine guns on the aircraft? Start learning how to use it, as a next war is imminent, and by then your Fokker will already be a relic..."*

In September 1927, the secret fighter *yato* – the sole Fokker D.VII included – took part in the autumn army manoeuvres, the first post-war military exercises in Bulgaria involving aviation.

The sad end of Bulgaria's air fleet of WW 1, which was scrapped on the order of the victorious Allies. Only a very few aircraft escaped the axe, including a single Fokker D.VII.

The lone Fokker D.VII crashed on 12 January 1928 with pilot *Poruchik* Nikola Kokilev at the controls, and was subsequently written off. The pilot survived, and went on to have a long career[9] lasting to shortly after the war, when he was fired from the air force, along with many other 'royalist' airmen.

Nevertheless in its short and lacklustre career, this lone Fokker symbolised that in the 1920s Bulgarian airspace was not totally defenceless. It also kept alive the hope of Bulgarian fighter pilots that one day their activity will officially resume and the fighter arm will re-emerge. They had to wait until 1937 for that cherished moment to arrive...

Camouflage and markings

The Fokker D.VIIs arrived in typical German camouflage scheme and markings (see Camouflage and Identification Markings sections of the Annex). Following the cessation of hostilities in late 1918, the German 'beam crosses' were overpainted, and a cockade – often referred to as 'Entente occupation marking' – made of the Bulgarian tricolour (white outer ring, green middle ring and red centre dot), was applied over the crosses, in six positions. The tail surfaces remained white, with no markings. All

Sometime in the early 1920s, a sole Fokker D.VII that somehow had avoided the Entente axe emerged from hiding. Initially, it did not bear any markings or codes, only a dark coloured four-leaf clover on the wheel covers.

---

9   As a side story, the family of Mr. Kokilev claims that he actually flew the Messerschmitt Me 262 jet aircraft in 1944, and presents a German language document, purportedly issued by the RLM, as proof (see page 71, bottom). However, the Author believes the veracity of this document is questionable.

Later on, after Bulgaria was officially allocated civilian aviation registration letters in June 1923, the Fokker was identified as B-BIXP, applied in black on the fuselage and both wing surfaces, directly over the airframe's crème colour. Notice the covered dummy rear cockpit, which was intended to disguise the single-seat fighter as a two-seat trainer.

Soon after, the black civilian registration was applied over a black bordered white rectangle (on the fuselage only). The civilian marked fighter, based at the main military airport of Bozhurishte, was "occasionally" fitted with a pair of machine guns and sent to intercept intruding foreign aircraft, which flew with impunity over Bulgarian skies. It was intended to be a message that Bulgaria was not "a house without dog" – as a veteran pilot aptly put it. Depicted is B-BIXP in its element, flying in the vicinity of Bozhurishte base airfield, in 1926 (as identified by the writing on the original negative's top right corner).

Bulgarian airmen flock near the pseudo-civilian Fokker after the successful completion of a test flight on 7 October 25, with Kpt. Marinov at the controls, which established a record altitude of 7000 m.

other factory markings and codes remained unchanged. This marking lasted until the air clauses of the Neuilly peace treaty were implemented in September 1921. On a photo of a D.VII sporting a cockade, a horseshoe is visible on the main wheel covers.

The sole Fokker D.VII recovered and used in the 1920s was painted overall in cream (clear doped linen), with black engine cowling. Initially, it sported a dark colour four-leaf clover on its main wheel covers and no registration. Later on, when the 'clandestine' aircraft was made 'official', the clover leaf disappeared and the aircraft received civilian registration B-BIXP in black, applied on fuselage sides and both wing surfaces. Initially, the letters were applied on the fuselage directly over the cream base colour, but later they were applied over a black bordered white rectangle, as per official regulations. Despite official policy, the letter B (for Bulgaria), was not applied on the rudder. The engine cowling was semi-gloss black. The same colour covered the top fuselage area, in front of the windshield.

Annex

Detailed inspection of Fokker D.VII, No. 5324/18 (Alb.), performed by RAF Capt. F. Wells (from Salonika Aircraft Part) at Bozhurishte airfield, presumably in December 1918 (excerpt)

"Single-seater scout airplane. Fokker D.VII (Alb.), Military No. 5324/18, Makers No. 5923. 160 HP Mercedes No. 42990, 140 mm bore, 160 mm stroke, 1450 rpm. Guaranteed until 6-2-1919. Propeller: Garuda, No. 20114.

Span top plane: 27'-6", bottom: 23'. Chord top plane: 5'-3", bottom: 3'-11". Overall length: 22'-8". Overall height: 9'-3 ½". Wing area (main planes): 198 sq. ft, (tail plane): 15 sq. ft. Wheel track: 5'-9", 760x100 mm Gothania tyres.

Identification markings: 8 black crosses. Upper surface of top plane has 2 black crosses 5'-6" square x 8" wide, edged with 2 ¼" white. Lower surface of bottom planes 2 crosses 4'-0" square x 4" wide, edged with 1 ¾" white. One cross on either side of the fuselage. Centre of cross 6'-3" from stern post, 2'-7" square x 4" wide, edged 1 1/8" white. One cross on either side of rudder, 2'-1" square x 4" wide.

Camouflage: all fabric parts of machine, except rudder and fin, are covered with dyed camouflage fabric, the pattern being printed on the fabric, and consisting of rectangular and 5&6 sided figures of an average diagonal measurement of about 9" of various colours. Those on the sides and upper surfaces are fairly sub-dued, mostly heliotrope, light and dark green, dark blue and light brown. On the under surfaces more vivid colours are employed, consisting of light Prussian blue, pale crimson, buttercup yellow, and light green. The rudder and fin are painted white. Fabric of fairly good quality, insufficiently doped. (...) Very sensitive machine and difficult to land, not tiring to fly. Range of vision very fair. Strongly constructed [presumably the opinion of Bulgarian pilots, D.B.]. Armament consists of 2 Spandau guns, fixed, firing through the propeller, flexible drive, interrupter gears, driven off engine camshaft. 1918 type, starboard No. 7625, port No. 7611. 1000 rounds of ammunition, 500 each gun. 1 in 4 tracer.

Markings: Lower plane, rear spar dated 20/8/18, front spar dated ditto. Top plane dated 24/8/18."

Above: Bird's eye view of Sofia-Bozhurishte base airfield, in 1926 – home of the sole Fokker D.VII and practically all Bulgarian covert military aircraft of the 1920s.

Left: The sad remains of the crashed Fokker D.VII signal the end of the lacklustre decade-long career of Bulgaria's sole post-war fighter aircraft, which lasted from November 1918 until January 1928. At the time of its demise at the hands of Por. Kokilev, the black civilian registration was applied directly onto the airframe's crème base colour.

Below: German language document, purportedly issued by the Reichsluftfahrt-ministerium (RLM) in 1944, mentioning that Major 'Kokileff' (i.e., Kokilev) – who crashed the D.VII – flew the Messerschmitt Me 262 jet aircraft in total for 8,10 hrs. The authenticity of this document needs to be confirmed, though.

Deutsches Reich

Der Reichsminister der Luftfahrt

Aufgrund des Dokuments NR 634 von 1944, ausgestellt auf den Namen Major NIKOLA KOKILEFF werden diesem in Flug-und teilweise technischer Ausbildung am Flugzeug Me 262 8,10 Flugstunden bestätigt.

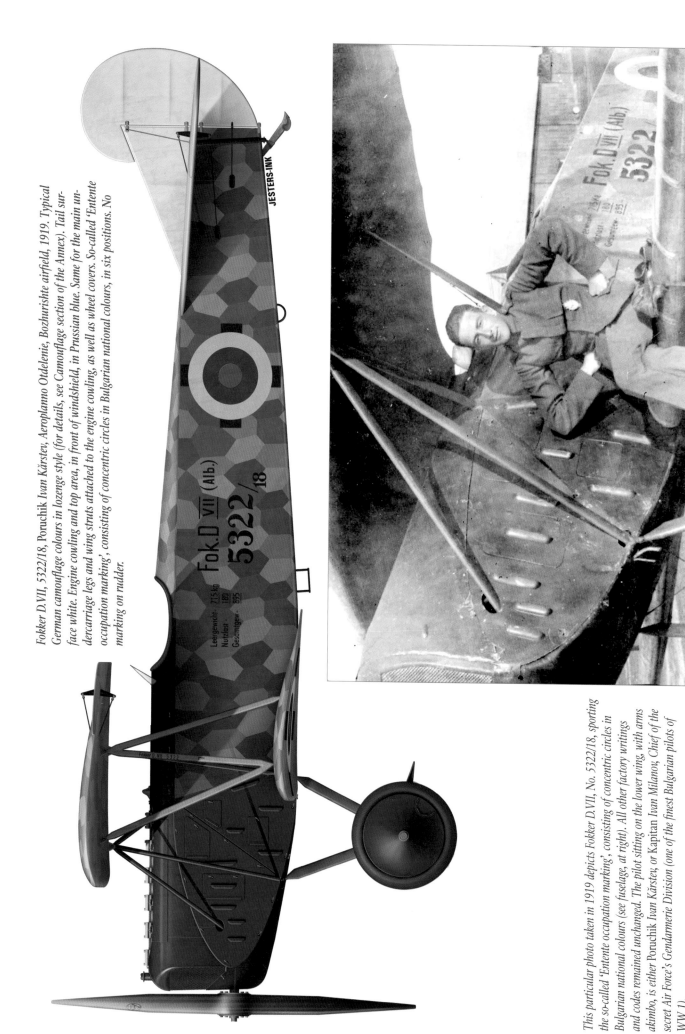

Fokker D.VII, 5322/18, Poruchik Ivan Kărstev, Aeroplanno Otdelenie, Bozhurishte airfield, 1919. Typical German camouflage colours in lozenge style (for details, see Camouflage section of the Annex). Tail surface white. Engine cowling and top area, in front of windshield, in Prussian blue. Same for the main undercarriage legs and wing struts attached to the engine cowling, as well as wheel covers. So-called 'Entente occupation marking', consisting of concentric circles in Bulgarian national colours, in six positions. No marking on rudder.

This particular photo taken in 1919 depicts Fokker D.VII, No. 5322/18, sporting the so-called 'Entente occupation marking', consisting of concentric circles in Bulgarian national colours (see fuselage, at right). All other factory writings and codes remained unchanged. The pilot sitting on the lower wing, with arms akimbo, is either Poruchik Ivan Kărstev, or Kapitan Ivan Milanov, Chief of the secret Air Force's Gendarmerie Division (one of the finest Bulgarian pilots of WW I).

Fokker D.VII, B-BIXP, Gendarmerie Air Otdelenie, Bozhurishte airfield, 1926. Overall cream (clear doped linen). Black engine cowling and top area, in front of windshield. Propeller also semi-gloss black. Civilian registration in black, applied on fuselage sides and both wing surfaces. On the fuselage, the registration was written over a black bordered white rectangle. No marking on rudder.

JESTERS-INK

Profile view of the unique Fokker D.VII that survived post-war destruction, and was subsequently put in service after Allied control eased in the mid-1920, registered B-BIXP. The second location, behind the pilot's, is fake.

DAR-5 *Brămbar*

The Sole Bulgarian Designed Fighter-Trainer

In 1929, under the lead of German *Dipl. Eng.* Hermann Winter[1], design work started at the DAR[2] Company, located in Bozhurishte, of a small single-seat biplane. It was officially intended to be used as high-altitude 'meteorological survey' aircraft. In fact, its covert role was fighter trainer, intended to kick-start the advanced training of would-be fighter pilots of the still secret Bulgarian air force. It is the only Bulgarian designed and produced aircraft type discussed in this book.

The airframe, of mixed, metal-wood construction, was powered by a five-cylinder Gnome&Rhône 5 *Titan* of 230 hp. The length of the sturdy little biplane was only 6.65 m, while the wingspan was 7.50 m. Wing surface area was 16.77 m². Empty weight turned out to be a mere 680 kg, while the take-off weight was 1,050 kg. The prototype's range was 745 km, cruising speed 165 km/h, while it could climb up to 6,000 m. Due to a fairly large fuel tank and low consumption, it could stay airborne for an impressive 4 hours and 45 minutes.

The prototype of the DAR-5 (construction number 44) was finalised by 1930, when it took off on its maiden flight, unmarked. Shortly after, it was officially registered as B-BUDA. The flying characteristics appear to be modest (max. speed was a mere 180 km/h), mainly due to the weak powerplant. Eventually, no order was secured by DAR for series production. Nevertheless, the sole aircraft was kept

---

The unmarked DAR-5 prototype, without the metal engine fairing, after it was completed at DAR Works. Here, the propeller is painted glossy black.

1 Aircraft designer Dipl. Eng. Prof. Dr. Hermann Winter, graduate of the famous *Technische Hochschule* (Technical Highschool, or Polytechnic) of Charlottenburg, Germany, arrived in Bulgaria in July 1925, at the invitation of the Bulgarian Government. He brought with him from Germany a handful of engineers and technicians. Under his guidance, the DAR Works were established in 1926. Several aircraft types were designed and manufactured under his leadership, one of the most notable ones being the DAR-5, subject of this chapter.

2 DAR was short for *Dărzhavna Aeroplanna Rabotilnitsa* (State Airplane Workshop).

in service by personnel of Bozhurishte airfield. From 1932, it was re-registered LZ-UDA. Later during service, the prototype's radial engine was enclosed in a special sheet metal cowling, designed by *Dipl. Eng.* Kiril Yakimov Petkov[3], finished in an eye-catching 'polished metal' look.

The *Brămbar*, or Beetle, as the unique DAR-5 was officially called based on Order No. 180 issued on 18 August 1937, was seen for many years at Bozhurishte, performing regular meteorological reconnaissance flights in the early mornings, and also occasional liaison duties, or pleasure flights. For example, *Kapitan* Ivan S. Ivanov flew LZ-UDA on 25 March 1936. The training flight originated from Bozhurishte airfield, and lasted one hour and ten minutes (from 8:20 to 9:30).

Last known sighting dates are 14 October 1941, when it was reported as extant with the 1st *Polk* (regiment), based at Bozhurishte. It is also listed in an undated VNVV document, most probably originated in late 1941, as reference to VNVV Commander Order No. 272/12.09.1941 is included, as one of the available training aircraft types (along with the PWS-26, Avia Bs.122, Fw 56, KB-5 and Fw 43a), described as 'D.A.R. 5'.

It has to be noted that there was an actual fighter aircraft project started by DAR engineers in January 1931 – called DAR-7 – which remained on paper only. The DAR-5 was the original source of this project. The design proposed a small biplane of mixed steel and wood structure, to be powered by a Gnome&Rhône 9A Jupiter radial engine of 480 hp. Wingspan was projected to be 8.80 m, length 7.00 m, wing surface area 21.00 m². Empty weight was calculated as 795 kg, while take-off weight

---

3   Kiril Petkov became head of the DAR design bureau in 1933. Previously, he lived and studied in the USA (including at the Michigan University) for seven years, prior to returning to Bulgaria in 1930. His first aircraft design was the DAR-7SS light liaison aircraft, the first Bulgarian monoplane construction. Only the prototype was built and flown.

was 1,390 kg. Maximum speed was anticipated at 268 km/h, with a range at 450 km. Armament was planned to consist of four 7.92 mm machine guns of unspecified type. As noted, the project never materialised.

Camouflage and markings

The aircraft was painted in cream (clear doped linen) overall. Initially, the 5-cylinder engine was left uncovered; however, later on it was covered with a shiny sheet metal cowling.

The prototype received civilian registration, B-BUDA. It was applied in black, on the fuselage sides and both wing surfaces. The last four letters were underlined, as per official regulations. From 1932, the registration changed to LZ-UDA, as depicted. The Bulgarian tricolour was applied on the rudder, in horizontal stripes.

The DAR-5 prototype parked on Bozhurishte airfield in 1938, prepared for an exhibition flight (hence the Bulgarian flag attached to its wing struts). This time, the aircraft is fitted with the metal engine fairing covering the G&R 5 Titan radial engine. The propeller is made of wood, covered by a layer of transparent lacquer.

Side view of the aircraft. A lacquered wooden propeller is attached to the engine shaft.

DAR-5 (c/n 44), LZ-UDA, 1st Polk, Bozhurishte airfield, 1938. Overall cream (clear doped linen). Engine fairing in 'polished metal' finish. Civilian registration in black, applied on fuselage sides and both wing surfaces. Bulgarian national colours on rudder.

10 o'clock view of the DAR-5 prototype, with snow-covered mountain peaks giving a majestic background.

Heinkel He 51 *Sokol*
Bulgaria's First True Fighter

A military agreement dated 27.05.1936, signed in Berlin by German and Bulgarian officials, stipulated the delivery of twelve two-seater reconnaissance Heinkel He 45s (equipped with BMW VI 7.3 ZU engine), twelve single-seater fighter aircraft, type Heinkel He 51 (with BMW VI 7.3 ZU engine), as well as six two-seater training aircraft, Heinkel He 72 *Kadett* (with Siemens Sh 14A engine). An updated version, signed twelve days later, enlarged the scope of the contract. Now it was calling for the speedy delivery to Bulgaria of six Fw 44, six Fw 56, six He 72 and two Fw 58 trainers, as well as the aforementioned twelve He 45s and twelve He 51s. Of these aircraft, only the last two Heinkel types were actual combat warplanes, and only the He 51 was a fighter. This way, the Heinkel He 51 became the first true fighter aircraft of the Royal Bulgarian Air Force (VNVV).

These two Heinkel combat aircraft types certainly breached the restrictions imposed upon the defeated Bulgarian Kingdom by the post-WW1 Neuilly Peace Treaty. The warplanes' arrival in Bulgaria in late 1936 represented the beginning of a new era, when the VNVV openly started to re-arm and attempted to catch up with the air forces of the surrounding, mostly hostile, countries (Yugoslavia, Rumania, Turkey and Greece).

As noted, the aforementioned agreement listed a dozen He 51s among the aircraft to be exported to Bulgaria. The precise aircraft type was He 51C[1], sold for a unit price of 71,117 *Reichsmarken*. The airframe was fitted with a BMW VI 7.3 ZU type V-12 in-line engine of 750 hp, which gave a

---

1   After a few prototypes in the V series, also known as He 51a and He 51b, which flew first in 1933, the series production was called He 51C (land version) and He 51D (sea version). The last sub-type, equipped with floats, could easily be changed into a land version, equipped with wheels. Both serial production versions (C and D) were armed with machine guns and could be fitted with racks for light bombs (as well as an auxiliary underbelly fuel tank). No series produced A or B versions existed, despite various claims published in many books and articles. Total production for the RLM was, as follows: 473 pcs. He 51C (145 by Heinkel, 69 by Arado Brandenburg, 80 by Erla, 102 by Fieseler and 77 by AGO) and 33 pcs. He 51D Sea (31 by Heinkel and 2 by Arado Brandenburg). In total, 506 units. In addition, there were 29 pcs. „*Zivil und Export*", Bulgaria included.

Before selecting the Heinkel He 51 as Bulgaria's premier fighter aircraft, a number of other types were tested in Bulgaria. One of them was Curtiss P-6A 'Hawk I', c/n 17, NR9110, depicted here during a stop at Sofia during a European sales tour, in the early 1930s. Famous aviation pioneer and future USAAF General James Harold "Jimmy" Doolittle is sitting in the cockpit (hence this aircraft is sometimes called "Doolittle Hawk"). The military version was offered with a pair of Browning machine guns of 7.62 mm (0.3 in) calibre. This particular demonstrator was purchased by the Dutch in 1934.

A group of German and Bulgarian airmen and technicians gather in front of a Heinkel He 51 at the headquarters of the Ernst Heinkel Flugzeugwerke A.G. in Rostock, probably in mid-1936. At centre left, the short man with spectacles is Prof. Ernst Heinkel. The tall man in dark suit, second from right, is a Bulgarian pilot. Notice the German language black service stencils on the rear fuselage of the He 51, indicating that this was not one of the aircraft intended to be sold to Bulgaria.

330 km/h top speed at ground level. The armament consisted of a pair of cowling-mounted 7.9 mm MG 17 machine guns with 500 rounds each. Although bomb racks could also be fitted to the airframe, and Bulgarian sources occasionally refer to a 60-kg bomb load, there is no photographic evidence the Bulgarian airframes were actually equipped with such a feature.

A document by Ernst Heinkel *Flugzeugwerke* AG, dated 17 September 1936, mentions that an order has been placed by the Bulgarian Government on 8 June 1936, calling for 12 He 51 *Zerstörer* (sic!), each powered by a BMW VI engine of 750 HP. The *Antrag Reichsbürgschaft* of 1 August 1936 reinforces the details in the original contract and places the delivery in 5 to 7 months. In fact, all aircraft arrived in Bulgaria by the end of that year, as detailed below.

Most of the few published sources mentioning the He 51 biplane fighter in Bulgarian service classify it as obsolescent, at best a 'hand-me-down' type Germany wanted to get rid of. The Author believes such statements are inaccurate and unjustified; the use of hindsight to deliver judgment is inappropriate in a historical context. If one takes into consideration the fighter aircraft types the smaller European air forces, and not only such, were equipped with in 1936, it quickly becomes clear not only that the He 51 was not 'obsolescent', but it actually 'outclassed' the main fighter type(s) of several countries Bulgaria was expecting to be involved in any war with. For example, Yugoslavia, a country which would actually attack Bulgaria in early April 1941, ordered in 1936/1937 the Hawker Fury, which was slightly

Five He 51Cs depicted on 'Sofia' (probably Bozhur-ishte) airfield shortly after their arrival in late December 1936. One of the German ferry pilots, Plewig, was the third man from left. The aircraft were painted in Dark Green camouflage colour on the fuselage and upper wing surfaces, and carry civilian ferry registration in black. Only the last letter of this registration is legible on the first (A), second (V) and last aircraft (M), while the third aircraft shows the full registration except for the last letter (D-IZJ_). The washable black paint the registration was applied on the fuselage has already begun to chip off.

underpowered when compared to the He 51, and the flying characteristics were no better, either. The Greek air force, another potential enemy, was even worse equipped, the sole fighter types available being a couple of Czech-made early Avia B.534s and five Avia BH.33s – a negligible force. Finally, Turkey, the Bulgarians' arch rival, had a matching fighter type, the Polish-made PZL P.24, which entered service also in 1936, while the existing Curtiss Hawk can be considered as slightly inferior to the He 51. Finally, Bulgaria's larger neighbour to the north, Rumania, did have a sizeable fighter force; however, despite having a territorial issue (*Dobrudzha*), it was not on collision course with Bulgaria. In conclusion, it can be stated that the Heinkel He 51 fighter was certainly not obsolescent at the time it entered Bulgarian service, and the only drawback was the limited number available, only a dozen, clearly not enough for the size and strategic aim of the resurgent VNVV.

Once the agreement was signed in June 1936, *Ernst Heinkel Flugzeugwerke* A.G., headquartered in Rostock, received the order for the twelve He 51Cs. The aircraft set aside against the Bulgarian order were new units, built under licence by Fieseler *Flugzeugbau*, located in Kassel. Their construction numbers ranged from 891 to 902. Once ready, at least a few were delivered by air, while others, according to a Bulgarian source, came by train. The logbook of Vienna airport recorded on 7 December 1936 the arrival of two He 51s en-route to Bulgaria, namely D-IZLA and D-IXFY (ferry registrations). German sources give three dates for the dispatch of the dozen He 51s, as follows: four on 6 December, two on 7 December and six on 11 December 1936. The British aero magazine *Flight* promptly reported in its 10 December 1936 issue: *"Six German military aircraft are on their way to be delivered to Bulgaria."*

All twelve He 51s were handed over to the Bulgarian air force in mid-December 1936 (officially, the *Sokols* were accepted from the German supplier on 15.12.1936), they entered actual service early the next year. However, they were officially unveiled to the public only on the occasion of the traditional military parade held on 'St. George's Day' (National Day of Bravery and of the patron-saint of the Bulgarian Armed Forces) on 6 May 1937, when they flew over the cheering crowd assembled in the centre of the capital, Sofia. On 27 June, Bulgaria's Tsar Boris III handed over the battle standard to the venerable *Mahyor* Georgi Drenikov, the commander of the newly formed 3. *Armeyski Orlyak* (3rd Army Aviation Group).

This very moment is considered as the formal rebirth of the Bulgarian air force.

On the last day of the next month, Bulgaria signed the so-called 'Salonika Agreement' with previously hostile countries of the 'Balkan Entente', which removed any legal obstacles to Bulgaria arming itself. This agreement also meant the existence of the Bulgarian air force was now official internationally as well.

The Heinkel He 51 biplane was particularly liked by Bulgarian pilots for its pilot-friendly controls, outstanding manoeuvrability and adequate speed for the late 1930s. However, they considered the two small calibre machine guns as insufficient. The mixed wood-metal construction airframe was easy to maintain and repair, and the BMW engine was robust, although more power would certainly have been welcomed.

In combat service, the Heinkel He 51Cs received the newly introduced roundel-style air force marking (the so-called 'Tsarist roundel'), and were identified by two white numbers, one applied on the rear fuselage (believed to be the *krilo* number) and the other one on the fin (believed to be the aircraft's individual number within the *krilo*). Sometime in mid-1940 this numbering system was abandoned and

On 27 June 1937, Bulgaria's Tsar Boris III handed over the battle standard to the commander of the air force and individual orlyatsi (groups), during an elaborate and pompous military ceremony held on the main Bozhurishte airfield. The centrepiece of the display of the newly acquired warplanes was He 51C, No. 11-7, placed over a floral arrangement depicting an aviation symbol. The freshly awarded five combat standards were placed into the cockpit.

replaced with the standard one, consisting of a serial number running from 2 to 12 (No. 1 was omitted due to an earlier fatal crash). This switch may have been done simultaneously with the Bulgarian air force's military marking change in late June 1940. All available photos show He 51s either with the *krilo*/individual numbers and the early style roundel marking, or with the running serial numbers and 'black-X-in-white-square' type marking.

Even before the Heinkel fighters formally started their service, on 18 August 1937 a code name was officially selected for the type, as was customary with the VNVV, namely *Sokol*, or Falcon. Later on, sometime in late 1939, a so-called *Nomenklaturen Nomer* (NN, or Register Number) was assigned to the He 51C, identifying the aircraft type as 7007[2]. This was the first registration number allocated to a fighter. Indeed, the He 51C was the first fighter type of the Bulgarian air force.

---

2   Of the four-digit NN code, the first one (a 7) identified the item as a powered aircraft, the last one (a 7) as a fighter type. These two numbers stayed the same for all fighter types. The second and third digits meant the one- or two-digit sequential order number of the particular aircraft type in the series of fighters in service.

Not long after the first Heinkel He 51s arrived from Germany, the seven best Bulgarian fighter pilots were sent to Germany in June 1938, to the renowned Werneuchen Fighter Pilot School (Jagdfliegerschule)[1], to hone their piloting skills. One of the German aircraft types they often flew was the venerable He 51 biplane. Depicted is this first group of Bulgarian fighter pilots, as follows (from left to right): Podpor. Dimităr Tamahkyarov, Podpor. Asen Kovachev, Podpor. Aleksandăr Gunchev, Podpor. Nikolay Yordanov, Podpor. Stoyan Stoyanov, Richard Leppla (German flying instructor), Podpor. Vasil Shishkov and Podpor. Dimităr Lazarov. Sitting is Luftwaffe Oberleutnant Hans-Carl Röders. Original photo processed by 'Foto Grünberg' in Werneuchen, Germany.

---

1   Formed on 1 November 1937, under command of the venerable WW 1-pilot *Oberst* (Col.) Theodor Osterkamp. On 15 January 1940, the school was re-named *Jagdfliegerschule* 1, while on 15 December 1942 it became *Jagdgeschwader* 101.

When all He 51s had been accepted from the German team and impressed in service in early 1937, they constituted the fighter arm of the fledgling VNVV, the only fighter aircraft available at that time.

In January 1937, He 51 Nos. 11-5, 11-6, 11-7 and 11-8 were assigned to the 1st *Yato* (Squadron) of the 3rd *Iztrebitelen Orlyak* (Fighter Group), Nos. 22-5, 22-6, 22-7 and 22-8 were assigned to the 2nd *Yato* of the same *orlyak*, while Nos. 33-5, 33-6, 33-7 and 33-8 were assigned to the 3rd *Yato* of the same *orlyak*. The He 51s' allocated task was interceptor fighter. As such, in August 1939, the *Sokols* were deployed to the volatile Turkish border, to Yambol landing ground, from where they performed border patrol flights. On several occasions, ground fire coming from Turkish border positions targeted the low flying Bulgarian biplanes, without any serious hits being recorded, though.

This 'front fighter' task lasted only until the ex-Czechoslovak Avia B.534s arrived in great numbers and were put into service in early 1940. At this point, the newcomers took over this crucial role. The surviving He 51s were assigned to 2. *Ucheben Orlyak* (Training Group), based at Dolna Mitropoliya, to serve as advanced trainers for would-be fighter pilots.

On 18 November 1939, the existing eleven He 51s were planned to be distributed as follows:

- 2-i *Iztrebitelen Orlyak* (Fighter Group), C/O *Mahyor* Krăstyu M. Georgiev,
- 2-i *Ucheben Orlyak* (Training Group), C/O *Kapitan* Stefan I. Măndev,
- 22-o *Uchebno Yato* (Training Squadron), C/O *Poruchik* Krăstyu A. Atanasov: 8 *Sokol* (Nos. 11-6, 11-7, 11-8, 22-5, 22-6, 22-7, 22-8 and 33-5),
- *Shkola za vissh pilotazh* (High Aerobatics Piloting School) C/O *Poruchik* Krăstyu A. Atanasov, Deputy C/O *Poruchik* Chudomir M. Toplodolski: 3 *Sokol* (Nos. 33-6, 33-7 and 33-8).

The following *podporuchik* instructors were listed with the Aerobatics School: Lyuben I. Stoyanov, Vasil P. Shishkov and Dimităr G. Tamahkyarov. The 'krilo' commanders were (all with the rank of *podporuchik*): Aleksandăr H. Gunchev, Dimităr C. Lazarov, Asen D. Kovachev, Nikola G. Yordanov, Bogdan Y. Iliev and Dimităr S. Spisarevski. At that time, the following officer students (all with the rank of *podporuchik*) were attending the courses of the aerobatic school: Ivan I. Rusev, Ivan V. Boyadzhiev, Petăr V. Dimov, Hristo K. Pazvantov, Zahari G. Pernikliyski and a certain 'Detăr D. Manolov' (most probably

One of the He 51s purchased from Germany was reportedly paid for by the coal miners of the town of Pernik. To honour the financial effort of the miners, the word "Min'or" (Miner) was painted on the under surface of the lower wing in large, black capital letters (мин to the starboard and ьорЪ to the port wing under surface), as depicted on this head-on photo. Reportedly, the aircraft was presented to the miners and locals by Tsar Boris himself on 24 May 1937, although it must have been a fly-by only as the town does not have an airfield.

Petăr D. Manolev)[3]. Between April and June 1940, the following *Sokol* were on duty at the *Shkola za vissh pilotazh* (High Aerobatics Piloting School): 11-8, 22-5, 22-6 and 33-6.

The first, and only, fatal accident involving a *Sokol* happened on 19 April 1939, when *Feldfebel* Vălyu Videv Hristov crashed to his death near the village of Kostinbrod, not far from Bozhurishte main base. The investigation revealed the main cause as "violation of air discipline". Although the document does not list the individual serial number of the aircraft, by eliminating the aircraft extant after this date it can be ascertained that it must have been No. 11-5. A document dated 17 January 1940, refers to the scrapping of this particular aircraft and its BMW engine, No. 19788, as part of 1st *Lineen Orlyak*.

Another accident, albeit of lesser consequence, happened on 8 May 1939, when pilot *Feldfebel* Atanas A. Matev crash-landed his mount on Bozhurishte airfield. The aircraft, curiously identified in a period document as 'P-8' (perhaps 11-8, as the P in Cyrillic is written П), could be repaired and eventually resumed service.

Four flying accidents were recorded for 1941, all in March and all at Marno-Pole (Karlovo) airfield, as follows: on the 18th, *Sokol* No. 7/7007 of the 5th [sic!] Air Regiment (*Polk*) belly landed with *Podofitser* Velcho G. Raichev at the controls, causing 35% damage. On the 29th, two *Sokols* collided while taxiing. No. 5/7007 veered off course while landing and crashed into No. 10/7007, which was stationed 20 m from the tower with a punctured tyre. Both aircraft could be repaired. Finally, on the same day, aircraft No. 11/7007 overturned while landing. *Kandidat podofitser* Stefan D. Petrov escaped with minor injuries, and the aircraft was taken to the repair shop.

At the end of 1941, of the eleven He 51s available, five were damaged in accidents, all repairable. In a document dated 14 October 1941, the existing eleven *Sokols* and 32 BMW VI engines are listed as scheduled to be maintained by *Parkova Rabotilninitsa Kăm 1-i Văzdushen Polk* (Workshop of the 1st

---

3   All these six officers were pilots from the 58th Class of the Military School. The 58th Class graduated on 16 June 1939, being promoted to the first officer rank, i.e. *Podporuchik* (2nd Lieutenant).

Tsar Boris (to the left, with his head bowed) is reviewing a row of He 51s assembled at Bozhurishte main air base, in 1939. The high-ranking delegation is led by Lt. Gen. Teodosi Daskalov, Minister of War, while Tsar Boris is at centre, with his head bowed. Col. Vasil Boydev, Commanding Officer of the VNVV, is walking at left. The 'Sokol' at right is No. 11-7, while the one near him is No. 33-8.

Yet another row of He 51s, flanked at left by a Fw 56 trainer, prepared for a parade. The row is led by the aircraft baptised "Min'or" (Miner).

These He 51s (at right) and PZL P.24s (at left), flanking three Fw 56s (top, centre), belonged to 2-i Iztrebitelen Orlyak (Fighter Group). The presence of No. 11-5 (the 3ʳᵈ aircraft from right) dates this photo prior to 19 April 1939, when that particular aircraft crashed, killing the pilot, Feldfebel Vălyu V. Hristov. The twelve fighter pilots are lined up for this official photograph.

Air Regiment) in Bozhurishte, where 120 workers were assigned to the airframe and 50 workers to the engine repair section.

A comprehensive VNVV order of battle from 26 May 1941 lists *Sokol* Nos. 2, 3 and 7 at 6th Fighter Regiment (*Polk*), while Nos. 4, 9 and 11 were under repair at the Main Repair Shop in Bozhurishte.

A document listing trainer aircraft, dated 24 December 1943, reflecting the situation extant on 23 November, lists the following *Sokol* as 'in use': 2, 3, 4, 5, 6, 7, 8 and 12.

On 27 December 1943, the following four 'BMW 6' engines were scrapped: 18159, 18638, 18720 and 18713. On 28 June 1944, along with *Sokol* No. 7, the following two 'BMW 6d' engines were scrapped: 19772 and 18076. On 1 November 1944, 'BMW 6d' No. 17656 was written off. One more 'BMW 6d' engine was struck off charge on 24 December 1944, namely 17474. Four days later, it was followed by another one (this time without the 'd' suffix), No. 23137.

In the logbook of Petăr Manolev the following flights are listed with *Sokols* at *Shkola za Iztrebitelni Letsi* (Fighter Piloting School) – only selected He 51 flights are mentioned: 1.12.1939: 11-8, 5.12.1939:

33-6, 12.02.1940: 33-6, 13.02.1940: 11-7, 22.02.1940: 22-6, 24.02.1940: 22-7, 28.02.1940: 11-7, 29.02.1940: 22-8, 6.03.1940: 33-5, 23.03.1940: 22-7 (then he switched to the *Dogan*). Next time he flew the *Sokol* was as instructor at *Shkola za Iztrebiteli* (Fighter School), located at Marno-Pole, as follows (only selected flights are listed): 18.06.1941: 7, 28.06.1941: 5, 5.07.1941: 8, 8.07.1941: 12, 3.11.1941: 12, 13.11.1941: 8 (from April 1942, he was located on Dolna Mitropoliya airfield) 1.06.1942: 3, 4.06.1942: 4, 8.07.1941: 4, 9.07.1941: 10, 23.07.1941: 8, 14.10.1942: 5, 22.10.1942: 3, 6.11.1942: 4, 10.12.1942: 5, 24.02.1943: 5, 20.03.1943: 4, 8.04.1943: 10, 14.04.1943: 5, 31.05.1943: 4, 25.10.1943: 6 and 7, 18.02.1944: 3, 1.03.1944: 8 and 12, 6.03.1944: 6 and 8 (this is the last date when he flew the *Sokol* at Dolna Mitropoliya). He then made his final flight on No. 5 at Bozhurishte, on 25.07.1944.

Student pilot Zhelyu Zhelev flew at *Iztrebitelna Shkola* in Dolna Mitropoliya *Sokol* No. 3 on 19.02.1944 and on 8.03.0944, then No. 7 on 12.03.1944, before switching to the Dewoitine D.520 fighter.

On 28 December 1944, seven He 51s (Nos. 2, 4, 8, 9, 10, 11 and 12) were ordered to be scrapped at *Glavnata Remonta Rabotilnitsa* (Main Repair Shops) in Bozhurishte (No. 2 might be a typo).

On 27 July 1945, four He 51s were still extant (probably Nos. 2, 3, 5 and 6). However, they soon ended up on the scrap heap as well. The penultimate extant aircraft, No. 3, was officially scrapped on 12 November 1945, while the very last one, No. 6, on 22.03.1946. This event marked the 'fall of the curtain' for the first Bulgarian fighter type's time in a decade-long service career.

A three-aircraft krilo – basic flying element in the late 1930s/early 1940s – in flight.

Line-up of nine 'Sokol', with No. 11-6 opening the row. A German document dated 1 June 1940 lists ten unarmed extant He 51s, and categorises the fighter type as 'veraltet' (outdated).

Colours and markings

Based on available black/white photographs, the Heinkel He 51Cs delivered to Bulgaria in December 1936 may have arrived in two distinctive painting schemes. One consisted of Dark Green (possibly *grün für camouflage* BC.6954/6663 by Herbig-Haarhaus, or HH) upper surfaces over Light Blue (possibly *blau* BC.6954/6663 by HH), or less likely Silver (possibly *silber* BC.6954/6663 by HH). The other, less probable, scheme may have consisted of overall Light Grey [possibly DKH L40/52 *hellgrau*, or Avionorm *Nitrodecklack* (nitro covering paint) 7375, known later on, after RLM standardisation, as RLM 63[4]][5]. Another possibility for the Light Grey colour on Bulgarian aircraft is *taubengrau* (pigeon grey) BC.6954/6663, also by HH. It has to be noted though that of the two photos showing all-grey He 51s reportedly built for Bulgaria, published in Bulgarian books, one has the service writing in German (in contrast to green/blue aircraft seen in Bulgaria, which clearly have the writing in Bulgarian language), and the other one, published with the legend *"The first He-51B [sic!] Sokol after assembly at Bojurishte in 1936. Note the lack of insignia and underbelly drop tank,"* has the black German civilian markings on the fuselage retouched and the pre-August 1936 tricolour stripes added to the tail surface. Therefore both images apparently show He 51s that did not actually end up in Bulgaria.

The definitive answer whether the airframe surface finish was in Green over Blue (or Silver), or Light Grey overall would be given by the Bulgarian edition of the aircraft maintenance guide, which had a special chapter dedicated to repair paints, where the precise paint types and manufacturers were usually given. However, the Author had no access to this document. In fact *all available photos depicting the He 51 in Bulgaria show the airframe painted in Dark Green over, most probably, Light Blue livery*.

If a modeller ponders which colour shades available on the market should be used on his/her scale model of a Bulgarian He 51C, the Author recommends RLM 62 (Green) and RLM 65 (Light Blue), without being able to positively prove the veracity of these hues being the ones actually used, however.

At the moment of entering service, the Heinkel He 51Cs received the newly introduced roundel-style air force marking, which consisted of a large, white dot, featuring in the centre the Bulgarian Order of Bravery, in red and gold. This military marking was applied in six positions, on the mid-fuselage and on both wing surfaces. The rudder received Bulgaria's national colours, in three equally wide horizontal stripes (White on top, Mid-Green in centre and Blood Red on bottom). The engine cowling was painted in Red all around, extended rearwards by a tapered horizontal flash along the fuselage that ended

---

4 The painting guide for Heinkel He 51C/D, dated late 1936, lists Celesta *Flugzeugüberlack* 2002, *grüngrau* 63, i.e., RLM 63, for fabric covered areas, while for metal parts the Avionorm *Nitrodecklack grau* 7007 is recommended. Obviously, these two light grey shades must have been visually identical, as no visible difference in shade can be observed on quality black/white photos.

5 The Heinkel He 50G *Handbuch* (manual) from 1936 (L.Dv. 313) gives following top coat paints:
Fabric surfaces: „*Cellesta-N-Flugzeugüberzugslack* 2000/63", *Hersteller* (manufacturer) Atlas-Ago.
The topmost paint coat is described as: *"Lasurlack Nr. 2910/63, Flugzeugüberzugslack 2000/63, Ausgleichsflüssigkeit Nr. 1611; Überzugslack, farblos Nr. 1606."* Notice the reference to colour No. 63 (after the slash), which was RLM 63 *hellgrau* (Light Grey).

Another, albeit shorter, line-up of Sokols, featuring three pilot buddies posing for eternity (the middle one is Poruchik Lyuben Kondakov). Notice the inverted colour spinner attached to the first and last Sokol. The latter fighter does not have the customary underbelly auxiliary fuel tank attached. The wheel spats had been removed for easier service.

underneath the tail plane. Additional artwork, representing stylised hawk's claws, was painted on the wheel spats, also in Red. Later on, this colour changed to Yellow on some aircraft. Also, the tricolour on the rudder was eventually overpainted with yellow in April of 1941. Even later, probably in 1943, the survivors had their lower wingtips painted in yellow. The auxiliary underbelly fuel tank remained in shiny metal colour.

Without doubt, the Bulgarian Heinkel He 51s featured a very vivid, eye catching colour scheme.

Initially, the Heinkel 51s were identified by two groups of numbers, one applied on the rear fuselage and the other on the fin. The two-digit numbers on the fuselage (Nos. 11, 22, or 33) are believed to have represented different *yata* (squadrons), i.e., 11 referring to the 1st *Yato*, 22 to the 2nd *Yato*, while

33 to the 3rd *Yato* of a particular fighter group (in the early case, 3. *Iztrebitelen Orlyak*). The single-digit number on the fin (from 5 to 8) represented the serial number of the individual aircraft within a particular four-aircraft *krilo* (flight/squad) of a particular *yato* (squadron). For example, aircraft No. 11-5 was the first aircraft of the He 51 flight/squad of first squadron, while aircraft No. 33-8 was the last aircraft of the He 51 flight/squad in the third squadron[6]. Other fighter, or fighter-trainer, aircraft types using the same numbering style[7] were the PZL P.24 *Yastreb* (same fuselage numbers and tail numbers from 1 to 4) and the Focke-Wulf Fw 56A *Komar* (same fuselage numbers and tail numbers from 9 to 10).

Sometime in mid-1940, this numbering system was abandoned and replaced with the regular VNVV one, consisting of a serial number running from 2 to 12 (No. 1 was omitted due to an earlier fatal crash), applied on the fuselage, in white, and on the underwing surfaces, in black (inside, or outside of the military marking). This switch may have been done simultaneously with the Bulgarian air force's military marking change in late June 1940, when the 'Black-X-in-White-Square' type of marking was introduced. This new marking, more in line with the Axis standards, was also applied in the same six positions, right over the former roundels.

When the new He 51 fighters were officially unveiled in June 1937, they represented a true novelty not only to the general public, but to military personnel as well. At least one of them carried the name of Tsar Boris' newborn son, *Simeon*, in large black capital letters on the under-wing surface (СИМ under the starboard wing and ЕОНЪ under the port wing surface). This was undoubtedly a propaganda manoeuvre, to popularise the tsar's family among the Bulgarian people, very effective when overflying crowds at low altitude.

All service texts were written in Bulgarian, in White over Dark Green and in Black over Light Blue, or bare metal. The detailed text applied to the rear fuselage is believed to contain the following characters:

ТЕГЛО ПРАЗЕНЪ - 1474 кг
ОБЩЪ ТОВАРЪ - 425 кг
ДОПУСТИМО
ТЕГЛО НА ЛЕТЕНЕ - 1900 кг
ГРУПА НА НАТОВАРВАНЕ
ПОСЛЕДЕН ПРЕГЛЕДЪ - X.X.1937 г.

These factory inscriptions were later on overpainted during general overhaul. The yellow fuel octane triangle, usually visible on the port fuselage side, in front of the windshield, was not applied on Bulgarian machines, nor the white oil triangle located on the engine cowling. However, the Red Cross symbol (showing where the first aid kit was located) was present just aft the fold-down cockpit entry door.

The hand writing on the reverse side of this original print – done well after the camera's release button was pressed, judging by the modern ball pen used – dates the photo to 20 July 1940. However, the greatcoat worn by the two airmen in the foreground casts doubt if this photo was indeed taken in the heat of the summer. Instead it was most probably taken earlier the year, during a cold late winter/early spring day. Also, by that date, the numbering style of the Heinkels may have already changed to the standard VNVV one. One detail given on the print's verso is certain, namely that the photo was taken at Marno Pole/Karlovo main air base, identifiable by the tower seen in the background.

6   For confirmation of this theory, please see the organization in early January 1939.

7   Similar numbering style was also used by Heinkel He 45s, Focke-Wulf Fw 58s and Dornier Do 11s.

Annex

No.	Engine	Photo	Unit/Date	Damaged	Destroyed	WFU	Notes
Initial serial numbers							
11-5	19788	Yes	1. *Lineen Orlyak*/19.04.1939		19.04.1939	12.12.1939	The sole deadly accident. Probably would have been renumbered No. 1
11-6		Yes	*22-i Uchebno Yato*/18.11.1939			N/A	
11-7		Yes	*22-i Uchebno Yato*/18.11.1939			N/A	
11-8		Yes	*22-i Uchebno Yato*/18.11.1939	8 May 1939		N/A	S/N of the damaged A/C listed as 'P-8' (possibly 11-8)
22-5		Yes	*22-i Uchebno Yato*/18.11.1939			N/A	
22-6		Yes	*22-i Uchebno Yato*/18.11.1939			N/A	
22-7			*22-i Uchebno Yato*/18.11.1939			N/A	
22-8		Yes	*22-i Uchebno Yato*/18.11.1939			N/A	
33-5		Yes	*22-i Uchebno Yato*/18.11.1939			N/A	
33-6		Yes	*Shkola za vissh pilotazh*/18.11.1939			N/A	
33-7		Yes	*Shkola za vissh pilotazh*/18.11.1939			N/A	
33-8			*Shkola za vissh pilotazh*/18.11.1939			N/A	
New serial numbers							
1						N/A	Probably not assigned (ex-11-5)
2						28.12.1944/ 5.11.1945	
3		Yes				12.11.1945	
4		Yes				28.12.1944	WFU given also as on 28.2.1945
5		Yes				11.09.1945	
6		Yes				22.03.1946	Still extant on 27.07.1945
7		Yes				28.06.1944	
8		Yes				28.12.1944	WFU given also as on 29.1.1945
9		Yes				28.12.1944	WFU given also as on 29.1.1945
10		Yes				28.12.1944	Also mentioned as written off in a document dated 30.04.1946
11						28.12.1944	WFU given also as on 29.1.1945
12						28.12.1944	WFU given also as on 29.1.1945

Additional info see:
http://mmpbooks.biz/assets/ BFC/01.pdf

A well-tanned pilot (in uniform, in centre) smiles broadly at the camera, while the technicians surrounding him try to appear serious, business-like. Notice the Bulgarian pilot's wings embroidered over the right pocket of the officer's uniform.

By the time of the marking change, the He 51 was relegated to the secondary role of fighter trainer. Notice the stripe-painted propeller of the machine at right, in contrast to the other ones, which have the propeller blades in grey (including the Ar 65F at extreme left). All these aircraft wear yellow engine cowling and rearward tapering fuselage stripe.

When the military marking of the Bulgarian air force switched to a pro-Axis style in late June 1940, featuring a prominent black cross on a white square background, all other markings stayed unchanged for a short while.

These four airmen took the opportunity to pose for a photograph while the auxiliary belly tank is being refuelled on Bozhurishte airfield.

This photo of He 51C, No. 6, was snapped by its 'dvoyka' pair at close range.

No. 10 (centre) is lined up along with other Heinkel fighters, probably for one of the frequent parades and reviews.

The chrome yellow nose of the He 51 is prominent on this photo taken in front of the hangar at Bozhurishte main air base. The elaborate "bird's claw" artwork has disappeared from the wheel spats. No. 3 is in the background.

These three photos depict No. 8, parked on Bozhurishte airfield, sometime in 1943. Notice the yellow stripes on the lower wingtips.

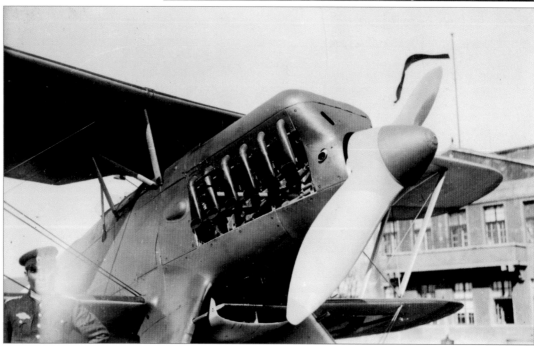

Scenic view of a landing ground with majestic, snow-capped mountains in the background.

From 1943 on, the surviving He 51s (No. 4 is depicted at right) could be found in the fighter school and training units, alongside the similarly outdated Avia B.534s (at left).

No. 3 was one of the last survivors. It was officially scrapped on 12 November 1945.

Heinkel He 51C Sokol, No. 22-6, pilot Kapitan Ivan S. Ivanov, Bozhurishte airfield, 6 May 1937. Camouflage colours: Dark Green over Light Blue. Wing struts also Light Blue. Engine cowling Red all around (except for the rectangular panel on the lower area, which stayed metal), extended rearwards by a tapered horizontal flash along the fuselage. Artwork on the wheel spats also in Red. White-Green-Red rudder. Outside surface of propeller blades Grey, inside dull Black, tips Red. Decal with the Heinkel factory logo on the outer propeller blade surface. Early style VNVV military marking in six positions. Serial numbers White. Auxiliary underbelly fuel tank in shiny natural metal.

Once the He 51s were officially taken over by the Bulgarian air force in early 1937, they received full VNVV military markings and identification numbers, as depicted in this superb profile view of No. 22-6. The engine cowling was painted in Red all around, extended by a tapered horizontal flash along the fuselage that ended underneath the tail plane. Additional artwork, representing stylised hawk's claws, was painted on the wheel spats, also in Red. Undoubtedly, the Bulgarian Heinkel He 51s featured a very vivid, eye catching colour scheme.

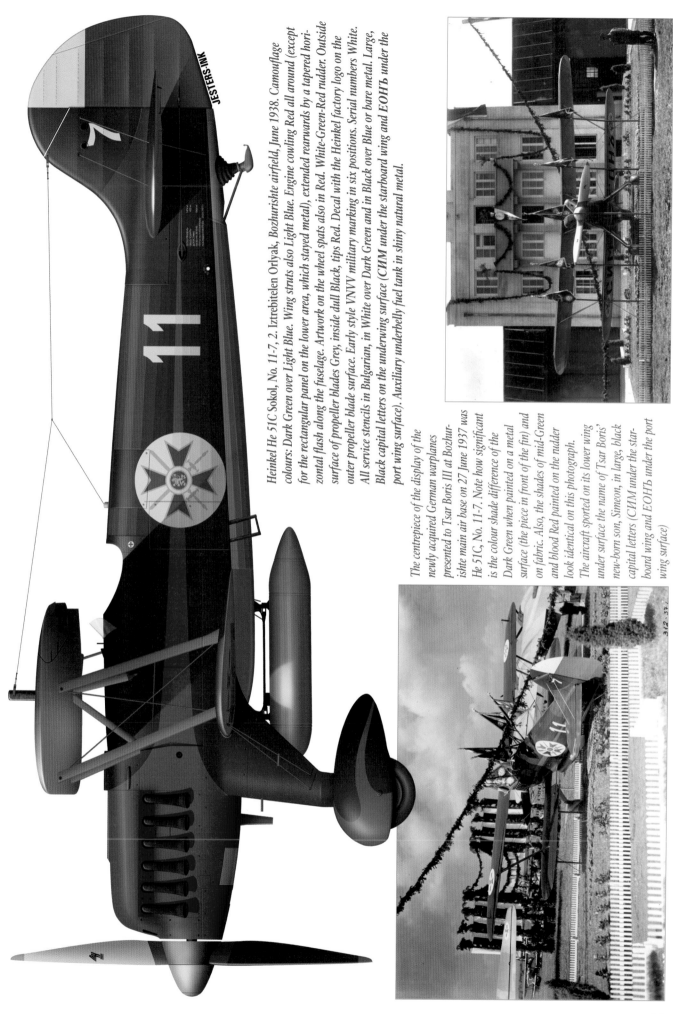

Heinkel He 51C Sokol, No. 11-7, 2. Iztrebitelen Orlyak, Bozhurishte airfield, June 1938. Camouflage colours: Dark Green over Light Blue. Wing struts also Light Blue. Engine cowling Red all around (except for the rectangular panel on the lower area, which stayed metal), extended rearwards by a tapered horizontal flash along the fuselage. Artwork on the wheel spats also in Red. White-Green-Red rudder. Outside surface of propeller blades Grey, inside dull Black, tips Red. Decal with the Heinkel factory logo on the outer propeller blade surface. Early style VNVV military marking in six positions. Serial numbers White. All service stencils in Bulgarian, in White over Dark Green and in Black over Blue or bare metal. Large, Black capital letters on the underwing surface (СИМ under the starboard wing and ЕОНЪ under the port wing surface). Auxiliary underbelly fuel tank in shiny natural metal.

The centrepiece of the display of the newly acquired German warplanes presented to Tsar Boris III at Bozhurishte main air base on 27 June 1937 was He 51C, No. 11-7. Note how significant is the colour shade difference of the Dark Green when painted on a metal surface (the piece in front of the fin) and on fabric. Also, the shades of mid-Green and blood Red painted on the rudder look identical on this photograph.

The aircraft sported on its lower wing under surface the name of Tsar Boris' new-born son, Simeon, in large, black capital letters (СИМ under the starboard wing and ЕОНЪ under the port wing surface)

95

JESTERS-INK

In late June 1940, the VNVV changed the military marking to align it with Axis standards. The new marking was apparently crudely applied on the fuselage of No. 7. The horizontal arm of the numeral is unusually long. The 'cheatline's colour had changed from red to yellow, to conform more to the Axis recognition system.

Heinkel He 51C Sokol, No. 7, Shkola za vissh pilotazh, pilot Poruchik Chudomir M. Toplodolski, Karlovo airfield, late 1941. Camouflage colours: Dark Green over Light Blue. Wing struts also Light Blue. Engine cowling Yellow all around (except for the rectangular panel on the lower area, which stayed metal), extended rearwards by a tapered horizontal flash along the fuselage. Artwork on the wheel spats also in Yellow. White-Green-Red rudder. Outside surface of propeller blades Grey, inside dull Black, tips Red. Decal with the Heinkel factory logo on the outer propeller blade surface. Axis style VNVV military marking in six positions, crudely applied onto the airframe. Serial number on fuselage in White, Black on wing under surface (inside of the marking). Triangle on fin White. All service stencils in Bulgarian, in White over Dark Green and in Black over Light Blue or metal. Auxiliary underbelly fuel tank in shiny natural metal.

JESTERS-INK

Heinkel He 51C Sokol, No. 3, Shkola za Iztrebiteli, pilot Podporuchik Petăr D. Manolev, Dolna Mitropoliya airfield, June 1942. Camouflage colours: Dark Green over Light Blue. Wing struts also Light Blue. Engine cowling Yellow all around (except for the rectangular panel on the lower area, which stayed metal), extended rearwards by a tapered horizontal flash along the fuselage. Yellow rudder. Outside surface of propeller blades Grey, inside dull Black, tips Red. Axis style VNVV marking in six positions. Serial numbers on fuselage in White, Black on wing under surface (outside of the marking). Triangle on fin White.

Following the invasion of Yugoslavia by the German Wehrmacht in April 1941, Bulgarian warplanes displayed even more 'Axis' yellow on the airframe. Accordingly, the Bulgarian national colours on the rudder were overpainted with yellow. Later, the lower wingtips were painted yellow as well. No. 3 was the second to last survivor, being officially scrapped on 12 November 1945.

97

PZL P.24 *Yastreb*
Bulgaria's Most Powerful Pre-War Fighter

One of the many avenues the Bulgarians attempted to follow in order to purchase fighter aircraft was Poland.

Following a live demonstration of the PZL P.24/II prototype (registered SP-ATO) by factory test pilot Bolesław Orliński in January 1936, in front of several military attachés from the Balkan countries accredited to Poland, including the Bulgarian one, the aircraft and its pilot were invited to visit Bulgaria. The request was quickly honoured, and the khaki-painted 'civilian' P.24/II demonstrator landed on Bozhurishte airport the next month, with the same Orliński at the controls. The air displays and test flights must have left a lasting impression on the Bulgarian air force decision makers[1], as on 9 April 1936 Sofia placed an order[2] calling for twelve[3] aircraft of the would-be series production (which had not even commenced at that point).

Of the two models marketed by the PZL Works[4] internationally (the P.24a armed with two MGs and two cannon, and the P.24b fitted with four MGs), the Bulgarians opted for the latter. The airframe was to be powered by a French fourteen-cylinder Gnome&Rhône G&R 14 Kfs radial of 900 hp, which turned a 2.6 m diameter, narrow-blade G&R metal propeller. The armament consisted of four 7.9 mm calibre Colt-Browning MG 40 machine guns mounted in the wings, complemented by four 12.5 kg bombs that could be attached in pairs to under-wing racks.

The dozen ordered aircraft were to be delivered on 15 November 1936. However, the first aircraft for the Bulgarian order only flew for the first time in October, a mere month before the deadline. Delivery was further delayed by a landing accident at Okęcie factory airfield in November 1936, when one of the Bulgarian P.24bs turned over while taxying on snowy terrain. Following a test flight in cold weather, ice had accumulated in the gap between the main wheels and the aerodynamic spats, blocking the wheel and causing the aircraft to somersault. The factory test pilot, Jerzy Widawski, was not hurt, and the aircraft sustained only minor damage. This mishap prompted the designers to reinforce the wheel spats. The damage caused by the accident to the unlucky aircraft were quickly repaired and the aircraft was set for delivery, along with the others, slated for 20 December 1936.

Actual dispatch of the crated aircraft suffered a further setback due to the international tensions in Europe in those turbulent times (the war in Spain had broken out in July 1936), which made the cheaper delivery by sea risky. Instead, the crates had to be transported by train. Despite the series of issues plaguing delivery, the P.24bs finally arrived in Bulgaria in early 1937. Minutes taken on 9 June 1937 mention two aircraft batches and their respective construction numbers: "*on 01.05.1936* [1937, probably a typo], *the PZL 24Bs with construction numbers 756, 761, 726, 760, 753 and 752 were accepted, while on 31.5.1937, PZL 24Bs with construction numbers 751, 754, 755, 757, 758 and 762 were accepted* [presumably by the Bulgarian party]". It can be observed that only one construction number does not fit the 751-762 series, namely No. 726. This might have been a replacement aircraft, instead of a possibly damaged or otherwise undeliverable No. 759.

---

1   PZL P.11c, SP-AYZ (c/n 628) was among the three Polish warplanes displayed at the International Air Show, held at Sofia, from 18 to 20 June 1936 (the two others were PZL.23A, SP-BCT, c/n 901, and P.W.S. 16bis, SP-BCX, c/n 024). Therefore, Bulgarian specialists became acquainted with the new fighter type's predecessor, the P.11, too.

2   An identical number of PZL.43 light bomber/ground attack aircraft, to be powered by a G&R 14Kirs engine, was also included in the deal signed on 9 April 1936. The total price of the contract was 5.080.286 zloty.

3   An otherwise well-informed Polish source mentions 14 P.24b's ordered by the Bulgarians in April 1937 [DESZCZYŃSKI, Marek Piotr: 'Polski eksport sprzętu wojskowego w okresie międzywojennym (Zarys problematyki)', Polish Export of Military Equipment in the Interwar Period (Outline of Problems), in Przegląd Hystoriczny, No. 85/1-2, 1994]. However, in a book co-authored by the same researcher, published in 2004, the number of exported P.24b's is reduced to twelve [see Bibliography for details of the book].

4   PZL stands for *Państwowe Zakłady Lotnicze*, i.e. State Aviation Works.

Two shots of PZL P.24/II, SP-ATO, during its presentation to foreign military attachés at the factory airfield, in January 1936. At that time, the fighter type represented 'cutting-edge' technology. Note that the aerodynamic wheel spats were removed during operations from unpaved taxiing ground.

The fighters were assembled at Bulgaria's main airfield, Bozhurishte, during the spring of 1937. Officially, the final acceptance happened on 31 May 1937. They were then assigned first to the 3rd *Iztr. Orlyak* (four aircraft to each *yato*), then to the 1st *Armeyski Orlyak* (Army Air Group), formed on 15 July 1937, along with a dozen PZL.43A attack aircraft, also of Polish manufacture. Each warplane type equipped one *yato* (squadron).

Based on Order No. 180, issued on 18 August 1937, the P.24b was code-named *Yastreb* ('Kestrel') in Bulgarian service and received *Nomenklaturen Nomer* (Register Number) 7017 (i.e. the second fighter type included in the VNVV warplane roster, after the Heinkel He 51, which was NN 7007). It has to be stated that the P.24b was the most powerful fighter aircraft of the Bulgarian air force in the pre-war time period. Thus, besides training, the *Yastreb* was also tasked with the defence of the capital, Sofia, until a better performing fighter type would eventually enter service with the VNVV.

The second PZL P.24 prototype (SP-ATO) is depicted at Tatoi air base in Greece during the fighter type's Balkan sales tour, in January 1936. Next stop would be Bulgaria's capital, Sofia. Standing near the aircraft is Polish factory test pilot, the venerable Bolesław Orliński.

Less than a year after the type entered combat service, the first and only fatal accident occurred. On 6 June 1938, during a routine training flight from Bozhurishte airfield, PZL P.24b No. 22-3 caught fire in mid-air, due to a leaking fuel tank (reportedly, the tank's cap came off during flight). Flames coming from the exhaust pipes set the pouring fuel on fire and also generated thick smoke. The pilot, *Poruchik* (1st Lieutenant) Vasil Marinov Benchev, reportedly suffocated in the aircraft's cockpit. The uncontrolled aircraft crashed near the village of Brigadir, near Pernik[5]. This was one of the very first fatal accidents of the fledgling VNVV.

The existing eleven aircraft were planned to be allocated to the 3-o *Obraztsovo Iztrebit. Yato*, as per a draft Order of Battle plan, dated 18 November 1939. Indeed, Order No. 351, issued by the Bulgarian Ministry of War on 10 November 1939, established *'Obraztsov Orlyak'* (literally, Model, or Exemplary Group; in fact, an Instructor Training Group, a sort of 'Top Gun' unit), based at Sofia airfield. *Kapitan* Pencho Mitev was named commanding officer, while his deputy was *Poruchik* Georgi Aladzhov. The main unit had three *yata* (squadrons), the 901st (equipped with PZL.43 *Chayka* attack aircraft), the

---

5   The aircraft was officially struck off the VVNV inventory only on 15 December 1938.

The PZL P.24d version, fitted with four 'heavy' machine guns and the possibility to be fitted with the locally-made G&R K14 radial engine, was offered to the Hungarians. Őrnagy (Major) Kálmán Csukás test flew the type in 1937. However, due to diplomatic pressure by Rumania – Poland's long-time armament customer and military ally, and arch-enemy of Hungary – the deal eventually fell through.

One of the first PZL P.24bs seen during acceptance trials at PZL's Okęcie factory airfield, Poland, in late 1936. Note the Bulgarian tricolour segments are painted with slanted edges. The fuselage flash is missing. The quick-release locks on the engine cowling side are unpainted. The golden rampant lion doesn't seem to be applied to the centre of the wing marking. All these errors were corrected by the time the aircraft entered active service with the VNVV in the Spring of 1937.

902nd (equipped with P.24b *Yastreb* fighters) and 903rd (equipped with He 45B *Shtărkel* reconnaissance aircraft). This *orlyak* gathered the best Bulgarian flying instructors available, hence its name.

Order of Battle of *Yato* No. 902 (10 November 1939)
Pilots
Yato Commander: *Poruchik* Doncho Nikolov Dimitrov,
1st *Krilo* Commander: *Podporuchik* Nikola Savov Vălchev,
2nd *Krilo* Commander: *Podporuchik* Viktor Evstatiev Pavlov,
Pilot: *Podofitser* Dako Petkov Dakov,
Pilot: *Podofitser* Tsvetan Dimitrov Gruev,
Pilot: *Podofitser* Hristo Krumov Tanev,
Pilot: *Podofitser* Ivan Dimitrov Kostov.
Aircraft
'Yastreb' No. 11-1, at D.S.F.[1]
'Yastreb' No. 11-2
'Yastreb' No. 11-3
'Yastreb' No. 11-4, at 3rd *Raz. Orlyak*[2]
'Yastreb' No. 22-1
'Yastreb' No. 22-2
'Yastreb' No. 22-4, at 3rd *Raz. Orlyak*
'Yastreb' No. 33-1
'Yastreb' No. 33-2, at D.S.F.
'Yastreb' No. 33-3, at 3rd *Raz. Orlyak*
'Yastreb' No. 33-4, at D.S.F.
Note: The missing number, 22-3, was the one that had crashed the previous June with *Por.* Benchev at its controls.

---

1   D.S.F. is short for *Dărzhavna Samoletna Fabrika*, or State Aircraft Factory, at that time based at Bozhurishte, near Sofia (today part of Sofia).
2   *Raz. Orlyak* is short for 3. *Razuznavatelen* (reconnaissance) *Orlyak*, based at Yambol.

Order of Battle of *Yato* No. 902 (19 July 1940)
Crew #1: Yastreb No. 11-1, pilot: *Poruchik* Doncho Nikolov Dimitrov
Crew #2: Yastreb No. 11-2, pilot: *Podporuchik* Viktor Evstatiev Pavlov
Crew #3: Yastreb No. 11-3, pilot: *Podofitser* Hristo Krumov Tanev
Crew #4: Yastreb No. 11-4, pilot: *Podofitser* Tsvitan Dimitrov Gruev
Crew #5: Yastreb No. 22-1, pilot: *Podofitser* Dako Petkov Dakov
Crew #6: Yastreb No. 33-1, pilot: *Podofitser* Stefan Nikolov Stefanov
Crew #7: Yastreb No. 33-3, pilot: *Podofitser* Atanas Atanasov Matev
Crew #8: Yastreb No. 22-3, pilot: *Podofitser* Aleksandăr Georgiev Haralampiev

Jagdeinsitzer *P. Z. L. P-24* ²)

¹) *Muster deutscher Herkunft.* ²) *Muster polnischer Herkunft.*

This retouched photo was included in a German brochure listing the most important Bulgarian war-planes, P.24 included. Page scanned from an original copy of Die Kriegsflugzeuge der Staaten Südost-Europas *(Warplanes of the Countries of South-Eastern Europe), edited by der* Oberbefe-hlshaber der Luftwaffe, *published in December 1940.*

The first time the PZL P.24s – along with the other Bulgarian warplanes, all sporting the new military markings – were openly shown to the public, revealing the existence of the Văzdushni na Negovo Velichestvo Voyski *(VNVV), or His Majesty's Air Force, was during the 'open door' event organised at the main military airfield of Bozhur-ishte on 27 June 1937.*

In 1941, a total of 11 P.24s were available. Of these, two were damaged in accidents during the year. In February 1941, the eleven P.24s were assigned to the 1/6. *Orlyak* of the 6th *Iztrebitelen Polk* (Fighter Regiment), forming a separate *yato*, the 672nd. The unit was based on Asen airfield, in central Bulgaria (north-west of Kazanlăk). This was most probably the last operational assignment of the P.24 as a first-line fighter aircraft. The type was eventually replaced by the much superior Messerschmitt Bf 109E.

After this date, not much was heard of the *Yastrebs*. They soldiered on as trainers, usually based on Marno Pole/Karlovo main air base. Their swift end came in the summer of 1944. On 12 June 1944, at 01:50, three groups of 15-20 RAF bombers of the 205th Bomber Group⁶ attacked Karlovo. The airfield was illuminated first with flares. Soon after, about 100 explosive and many incendiaries were dropped from 1,500 m. Based on Bulgarian sources, eight Bulgarian aircraft parked on the airfield were de-

6   No. 205 Group of RAF was part of the Mediterranean Allied Strategic Air Force (MASAF), alongside the US 15th AAF.

The same aircraft, No. 1, depicted at the same event. Combat flags of the now openly existing air force units are stacked into the cockpit of a P.24b, which had its canopy removed. The stylised Cyrillic letter B embroidered in each corner of the flags stands for [Tsar] Boris (and not for Bulgaria).

This specially marked P.24b, No. 1, adorned with garlands and tiny Bulgarian flags, is being blessed with holy water by an Orthodox priest during a ceremony.

stroyed, five were heavily damaged and three were damaged only lightly. Thirty men were killed and 72 wounded[7],[8]. The attackers lost a bomber of the 231 Wing, 70 Squadron, a Wellington Mk. X, LN870[9]. The aircraft's pilot, Warrant Officer B.E. Marstin, became disoriented and crashed the bomber before it could reach its target. Five crew members were killed[10].

---

7   The victims were mainly soldiers from a searchlight platoon. Their commander was absent. They were sleeping in barracks, having orders to run for cover to a nearby forest in case of aerial attack. They did exactly that, but lots of bombs hit exactly that very forest, killing and wounding many of them. The careless commander was one of the main protagonists of the 9 September 1944 leftist coup d'état.

8   A German report lists 14 Bulgarian aircraft destroyed, 9 Bulgarian and 1 German aircraft damaged, 20 killed and 60 wounded.

9   The aircraft crashed between the villages of Krivodol and Stalyska Mahala.

10   The mangled remnants of the five fallen airmen (three Australian and two British) were exhumed on 16 October 1946, and are currently interred in the War Cemetery at Sofia.

The Bulgarian Tsar, Boris III (centre), is flanked by Prince Kiril, the Tsar's younger brother (left), and General Major Hristo N. Lukov (right), Minister of War (23.11.1935-4.01.1938). This time, the cockpit canopy of the specially adorned P.24, No. 1, is in place.

The first P.24 is dedicated to the new-born son of Tsar Boris, Crown Prince Simeon Tărnovski (born on 16 June 1937). The white Cyrillic writing on the fuselage side spells: "Симеонъ Князъ Търновски" ("Simeon Knyaz Tărnovski"), knyaz meaning prince.

Former fighter pilot and unit commander, *Kapitan* Asen Kovachev, who was stationed in Karlovo at that time, remembers: *"Following the night raid (...) the material damage was not big, just 8-9 old PZL 24 fighters burned on the ground. We had left them lined on the airfield as decoy".*

Later that month, Karlovo airfield was targeted again by Allied bombers, this time by the USAAF, in a daytime raid. On 28 June, at noon, 138 B-24 heavy bombers of the 304th Bomber Wing, 15th AAF, escorted by 36 P-47s from the 332nd Fighter Group and 39 P-38s from the 14th Fighter Group, bombed the airfield and its perimeters. The attackers claimed 22 aircraft destroyed on the ground, as well as heavy damage to workshops, hangars, barracks, the administration buildings and fuel storage tanks. Indeed, the whole airfield was practically destroyed. However, because of an earlier evacuation order, only three fighter aircraft were actually destroyed and six more damaged. One officer and six technicians were killed, six more technicians wounded.

Frontal view of one of the freshly delivered PZL gull-wing fighters. Notice the unequal width coloured stripes painted on the rudder of the unidentified aircraft type, at left.

Former *Kapitan* Asen Kovachev recalls the American raid: "*On 28 June, a Bf 109 krilo* [flight of four] *was up in the air performing training, as usual. Suddenly, the air warning siren started - Alarm! I immediately rushed to the Headquarters with my car* [he had a Ford Eifel, bought during his training in Germany] *and met at the stairs the German instructor, Major Kyule* [Kühle]. *He told me that from the Boyana commanding centre they had informed him that there was no immediate danger for the airfield* [Karlovo]. *Despite this, I went to the office and the telephone operator met me anxiously: <<Mr. Poruchik, from Pirdop* [a nearby town] *they report a large group of bombers heading to the airfield!>>. Hearing that, Major Kühle[11] immediately ran, together with Luftwaffe Captain Halveg* [Hollweg][12], *to their powerful motorcycle. Because the Bf 109s that were in the air had no radio connection with the ground, I ordered immediately a red rocket to be fired up, which means <<landing!>>. Together with Pavel Pavlov and Georgi Kirovski we got in my car and headed for the landing strip to meet the landing aircraft and redirect them to the nearby*

---

11 *Luftwaffe* Major Helmut Kühle, former *Gruppenkommandeur* of II./JG 52, was the actual commander of the Marno Pole/ Karlovo fighter training base.

12 *Luftwaffe* Major Hermann Hollweg, who formerly led I./JG 104, was the commanding officer of the German training mission in Bulgaria.

Aircraft of the Obraztsov Orlyak *(literally, Model, or Exemplary Group; in fact, an Instructor Training Group, a sort of 'Top Gun' unit) are lined up on Sofia airfield, sometime in 1939. Seven P.24b are at left, six He 51s are at right, while three Fw 56s are at the far end, centre. A dozen fighter pilots line up in a circle segment in the foreground.*

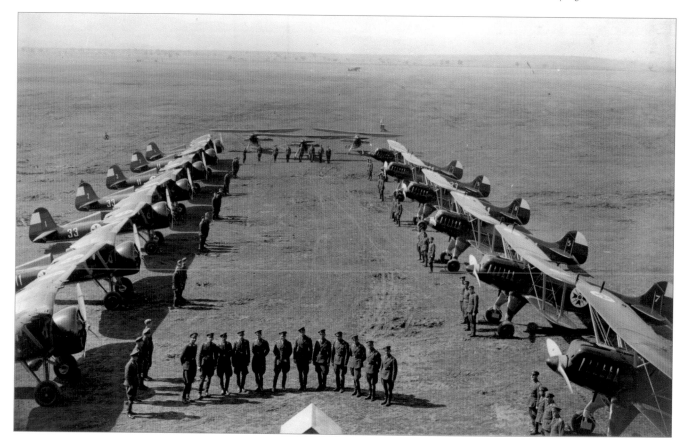

airfield at Asen. The airplanes were landing one after another, and immediately took off to the afore-named airfield. We just sent away the 4th one when bombs started to fall on the airstrip. We jumped out of the car and hit the ground, but Poruchik *Kirovski was killed by shrapnel* [it seems he tried to escape with the car, but some shrapnel hit the car, one went through his body]. Poruchik *Pavlov and I were wounded by small shrapnel fragments. As the bombs stopped exploding, we all ran and hid in the trenches. A little later a new wave of bombers flew by, and one bomb, falling close to us, threw soil on us. Then all went silent. The remains of the discarded PZL 24s, used as decoys, were crackling in flames.*"

As described by the eye witness, most of the eleven destroyed aircraft were obsolete PZL P.24s, left in the open field as decoys. Indeed, following these raids, all of them were written off (five on 12 June, one on 15 July and the rest on 31 August, see Annex, available on-line, see next page). A comprehensive list of the available VNVV aircraft, dated 1 September 1944, does not list a single P.24. With this, the lacklustre career of the Polish gull-wing fighter came to an inglorious end.

It has to be noted that a number of the more powerful version of the P.24 fighter, model "j", to be fitted with a Gnome&Rhône G&R 14N-01radial engine of 950 hp nominal output, was also set to be sold to Bulgaria in late 1939 (twelve units). The Bulgarians sent to Poland a spare engine, used on PZL PZL.43 bombers, to be fitted to the prototype. The prototype was actually finished at the PZL Plant in Warsaw, in the summer of 1939. However, due to the war no deliveries took place, and the engine-less fuselage of this single prototype was captured by German troops on Okęcie airfield, in September (as seen in photographs). A Bulgarian document dated on 25.11.1939, listing undelivered aircraft and various matériel from Poland due to the outbreak of war, includes – besides a number of PZL.43s – a single P.24, construction number 17846.

Reportedly, there were plans to produce the type in Bulgaria under licence, at the D.F.S. Plant in Lovech; however, no actual production took place due to the war.

Camouflage and markings

The PZL P.24s built for the Bulgarian order were finished in standard Polish air force camouflage colours of olive green (khaki) on the upper surfaces over light blue-grey on the under surfaces. The wing leading edge was also completely painted in khaki, extending to the outer wing spar on the under surface. The rudder was in the Bulgarian national colours of white (top), green (middle) and red (bottom). Interestingly and uniquely, the colours were initially painted angularly, at about 30 degrees to the horizontal. Bulgarian military markings were applied on both wing surfaces and on the mid-fuselage, in six positions. The factory logo appeared on the mid-fin, in red, while the aircraft type on fin top was in the same colour. Test flights were performed on aircraft wearing this standard camouflage scheme.

A photo taken in Poland shows an aircraft adorned with a light-coloured tapering flash line that ran along the fuselage. Polish sources identify the colour as light blue. However, there is no evidence of this colour being actually used on Bulgarian fighter aircraft, only red (and later on yellow). Therefore, the Author believes the colour identification is erroneous, and it was actually red that appears light in Polish period photos. The engine cowling was completely painted in the same colour. Stylised bird of prey claws were painted on the wheel spats, in the same colour. Strangely, the Bulgarian military markings were not applied on this particular aircraft, and the rudder is also khaki, not the customary tricolour.

Once in Bulgaria, the aircraft were identified with white serial numbers, 11, 22, or 33 applied on the rear fuselage, and 1 to 4 on the mid-fin. The meaning of these numbers is not fully understood; however, the Author believes the fuselage numbers may have represented different *yata* (squadrons), i.e. 11 referring to the 1st *Yato*, 22 to the 2nd *Yato*, while 33 to the 3rd *Yato* of a particular *orlyak* (group). The single-digit number may have referred to the place the machine had in the particular four-aircraft *krilo* (flight/squad), 1 to 4, of a particular *yato* (squadron). For example, aircraft No. 11-1 was the first aircraft of the P.24 flight/squad of the first squadron, while aircraft No. 33-4 was the last aircraft of the P.24 flight/squad in the third squadron. Other fighter and fighter-trainer aircraft types using the same numbering style[13] were the Heinkel He 51 *Sokol* (tail numbers from 5 to 8) and the Fw 56 *Komar* (tail numbers 9 and 10).

Later, this early style numbering was replaced by the standard Bulgarian aircraft identification, consisting of only an Arabic number applied in white on the fuselage aft the military marking, and in black on the wing under surfaces. Simultaneously, the peculiar Bulgarian identification triangle also appeared on the mid-fin, in place of the former Arabic numeral. The sole photograph depicting a P.24 in this identification scheme shows the engine cowling and the tapered flash along the fuselage, as well as the rudder, in yellow. This was the livery the surviving aircraft wore at the moment of their destruction by Allied bombs at Karlovo airfield, in June 1944.

The Bulgarian air force commanders apparently liked parades; therefore, many photos show such ceremonial events. This particular photo, depicting seven neatly lined up P.24s, headed by an Fw 56 (at right) was taken during such an occasion. The French propeller maker's rectangular logo (Gnome&Rhône) is clearly visible on the bare metal blades. The diameter of the propeller blades' inscribed circle was 2.6 m.

Additional info see:
http://mmpbooks.biz/assets/BFC/02.pdf

---

13 Similar numbering style was also used by Heinkel He 45s, Focke-Wulf Fw 58s and Dornier Do 11s.

Similar line-up of P.24s, led again by a Fw 56, is depicted in this photo as well. Several fighter pilots – some faces being familiar, often seen on other photos – casually pose for this shot taken at Bozhurishte airfield, in 1939. The complete photo depicting all eleven airmen, can be seen on page 140.

Another group of Bulgarian pilots, this time clad in flying overalls, complete with goggles, pose in front of a P.24b. The aircraft's pilot, seated in the cockpit, warms up the engine prior to take-off for a training sortie, sometime in the late 1930s. Notice the four wing-mounted 7.9 mm calibre Colt-Browning MG 40 machine guns, protruding from the wings' leading edge.

Three fighter pilot buddies are posing for eternity in front of a Yastreb (they appear the same people featured in a similar three-pilot memory shot in front of a row of Sokols. The pilot in centre is future Bf 109G-pilot, Podporuchik Lyuben Kondakov). Based on the large military tent seen in the background, at right, this field must have been one of those landing grounds used during military manoeuvres, like Buhovtsi.

A four-aircraft P.24b krilo (33-1, 33-4, 22-4 and 22-1) is seen during the visit of a delegation of Polish P.37A and B bombers (seen in the background), led by Gen. Ludomił Rayski, Commanding Officer of the Polish Air Force, on 28 August 1938. A German Ju 52/3m airliner of the Lufthansa (D-AMFR) is also parked on Sofia-Bozhurishte airfield.

Discarded PZL P.24j (?) wreck pushed against the wall, photographed by a German soldier on the PZL factory airfield at Okęcie on a gloomy late September day of 1939. Details surrounding the second batch of P.24s ordered by the Bulgarians, which remained undelivered due to the war, are unclear.

Another photo of the same derelict P.24j seen through a German soldier's camera. A Bulgarian document dated 25.11.1939, listing undelivered aircraft from Poland, includes one single P.24, Construction No. 17846. This might be that very aircraft.

The elegant silhouette of the gull-wing PZL P.24 is show in its splendour, in the element she belongs to: the air. The machine guns had been removed, as was the cockpit canopy – a common occurrence during training flights.

The elegance of the Polish-designed aircraft type was equally obvious on the ground. The cockpit canopy is again missing; however, the machine guns are in place. Notice the red factory emblem and aircraft type stencilled onto the top fin. A German document dated 1 June 1940 lists eleven extant PZL P.24s and categorises the fighter type as '1ˢᵗ Class' (the same category as the Bf 109E).

An Army soldier (there are no wings surrounding the cockade on his cap) poses in front of a P.24b. The engine cowling appears to be black; in fact, it was dark red. Aircraft No. 1 can be seen in the background.

Below, left: This page of an official Bulgarian aircraft silhouette recognition manual, scanned at the Bulgarian military archives at Veliko Tărnovo, shows the PZL P.24b, identified by its official air force code name ястреб (i.e. Yastreb). The depicted sample aircraft already sports the Axis style 'black St. Andrew's cross in white square' type military marking.

ЯСТРЕБЪ

Left: Prominent fighter pilot and instructor Lt. Asen Kovachev, assigned to Karlovo air base in June 1944, witnessed the destruction of the last surviving P.24s, as described in his memoirs.

Below: The charred remains of the P.24s, which had been lined up on Marno Pole/Karlovo airfield to serve as decoy, are shown after either the RAF night bombing of 12 June 1944, or the USAAF daylight bombing raid of 28 June 1944. With this unglamorous scene, the Polish fighter type exited from the annals of the Bulgarian air force.

111

PZL P.24b Yastreb, 'White 1', 1. Armeyski Orlyak, Bozhurishte airfield, July 1937. Camouflage colours: Polish Air Force Khaki (FS 34088) on upper surfaces, Light Blue (FS 26329) on under surfaces. Engine cowling and tapering flash along the fuselage Red. Stylised lines on wheel spats also in the same colour. Bulgarian national colours White (top), Green (middle) and Red (bottom) on rudder. Propeller blades in natural metal. Factory markings on fin Red.

Simon Schatz
in cooperation with
Maciej Noszczak

The port side of the same aircraft, shown during an air force ceremony in 1937. The metal rectangle over the Cyrillic letter E is a factory service plate, attached to all aircraft. A couple of all-grey Dornier Do 11 bombers are visible in the background.

While the pilot adjusts his flying gear, the mechanic, sitting in the cockpit, warms up the engine of the first PZL P.24b that entered Bulgarian service. As noted earlier, this particular aircraft was dedicated to the new-born son of Tsar Boris, Crown Prince Simeon Tărnovski (born on 16 June 1937). The white Cyrillic writing on the fuselage side spells: "Симеонъ Князъ Търновски" ("Simeon Knyaz Tărnovski"). Notice the red PZL factory logo over the aircraft's white serial number located on the fin.

PZL P.24b Yastreb, 'White 11-2', 902. Yato, pilot: Podporuchik Viktor Evstatiev Pavlov, Bozhurishte airfield, June 1940. Camouflage colours: Polish Air Force Khaki on upper surfaces. Light Blue on under surfaces. Engine cowling and tapering flash along the fuselage Red. Stylised lines on wheel spats also in the same colour. Bulgarian national colours White (top), Green (middle) and Red (bottom) on rudder. Propeller blades in natural metal. Factory markings on fin Red.

Simon Schatz
in cooperation with
Maciej Noszczak

The elegant silhouette of the PZL P.24 is nicely shown in this perfect side view photo. The aircraft wore typical Polish camouflage colours of khaki on the upper surfaces, over light blue. The engine cowling and the tapering red flash along the fuselage side were blood red. Following the deadly in-flight accident of Poruchik Vasil M. Benchev, who reportedly suffocated in the aircraft's cockpit following an engine fire in June 1938, the centre window of the cockpit canopy was removed on all aircraft.

PZL P.24b Yastreb, 'White 5' (5/7017), 1/6. Orlyak, 6. Iztrebitelen Polk, Asen airfield, April 1941. Camouflage colours: Polish Air Force Khaki on upper surfaces, Light Blue on under surfaces. Lower engine cowling and tapering flash along the fuselage Yellow. Rudder in the same colour. Propeller blades in natural metal. Factory markings on fin Red.

Simon Schatz
in cooperation with
Maciej Noszczak

This is the only known P.24b showing the entire aircraft and all codes that was photographed wearing the pro-Axis military markings. Luckily for the artist, this nice profile view allows all details to be properly represented in the artwork. The lower engine cowling and the tapered flash along the fuselage, as well as the rudder, were yellow. Note the typical VNV triangle applied on the fin, which identifies the fighter type's Nomenklaturen Nomer (Register Number) as 7017, meaning that it was the second fighter aircraft type in Bulgarian service (the first one, No. 7007, was the Heinkel He 51).

Arado Ar 65 *Orel*
The Old 'Eagle' of Bulgaria

The red-silver, three-engine Junkers Ju 52/3m transport D-ABAQ[1] slowly descended upon the grassy runway of Sofia international airport on Sunday, 26 May 1937, a fine, sunny day. After coming to a stop, the door opened, and a chubby man emerged in an all-white suit, wearing matching white shoes and black bow tie. He held a carved walking cane in his left hand, and joyously waved to the crowd with the right one. His importance was obvious, as he was greeted by no other than the Bulgarian monarch, Tsar Boris III, and his entourage (the Prime Minister, the Minister of Foreign Affairs, the Minister of Home Defence and the Minister of Railways, who was also in charge of aviation). Bulgaria's ruler also wore a white uniform, with the Iron Cross 1st Class pinned to his right breast pocket above a large Bulgarian cross-shape medal, the Bravery Order. The guest was none other than Hermann Göring, commander-in-chief of the resurgent German Air Force (*Luftwaffe*). He arrived from Budapest, heading a large delegation, part of which was transported by another similarly adorned Ju 52/3m[2].

Next day, Göring and the German delegation had a conference with the heads of the Bulgarian Government. After a lavish lunch, he departed for a hunting session with Tsar Boris at his palace at Vrana,

1   Junkers Ju 52/3m, W.Nr. 4066, D-ABAQ, called 'Manfred von Richthofen II'. Göring's travelling aircraft used until 1943. His personal pilot was a former Lufthansa Captain, *Flieger-Oberstabsingenieur* Friedrich Hucke.
    This particular aircraft had an oversized seat specially for Göring, located immediately at the main cabin door.
2   D-ABIK (W.Nr. 4069), called 'Manfred von Richthofen I'. That Junkers was equally painted mostly red, with metal/silver portions on fuselage and wings, and with black/silver striped ailerons and flaps.

Hermann Göring, head of the Luftwaffe *(centre, in white suit), and Tsar Boris III, monarch of Bulgaria (at right), greet each other upon the former's arrival at Sofia airport on Sunday, 26 May 1937. Göring's travelling machine, the red-silver Junkers Ju 52/3m, registered D-ABAQ, is seen in the background, while sister ship, D-ABIK, is visible behind. Göring offered twelve Arado Ar 65 biplane fighters and twelve Dornier Do 11 high-wing bombers as gift to the Tsar, with the veiled intention to of attracting the Balkan country to the Axis side. He eventually succeeded; Bulgaria becoming one of the Axis powers from 1 March 1941.*

located in the outskirts of Sofia, having there again confidential tête-à-tête talks with the Bulgarian monarch. On the 28th, Göring and his entourage departed for Mostar, Kingdom of Yugoslavia, amidst the cheers, waving and straight-arm 'German salute' of his Bulgarian hosts, as well as the German ambassador to Bulgaria, Eugen Rümelin.

The head of the *Luftwaffe* did not come to visit the Tsar empty handed. As a token of German-Bulgarian friendship, Göring presented Boris with twelve Arado Ar 65 fighters and an identical number of Dornier Do 11 bombers. Although both warplane types were considered by the *Luftwaffe* as outdated and obsolete, they were most welcomed by the Bulgarians, who badly needed any combat aircraft for their fledgling, but still secret, air force. Obviously, Göring's generous gesture had political connotations, and fitted into Berlin's strategy. The Third Reich wanted to extend its influence in the Balkans, to the detriment of Italy, which considered the territory as its traditional area of influence. Besides political ties, the Germans also wanted to sell increasingly obsolescent arms, including aircraft, to the Bulgarians, at top prices. They succeeded in both goals, as Sofia gravitated ever closer to Berlin, and also the supply of German weapons started to flow towards the Balkan country.

The promised gifts arrived promptly. The dozen Arado Ar 65F[3] fighters, powered by twelve-cylinder BMW VId engines of 550 hp[4], landed on Sofia main airfield, ferried by German pilots dressed in civilian clothes[5].

The light grey painted biplanes wore black German civilian registrations, as follows:

Weeks later, the aircraft type and serial number were applied on the fin, in white. 'Ap.65-106' can be deciphered as follows: 'Ap' is the Cyrillic version of Ar, which is short of Arado. '65' is the aircraft type, while '106' is this particular machine's individual serial number within the VNVV.

Factory	Manufactured	W.Nr.	Register	Previous owner
AGO	1935	6	D-IJAA	JFS Schleißheim
AGO		19	D-IVUA	JFS Schleißheim
Erla	1935	41	D-IJIO	JFS Schleißheim
Ar. W		335	D-IZUP	JFS Schleißheim
Ar. W	1934	633	D-ITYH	JFS Schleißheim
Ar. W		652	D-IXUZ	JFS Schleißheim
Ar. W		875	D-ISYZ	
Ar. W		878	D-I???	
Ar. W		888	D-IMIZ	
AGO	1936	2172	D-IHNO	FlGr. Schleißheim
AGO	1936	2179	D-I???	
AGO	1936	2180	D-IJKI	

Key: Ar. W=Arado Warnemünde

Note: All these aircraft were in a used condition, previously being employed by various *Luftwaffe Flugzeugführerschulen* (i.e. piloting schools). Some were involved in minor accidents (e.g. D-IZUP had a mid-air collision in January 1935), and after repair were sold to Bulgaria

On 26 July 1937, at a pompous ceremony held at the Bozhurishte airport, Tsar Boris III handed over the battle standards to the combat units of the embryonic air force. On the same occasion, he officially 'donated' the twelve Ar 65 fighters, along with the same number of Do 11 bombers, to his air forces, i.e. to the Royal Bulgarian Air Force, in other words His Majesty's Air Forces (VNVV). All these warplanes defiantly wore full military markings, denoting that they'd shed the veil of secrecy set to circumvent the harsh clauses of the post-war Neuilly peace treaty imposed upon Bulgaria. They also displayed a large, colourful tsar's cipher on their fuselage, symbol of the royal gift.

---

3   The F sub-type was the final version of the Ar 65, of which three prototypes and 192 series units were built in total.

4   The first aircraft D-IJAA, was fitted with engine No. 18707.

5   One of the ferry pilots was Johann Bungartz, an AGO employee.

The aircraft type was not new to several Bulgarian pilots, as they had the chance to fly it while training in Germany. One of those trainees, who flew the type at the Kaufbeuren piloting school, was Dimităr S. Lazarov, future commander of the 692nd Fighter *Yato*. He shared his experiences with the Author at his Sofia home, on 22 May 2004. Another pilot who flew the Arado biplane while in Germany was Stoyan I. Stoyanov, future top scoring Bulgarian fighter pilot.

The Arado Ar 65F fighter type was impressed in Bulgarian military service with the *Nomenklaturen Nomer* (Register Number) 7027 and assigned the code name *Orel* (Eagle), on 18 August 1937. Royal Order of 15 July 1937 introduced a new organization for the Bulgarian Army and Air Force. Based on this directive, the Ar 65Fs were allocated to the 2nd Army *Orlyak* (Group), based at Plovdiv airport, where they formed a fighter *yato* (squadron). The *Orels* participated in the autumn 1938 manoeuvres, along with the other newly acquired German and Polish warplanes. The first-line service of the Arado fighter was to be short, however. On 1 August 1939, by the Order of VNVV Commander, *Polkovnik* (Colonel) Vasil T. Boydev, *Shkola za vissh pilotazh* (High Aerobatics Piloting School) was established (later on, it became known as the *Shkolata za Iztrebiteli*, i.e. Fighter School). *Poruchik* Krăstyu Atanasov was appointed as commander. The twelve Ar 65s were assigned to this élite school as fighter trainers.

Soon after the Arados started their second lives as fighter trainers, the first – and only – tragedy struck. On 6 September 1939, *Orel* No. 102[6] crashed near Kar-

All Ar 65 fighters (and Do 11 bombers) wore on their fuselage sides the so-called 'royal cipher' of Boris III, as a colourful sign denoting that these warplanes were donated to the air force by the monarch. The cipher was applied in front of the marking of the Royal Bulgarian Air Force (VNVV), the so-called 'Tsarist Roundel'.

lovo air based, killing the student pilot, *Podofitser* Ivan Dimitrov Pashov. The post-accident investigation revealed that the crankshaft broke and the subsequent engine failure caused the powerless biplane to crash into the ground. In 1940, the High Aerobatics School was renamed Fighter School, and moved to the airfield of Marno Pole, near Karlovo. Here, the Ar 65s kept their role as advanced trainers for future fighter pilots. In 1941, a total of eleven Ar 65s were available. Of these, one was damaged in an accident. The aircraft inventory of 26 May 1941 lists *Orel* No. 6/7027 in service with the 6th *Polk*, while Nos. 5, 8 and 10 were at the Main Workshop awaiting their turn to be repaired. No. 12 was flown once by *Podofitser* Dimităr D. Raynov at Karlovo, on 30 May 1941. On 27 December, *Orel* Nos. 11 and 12 were parked at Kazanlăk, for the winter period.

In April 1942, the piloting school moved to Dolna Mitropoliya, including all existing *Orels*. Once there, the Arados soldiered on, assisting generations of fighter pilots to hone their skills. *Poruchik* Petăr Manolev, chief instructor at the piloting school, flew a number of *Orels* for four and a half years, between November 1939 and April 1944, as listed in the annexes (available on-line, see page 121).

By the end of 1943, most of the Arado Ar 65s were retired from active service. A few were repaired and their lives extended, but most were not. A document listing trainer aircraft, dated 24 December, reflecting the situation extant on 23 November, lists Ar 65, Nos. 7, 8, 9 and 11[7], with the following note *"aircraft still in use; to be checked at the next scheduled overhaul if they should be repaired, or scrapped"*. Indeed, most of the surviving *Orels* were scrapped the next year. First to be struck off charge was No. 7, on 28 June, along with two BMW VI d engines, Nos. 19772 and 18076. The following eight aircraft had to be scrapped on 28 December, as *"they presented low security in flight"*: Nos. 1, 3, 5, 6, 8, 9, 10 and 11. They were to be sent to the aviation workshop (GRR) in Bozhurishte for scrapping. Interestingly, some of these aircraft were officially scrapped again on paper, also in 1945, at a different date: No. 6 on 10 August, Nos. 1, 3, 5 and 10 on 24 August, while Nos. 8 and 11 on 25 September. A couple of *Orels*, Nos. 9 and 12, finally laid down their wings on 1 November 1945. Aircraft No. 4/7027 was removed from the lists on 30 April 1946.

In reality, by then the days when the 'Eagle' (*Orel*) soared in Bulgarian skies were long gone.

---

6   Aircraft No. 102 was officially written off on 10 June 1940.

7   Aircraft No. 11 was flown by *Ppor.* Asen D. Gigov at Dolna Mitropoliya Fighter School on 15 October 1943.

Orel No. 110 and its pilot are prepared for a morning training flight. Interestingly, the last digit (0) is missing from the rudder. One possible explanation is that it's a replacement rudder, and there was no time, or will, to repaint the number 0.

Colours and markings

All twelve Arado Ar 65Fs were apparently painted in light grey overall. There are two possible versions of the actual paints and shades used:

1, DKH[8] **L40/52**, or Avionorm *Nitrodecklack* (nitro covering paint) 7375, which was a light grey. This colour was later on, after RLM standardisation, known as **RLM 63 *Hellgrau***, or light grey[9].

2, Zöllner *Decklack* (covering paint) RLM *grau* Rh 9069, covered by Zöllner *Lasurlack* (varnish) RLM *grau* Rh 9070 – as recommended in the manual for the Ar 68F, dated 10 February 1936. '*RLM Grau*' refers to **RLM 02 *RLM-Grau*** colour, which was also a light grey – albeit slightly darker than the RLM 63 – but with a distinct greenish hue.

If the aircraft were specially refurbished and repainted for export, variant no. 1 is more plausible, while if the aircraft wore their standard colour, used in *Luftwaffe* schools, then variant no. 2 is more probable. Different aircraft manufacturers may have used different paint suppliers (note that the dozen Ar 65Fs were built by three different factories). The definitive answer whether the airframe surface finish was in RLM 02 or RLM 63 would be given by the Bulgarian edition of the aircraft maintenance guide, which had a special chapter dedicated to repair paints, where the precise paint types and manufacturers were given.

As described in the chapter's main text, at the time of the fighters' official start of VNVV service, on 26 July 1937, they wore full military markings, and displayed a large, colourful tsar's cipher on their fuselage, symbol of the royal gift. This royal cipher consisted of a yellow Cyrillic letter B, symbolising Boris, topped with a crown. It was applied in the centre of a crimson-colour crest-shape background, framed by green and white lines – symbolising Bulgaria's national colours.

Besides the VNVV military roundels, applied in six positions, the aircraft type and serial number were displayed in white on the mid-fin, contrary to Order No. 53/14.04.1938, which stipulated that the number should be applied on the white area of the rudder. The engine cowling was painted in an eye-catching bright red colour, which was continued in a rearward tapering flash line, running along

---

8   DKH= Dr. Kurt Herberts, German paint and lacquer manufacturer.

9   As comparison, the painting guide for Heinkel He 51C/D, dated in late 1936 – thus the closest to the date the Ar 65Fs were exported to Bulgaria – lists Celesta *Flugzeugüberlack* 2002, *grüngrau* 63, i.e. RLM 63, for fabric covered areas, while for metal parts the Avionorm *Nitrodecklack grau* 7007 is recommended. Obviously, these two light grey shades must have been visually identical, as no visible difference in shade can be observed on quality black/white photos.

the fuselage, as far as the horizontal stabiliser strengthening strut. The rudder was divided horizontally in three equal areas, painted in the Bulgarian national colours: white (top), green (middle) and red (bottom).

Based on an official decree dated 14 April 1938, the last digit(s) of the individual serial number was painted in large black numerals on the fin (and on the rudder, in case of two-digit numbers), so the aircraft could be identified from a distance. In late June 1940, the so-called 'Tsarist Roundel' type military marking was replaced by the 'St. Andrew Cross' type one, consisting of a black X in a white square. The new marking was also applied in six positions, usually directly over the previous roundel. For a little while, all other markings and codes remained unchanged.

At one point in mid-1941, the white aircraft type and large black serial number disappeared from the fin (and rudder), the peculiar Bulgarian triangle being applied instead on the mid-fin. The aircraft's serial number now consisted of only the last one or two digits (1 to 12), instead of the previous three digits (101 to 112). The Bulgarian tricolour was overpainted in grey, as was the royal cipher, to reduce visibility. Later on, in 1942, the light grey livery gave way to the more military livery of dark green (of unidentified provenance and hue). The bottom surfaces stayed light grey. The wraparound engine cowling, along with the rearward tapering flash along the fuselage, became 'Axis yellow' instead of red. This was the camouflage scheme the last surviving *Orels* wore until they were scrapped in 1944/1945.

Two rows made of six fighter trainers each (Ar 65 Orel at left, Fw 56 Komar at right) are facing each other during a ceremony held at Karlovo airfield, in 1939.

Additional info see:
http://mmpbooks.biz/assets/ BFC/03.pdf

Ten Arado Ar 65s are lined up in front of one of Karlovo's hangars, during late 1939. The eleventh one (at far left) is taxiing towards the runway. The twelfth one had crashed in September and would be written off.

The only fatal accident involving an Orel *happened on 6 September 1939. That day, aircraft No. 102 crashed near Karlovo air based due to engine malfunction, killing the student pilot, Podofitser Ivan Dimitrov Pashov.*

Before a scheduled training flight, the details of the flight plan are being discussed.

Early morning engine start of an Orel. Judged by the large number of onlookers, it must have been a special event – possibly the first time the fighter type was presented to that particular unit.

One of the Orels is being readied for a training flight.

The engine is being checked prior to flight.

Once ready, the ground crew spins the propeller start the powerplant.

With the engine now roaring, the Orel pilot rolls towards the runway for takeoff.

Two group photos taken in front of Orel No. 107 at the same time. The moustachioed airman at right and centre, respectively, is Podporuchik Stoyan Stoyanov, future top scoring Bulgarian fighter 'ace' pilot.

A couple of Arado fighters is prepared for a dawn mission. A Dornier bomber, barely seen at right, under the upper wing, took off just a couple of minutes earlier.

Two airmen pose in front of an Ar 65F parked in front of the main hangar of Marno Pole/Karlovo air base. The pilot at left is Ppor. Atanas Borisov Atanasov – brother of fighter pilot Anton Borisov Atanasov, called 'Schwarz'. Atanas Atanasov passed away in 2000. The black diagonal line aft the so-called 'Tsarist Roundel' type marking is not an error on the print, as it can be observed on other photos as well.

Some sort of ceremony is being held in front of a parked and anchored Orel, in mid-1938. The still was captured during royal manoeuvres of the army, the so-called Strelkovi manevri, or Shooting Manoeuvres.

The broken propeller and damaged port lower wing leading edge point to a minor accident that may had occurred when the port wheel struck a hard object, or pothole, during low speed taxiing, pushing the airframe on its nose, leaning towards left.

The usual 'souvenir shot' taken in front of an Orel parked at Bozhurishte airfield, in 1939. A German document dated 1 June 1940 lists eight unarmed extant Ar 65s, and categorises the fighter type as veraltet (outdated).

Based on an official decree dated 14 April 1938, the last digit(s) of the individual serial number was painted in large black numeral on the fin, so the aircraft could be identified from a distance. This feature can be observed on these machines lined up on Marno Pole/Karlovo main air base.

In late June 1940, the so-called 'Tsarist Roundel' type military marking was replaced by the 'St. Andrew Cross' type one, consisting of a black X in a white square. The new marking was also applied in six positions, usually directly over the previous one. This (partial) overlapping of the new/old markings can be clearly observed on the lower surface of the lower wing of Orel No. 10. All other identification symbols stayed unaltered – for a while.

'Still life' with Arados. Two Ar 65Fs trainers are parked on the airfield of Dolna Mitropoliya fighter school in 1943. The yellow rearward tapering 'cheatline' is present on the fuselage of both aircraft; however, it's only faintly visible on the rear one.

The large, black numerals written on the tail surface, the red nose and the 'St. Andrew Cross'-style military marking date the photo from the spring of 1938 up to about mid-1941. Aircraft Nos. 11, 12, 9 and 4 are lined up on Marno Pole/Karlovo main air base.

Serene scene, featuring an Orel and two ground technicians, waiting for the take-off signal, so they could prepare the trainer for a sortie. The text written on the back of this original photograph says: "Старта самолет 'Орел', изтр. школа, лет. Карлово, 1941" (Start of airplane 'Orel', Fighter School, Karlovo airfield, 1941). The 'Royal Cipher' on the fuselage survived even after the new marking was introduced in late June 1940 – but not for too long. At one point, this colourful symbol was overpainted (see photo below), possibly to diminish the aircraft's visibility.

At a casual look at this mediocre quality photo it might appear that these Arados do not have the coloured nose and fuselage flash applied, which would be highly unusual. In fact, the colour is there; however, it's not red, but yellow. The switch of colours happened sometime in mid-1941.

Sometime in the Summer of 1941, the white aircraft type and large black serial number disappeared from the fin (and rudder), the peculiar Bulgarian triangle being applied instead on mid-fin. The Bulgarian tricolour on the rudder was overpainted in grey, as was the 'royal cipher', most probably to reduce visibility. Soon after, the surviving aircraft were repainted in Dark Green on their upper surfaces, over the original Light Grey, during their scheduled overhaul, or unscheduled repair work. The wraparound engine cowling, along with the rearward tapering flash along the fuselage, was repainted yellow instead of red. This is the livery used by the last serviceable Arado Ar 65Fs until they were scrapped in 1944/1945.

Orel No. 1 undergoing maintenance nearby a hangar, waiting for the propeller to be installed. The second man from left, in flying overalls, is Podporuchik Petăr Bochev – second-highest scoring Bulgarian fighter pilot. He flew the type during his fighter training course in 1942. The rudder, elevators, engine cowling and fuselage flash are yellow.

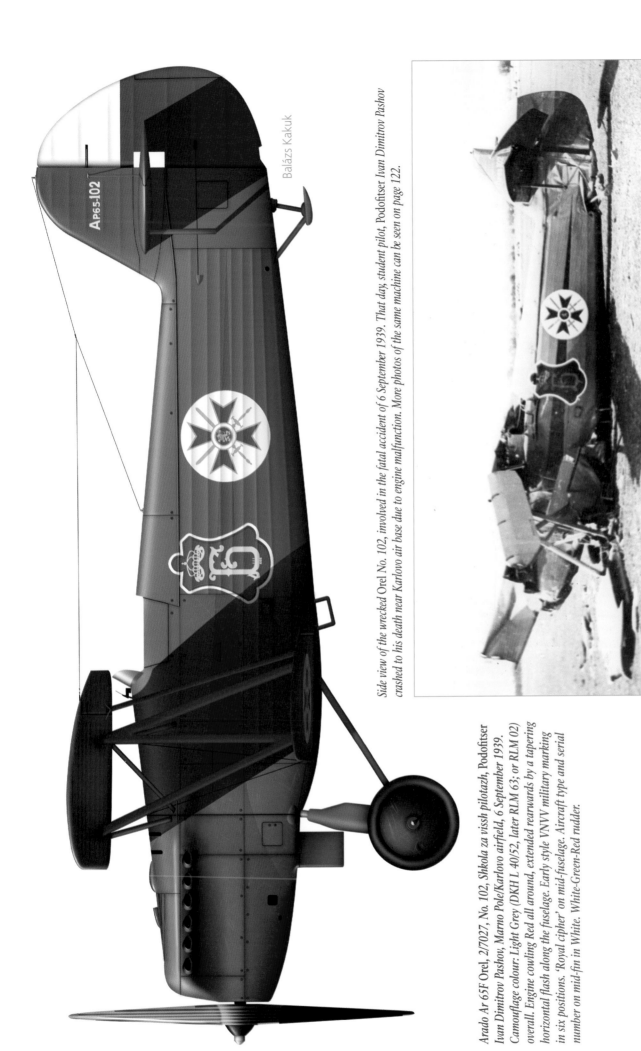

Balázs Kakuk

Side view of the wrecked Orel No. 102, involved in the fatal accident of 6 September 1939. That day, student pilot, Podofitser Ivan Dimitrov Pashov crashed to his death near Karlovo air base due to engine malfunction. More photos of the same machine can be seen on page 122.

Arado Ar 65F Orel, 2/7027, No. 102, Shkola za vissh pilotazh, Podofitser Ivan Dimitrov Pashov, Marno Pole/Karlovo airfield, 6 September 1939. Camouflage colour: Light Grey (DKH L 40/52, later RLM 63; or RLM 02) overall. Engine cowling Red all around, extended rearwards by a tapering horizontal flash along the fuselage. Early style VNVV military marking in six positions. 'Royal cipher' on mid-fuselage. Aircraft type and serial number on mid-fin in White. White-Green-Red rudder.

131

Balázs Kakuk

Arado Ar 65F Orel, 5/7027, No. 105, 'Black 5', Shkola za vissh pilotazh, Marno Pole/Karlovo airfield, late 1939. Camouflage colour: Light Grey (DKH L 40/52, later RLM 63; or RLM 02) overall. Engine cowling Red all around, extended rearwards by a tapering horizontal flash along the fuselage. Early style VNVV military marking in six positions. 'Royal cipher' on mid-fuselage. Aircraft type and serial number on mid-fin in White. Last digit of the serial number repeated in black, also on fin. White-Green-Red rudder.

Detail of a larger photo (see page 127) showing a row of Ar 65Fs lined up on Marno Pole/Karlovo airfield in late 1939, including No. 5. All features characteristic of the early livery worn by the Arado fighter trainers are visible (for details see Colours and Markings sub-chapter). The only exception is the individual number, applied in large black character on fin, contrary to Order No. 53/14.04.1938, which stipulated that the number should be applied on the white area of the rudder.

Balázs Kakuk

Detail photo of 'Black 12', parked on Marno Pole/Karlovo main air base in late summer of 1940. (The complete photo can be seen on page 128).

Arado Ar 65F Orel, 12/7027, No. 112, 'Black 12', Shkola za vissh pilotazh, Marno Pole/Karlovo airfield, late summer of 1940. Camouflage colour: Light Grey (DKH L 40/52, later RLM 63; or RLM 02) overall. Engine cowling Red all around, extended rearwards by a tapering horizontal flash along the fuselage. Axis style VNVV military marking in six positions. 'Royal cipher' on mid-fuselage. Aircraft type and serial number on mid-fin in White. Last two digits of the serial number repeated in black, on fin and rudder. White-Green-Red rudder.

Balázs Kakuk

134

Arado Ar 65F Orel, 5/7027, Shkola za vissh pilotazh, Marno Pole/Karlovo airfield, autumn of 1941. Camouflage colour: Light Grey (DKH L 40/52, later RLM 63; or RLM 02) overall. Engine cowling Red all around, extended rearwards by a tapering horizontal flash along the fuselage. Axis style VNVV military marking in six positions.

Two different tail marking styles can be observed on these lined up Arado Ar 65F's. In centre, Orel No. 10 still sports the early war high-visibility tail marking. By contrast, the two Orels seen in front and rear already sport low visibility tail (aircraft No. 5/7027 is closest to the camera). Photo taken on the landing ground of Marno Pole/Karlovo in the Autumn of 1941.

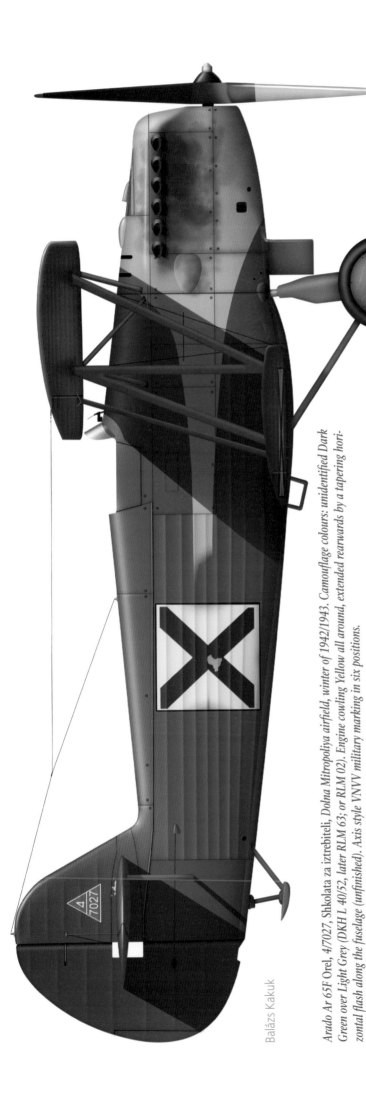

Balázs Kakuk

Arado Ar 65F Orel, 4/7027, Shkolata za iztrebiteli, Dolna Mitropoliya airfield, winter of 1942/1943. Camouflage colours: unidentified Dark Green over Light Grey (DKH L 40/52, later RLM 63; or RLM 02). Engine cowling Yellow all around, extended rearwards by a tapering horizontal flash along the fuselage (unfinished). Axis style VNVV military marking in six positions.

At one point in 1942, the light grey overall livery gave way to the more military-like dark green (the bottom surfaces stayed light grey). The wraparound engine cowling, along the rearward tapering flash along the fuselage, became 'Axis yellow' instead of red. This was the camouflage scheme the last soldiering Orels wore until they were scrapped in 1944/1945. Notice how the original light grey colour the mid-fin triangle had been applied on remained unpainted.

Focke-Wulf Fw 56 *Komar*
Bulgaria's First German Fighter-Trainer

The Fw 56 was developed by Focke-Wulf *Flugzeugbau AG* to meet the demand of the Reich's Air Ministry (*Luftfahrtministerium*) for an advance training aircraft, which could also be used, if needed, as 'light home defence fighter.' The nimble little aircraft, baptised *Stößer* (sparrow hawk) by its designer, Dipl.-Eng. Dr. Kurt Tank, Focke-Wulf's chief engineer, which could be fitted with a pair of machine guns, took off for the first time in November 1933. Subsequently, a total of 495[1] Fw 56s were built, including all export units[2], by the end of 1936.

One of the first foreign powers to be interested in purchasing the *Stößer* was Bulgaria. The negotiations soon led to signing a contract with Focke-Wulf *Flugzeugbau* GmbH on 8 June 1936. The contract called for six aircraft, sold for a unit price of 37,007 RM, to be delivered by February 1937. An *Antrag Reichsbürgschaft*, dated 14 July 1936, reinforces the details included in the contract. Delivery was set to February 1937. In fact, all Fw 56A-1s[3], powered by an Argus As 10C-3 V8 engine of 240 hp, were shipped to Bulgaria[4] earlier, on 1 December 1936, and arrived in Sofia ten days later.[5] The aircraft

---

1   This data is retrieved from original Focke-Wulf production figures. Other sources mention a total of 394, or 445 aircraft, including all exports, which are erroneous.

2   Little known fact is that three regular production aircraft – having duplicate production numbers, with a J suffix! – originally ordered by Yemen in 1936, eventually ended up in Spain, in the Republican camp. Other export sales: 1 to Bolivia, 30 to Hungary, 9 to Austria, 1 to Brazil.

3   Interestingly, these Bulgarian export aircraft were not officially assigned with the K suffix, as other European export Fw 56s were (e.g., KA-1 and KA-2 to Hungary, and KD-1 to Austria).

4   Excerpt from export document: „*To be delivered with 1 parachute, 1 gun installation (1 magazine), 1 bomb rack.*"

5   Hefty commissions have been paid by Focke-Wulf AG to Dr. Eng. Christo Gheneff (1000 RM), Georg Georgieff (1524 RM) and *Generalkonsul* Albert Gorgas, Sofia (8% on material cost and 2% on parts, 1% advance payment paid, 4574 RM).

High Army brass inspect the recently delivered Fw 56A-1s in early 1937. Notice the absence of wings (gold for generals, silver for officers) flanking the standard tricolour oval cap cockade on the officers' service caps that would identify them as air force officers.

136

selected to be exported to Bulgaria had the following *Werknummern* (construction numbers): 1853, 1854, 1981, 1982, 1983 and 1984.

As soon as they arrived in Bulgaria and were handed over on 14 December 1936, the Focke-Wulf fighter trainers were assigned to the 3. *Iztrebitelen Orlyak* (two aircraft to each of the three *yata*). Later, they moved to a top training unit of the VNVV, namely *Shkola za Vissh Pilotazh* (High Aerobatics Piloting School). This élite piloting school was part of the *2-i Iztrebitelen Orlyak* (2nd Fighter Group), based at Marno Pole/Karlovo airfield. It was headed by *Poruchik* Krăstyu A. Atanasov, seconded by his deputy, *Poruchik* Chudomir M. Toplodolski. Among the flying instructors of the school were the following *Podporuchiki*: Lyuben Z. Kondakov, Stoyan I. Stoyanov (future top scoring Bulgarian 'ace'), Vasil P. Shishkov and Dimităr G. Tamahkyarov. The six machines were allocated to the *Ucheben Orlyak* (Training Group). Although trainers, the *Komars* received the same numbering system as the two fighter types in service at that time, the P.24 *Yastreb* and the He 51 *Sokol*.

As usual with the new aircraft types that entered service with the VNVV, the Fw 56 (identified in early Bulgarian documents as the untranslatable Щоселите, or *Shtoselite* – possibly reference to the original German name *Stößer*, i.e., sparrow hawk – or simply FKW), also received a code name, *Komar* (Gnat) on 18 August 1937. Soon after, the type was assigned with the *Nomenklaturen Nomer* (NN) category of 7003, which identified the type as 'fighter-trainer' (last digit 3). As seen by the NN, the Fw 56 was the first fighter-trainer type of the Bulgarian air force.

The Fw 56 proved to be an instant success with Bulgarian pilots, instructors and students alike. Its outstanding flying characteristics were much appreciated, as was the easy handling by beginners. The added feature of the possibility to fire machine guns was a welcome bonus. Therefore, the *Komars* were used extensively for training, including 'dogfighting' drills.

Based on his logbook, 'old hand' *Kpt.* Dimităr I. Makazchiev, born in 1909, flew aboard *Komar* No. 22-10 at Bozhurishte main air base between 24 and 27 July 1938. Renowned pilot instructor *Ppor.* Petăr D. Manolev flew the *Komar* for the first time on 6 November 1939. He took the same No. 22-10 in the morning on a 20 minutes accommodation flight. Manolev repeated the flight in the afternoon, with the same aircraft, which also lasted 20 minutes. In the next weeks and months, Petăr Manolev flew the *Komar* often, as detailed in Annex 2 (available on-line, see page 141).

Five out of six Fw 56s line up on the snow covered landing ground on a sunny winter day. One would initially assume the sole aircraft that was destroyed in a crash, 22-9, is missing; however, a close look at the photo reveals that this very aircraft is the middle one. The steel skeleton of a large hangar being built can be observed in the background, at right.

Engine on! A pilot prepares for takeoff, while another one receives last-minute instructions prior to his own takeoff.

The student pilot of a Komar performs a low level bank to the right during an early morning training flight.

On 16 February 1943, Poruchik Nikola Vălchev of the 6th Fighter Regiment was flying Komar No. 1 *on a routine flight from Marno Pole to Kazanlăk, when the engine quit in mid-air. The pilot tried to land with his powerless aircraft; however, it turned over upon attempting to taxi in thick snow. The wing under surface looks very dark, in contrast to the clearly light blue painted wing struts. This is not in line with the other photos that show it as painted in a shiny light colour .*

On 18 November 1939, the following five *Komar* trainers were part of the aforementioned piloting school: 11-9, 11-10, 22-10, 33-9 and 33-10. Of these, only two were serviceable (11-9 and 22-10), while the other three were at the DSF Workshop for overhaul. The sixth *Komar* (22-9) is missing from the list; it had most probably been destroyed earlier. Officially, it was written off only on 10 June 1940; however, as usual with the cumbersome bureaucracy within the Bulgarian army, the actual incident had happened much earlier, only the write-off paperwork was filled at this date.

In 1941, a total of four Fw 56s were available. Of these, two were damaged in accidents. On 27 December 1941, *Komar* NN 5/7003 was located at Kazanlăk airfield. As it turns out, this particular Fw 56 will be the last one to soldier on until beyond the war's end.

The sole accident we have details about happened on 16 February 1943. *Poruchik* Nikola Vălchev of the 6th Fighter Regiment was flying *Komar* 1/7003 on a routine flight from Marno Pole to Kazanlăk, when the engine quit in mid-air, at around 11:30. The pilot tried to land with his powerless aircraft; however, it turned over upon attempting to taxi in thick snow south of Kazzanlăk. The pilot was lucky, as he escaped alive. Based on the post-accident photos, the aircraft was repairable. (See photos on the bottom of the page).

A report dated 28 Dec. 1944 lists, among other old trainers, *Komars* Nos. 1 and 6 as *"really worn, low security in flight, therefore they are already considered as unserviceable, thus have to be written off."*

Radiogram (radio transmitted telegram) dated 23 August 1945 lists the cipher (code letter) assigned to each aircraft type, for briefer communication. *Komar* was assigned with the letters 'Ko'.

The last Focke-Wulf trainer, 5/7003, was written off on 15 October 1946, closing the chapter of this nimble little aircraft in Bulgarian service. The choice made in mid-1936 proved to be the right one, as the *Komar* turned out to be an excellent tool in preparing Bulgarian fighter pilots for combat activity.

Camouflage and markings

As with the other aircraft types in Bulgarian service, there is no concrete information available linking the Fw 56 *Komar* to any particular paint, or colour shade. Nevertheless, one can assume that the Dark Green over Light Blue livery carried by these aircraft on arrival in Bulgaria were standard German colours available at that time, possibly supplied by company Herbig-Haarhaus. Therefore, the Author *assumes* the standard early *Luftwaffe* hues were used: RLM 62 Green and RLM 65 Blue. Obviously, this is only an assumption, which can be overruled if quality colour photos are unearthed, or more detailed information becomes available from Bulgarian archives. Therefore, no further details are given in the legend of the colour profiles other than the general colour hues (Dark Green and Light Blue).

The Dark Green colour was possibly obtained by using the following paint: *grün für camouflage* BC.6954/6663 by Herbig-Haarhaus (HH), while the Light Blue by possibly using the following paint: *blau* BC.6954/6663, also by Herbig-Haarhaus.

The Bulgarian tricolour was applied on the rudder using the following Herboloid paints: *'fahnengrün'* (Flag Green), *'fahnenweiss'* (Flag White) and *'carminrot'* (Crimson Red), all of the same BC.6954/6663' type finishing paint. Colour *'schwarz'* (black) of the same paint family was used for lettering and markings. After March 1941, the yellow Axis ID markings were brushed on the engine cowling, rudder and elevators using *'gelb-schwach-orange'* (Light Orange Yellow) paint. Interior surfaces may have been painted with *'grau'* (Grey) BC.9022, or *'silber'* (Silver) BC.6954/6663. The diluent (thinner) used for all these aircraft paints was identified by Herbig-Haarhaus as BC.2787. Later on, from about April 1942, the more advanced single-layer BC.12431 type of aircraft finishing paints and lacquers by the same German manufacturer were most probably used as the top layer of the airframes that needed a new coat of paint.

As for markings and codes, the Fw 56s were identified with white serial numbers, 11, 22 or 33, on the rear fuselage, and 9 or 10 on the mid rudder. The meaning of these numbers is not fully explained; however, the Author believes the fuselage numbers refer to different *yata* (squadrons), i.e. 11 referring to the 1st *Yato*, 22 to the 2nd *Yato*, while 33 to the 3rd *Yato* of a particular *orlyak* (group). The number on the rudder may have referred to the place a particular machine had in a particular *dvoyka* (pair). For example, aircraft No. 11-9 was the first aircraft of the Fw 56 pair of the first squadron, while aircraft

Another line up of a Komar trio at dawn (notice the long shadows), this time including (from right to left) 33-9, 11-10 and 33-10. The engine of the first aircraft is already running, and the entrance door is opened, ready to accommodate the pilot.

Line-up of Heinkel He 51 fighter biplanes, led by a Focke-Wulf Fw 56 trio, in preparation for one of the many parades. In centre, Komar No. 33-10, is visible. Eleven fighter pilots – some faces being familiar, often seen on other photos – casually pose for this shot taken at Bozhurishte airfield, in 1939.

No. 33-10 was the last aircraft of the Fw 56 pair in the third squadron. A couple of fighter aircraft types using the same numbering style[6] were the PZL P.24 *Yastreb* (tail numbers from 1 to 4) and the Heinkel He 51 *Sokol* (tail numbers from 5 to 8).

By late 1940, this early style two-code numbering system gave way to the standard Bulgarian aircraft identification, consisting of only an Arabic number for a particular aircraft type (identified by its NN). It was applied in white on the fuselage, aft of the military marking, and in black on the wing under surfaces. Uniquely to the Bulgarian air force, the typical VNVV identification triangle was not applied

6   Similar numbering style was also used by Heinkel He 45s, Focke-Wulf Fw 58s and Dornier Do 11s.

Another line-up led by two Fw 56s, also in company of He 51s, six of them. Although the identity of the Komar, 33-9, is apparent, the He 51 near it can be identified only by its unique writing on the lower wing's undersurface: мин on the starboard and борЪ on the port side. When read together, it means Miner, and was written in honour of the coal miners of Pernik, who reportedly paid for the aircraft.

on the tail surface (usually on mid-fin) of the Fw 56s, as this particular aircraft type did not have a fin per se. For the few aircraft that survived long enough to be serviceable after the Bulgarian about-face of 9 September 1944, a white band must have appeared on the fuselage, along with white wingtips, although there is no photographic evidence that supports this plausible scenario.

Additional info see:
http://mmpbooks.biz/assets/
BFC/04.pdf

This pair of scans of original negatives depicts Komar 33-10 during a work day on the airfield.

Above: Another original negative that depicts a Fw 56, possibly 33-10. The airman in front of the Komar is Svetoslav Spirov, future pilot in the 5ᵗʰ Bomber Group and active member of the post-war veterans' association.

Left: Yet another line-up of a Komar trio, this time 11-10 (subject of a colour profile), 11-9 and one of the two aircraft that had 22 on its fuselage. Snapshot taken on Marno Pole/Karlovo airfield, in late 1930s.

Some sort of ceremony is being held at Yambol landing ground, in 1937, as confirmed by the writing on the original photo's back. In the background, centre, three Fw 56s can be identified. Each of them has different pair of numbers on their fuselages: 11, 22 and 33. At right, two domestically produced DAR-3, Series 2, trainers are visible. LZ-DIO was the last unit of the second short series of six aircraft (c/n 74).

Another ceremony, involving a priest, this time the Komar being the protagonist.

This time, a Fw 56 Komar fighter trainer, at right, is depicted in company of a Bücker Bü 131 primary trainer (LZ-BUM), at left. The presence of the women points to the possibility of some sort of 'open day' at the airfield.

Preparing a Komar for a training sortie from Bozhurishte airfield, in 1939. The pilot's parachute is lying on the ground.

143

After all training flights were concluded, student pilots and their instructors gather for a group photo near one of the piloting school's Komars. The yellow wraparound engine cowling reveals that the photo must be taken after April 1941.

This is probably the last known photo of a Fw 56 with the so-called 'Tsarist roundel' type of military marking. Luckily, the precise date and location were recorded on the print: Karlovo airfield, 12 March 1940. At left, the aircraft type is also given: Komar. A couple of Arado Ar 65Fs are visible in the background.

In late June 1940, the new military marking was introduced, symbolising 'St. Andrew's Cross', in line with other Axis air forces. Shortly after, the early style two-code numbering system gave way to the standard Bulgarian aircraft identification, consisting of only an Arabic number for a particular aircraft type. This new configuration is illustrated by this photo, featuring No. 1 (NN 1/7003) closest to the camera. It's interesting to note that this aircraft type was the only one in VNVV service that did not have the typical triangle applied on the tail surface, as the airframe construction lacks a rudder, the typical location the triangle was applied on.

This photo, scanned form an original negative from the Popganchev collection, shows Komar No. 1, which bellied in a maze field at an unspecified date.

Three-quarter view of Fw 56, No. 5. This time, the flash along the fuselage is yellow.

Silhouette study of the port side of the same machine, No. 5, taken sometimes in April–May 1941. At this time, the fuselage flash was painted in Axis yellow. This particular Fw 56 was the last one to soldier on until beyond the war's end.

Balázs Kakuk

Focke-Wulf Fw 56A-1 Komar, 11-10, pilot Kpt. Ivan S. Ivanov, Bozhu-rishte airfield, 1 February 1937. Camouflage colours: Dark Green upper surfaces, Light Blue under surfaces. Roundel-style national marking in six positions. Rudder in Bulgarian tricolour (White, Green, Red). Red wrap-around engine cowling and fuselage flash. Spinner Black/Red.

Fine silhouette study of the starboard side of Fw 56A-1, 11-10, which reveals the VNVV markings and codes used in the early phase of service. Another, better quality view of the port side of the same aircraft can be seen on pages 139 and 142.

Balázs Kakuk

Focke-Wulf Fw 56A-1 Komar, 5/7003, 'White 5', 6. Iztrebitelen Polk (6th Fighter Regiment), Kazanlük, 1943. Camouflage colours: Dark Green upper surfaces, Light Blue under surfaces. Cross-style national marking in six positions. Yellow engine cowling and rudder. Red fuselage flash. Spinner Black/Yellow.

The tree-quarter view of Komar No. 5 reveals the marking and code applied on the lower wing surface. The engine cowling and rudder had been painted in yellow Axis recognition colour. The fuselage flash is in red.

Avia B.534 *Dogan*
The Ageing Czech Biplane

Following the occupation by Wehrmacht troops of what was left of Czechoslovakia on 15 March 1939, a large number of ex-Czechoslovak Air Force (Československé vojenské letectvo) aircraft ended up in German custody. This huge spoil of warplanes included over 350 Avia B.534 fighters of various models, in various conditions. Seventy-two of these in airworthy status were eventually sold to Bulgaria in November 1939, at deep discount, along with six more intended for spare parts. Depicted is a freshly captured Avia B.534-IV, with hastily applied Luftwaffe crosses (without the customary white borders) on its wings. Pilsen (Plzeň) airfield, late March 1939.

"*I rubbed my eyes in total disbelief. Which war was this anyway? World War One? It was like entering a time warp. Suddenly, these little biplanes appeared, for all the world, like old Curtiss Hawks. I was so surprised that, by the time I realised that they are firing at us, they were gone!*" – so remembers a B-24D 'Liberator' waist gunner describing his incredulous sighting over Bulgaria while returning from the epic Operation 'Tidal Wave' of 1 August 1943. There was nothing wrong with his eyesight; those enemy aircraft that attempted to intercept the US bombers were indeed biplanes. Unbeknown to the American airman, that particular interception was performed by ex-Czechoslovak Avia B.534 biplane fighters of the 1/6. *Iztrebitelen Orlyak*, based at the two military airfields nearby Sofia, Bozhurishte and Vrazh-debna. It was their second attempt, as they had also scrambled in the morning, when the 'Liberator' armada headed towards the Rumanian oilfields around Ploeşti. At that time, the Bulgarians were unsuccessful in catching up with the fast flying intruders. However, they were now waiting for them to return, to make a second attack. Indeed, scrambled in time, the biplanes managed to gain enough height to get up close to the bombers and fire their rifle calibre machine guns upon the huge 'furniture vans'[1]. The damage done by the 7.92 mm bullets was negligible, however. Nevertheless, it was the first time the Bulgarian Avia biplanes could fire their guns in anger.

* * *

How did the nimble Czech fighter type end up in Bulgaria? By pure chance, one could argue. It was 'thanks' to the German invasion of what was left of Czechoslovakia, on 15 March 1939, that a large number of ex-Czechoslovak Air Force (*Československé vojenské letectvo*) aircraft ended up in German custody. This large spoil of warplanes included about 350 Avia B.534 fighters of various models, in various conditions. Additionally, production of the 'standard' B.534 at the Avia Company (*Avia akciová společnost pro průmysl letecký Škoda*), a branch of the enormous Škoda Works (*Škodovy závody*) heavy machinery and military industrial enterprise, continued under German supervision up until April 1939, while manufacturing of the cannon-fitted version, the Bk.534, lasted until March 1940. In total, 445

---

1   *Möbelwagen – Luftwaffe* code name for the US four-engine bombers.

Famous Bulgarian aviator and test pilot Kapitan Inzh. (Capt. Eng.) Petko N. Popganchev enjoys a moment of tranquillity and reads a hand-written letter in front of a freshly assembled Avia B.534, still devoid of any markings. The peculiar Bulgarian identification triangle had been applied on mid-fin; with the Nomenklaturen Nomer (7037) barely visible in the triangle's denominator. A second still reveals the aircraft's individual serial number, written on the top of the triangle: 16. Based on his logbook, Kpt. Popganchev test flew Dogan No. 16 off Bozhurishte air base on 17 April 1940 – the likely date this particular photo was taken.

B.534s (all variants, c/n 001-445, not including two for Greece) and 121 Bk.534s (regarded as separate type, c/n 501-621) were produced by Avia[2].

As noted above, of the total number of Avia B.534s extant in March 1939, about 350 ended up in German hands during the invasion, the number completed by about 140 units produced under German supervision. These 'trophies' were concentrated at the airfields of Merseburg, Erding and several others, from where they were later assigned to their new owners. Many of these biplanes ended up in *Luftwaffe* service, first as stop-gap fighters[3], for a brief period – three were actually used as carrier-based test aircraft – then as fighter trainers, or glider towing machines, but a sizeable number proved to be superfluous. Of these, over 90 ended up in Slovak service[4], while the Chinese deal fell through. Not having an immediate customer, Berlin decided to offer them to one of its steady allies – Bulgaria. On 13 September 1938, the Bulgarian Military Attaché in Berlin cabled Sofia the good news, that GFM Göring had approved the sale of airplanes to Bulgaria, by a credit of 4 million *Reichsmarken*. The Bulgarians, desperate to fill in the gap of a first-line fighter type, but short on cash, argued for a while and finally struck a bargain. The deal called for slightly over 200 warplanes (including a significant number of Avia B.534 fighters), 50 spare aero engines and 143,000 bombs of various calibres, to be delivered in several batches[5]. The initial main deal was completed later on by several smaller ones. From the German side, it was the *Wirtschaftsgruppe Luftfahrtindustrie*, located in Berlin, which was in charge with the German armament exports.

There is a significant controversy in the published literature of the total number of Avia B.534s in active Bulgarian service. The number ranges from 48 to 100. However, only two are most often quoted by otherwise reliable printed sources: 72[6], or 78[7] units[8]. Nonetheless, the Author firmly believes it is a third number, namely 77, which is the correct one. The reasoning behind this statement is the follow-

---

2   At the time of the so-called 'Munich Crisis' of September 1938, about 370 of these aircraft were still extant by the ČVL of the 420 pcs. manufactured by then. Several defected to the Soviet Union. One ended up in Hungary, another one in Spain.

3   The *Luftwaffe* even organized conversion courses to the Czechoslovak fighter type, called Avia *Lehrgang*, located at Herzogenaurach and Bad Aibling.

4   79 B.534 and 11 Bk.534 are identified as in service with the SVZ, or Slovak Air Force.

5   Information from *Lieferungen von deutschen Flugzeugen und Flugmotoren an verbundete und neutrale Staaten vom 1.1.1936 bis 30.9.1942* and *Aus beutebestanden des Reichsluftfahrtministeriums gelieferte Flugzeuge und Motoren (bis 10.12.1942)*

6   e.g. Yordan Milanov: *Văzdushnite Voyski na Bălgaria prez voynite*, 1912-1945, 'Eăr Grup 2000', Sofia, 2008, p. 209.

7   e.g. Dimitar Nedialkov: The History of Bulgarian Air Power, Albatros MDV, Sofia, 2012, p. 131.

8   A German letter dated 09.12.1942 lists among the 204 Czech aircraft purchased by the Bulgarians in 1939: *"Jäger B 534 – 75 Stück."* (i.e., B 534 fighter- 75 pcs.). Unfortunately, this information does not really help in clarifying the total number of Avia B.534s sold to Bulgaria, as it does not fit any calculus.

Page scanned from an original copy of Die Kriegsflugzeuge der Staaten Südost-Europas *(Warplanes of the Countries of South-Eastern Europe), edited by* der Oberbefehlshaber der Luftwaffe, *published in December 1940, depicting an Avia Bk.534 with false Bulgarian markings. This particular retouched factory photo was copied post war and used by various authors to prove the existence of the cannon-armed version of the Avia fighter in Bulgarian service – which was not the case, however.*

Anlage 23

Bulgarien

Jagdeinsitzer Avia B. 534

Snapshot of a Bulgarian pilot taken in a freshly assembled Avia B.534 on a cloudy day in the late winter of 1940. There are no markings visible on either depicted aircraft. Notice the three silver coloured underwing bomb racks mounted on both wing surfaces, suitable for 10 kg splinter bombs.

ing: it is now known that in total four (or even five) protocols were signed between the German and Bulgarian partners. Three of them are known from German sources, the ones signed on the following dates: 19.8.1939, 26.2.1940 and 2.3.1940. There are references to a fourth and a fifth one as well, with only scant details being available, however. The first protocol called for 60 "used Ba 534 fighters" to be delivered (along with 20 Avia 12 Ydrs engines), the second one for eight more, while the last one for four more. In total: 72 aircraft. This number is reinforced by a comprehensive list of German aircraft export-ed to friendly and neutral states[9], which also mentions 72 "Bn 534 fighters", delivered in 1940 – and nothing more for the next years. Alongside aircraft, 32 HS 12Ydrs spare engines were delivered as well. Luckily, details of the elusive fourth protocol can be found in a Bulgarian air force document, dated 26 September 1940. It is mentioned in it that five Avia B.534s, delivered by the protocol of 4 December 1939 (sic!), were refurbished at a DSF Workshop instead of being scrapped. Most interesting is their listed serial numbers: Nos. 73-77! This document, signed by *Polkovnik letets* (aviation colonel) Konstantin Uzunski, Chief of Air Force HQ, reveals several highly interesting details, namely that the so-called 'fourth' protocol was, in fact, the second one, based on the date of the signature. Also, it suggests that the mentioned five Avia B.534s had to be extensively refurbished, meaning that they arrived in a poor state. The author argues that these battered airframes were sold by the Germans as spare parts only, that is why they do not show up in the comprehensive (airworthy) aircraft export list, quoted above.

Line-up of six recently delivered Avia B.534s at Marno Pole/Karlovo main fighter air base (the tower typical of this airfield is visible at right, which would be covered in camouflage paint later on). Only a half yato (squadron) is seen on the photo, the other half is probably lined up at left, facing this row, outside the camera's lens. Closest to the camera, without wheel covers, is No. 5/7037, while the second one might be No. 18, or 19/7037.

---

9   Source: *Lieferungen von Flugzeugen, Flugmotoren und Bomben (einschlieslich Lieferungen aus Beutebeständen) an das verbündete und neutrale Ausland in der Zeit vom 1.1.1937 bis 31.8.1943.*

Based on Bulgarian sources, there was a possibly fifth protocol, more precisely an appendix 3B to the original protocol of 18.08.1939, dated 22.11.1939. The date makes it the second protocol in chronological order. This one lists spare parts purchased for the following airplane models: "*BN 534, S 328, B 71, MB 200 and BS 122*". Additionally, the following airplanes with damaged engines were also shipped as spare parts: "*1 pc. BN 534 and 5 pcs. S 328.*" It is uncertain if this single Avia B.534 was ever restored to flying status, or it was actually used for spare parts, as per the original intention. Certainly, the five Letovs were not restored to flying condition, as the overall number would not match the total number actually in Bulgarian service. The Author believes the Avia had the same fate. Had this single Avia been restored to flying status, it must have happened before the five units listed in the afore-quoted fourth protocol; therefore, the numbering of the last batch of five aircraft would have started with 74. But it did not; it started with 73 and ended in 77. The confirmation of this theory would make the difference between a total of 77 or 78 Avia B.534s in actual Bulgarian service.

Let's recapitulate the protocols listed by chronological order, and the number of B.534s included in them:

- Protocol #1. Date: 18.8.1939. No. of B.534s: 60 (used, in flying condition). VNVV S/N 1-60 (confirmed).
- Protocol #2. Date: 22.11.1939. No. of B.534s: 1 (sold as spare parts). VNVV S/N (?, probably none).
- Protocol #3. Date: 4.12.1939 [referred to on 26.09.1940]. No. of B.534s: 5 (initially sold as spare parts, but restored to flying condition in mid-1940). VNVV S/N 73-77 (confirmed).
- Protocol #4. Date: 26.2.1940. No. of B.534s: 8 (used, in flying condition). VNVV S/N 61-68 (probable).
- Protocol #5. Date: 2.3.1940. No. of B.534s: 4 (used, in flying condition). VNVV S/N 69-72 (probable).

Total: 72 used aircraft in flying condition (matches the overall number given in the German export overview), plus 5+1 = 6 pcs., sold as spare parts only. Of these, five aircraft were confirmed as restored to flying condition, while the status of the last one is in limbo, believed by the author that it was actually used as spares. Thus: 78 airframes sold, in total, by the Germans, of which 77 were restored to flying condition (VNVV s/n 1-77).

The confirmation of the theory put forward by the author comes from an unexpected source: US intelligence files. A confidential report originating from the US Embassy in Turkey by the military attaché Maj. Louis J. Fortier, dated 9 July 1940, refers to a comprehensive list of aviation matériel originating from Germany and Italy, which was transported across Yugoslav territory and delivered to Bulgaria in the period of 1 September 1939 and 31 May 1940. This document dated 6 June 1940 – coming from Yugoslav Army General Staff through a spy, and categorised by the US functionary as 'extremely reliable' – mentions 73 "Avia BH-534s". The numbers indeed add up: 60 (first protocol), 1 (second protocol, as the customs officials were not interested in the technical state of the airframes found on railway wagons, they counted pieces), 8 (fourth protocol) and 4 (fifth protocol). In total 73 units. Apparently, the last five aircraft contained in the third protocol were delivered later on, after 31 May 1940, which is in line with the VNVV letter dated only on 26 September.

There is trace in Bulgarian documents of Avia No. 77[10, 11], and a photograph that almost certainly shows number 77 on an Avia airframe exists as well. In contrast, the author found no trace of aircraft No. 78. The above demonstration settles the issue of the number of aircraft in active Bulgarian service, as far as the author is concerned. Summing up: in total, 78 Avia B.534 airframes arrived in Bulgaria, but only 77 became operational.[12]

Another controversial issue related to the Avia B.534s sold to Bulgaria is their actual sub-type. Again, various conflicting information circulates in the printed and electronic media. It is often mentioned that alongside the machine gun armed models (version IV and V), the cannon-armed Avia Bk.534 also ended up wearing Bulgarian markings. To illustrate this claim, Czech authors (and at least one prominent Bulgarian one as well) publish a photo of this sub-type, easily recognisable by its single cannon trough running along the front fuselage side, in contrast with a pair of such troughs peculiar to the machine gun equipped 'standard' B.534. However, on the 'proof' photo the Bulgarian markings visible on the rear fuselage were actually retouched.

---

10 Prominent airman and test pilot, *Kpt.* Petko Popganchev flew No. 77 on 19.08.1940.

11 Aircraft No. 77/7037 was officially written off on 28.12.1945.

12 After the manuscript had been closed, prominent Czech researcher Jaroslav Kreč, who studied *in extenso* the story of the service of Avia B.534 in Bulgaria, confirmed to the Author that he also identified 77 *Dogans* in VNVV service. The only difference between the two independently performed researches is that Mr. Kreč didn't find the 78th airframe being sent to Bulgaria. He originates this difference to a typo made in a key Bulgarian document, when compared to the original German document (the Author had no access to).

The lower engine cowling of this Dogan was completely painted with a fresh layer of dark green that appears slightly darker than the fuselage's original Czecho-slovak-era greenish khaki. The rudder is dark painted, probably khaki like the airframe. The aircraft already carries the St. Andrew Cross-type military marking, consisting of a black X in a black bordered white square, introduced on 26 June 1940. There is no white serial number visible on the fuselage side. These details place the time the photo was taken in 1940, possible in the autumn, due to the warm clothing the airmen are wearing. The other airplane whose nose is seen in the hangar door, at left, also has the lower engine cowling painted in dark green.

The author managed to buy an original copy of an official wartime German booklet published in December 1940, which lists the major aircraft types of South-East Europe, including Bulgaria[13]. To his great surprise, the very same retouched photo of a Bk.534 in false Bulgarian markings (see photo on page 150) was used to illustrate the type's service in the Bulgarian air force! Apparently, this booklet was the original source, taken at 'face value' by post-war Czech and Slovak historians, then spread around unchecked. Therefore, it can be stated that the author found no credible proof of Bulgarian service of the cannon-armed Avia biplane. This makes sense, as except for the first three units, all cannon-armed Bk.534s were manufactured after Czechoslovakia was occupied by German troops. These brand-new aircraft were then used by the *Luftwaffe*, rather than be sold to the poor Balkan ally, which received only used aircraft – fair enough, at a deeply discounted price.

Finally, a few words about the various sub-types mentioned in German documents: Ba.534, Bn.534, BH-534, etc. The letter 'n' stands for 'night equipment'. However, not only the newer versions (the second half of production model IV and all model V) were capably of flying at night (or poor visibility conditions), but some older machines were upgraded to Bn.534 standard, their construction numbers remained the original ones. Moreover, there are only minor visual exterior differences between the standard B.534 and the Bn.534 version, in the form of small lamps on the rudder and on the lower wingtips, difficult to spot in photographs. Therefore, the author does not differentiate between these sub-types, unless quoted as such in documents. It has to be noted that the occasionally used Ba.534 and BH-534 sub-types are spurious.

In total, there were five production models, ranging from I to V. Bulgaria received mainly model IV (total number built: 229), but also a few model V (total number built: 41) and at least one model II ended up in VNVV service (total number built: 46). The latter model is easily recognisable by its shorter rear fuselage spine and bubble canopy (initially, this sub-type featured an open cockpit). The visual exterior difference between B.534, version IV and V, consists of the small window aft of the side canopy window. In series IV the rearward facing side window is oval, while in series V it is rectangular. The cannon-armed version was a separate series, called Bk.534 (k stands for cannon), irrelevant to the Bulgarian topic.

In VNVV service

The first connection between the Avia B.534 and Bulgaria the Author could identify is a brief entry in the logbook of a Bulgarian pilot. Based on this document, *Feldfebel-shkolnik* Georgi Stoyanov Geor-giev took part in a mission to inspect and test fly ex-Czechoslovak aircraft gathered at Merseburg, Germany. During his stay at this air base between 18 August and 18 October 1939, he performed twelve

---

13 *Die Kriegsflugzeuge der Staaten Südost-Europas* (Warplanes of the Countries of South-Eastern Europe), edited by *der Oberbe-fehlshaber der Luftwaffe, Führungsstab IC,* published in December 1940.

The first 'real' operation the Bulgarian Avia fighters were involved in was the recovery of Southern Dobrudzha (also called Quadrilateral) in September 1940. During the operation, Avia B.534s of 442ⁿᵈ Fighter Yato (Squadron), belonging to the 4ᵗʰ Army Air Polk (Regiment), flew missions over Dobrich and other cities located in the disputed region, as well as the roads where Bulgarian troops were advancing towards the new Rumanian border. Notice that none of the eleven Avias lined up at the edge of Buhovtsi airfield carry any individual numbers on fuselage, or rudder; they can be identified only by the small serial number applied in the triangle numerator on mid-fin.

landings aboard a *Dogan*[14], with a total flying time of two hours and forty minutes. These brief test flights were performed at 500 m altitude. Unfortunately, no further details are given.

The first shipment of 60 Avia B.534s arrived in Bulgaria in October 1939[15]. The disassembled airframes were packed on railway wagons. Upon their arrival, the crates were shipped to DSF Bozhurishte for assembly, refurbishment (as all aircraft were previously used) and test flight. Once airworthy and officially accepted, the Avias were registered with serial numbers ranging from 1 to 60, the number written in the standard triangle applied on mid-fin. Two other shipments of a dozen Avias in flyable condition had arrived in Bulgaria by May 1940. These became Nos. 61-72. They were followed in the summer by the aforementioned five worn units, originally intended as spare parts. After their lengthy

---

14 Besides the *Dogan*, Georgiev also test flew the *Vrana* and the *Osa*.

Neat row of nine AviaB.534s prepared for inspection at Bozhurishte airfield, probably in the Autumn of 1940.

15 An Avia B.534, carrying D-IWNF temporary civilian registration, was reported at *E-Stelle* Travemünde test centre in 1939. It could be that it was one of the aircraft eyed to be exported to Bulgaria (Note: this particular aircraft is not to be confused with the couple of Avia B.534s, also located at *E-Stelle* Travemünde – also wearing German civilian registers, D-IUIG and D-IUIO – involved in trials as carrier-borne aircraft, specifically intended for service aboard the abortive Graf Zeppelin carrier ship).

refurbishment, they were handed over to the air force only in July-August 1940, with the serial (board) numbers 73 to77[16].

Based on the little concrete information existing on the previous life of these Avias, they were of older production, as one would suspect. For example, aircraft NN 63/7037, involved in an accident on 11.09.1942, was built in 1937, while Nos. 30, 40, 50 were all built in 1938. Based on their serial numbers, the five worn B.534s, refurbished at DFS by September, were all built in 1938.

Not long after the first shipment of Avia B.534s, the aircraft type was officially assigned with a code name, *Dogan* (hunting falcon) (Order No. 116/16.11.1939). A *nomenklaturen nomer* (NN, registration number) was also assigned to the aircraft type, namely 7037. This means that the Avia B.534 was the fourth fighter type introduced in VNVV service. From then on, the Avia B.534 was mentioned in Bulgarian documents mostly by its code name and its NN, e.g. *Dogan* 7/7037, and only rarely as 'Авиа 534' (Avia 534), or 'Авиа Bn.534' (mixed Cyrillic and Latin letters).

It has to be highlighted that the Avia B.534 biplanes were delivered in the same time span as the Messerschmitt Bf 109E all-metal monoplanes, a type that represented a totally different class and was undisputedly superior to the nimble, but obsolescent, Czech biplane of mixed construction. Nevertheless, the total number of aircraft placed in service in Bulgaria made *the* difference. Of the Bf 109Es only 19 entered active duty with the VNVV, while of the Avia B.534 – as stated above – 77 units served. The

16 Prominent pilot *Kpt*. Petko Popganchev test flew No. 73 on 2 July 1940, while No. 77 on 19 August 1940.

An unidentified Dogan, seen from 11 o'clock. It may have been part of one of the fighter yata *of the four army-assigned air* polkove, *operating the Avia B.534. This possibility is supported by a variety of single- and multi-engine aircraft types seen in the background, just over the lower wing (a Junkers Ju 52 wing at extreme right, an Avia-MB.200 at right with an Avia B.71 near it, while at left a Letov Š.328 and a PZL.43 can be observed, just underneath the propeller blade). There is no yellow Axis identification colour applied yet, dating this photo pre-April 1941.*

Avia biplane remained the mainstay fighter aircraft of the VNVV until the arrival of the vastly superior Messerschmitt Bf 109G series, the ultimate fighter type the Bulgarians ever had in this period.

In anticipation of the influx of the large number of warplanes coming from Germany (occupied Czechoslovakia included), the VNVV commander detailed in Order No. 118 of 18 November 1939 the planned new structure of the air force. Accordingly, the existing mixed task army air groups (*orlyatsi*) were replaced by specialised *orlyatsi*, with specific tasks. As far as fighter aviation concerns, the existing 2nd Army Air *Orlyak* was renamed 2nd Fighter *Orlyak*, and was envisaged to have four fighter squadrons (*yata*), each equipped with 12-15 Avia B.534s, along with a training squadron. The advanced piloting school was also to be attached to this fighter group, unit which would also receive a number of Avia fighters. In total, a maximum of 65 Avias B.534s were to be allocated to this group.

The date of the first flight of an Avia B.534 in Bulgaria is uncertain. However, it must have happened

Planned Order of Battle of 2. *Iztrebitelen Orlyak* (Fighter Group) and *Shkola za Vissh Pilotazh* (Advanced Piloting School) (23.11.1939)

Personnel

Orlyak Commanding Officer: *Mahyor* Krăstyu M. Georgiev
Adjutant Officer: *Podporuchik* Marin G. Petrov
Training *Orlyak* and Advanced Piloting School Commanding Officer: *Kapitan* Stefan I. Măndev
Airfield *Yato* commander (2. *Let. Yato*): *Kapitan* Nikola D. Semerdzhiev
First fighter *yato* commander (212. *Yato*): *Kapitan* Kiril Y. Brăchkov
Second fighter *yato* commander (222. *Yato*): *Poruchik* Todor G. Yordanov
Third fighter *yato* commander (232. *Yato*): *Poruchik* Lyuben K. Shoroplev
Fourth fighter *yato* commander (242. *Yato*): *Poruchik* Vălyo T. Bozhikov
Training *yato* & advanced piloting school commander (22. *Uch. Yato*): *Poruchik* Krăstyu A. Atanasov
Advanced piloting school deputy commander: *Poruchik* Chudomir M. Toplodolski
Krilo commanders: *Podporuchiki* Aleksandăr H. Guntsev, Dimităr S. Lazarov, Asen D. Kovachev, Nikola G. Yordanov, Bogdan Y. Iliev, Dimităr S. Spisarevski.
     (...)
Equipment

First fighter *yato* (212. *Yato*): 12 'Dogan' (plus 3 reserves)
Second fighter *yato* (222. *Yato*): 12 'Dogan' (plus 3 reserves)
Third fighter *yato* (232. *Yato*): 12 'Dogan' (plus 3 reserves)
Fourth fighter *yato* (242. *Yato*): 12 'Dogan' (plus 3 reserves)
Training *yato* (22. *Uch. Yato*): 8 'Sokol', 4 'Osa'
Advanced piloting school: 5 'Komar', 3 'Vrabche', 6 'Lastovitsa', 11 'Orel', 8 'Osa', 3 'Sokol', 3-5 'Dogan'
Additional stock: 5 'Chuchuliga III'

in the early days of 1940, from Bozhurishte airfield, where the DSF Aviation Workshop was located. Completed aircraft were then flown to Marno Pole/Karlovo main air base, located in the centre of the country, home of the 2. *Iztrebitelen Orlyak* (Fighter Group). This happened sometime from February

1940 on. By the time all *Dogans* reached Marno Pole it was April. Each *yato* received twelve aircraft, plus reserves. The *Shkola za Vissh Pilotazh* (Advanced Piloting School), also working under command of the 2nd *Orlyak* at Marno Pole/Karlovo, was allotted a few Avia B.534s as well (one source puts the figure at ten).

Additionally, the 4th Army Co-operation *Orlyak*, based at Gorna Oryahovitsa, also had a fighter *yato*, with twelve Avia B.534s – at least based on a US military intelligence report[17], reflecting the situation existing in April 1940. According to the report, the 2nd *Orlyak*, based at "Karlovo-Levsky" airfield, had only three *yata* at that date, with 36 Avia B.534s in total, while the fighter training squadron, located at the same air base, had no B.534s at all, only 11 'Avia 122s'. It is further mentioned that 12 'Avia 534s', along with 17 other ex-Czechoslovak warplanes, were actually stored in two hangars at Vrazhdebna airfield. The total of Avia fighters is thus put at 60, which is consistent with the number of airplanes of the first batch that arrived in Bulgaria.

Despite there being a fair number of new fighters in VNVV service by the spring of 1940, they could not be engaged in any combat activity if need arose, as the number of pilots trained on the type was very low, not enough to man even a squadron, let alone a group. Besides technical and tactical shortcomings, the airmen's strategic vision was mixed as well. Quoting again a US intelligence report[18], reflecting the situation existing in early 1940: *"For lack of qualified men on the spot, there is a tendency to rely on foreigners to form and perfect the navigation and technical personnel. We are going to find in the formation of the personnel this same lack of homogeneity which we observed in the material. In re-entering from training periods abroad which are organised at random depending on political developments, Bulgarian aviators lack unity in doctrine. Therefore, there are as many conceptions of aeronautical matters as there are countries. (...) Formed in an organization framework with vague contours, haphazard instruments, the fighting force of the Bulgarian crews would be at present exceedingly weak."* It's worth further quoting a couple of sentences about the affiliation of the military personnel, in early 1940: *"Bulgarian military circles with very rare exceptions are very Germanophile and the majority of them tied the future of their country to that of Germany. (...) They are told especially of the nefarious activity carried on by the representatives of the Balkan countries which surround them, by the French and by the English, but there is [sic!] almost never any questions of the Germans who benefit from special favor."*

The first actual operational flights aboard *Dogans* took place before all aircraft were commissioned by the 2nd *Iztrebitelen Orlyak. Podporuchik* (2nd Lt.) Petăr Manolev, located at *Shkola za Iztrebitelni Letsi* (School for Fighter Pilots), as recorded in his logbook – the informal name of *Shkola za Vissh Pilotazh* (Advanced Piloting School) – flew the *Dogan* for the first time on 27 March 1940 (aboard no. 23), followed by a second flight three days later, aboard No. 39. A month later, he already flown aircraft No. 60,

The mix of markings makes this photo difficult to date. It appears that the rudder is painted in Bulgaria's national colours, which points to an early time period. However, the serial number – in this case 70 – is already applied in large white numerals on the rear fuselage, as well as in black on the outer extremities of the lower wing – features peculiar to later time period. The engine cowling underside surface is painted dark, which is also quite unusual, unless it's wraparound yellow, a colour shade that sometimes appears on black/white photos as a very dark hue. The unpainted propeller blades, left in their original bare metal, is an uncommon sight. Photo taken at Marno Pole/Karlovo main air base.

---

17 Report No. 31/14 October 1941, signed by Lt. Col. C.C. Jadwin, G.S., military attaché. Source: Military Intelligence Division, War Department, General Staff, Military Attaché Report, Bulgaria. I.G. No. 9100.

18 Report No. 33/23 October 1941, signed by Lt. Col. C.C. Jadwin, G.S., military attaché. Source: Military Intelligence Division, War Department, General Staff, Military Attaché Report, Bulgaria. I.G. No. 9210.

---

1 Presumably Johann Pühringer, born on 17 October 1914, who later served as an *Oberleutnant* with III./SKG 10 and III./SG 4. He was killed by enemy fighters on 6 June 1944, while ferrying an Fw 190 A-7 in France.

then No. 59 later on the same day. In May, he logged flying time aboard the following aircraft: Nos. 57, 51, 59, 47, 48, 56 and 50. He stayed at the school until 15 June, when he was transferred to Krusheto landing ground (near Gorna Oryahovitsa).

On 15 June 1940, the 2nd Army Mixed Group (*Armeyski Smesen Orlyak*) was formed at Graf Ignatievo airfield, with three squadrons (*yata*), as follows: the 221st *Yato*, based at Krumovo (equipped with 9 PZL.43 *Chayka* attack aircraft), the 222nd *Yato*, based at Kaloyanovo (equipped with 12 Avia B.534 *Dogan* fighters) and the 223rd *Yato*, based at Graf Ignatievo (equipped with 8 Letov Š.328 *Vrana* reconnaissance and light bombers). The group staff, headed by the 45-year-old commanding officer *Polkovnik* (Col.) Petăr D. Sapunov, also stayed at Graf Ignatievo air base. This interim organisation lasted only two weeks, as the *orlyak* (group) officially expanded to *polk* (regiment) size, along with other *orlyatsi* (groups), as detailed below.

By 1 July 1940, all existing homogenous, single-task *orlyatsi* (groups) were expanded to *polk* (regiment) size, and their task was mixed again. Each mixed task *polk* now comprised two *orlyatsi* (groups) and five *yata* (squadrons) in total. Two *yata* were assigned with reconnaissance, one *yato* was a so-called 'lineen' (ad verbatim 'linear', meaning battle, i.e., close support), another one a fighter, while the last one was a training *yato*. The first four *polkove* (regiments) were subordinated to the four armies, one for each, and thus renamed army (air) regiments Nos. 1 to 4. The 1st Army Air *Polk* was based at Bozhurishte, the 2nd at Graf Ignatievo, the 3rd at Yambol, while the 4th one at Gorna Oryahovitsa. In contrast, the existing 5th (bomber) *Polk*, located at Plovdiv, and the newly established 6th (fighter) *Polk*, located at Marno Pole/Karlovo, became independent from the armies. They received their own command structure and now were directly subordinated to the Bulgarian Army HQ. The number of aircraft allocated to each *yato* was reduced to nine, in order to be able to equip the increased number of *yata*.

The army-assigned four air *polkove* had a fighter *yato* each, as follows:
- 1st Army (Air) *Polk*: 112th *Iztrebitelno Yato* (based at Bozhurishte, C/O *Por.* Lyuben K. Shoroplev)
- 2nd Army (Air) *Polk*: 222nd *Iztrebitelno Yato* (based at Kaloyanovo, C/O *Por.* Todor G. Yordanov)
- 3rd Army (Air) *Polk*: 332nd *Iztrebitelno Yato* (based at Yambol, C/O *Por.* Nikola M. Videnov)
- 4th Army (Air) *Polk*: 442nd *Iztrebitelno Yato* (based at Karlovo, C/O *Por.* Pavel L. Pavlov)

Initially, the 6th *Iztrebitelen Polk* comprised of two *orlyatsi* (1/6th and 2/6th) that included three first-line fighter *yata* and two training *yata*. Each fighter *yato* had theoretically nine *Dogans*, while the training *yata* also had several *Dogans* assigned. In total, seven first-line fighter *yata* were using *Dogans* (theoretically 63 aircraft), while the remaining ones were employed by the training *yata* and the fighter pilots' school, or were kept as reserve.

Just days before the reorganisation of Bulgaria's air arm, the first fatal accident involving a *Dogan* occurred. While performing a training sortie, the biplane flown by *Podofitser* Stefan Vasilev Iliev of the 2nd *Iztrebitelen Orlyak* fell into a tailspin and crashed near Marno Pole airfield on 11 June. It was the first Bulgarian pilot to die aboard the Avia fighter, probably No. 3, and the only known casualty for 1940.

On 25 September 1940, the air park of the VNVV consisted of 595 aircraft, of which 258 were first-line combat types. Of this number, 83 were serviceable fighters, of which the *Dogan* accounted for 85.5%. This number of warplanes could be considered as adequate for a country of the size of Bulgaria. However, quality wise the air park was very diverse, ranging from the state-of-the-art Bf 109E to the

obsolete Aero MB.200 bomber. The Avia fighter biplane already ranked, by that date, as obsolescent, but still could face a second-rate enemy, like Greece (about 45 fighters of the 160 combat aircraft), or Turkey (about 60 fighters of the 250 combat aircraft)[19], on equal terms. However, if attacked simultaneously by both these antagonistic neighbours, the Bulgarians would have certainly been in a very hard, desperate, situation, if left alone without allies. It the end, neither scenario happened.

The Wind of War Reaches Bulgaria

The first 'real' operation Bulgarian airmen took part in was during the recovery of Southern Dobrudzha (also called Quadrilateral) in September 1940. This area, with a mixed ethnic population, located on the shores of the Black Sea, was awarded to Bulgaria following the Treaty of Craiova, Rumania, signed on 7 September 1940. To ensure the territory recovery operation took place smoothly, the VNVV Commander ordered, in secret letter No. 503/12.09.1940, the formation of a *Smesen* (mixed) *orlyak*, based on the 4th Army Air *Polk* assets. It consisted of a staff *krilo*, one army co-operation *yato* to be located at Shumen airfield, and one fighter *yato*, to be located at Buhovtsi landing ground, in north-eastern Bulgaria, close to Shumen. Accordingly, *Dogans* of the 442nd *Iztrebitelno Yato* of the 4th

19 Figures of the combat aircraft park strength of Greece and Turkey available in 1940 are based on Bulgarian estimations.

Two photos depicting Bulgarian airmen horsing around, in the vicinity of a Dogan. The biplane has its propeller spinner and engine cowling painted in yellow. Based on the tent and the field conditions seen in the background, chances are these shots were taken at the same military airfield around Sofia photographed by a German soldier, shown on top.

Dogan pilot Podofitser Vasil Shterev, member of the 1st Army Air Polk, seen in the cockpit of his mount, in the second half of 1941. Notice the thin, yellow mid-fuselage band just aft of the cockpit and the heavy weathering of the Bulgarian national marking. The aircraft is already adorned with the rearward tapering yellow fuselage 'flash', typical of fighters and fighter trainers.

Army Air *Polk* moved to the assigned base in mid-September to provide air cover for the takeover operation. A couple of experienced trainer pilots were assigned to this task, too. One of them was *Podporuchik* Petăr Manolev, who moved from Marno Pole air base to Buhovtsi aboard *Dogan* No. 66 on 17 September 1940. The fighters flew missions over Dobrich and other cities located in the disputed region, as well as the roads where Bulgarian troops were advancing towards the new Rumanian border.[20] One of the prominent pilots who took part in this air cover operation was *Podofitser* Anton B. Atanasov (called 'Schwarz', or Black, in German), a member of the 442nd *Iztrebitelno Yato*. The three-*yata* strong mixed *orlyak* stayed on these temporary landing grounds in North-Eastern Bulgaria until the takeover of the acquired territory was completed in early October[21].

Just weeks later, war broke out on the southern borders of Bulgaria, heightening the already existing tension in the area. On 28 October 1940, Italian troops crossed the Greek border, and initiated what would be known as the Italo-Greek war. Intense air activity took place in the vicinity of Bulgaria's southern borders. Despite occasional airspace violations by foreign aircraft, particularly Italian, Bulgaria managed to stay away from this local conflict – for the time being. During one such occasion when unidentified aircraft were spotted inside Bulgarian borders, a *Dogan* pilot, *Podofitser* Nikola Bonev of the 222nd Fighter *Yato*, scrambled to intercept the intruders. Not being able to catch them in time, he decided to continue the pursuit over Greek territory. Not being successful in his endeavour, the frustrated pilot decided to strafe ground targets instead, firing volleys of bullets at a bridge guarded by Greek soldiers. This reckless act drew a prompt protest by Greek authorities, and the undisciplined pilot was reprimanded.

By the operational order No. 1/25.11.40 of the Commander of the Air Force, the number of the fighter aircraft on permanent alert was increased (one fighter *krilo* of three aircraft from each army air *polk*, while the 6th Fighter *Polk* had to assign for this duty three *krila* of three aircraft each). The number of *Dogans* on permanent combat alert was thus 21, located on five different airfields and landing grounds. On the airfields used by each army air *polk*, air observation ground posts were established to warn if foreign, or unidentified, aircraft appeared in their assigned airspace. To avoid shooting at their own aircraft, the flight of Bulgarian aircraft over the anti-aircraft firing zones was forbidden, except when the artillerymen were forewarned. Between 23 November and 1 December 1940, the first anti-aircraft de-

20 A prominent fighter pilot, *Ppor.* Dimităr S. Spisarevski of the 222nd *Iztrebitelno Yato*, was born in Dobrich on 19 June 1916, town which was about to be 'liberated' from Rumanian rule. Upon hearing the news that his native town will become again part of Bulgaria, Spisarevski performed aerobatics and low-level fly-byes over Plovdiv (near Graf Ignatievo, home base of 222. *Yato*), to the amazement of the local people. However, his commanding officer was not amused by this unauthorised 'show off', and grounded him for a month, assigning him to mundane duties, hardly suitable for a hot-blooded pilot as Spisarevski was (see portrait photo on page 165, top).

21 *Ppor.* Manolev flew his last sortie from Buhovtsi on 3 September, aboard *Dogan* No. 41. He resumed training flight on Marno Pole four days later.

fence exercises were held involving all four regions assigned to the four army *polkove*. Specially selected aircraft represented the 'targets' that had to be 'downed'. The exercise was deemed a success.

The year of 1940 was peppered with accidents involving *Dogans*. This aircraft type held the infamous record in the Bulgarian air force of being involved in the largest number of accidents: 32. This figure amounted to 20.4% of the total number of aviation incidents recorded throughout the year. And the *Dogans* started their operational service only in about May! Altogether, 42.9% of the entire *Dogan* fleet was involved in some sort of accident, or incident. However, as noted above, only one fatal accident is known. Overall, 158 accidents were recorded by VNVV annals (one for every 764 flight hours). Interestingly, 99 accidents (62.6% of the total) involved combat aircraft, the rest were trainers and secondary duty aircraft. The reasons for so many accidents with combat aircraft were: improper training of pilots (53.6%), lack of proper judgment of airmen (28.7%), disregarded orders (9.6%) and carelessness (7.9%).

Beautiful study of the silhouette of Avia B.534-IV, No. 74. Interestingly, the rudder is painted in Axis yellow (possibly the elevators as well), there is a yellow mid-fuselage band as well; however, the engine cowling is still green wraparound and the rearward tapering 'cheatline' is missing as well. This particular aircraft was officially written off on 4 September 1945.

The beginning of 1941 was quite dynamic for Bulgaria. During the meeting of the Bulgarian premier prof. Bogdan Filov with the *Führer* at Obersalzburg on 4 January, it became clear that there was no more space for political manoeuvres; Bulgaria could not stand aside in the upcoming European upheaval. Adolf Hitler promised Tsar Boris III that Bulgaria would receive all the territory she had lost after World War I, in return for Bulgaria joining the Axis. The Bulgarian monarch eventually accepted the offer. Accordingly, the government in Sofia decided to join the 'Tripartite Pact' on 20 January, which was actually signed by PM Filov on 1 March. Bulgaria was now on the path to war.

According to the plans of the *Oberkommando der Wehrmacht* (OKW) shared with the Bulgarian Army Staff, in the second half of February 1941 the bulk of the Bulgarian army were to relocate south and south-east, to cover the volatile Greek and Turkish borders, thus securing the flanks of the would-be main thrust direction of the *Wehrmacht* (German army). Most Bulgarian aviation units were mobilised as well. Changes were planned in the air force structure yet again. From the existing fighter units three separate *orlyatsi* were planned to be formed:

1/1. [i.e., no. of the *orlyak*/no. of the *polk*] *Iztrebitelen Orlyak*, consisting of three fighter *yata* equipped with Avia B.534s – the ones from the 1st, 2nd and 4th Army Air *Polk*[22]. This planned new *orlyak* was based at Bozhurishte main air base. This air group consisted of 34 aircraft. [Not actually implemented. The three fighter *yata* remained under command of the 1st Army Air *Polk*, headquartered in Sofia].

1/6. *Iztrebitelen Orlyak*, consisting of one Bf 109E *yato* and one PZL P.24b *yato*, based at Asĕn landing ground. This air group consisted of 21 aircraft.

2/6. *Iztrebitelen Orlyak*, consisting of two Avia B.534 *yata*, based at Dăbene landing ground, south of Karlovo. This air group consisted of 24 aircraft.

---

22 On 26 May 1941, the following *Dogans* were reported as serviceable with the four Army Air *Polkove*: 1st A.A.P.: Nos. 49 and 70; 2nd A.A.P.: Nos. 19 and 63; 3rd A.A.P.: Nos. 33, 34, 38, 42, 43, 44; 4th A.A.P.: No. 56. Additionally, the 6th Fighter *Polk* listed the following ones: 28 and 62 (1st *Yato*), 11 and 36 (2nd *Yato*) and 6 and 62 (sic!) (3rd *Yato*). The Main Workshops repaired the following *Dogans*: 13, 36 (sic!), 40, 48, 52, 61, 71 and 73.

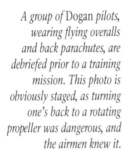

Nine Dogans *are lined up on the field, probably during manoeuvres, presumably in late 1941. They all have their nose sections painted yellow, which continued in a rearward tapering flash along the fuselage. There is no yellow recognition colour applied anywhere else. The aircraft's serial number is not yet painted on the fuselage side, aft the national marking, as it was the case later on.*

A group of Dogan *pilots, wearing flying overalls and back parachutes, are debriefed prior to a training mission. This photo is obviously staged, as turning one's back to a rotating propeller was dangerous, and the airmen knew it.*

Additionally, the 332nd *Iztrebitelno Yato* of 3rd Army Air *Polk*, equipped with 12 Avia B.534, strengthened with a Heinkel He 45 *yato* of the *Obraztsov* (Exemplary, or Model) *Orlyak*, was based on Okop landing ground, south of Yambol.

[Note: in total 34+24+12=70 *Dogans* were to be mobilised, along with other warplanes]

From 18 February on, a three-fighter *krilo* was kept 'on alert' in every *orlyak*, early air warning posts were established in different locations in case of enemy air intrusion and direct telephone connections were made with the command posts of every high unit.

On 28 February 1941, *Wehrmacht* units crossed from Rumania into Bulgaria over the River Danube. *Luftwaffe* units started their relocation on Bulgarian airfields as well. The German air units settled on many of the main airfields – e.g. Sofia, Plovdiv, Telish – but also on reserve airfields – e.g. Vărba, Kraynitsi, Belitsa, Krumovo, etc. The chief of the VNVV Staff ordered the commanders of his aviation units to report every 15 days about the German aviation units, their organization and structure, their equipment, down to single aircraft – all this for the sake of 'learning from the Germans' experience'.

The air defence of the Bulgarian capital was entrusted to the aforementioned 1st Army Air *Polk*, based at Bozhurishte, near Sofia. The fighter group mustered 34 Avia B.534s. The rest of the fighter units were kept on alert on various landing grounds around the country in case the potential enemy would attack from west, south, or south-east. The fighter element complemented the ground based anti-aircraft artillery element[23].

The first real combat activity of the *Dogans* happened during Operation 'Marita' – the *Wehrmacht* drive against Yugoslav and Greece. In early April 1941, the Avia B.534-equipped *yata*, deployed to various landing grounds, were placed on increasing alert. This was done in time, as enemy aircraft indeed penetrated Bulgarian airspace starting from the first day of war, 6 April. That day, at 08:35, a group

---

23 In April 1941, the ground based air defence of Sofia consisted of four Bulgarian heavy batteries, of four cannon each (two 8.8 cm and two 7.5 cm), five Bulgarian light artillery units (each with six 20mm cannon), two other 20 mm cannon-equipped units located at the two airfields (Bozhurishte and Vrazhdebna), three German heavy artillery batteries (8.8 cm), two German light batteries (20 mm), completed by three Bulgarian 150 cm and German 60 cm search lights.

of four Yugoslavian aircraft attacked Kyustendil (located only 20 km from the western border). The enemy bombers dropped eight bombs from 1,500 m height, which fell on the area of the rail station and on a nearby civilian district. An air alarm was not sounded, so there were many victims – 47 people and 11 horses killed, 95 people wounded (mostly civilians), many buildings destroyed. A little later, at 10:30, two Yugoslavian bombers dropped bombs over Gyueshevo as well. This time, there were no victims. In the afternoon, at 15:00, two more Yugoslavian aircraft flew across the border, north of Treklyano, near Kyustendil, in the direction of Radomir. One of these intruders dropped a bomb on the airfield at Vărba and later on the village of Sirishtnik, near

Pre-mission briefing of Dogan pilots during manoeuvres on what is believed to be Dăbene landing ground, located in the Karlovo area.

Radomir, again without victims. The other aircraft managed to reach Sofia and dropped eight bombs from 2,000 m height over the western part of the capital, then disappeared in the direction of Slivnitsa. Eight citizens were killed and twelve wounded, eight buildings were destroyed.

As darkness fell, from 20:05 to 21:10, unidentified enemy aircraft (actually British) dropped bombs on Petrich, Hotovo, on the Central rail station in Sofia and the nearby villages, on the German-used railway station, Delyan railway station and Boboshevo. In total, 43 bombs of 50 and 100 kg were dropped, along with a few incendiaries, in two distinct waves (20:05-20:20 and 20:55-21:10). The crews of the aircraft attacked the towns with machine gun fire, too. In total, 18 civilians were killed, 28 wounded, 14 buildings were destroyed and 3 fires were started. The panic was great, part of the population of the capital spent the night outside, fearing renewed air attacks. Bozhurishte airfield was targeted as well, with a total of 43 bombs of 50-100 kg calibre, 16 of which were duds. As noted earlier, there were 34 Avia B.534s based at Bozhurishte at that time. There is no information if any of them was destroyed or damaged by enemy bombs.

While Yugoslav bombers attacked in daylight, the night intruders were undoubtedly British. Air attacks against various Bulgarian targets continued over the next two days. After five days of lull due to bad weather, they resumed and continued on the 14th. That day, at 01:15 am, the railway station of Sofia was again attacked by a group of 8-10 bombers, from the attitude of 1,000-1,200m. Vrazhdebna airfield was attacked as well. In total, 64 bombs exploded (another 77 were duds), along with 20 incendiary bombs. Six more bombs fell on the nearby Busmantsi village, just east of the capital. Again, there is no information available if the bombs dropped on Sofia's second airfield destroyed or damaged any aviation matériel.

Bulgarian fighters attempted to intercept the daylight intruders. However, they were scrambled late and could not catch up with them. Anti-aircraft artillery was ineffectivet as well. Despite the preparations and air defence plans, the enemy could bomb Bulgaria with impunity.

On one occasion, a *Dogan krilo*, led by *Ppor.* Dimităr S. Spisarevski, chased Yugoslav Dornier Do 17K bombers, but could not catch up with them, as the biplane fighter's top speed was less than the bomb-

This eleven o'clock view of a lone 'Dogan' parked somewhere in the field does not reveal much details. Unfortunately, in this particular case the black serial number was not applied on the lower wing undersurface, thus the aircraft's identity remains unknown.

Group photo in front of a Dogan *parked at the edge of a concrete airstrip.*

er's[24]! *Podofitser* Anton B. Atanasov of the 222nd *Yato* also attempted to catch the Yugoslav intruders on 6 April, but he also did not manage it due to the low performance of his mount. Other interception attempts also remained ineffective. The first 'live' combat activity of the *Dogan* proved to be a failure.

Although the repeated bombings resulting in loss of life and significant damage to the infrastructure, Bulgaria eventually ended the brief Balkan war with significant gains. This was because what Sofia regarded as historical Bulgarian territories of 'Vardar Macedonia' and 'Western Thrace', as well as two major islands in the Aegean Sea, were taken over from the defeated and dismembered Yugoslavia and Greece, respectively. With these newly acquired territories, together with the country's pre-war territory, the so-called 'Greater Bulgaria' was now established. The territorial expansions southwards allowed Bulgaria long-sought access to the Aegean Sea. New air bases were set up, including one in Skopie, future home of Bulgarian fighters relocated to Macedonia, and Kavalla, located on the shores of the Aegean Sea.

Guarding the Black Sea

Following the Axis attack on the Soviet Union on 22 June 1941, the international situation in the vicinity of Bulgaria changed radically. Possible enemy intrusions were no longer expected from the south, but rather from the north-east. Indeed, on a few occasions unidentified bombers, undoubtedly Soviet, dropped a few bombs on Bulgarian territory on the right bank of River Danube and the southern Dobrudzha area, most probably in error, instead of Rumanian targets. For example, six bombs fell on Dobrich on 22 June, while on 12 August three localities suffered bomb damage.

Despite the *Wehrmacht* and its Rumanian, Finnish, Slovak and Hungarian allies achieving srunning victories on the Eastern Front, the Soviet Black Sea Fleet and its aviation dominated the Black Sea area.

---

24 The top speed of the Do 17Ka-3 at 3,850 m was 438 km/h and cruising speed 350 km/h; while the top speed of the Avia B.534 was only 380 km/h.

Pre-mission debriefing, with Dogan *line-up in the background.*

Soviet aircraft and submarines were active against German shipping and Axis bases along the Rumanian and Bulgarian coastlines. To counter this new threat, the Bulgarian air force HQ received the task to defend the Black Sea coastal area against Soviet air and sea activity. Initially, only Letov Š.328 reconnaissance and light bomber aircraft of the army air regiments took part in this activity, from 4 August on. However, the need for fighter air cover of the coastlines, to counteract enemy air activity, arose soon after. For this duty, a *Dogan krilo* was ordered to relocate close to the Black Sea coastline. Just days after the relocation, the first 'live' action took place. On 16 August, at 13:45, the crew of a *Vrana* biplane patrolling the Black Sea coastline discovered a submarine between the Kamchia River's mouth

Would-be Bulgarian national hero, Por. Dimităr S. Spisarevski, smiles broadly during autumn manoeuvres (see large tent in the background). Dogan No. 28, believed to be part of the 222. Orlyak, offers a suitable background. Notice the yellow rudder and port elevator.

and Cape Emine. The enemy submarine was about to attack an Axis vessel. The crew of the aircraft dropped its meagre bomb load and shot at the target with the onboard machine guns. Then it called the other aircraft on duty, including a pair of Avia B.534 fighters fitted with four 20 kg bombs. However, they arrived too late, the submarine had already submerged. It turned out to be the Soviet *Shtuka*-class submarine Sht-211, which on 11 August had dropped ashore, near the Kamchia River, a group of Communist saboteurs, led by Red Army Col. Tsvyatko Radoynov, of Bulgarian origin. Later, the Soviet vessel took ambush position between Cape Emine and Ilyndzhik, and waited for a proper target to strike. That is when it was spotted by the Bulgarian aircrews and chased away.

Another occasion when Bulgarian aircraft on stand-by were called to intercept a Soviet submarine was on 21 September. While escorting two Rumanian transports, guarded by five Rumanian military vessels, from Shabla to Varna, the crew of an Š.328 spotted a submarine at 10:07 near Cape Shabla, and called the aircraft on duty from the nearby airfield, *Dogans* included. They arrived late again, so the submarine managed to hide in the meantime; therefore, the bombs had to be dropped at random before landing 'empty handed'. Further counter-submarine missions were logged by Avia biplanes, all ending with negative results.

Despite the failure to destroy the spotted enemy targets, these cases proved that the need for such patrolling missions was well founded, as the attackers were thwarted in successfully carrying out their missions. This is how the Black Sea Air Defence was formed, including air units. According to the VNVV HQ secret letter No. I-2733/1.10.1941, a special fighter *orlyak* was formed, code name 'Galata'. Initially, it included a staff unit (located at the Chayka Sea airfield), the 682nd Fighter *Yato* (located at Balchik) and the 692nd Fighter *Yato* (located at Sarafovo). Both *yata* were from the 6th Fighter *Polk*, equipped with Bf 109Es. Later, the 442nd Fighter *Yato* of the 4th Army (Air) *Polk* joined as well, moving to Novgradets airfield (today called Suvorovo), close to Varna. It had six Avia B.534s. The reinforcement joined the mixed *orlyak*, already in service at Buhovtsi base, near Shumen.

At Balchik there was an air gunnery school, called *Strelkovata Shkola*, where the *Dogan* pilots could hone their firing skills when scheduled.

The general task of the three-*yato*-strong special 'Galata' Fighter *Orlyak* was '*to guard Varna and Burgas, also to defend Bulgarian airspace against intruding enemy aircraft*'. Each *yato* had permanently on high alert four aircraft, for a three-minute take-off, while the other serviceable aircraft had to be readied in 30 minutes. The alert started 30 minutes before sunrise and continued until 30 minutes after sunset.

The 'Galata' Fighter *Orlyak* existed until late 1942, when the situation on the Eastern Front prevented the Soviet air force from conducting long-range missions that could potentially reach the Bulgarian coastline. Information about the combat activity of this special unit is scarce, but it appears that no enemy aircraft were ever shot down and no submarines actually sunk.

Dogan No. 2 of the 442nd Yato, 4th Army (Air) Polk, patrols the area around Pomorie, over the shores of the Black Sea, in late 1941. The cockpit canopy is slid rearwards, for better visibility and audibility. Due to the type of the negative film, the yellow mid-fuselage band, rudder, elevators and engine cowling appear in very dark shade, almost the same as the greenish khaki upper camouflage paint.

Protecting the 'Greater Bulgarian' Airspace

In the autumn of 1941, from 13 to 17 September, the thus far largest military manoeuvres of the Bulgarian army were held in the south-eastern area of the country. The 'blue' side (the 'attackers') comprised the 2nd Army, while the 'red' side (the 'defenders') were the 3rd Army and a few other smaller army units. Attached air units to the 2nd Army included one fighter *yato* from the 6th Air *Polk*, with six Avia B.534s; while the 3rd Army was supported by one fighter *yato*, the 332nd, also with six Avia B.534s. Six Letov Š.328 *Vrana* of the 4th and 5th *Voyskovo Yata* also participated in the manoeuvres.

The pilots flying the defender *Dogans*, attached to the 3rd *Armeyski Manevr. Orlyak*, based on Yambol airfield, were the following:

Kpt. Dimităr D. Radev
Ppor. Petăr G. Kasabov
Feldf.-shkolnik Georgi D. Kyutsukov
Podof. Nedyu K. Dobrev
Podof. Georgi K. Yordanov
Podof. Todor N. Tonev

Although the manoeuvres were declared a success, in fact they could not simulate a real modern war. The participating forces were also not representative of the entire army and air force, as many units were on active duty along the enlarged borders. The fighter and army *yata* of the army air *polkove* and the best *yata* of the bomber and the fighter *polk* were fulfilling different combat tasks along the Black Sea and the White Sea coasts, as well as in Vardar Macedonia. Some aircrew were abroad for specialised instruction, others under training at home. The number of flying officers in the fighter *yata* was inadequate, as NCOs made up about 70% of the pilot roster.

Once autumn and bad weather set in, the yearly maintenance work of the air park commenced. Based on VNVV Order No. 127/14.10.1941, 70 *Dogans*, along with 171 Avia & SKD 12 Ydrs engines, were to be maintained as scheduled at Karlovo Main Repair Shop (*Glavni Remontni Rabotilnitsi*, or GRR)[25]. Of the balance of seven aircraft, four B.534s had to be written off. Indeed, the following write-offs were recorded in 1941: on 25 July *Dogan* No. 42/7037 was written off from 3. *Văzdushen Polk* assets, at Yambol (VNVV Order No. 90/19.07.1941). *Dogans* Nos. 1, 3 and 12/7037 were written off from 1. *Văzdushen Polk* assets, at Bozhurishte (VNVV Order No. 106/18.06.1941). The remaining three *Dogans* must have been in adequate shape, with no need of overhaul.

A document dated 18 December instructs the air units to return to their main bases for the winter period. Accordingly, all flying units of the 3rd Army Air Polk (including the 332nd Fighter Yato) had to move from Sarafovo to Yambol, while the 442nd Fighter Yato of the 4th Army Air Polk moved to Novgradets. The 222nd Yato had to stay on at Bozhurishte, subordinated to 1st Army Air Polk (instead of the original parent main unit, the 2nd Army Air Polk). The principal fighter regiment, the 6th, had to remain at Karlovo main air base, to consolidate its structure and prepare the newly formed Strela (Bf 109E) yata. On 27 December 1941, the following Dogans were reported by the respective airfield inspectorates: Yambol: 38/7037 (engine: Avia 1171), 34/7037 (engine: HS 374/1378), 31/7037 (engine: HS 23/523), 33/7037 (engine: HS 343/843), 44/7037 (engine: Avia 397), 32/7037 (engine: HS 324/824).

25　At that date, 340 workers worked on airframes and 140 on engines at GRR Karlovo.

A group of happy Dogan *pilots – including Ppor. Stefan N. Marinopolski, second from left, member of 2/6. Orlyak – in front of aircraft No. 40, sometimes in mid-1942. This particular* Dogan *was written off on 28 June 1944, the day of the devastating daylight bombing raid against Karlovo main fighter base.*

Dogan NN 75/7037 wears the most extensive yellow markings ever observed on Bulgarian warplanes: bottom and upper wingtips, wrap-around nose and fuselage 'cheatline', mid-fuselage band, rudder and elevators. The tallest airman (third from left) is the venerable Cpt. Petko N. Popganchev. This particular aircraft was officially written off on 4 September 1945.

The report mentions that the radio sets of the Avias didn't work properly despite the fact that there was an electrical engineer assigned to the airfield. The fighters' gunsights were damaged.

Novgradets: 47/7037 (engine: HS 183/683), 50/7037 (engine: HS 362/862), 55/7037 (engine: HS 110/610), 60/7037 (engine: HS 376/876), 49/7037 (engine: HS 361/861).

Gorya Oryahovitsa: 46/7037 (engine: HS 346/846), 59/7037 (engine: HS 375/875), 56/7037 (engine: HS 374/874).

Kazanlăk: 16/7037 (engine: HS 244/744), 41/7037 (engine: HS 360/860).

Sarafovo: none

Balchik: none

Kolyu Ganchevo: none

1941 was again a bad year as regards air incidents and accidents. In total, there were 13 accidents recorded, with the loss of 28 lives. Eight of these losses involved combat aircraft, while the balance was made up of trainers and second line aircraft. The first recorded incident involving a *Dogan* happened on 13 February at Yambol airfield, when aircraft No. 38 of the 3rd Army Air *Polk* reported a defective propeller (details are lacking). The same day, the venerable *Poruchik* Chudomir M. Toplodolski of the 6th Fighter *Polk* damaged *Dogan* No. 61 at Dăbene landing ground. On 19 March, *Feldfebel-shkolnik* Konstantin D. Petsev overturned on Bozhurishte air base with his mount, *Dogan* No. 10/7037. On the 27th of the same month, *Dogan* No. 56 was heavily damaged in hangar at Bozhurishte, along with two other aircraft, due

This and next page: *This series of four photographs depicting Dogan No. 9 was taken by a German officer, Oblt. Reinartz, probably while he was stationed in Bulgaria in the late spring of 1941. Various details, not usually seen in lesser quality photos, can be studied (including the ventilation scoop built into the upper windshield).*

to 'careless manoeuvring' of (i.e., playing with) a prime mover by a civilian volunteer (he did not know how to stop the machine). Next day, *Dogan* No. 43, piloted by *Podofitser* Georgi K. Yordanov, somersaulted while landing on Yambol, due to pilot error. On 18 May the second fatal accident occurred. *Podofitser* Petko G. Mirchev of the 6th Fighter Regiment lost orientation during aerobatics and crashed to his death near Karlovo air base. The aircraft's NN is not recorded[26]; however most likely it was one of the aforementioned four *Dogans* officially written off that year, probably No. 1.

It is recorded that at the end of 1941 a total of 73 B.534s were still available (this is only possible if the

Dogan destroyed in 1940 was actually written off only in 1941, which would not be an uncommon occurrence). Of these, 20 were in unserviceable condition. Another interesting piece of information refers to the Bulgarian designed and manufactured DAR-10A close air support aircraft. Reportedly, the prototype performed mock combat with an Avia B.534 in late 1941. Bulgarian sources claim the domestic DAR model was superior to the Czechoslovak design. However, this statement raises some questions, as the DAR-10A was not a fighter like the agile Avia biplane, thus its superiority is questionable.

A Dogan photographed prior to takeoff, captured from ground level, in 1942. This fighter biplane was reportedly part of the 622. Yato, 1/6. Orlyak.

New Year, New Reorganisation

In the spring of 1942, the bulk of the Bulgarian army, covered from the skies by the air force, was deployed again along the whole western, southern, south-eastern and eastern borders of the so-called 'Greater Bulgaria'. In these conditions, the VNVV was reorganised again in March. The main change[27] was the forming of a higher unit, called *Văzdushna Eskadra* (Air Division), which gathered all fighter, bomber and so-called 'lineen' (battle) *polkove* (regiments).

The *Văzdushna Eskadra* was envisaged as something like an operational-tactical higher unit, encompassing the élite squadrons, equipped with top warplanes, similar to the mixed aviation regiments of the front aviation. It included a Staff, the 2nd Battle, the 5th Bomber and the 6th Fighter *Polkove*. On paper, the fighter *polk* consisted of three *orlyatsi*, with three *yata* each. But shortage of available matériel and personnel forced the *orlyatsi* to have incomplete staff; the gaps remained to be filled later on.

Commanding Officer of the *Văzdushna Eskadra* became *Polkovnik* (Col.) Ivan Nozharov (until 14 March he was the Air Force Chief of the Staff), while *Podpolkovnik* (Lt. Col.) Vasil Vălkov assumed command of the 6th Fighter *Polk*.

In a secret report of the VNVV Commander it is mentioned that the main units of the *Văzdushna Eskadra* (the bomber, the battle and the fighter *polkove*) formed the so-called 'assault air force'. Their air bases (Plovdiv, Graf Ignatievo and Karlovo, respectively) were in the range of an envisaged Bulgarian-Turkish war zone. Also, it was mentioned that the central location of the *Eskadra*'s air bases was giving the opportunity for the use of these units in other war theatres as well.

As far as the *Dogans* were concerned, during the reorganisation they were redistributed as follows: 30 Avia B.534s were assigned to each of the 6th *Iztrebitelen Polk*'s first two *orlyatsi*, each *orlyak* comprising of a *shtab* and three *yata*.

Order of Battle of 6. *Iztrebitelen Polk* (Fighter Regiment), April 1942 (only *Dogan* units shown)
1/6. *Iztrebitelen Orlyak*:   *Shtab na orlyaka* (3 'Dogan')
  612. *Iztr. Yato* (9 'Dogan')
  622. *Iztr. Yato* (9 'Dogan')
  632. *Iztr. Yato* (9 'Dogan')

---

26 Another source mentions that Mirchev died aboard an Avia Bš.122; however, this cannot be confirmed. Yet another source gives the date of his demise as 19 May 1941.

27 The other details of this reorganisation are not discussed here.

Senior air force officers gather around a parked Dogan on a frigid day of 1941. The aircraft in the background wears the mid-fuselage band and yellow nose plus flash. Unfortunately, the officer leaning forward partially covers the aircraft's white serial number; however, enough of it is still visible to lead to the conclusion that it might be No. 24.

The training *yato* kept nine *Dogans*. Theoretical total: 69 Avias (the remaining few Avias were assigned to the Piloting School, which moved from Marno Pole main base to Dolna Mitropoliya airfield on 28 March).

Not much enemy air activity happened in Bulgarian airspace until mid-1942. Occasionally, RAF bombers dropped a few bombs at night, then disappeared unscratched. Some mine-laying activity over the River Danube also took place. Air supply missions for the chetnik guerrilla forces of Dragoljub "Draža" Mihailović, active in occupied Yugoslavia, was also performed by RAF transports without much opposition from the Axis. The situation changed radically with the arrival of American aviation units within striking distance from the Balkans. Its first units were transferred to North Africa in May–June 1942, then unified as the 9th Air Army. On 12 June, thirteen B-24D 'Liberator' bombers of the so-called HALPRO[28] detachment performed the first USAAF strike of World War Two against a strategic Axis object in Europe – the petrol storage tanks and refineries in Ploeşti, Rumania. The intruders were detected by Bulgarian air warning posts along the Black Sea shores by their engine noise, from 02:55 to 3:17 am. No damage was inflicted upon Bulgarian soil (the damage against Rumanian targets was also minimal). The major effect it had was the clear warning to the Axis that the Allies are now within striking distance. Accordingly, immediate measures were taken by the affected Axis countries' air defences.

As for Bulgaria, the air defence of the capital (which was not covered at that date by any fighter unit) was reinforced by two *yata* of the 1/6. *Iztrebitelen Orlyak* only ten days following the first USAAF intrusion. Accordingly, the *orlyak* staff unit and the 622nd *Yato* with eight *Dogans* deployed from Marno

---

28   After the commander's name: Col. Harry A. Halverson's Project (HALPRO)

Based on the caption written on the verso of the photograph, depicted are two brothers with their visibly proud father. Behind them is a Dogan, believed to be No. 68.

Dogan No. 44 is parked at the edge of the landing ground. The tarpaulin cover is removed from the engine and cockpit, which indicates the aircraft is about to be flown, or maintained.

Pole/Karlovo main air base to Vrazhdebna, while the 612th *Yato* with seven *Dogans* moved to Bozhurishte, both air bases located in the proximity of Sofia. The fighter *orlyatsi* were placed under direct command of the Commander-in-Chief of the VNVV. Parallel to this move, the Commander of the Air Force issued a special order calling for the organization of the anti-air defence of the capital, made by the 1st Fighter *Orlyak* and the 1st Anti-Aircraft Artillery (AAA) *Otdelenie* (Department), which had to operate in joint defence of Sofia's airspace (secret Letter No. 642/26.06.1942), even though the official message was: *"in the present military-political situation, enemy air strikes on the capital are inconceivable"*. Yet the declaration of war upon the USA and the UK (but not against the USSR!), issued by the Bulgarian Government on 13 December 1941 under German pressure and regarded only as a 'symbolic' act, was to reap a storm. While the UK returned the 'favour' twelve days later, it largely remained without consequences. The US Congress reciprocated the war declaration only about half a year later, on 5 June 1942[29]. American bombers then appeared unexpectedly in the vicinity of Bulgarian airspace only days later – as mentioned earlier – to the Bulgarians' utmost surprise. This totally unanticipated event prompted the strengthening of the air protection of the country's capital, detailed earlier, as well as other vital centres, both by interceptor aircraft and by anti-aircraft artillery. It was also stated that *"special attention must be paid at the directions along the Struma, Mesta* (in Greek Nestos) *and Maritza rivers"*.

Co-operation practice between AAA and fighters was quite interesting and not straightforward. The AAA had to direct the fighters to the targets with rows of signal shots, and the fighters had to report about the enemy (location, time, number, type, height, direction of flight, etc.). It was permitted for fighters to attack enemy aircraft in the zones of AAA fire, as the AAA had to hold fire until their own fighters were in a good position to attack the intruders. As this was too difficult for the artillery staff to determine, the fighters had to estimate themselves the danger of getting in the range of friendly AAA fire! Obviously, such clumsy and unrealistic co-operation between ground and air units could not successfully materialise in real combat situations.

There were two levels of alert for fighter crews. Those pilots who were assigned with high alert had only five minutes for take-off when the alarm was sounded. Those on a lower level of alert had 15 minutes to actually take off from the moment the sirens sounded. Despite these measures, the level of air protection of sensitive areas was inadequate, mainly due to the insufficient number of available fighter aircraft, as well as their low serviceability. Luckily for them, no 'real' alarm was sounded in the next year to come.

Even with the absence of combat operations in 1942, the Avia B.534-equipped fighter and training units suffered significant losses in accidents, due to mechanical failure or pilot error. The very first such event was also a fatal one. On 13 March, *Ppor.* Atanas A. Popov, reportedly attached to the 2nd Air Regiment, crashed to the ground during a training flight at Bankya (Lyulin rayon, just north-west of Sofia), destroying *Dogan* No. 23/7037, and died. Although the cloudy weather was not ideal for flying, the post-accident report concluded that the fatal crash was a result of indiscipline, of aerobatics performed

---

29   The dates of various declarations of war are based on *Allied Deliberations on Bulgaria World War II*, compiled and edited by Alfred M. Beck. American Research Center in Sofia, 2016, page 15. Other sources give contradictory dates.

This pair of photos depicts a Dogan krilo during drills at Marno Pole/Karlovo airfield, in the Summer of 1942. The three pilots of the krilo (i.e. three-aircraft basic formation) are saluting their commanding officer after receiving their orders. Depicted is Avia B.534, No. 77 – the highest serial number identified on photographs and in documents. In the background of the top photo, a couple of old PZL P.24bs are visible, lined up near the hangar.

at low altitude. Precisely one month later, on the 13th, it was the turn of a 662nd *Yato* pilot, *Zamestnik ofitser* (Warrant Officer)[30] Toni E. Tonev to suffer an accident at Marno Pole main air base, albeit a much lighter one. While landing, the *Dogan* No. 70/7037 ended up on its nose (15% damage). A similar accident involved *Dogan* No. 50/7037, which also ended up on its nose following a botched taxiing, also at Karlovo, on 20 April. The pilot, *Kandidat podofitser* Stefan D. Petrov of the 642nd *Yato*, escaped unhurt. On 29 May, the undercarriage leg and the lower starboard wing of *Dogan* No. 71/7037 were broken off during a bad landing at Marno Pole air base by *Kand. podof.* Georgi N. Atanasov of the 662nd *Yato*. While taking off, also from Marno Pole on 15 June, the engine of *Dogan* No. 44/7037 (c/n 425) lost power,

---

30 The rank of *Zamestnik ofitser* (Warrant Officer), 3rd, 2nd and 1st Classes, was an interim officer's rank assigned to NCOs who finished the fast-paced School of Officers in Reserve (Sh.Z.O.). It was meant to differentiate them from the career officers, graduates of the Military Academy, who were disturbed in seeing former NCOs being elevated to the officer's rank after a quick course. This short-lived rank category was introduced during early wartime, and gradually ceased at the end of the war following the pro-Communist coup September 1944. See also footnote in the Bf 109G *Strela* chapter about the '*Zapasni ofitser*' (Officer in reserve) rank.

Curiously, although the aircraft in the foreground has its serial number applied on the rear fuselage, the one in the rear (which was a B.534-V, not a B.534-II, or -III, as it may appear to the inattentive onlooker), has not. Photo believed to be taken at Buhovtsi landing ground, near Shumen, in 1941.

compelling the pilot, *Zamestnik ofitser* Mihail T. Uzunov of the 632nd *Yato*, to belly land his unpowered mount, causing 40% damage.

On 13 August, *Kand. podof.* Tsonyu P. Uzunov of the 632nd *Yato* taxied too long after landing on Daskal-Atanasovo airfield (located about 25 km SE from Stara Zagora). The biplane, No. 30/7037, built in 1938, broke its undercarriage and ended up on its belly, which caused 25% damage to the airframe. Next day, *Dogans* of the 662nd *Yato* were performing ground attack exercises nearby Daskal-Atanasovo airfield. Bf 109E *Strelas* of 3/6. *Orlyak* provided top cover. While taking off for an air escort sortie, *Strela* No. 7/7057 flown by *Podofitser* Dako P. Dakov of the 672nd *Yato* veered off course and crashed into a parked Avia B.534 *Dogan*, No. 35. Both aircraft had to be written off following the violent collision. Also on 14 August, another accident happened at Daskal-Atanasovo, this time involving *Dogan* No. 40, with *Podofitser* Petăr Bisov of the 652nd *Yato* at the controls. Finally, an old Avia B.534 (No. 63/7037), built in 1937, was slightly damaged in a tyre accident involving *Poruchik* Hristo Pazvantov of the 632nd *Yato*. The incident happened on Marno Pole/Karlovo main air base on 11 September 1942. This was to be the last recorded accident of the year involving the Avia B.534 fighter, available to the Author.

Todor 'Tedi' Vălkov, son of the Commander-in-Chief of the 6th *Iztrebitelen Polk* (Fighter Regiment), *Podpolkovnik* (Lieutenant-Colonel) Vasil P. Vălkov, witnessed many unusual events during the war, while loitering around airfields in his boyhood, having access everywhere due to his privileged status. One of the memories he recalled in May 2018 was the crash of the *Dogan*, flown by a family friend, *Podporuchik* Petăr Kirov Petrov of 2/6. *Orlyak*. On an unspecified summer day in 1940, or 1941, he was watching from Bozhurishte air base, together with his father, a number of *Dogans* on training flight. One of them flew towards the ground - they thought he would simulate a ground attack. However, he did not recover, but continue to dive. At one point, the doomed *Dogan* disappeared from sight, in the direction of the nearby village of Gurmazovo.

Vălkov sr. immediately ran to the ambulance car and told the driver to head for the place of the suspected crash. 'Tedi' jumped on his bicycle and also headed in the same direction, but cutting the road short, through the Bozhurishte horse breeding farm. As 'Tedi' reached the road, he saw the ambulance tilted sidewise in the ditch and his father cursing around it. In the hurry, the driver left the road and fell into the ditch. 'Tedi' rode the bicycle back to the airfield and came with another car, picking up his father. All of them headed towards the crash site. As they reached the location, they saw the *Dogan* flipped on its back, the fuselage twisted. However, Petrov, white as a paper sheet, sat near the wreck, visibly shaken, but alive. Lt. Col. Vălkov stepped to him, put his hand on his shoulder and told him, in official tone: Поздравявам те с новия ти живот! (I congratulate you for your new life!).

It turned out that the controls locked during flight, rendering the aircraft uncontrollable. As the aircraft was diving towards the ground, the pilot was desperately kicking and shaking all the controls. Right above the ground, in the last possible second, the frantic jerking of the control stick worked! The pilot managed somehow to pull up the biplane and avoid a vertical hit and what 'Tedi' was expecting to find, the pilot buried 3-4 meters in the ground, shredded to pieces – as he recalls 75 years later. However, the recovery was made too low and too late; the *Dogan* hit the ground rather violently, but horizontally,

Would-be Dogan *pilot, Rusi Rusev, is depicted early in his military career, as a Yunker (Cadet) in 'His Majesty's Military School'. On 1 August 1943, the day of the epic 'Tidal Wave' US bombing raid, he took part in the combat mission as commander of 622. Yato.*

173

Unfortunately, the full serial number of this Avia B.534-V is not seen on the photo; however, the last digit appears to be 9. If so, a photo included on page 167 shows a different style numeral on the rear fuselage. The third man from left, with arms akimbo (i.e., hands on hips), is Ppor. Nedelcho D. Bonchev of the 652ⁿᵈ Yato. Bonchev ended up sixth in the ranks of top Bulgarian fighter pilots, with two confirmed 'Fortresses' shot down and a 'Liberator' damaged, amounting to 8 victory points. This particular photo is often located by various Bulgarian publications to "Piacenza airfield, Italy", which was certainly not the case.

not nose first, which made all the difference! While hitting the ground, the aircraft jolted up, then fell back on its back, belly up. Despite the violent crash, the pilot could exit the twisted airframe, stunned, but alive. It was a lucky escape, made in the last split second.

In 1942, seven incidents (five of which were made by warplanes) claimed the lives of 16 airmen in total. Of these, only one involved a *Dogan*, as detailed above. Overall serviceability of the combat aircraft was low, about 40%. This unsatisfactory technical state rendered more than half of the existing *Dogan* fleet useless in case of a real enemy attack.

A letter dated 9.12.1942 asks Berlin for spare parts for the 204 existing ex-Czechoslovak aircraft from 1939. The list includes: *"Jäger B.534 - 75 Stück"*.

1943 – The Year When Guns Were Fired in Anger

During the winter period enemy air activity was very low. In the spring, however, more and more hostile aircraft intruded in Bulgarian airspace, not only at night, as it was customary until then, but in daylight as well. Consequently, the Army Chief of Staff wrote a secret letter, No. I-201/11.06.1943, addressed to the Air Force Chief of Staff, asking for countermeasures against enemy flights. In his reply (secret Letter No. 836/4.07.1943), the Chief of Staff explained that there are no night fighters in Bulgaria, the task being assigned to the German fighter aviation units located in Greece. However, Bulgarian AAA units were to be strengthened in Vardar Macedonia, which lies on the route of Allied bombers heading towards the northern Balkans region.

The question raised by the top officer of the army, questioning the air defence of Bulgaria, was well timed. On 24 July, at 11:30, 24 US B-24 'Liberators' performed a surprise strike against Sedes airfield, located 15 km east of Thessaloniki, Greece, not far from Greater Bulgaria's southern borders. This unexpected blow led to the further strengthening of the anti-air defence, particularly around the capital. In secret letter No. 970/2.07.1943, the Commander of the Air Force completed the orders he had detailed in his secret letter No. 642 of 1942. Accordingly, the 1/6ᵗʰ Fighter *Orlyak* and the units of the Air Warning Service were to be subordinated to commander of the 1ˢᵗ Air Defence Region. Furthermore, the best fighter unit the VNVV could muster – the 682ⁿᵈ *Yato*, equipped with the recently delivered 16 Bf 109G-2s – was to be transferred from Karlovo to the Sofia area, to better protect the capital. Eight Bf 109Gs were to move from Karlovo to Bozhurishte, while the other eight Bf 109Gs went to Vrazhdebna (i.e., one half *yato* to each airfield). According to this order, the Bf 109Gs had to be ready to perform air interdiction missions from 15 July. The Messerschmitts had to replace the Avia B.534-equipped 612ᵗʰ and 622ⁿᵈ *Yata* on duty at Bozhurishte and Vrazhdebna airfields. From then on, air protection of the capital was to be entrusted only to the potent Messerschmitts; the obsolete Avia fighters could retire to secondary roles. However, the change of guard was not performed by the time the long predicted massive air intrusion in Bulgarian airspace occurred.

Dogan No. 30 ended up on its belly following a botched landing on Daskal-Atanasovo airfield on 13 August 1942. The pilot, Kand. podof. *Tsonyu P. Uzunov of the 632ⁿᵈ Yato, escaped unhurt, but most probably was punished for the error he made. The aircraft does not seem to sport the tapering yellow flash along the fuselage.*

In the early morning of 1 August 1943, a Sunday, German early warning systems located a huge air armada approaching south-eastern Europe. The warning reached Sofia as well – the Bulgarian high command thought the incoming attack would target the capital – so fighter units were scrambled in an attempt to intercept the incoming intruders. The alarm was sounded at 12:30 EET, when the enemy bombers were approaching the Slivnitsa–Babushnitsa axis, located on the western border region of Greater Bulgaria. In total, 20 Bulgarian fighters took off to intercept the unexpected enemy. These were six Avia B.534s of the 622ⁿᵈ *Yato* from Vrazhdebna and four more of the 612ᵗʰ *Yato* from Bozhurishte, both of the 1/6ᵗʰ *Orlyak*. Additionally, ten Bf 109Gs of the 3/6ᵗʰ *Orlyak* took off from Karlovo.

The first fighters to be ordered to take off were the *Dogans*. However, they took off too late, so they could not catch up with the 'desert pink' painted bombers flying high, at around 5,000 m altitude. It turned out that the Americans did not target Bulgaria after all, as originally thought. Rather, they continued their epic journey north-east, towards the Danube, the natural frontier with Rumania. The report of the VNVV Commander addressed to the Army Staff (No. IV – PS – 6470 from 02.08.1943) mentions the following: "*Only Podporuchik [Velcho S.] Vaptsarov and Podporuchik [Dimităr S.] Daska-lov [actually, Podofitser, D.B.] from the Vrazhdebna-based yato could engage in air combat over Vratsa. The other aircraft could not reach the enemy because they were flying with superior speed towards North-East*". There is no data available about this first interception mission of the VNVV against USAAF, as the

An Avia B.534 is being serviced in field conditions. At left, a German soldier watches the activity. Due to removed side panels, the on-board machine guns and various auxiliary equipment can be seen to advantage.

1/6. *Iztrebitelen Orlyak* kept no combat diary for this period. However, it can be safely assumed that the aforementioned two *Dogan* pilots of 612. *Yato* made only visual contact with the Americans, at most. They could not close in enough to fire their machine guns effectively.

The impression of an American crewman, S/Sgt. Gola Gibbey, positioned in the top turret of 'Buzzin Bear' of the 44th BG, was recalled post-war, as follows: "*it was a fleeting encounter, as the older Bulgarian fighters couldn't get high enough to intercept the bombers before they outdistanced the old fighter planes*[31]". Another US member of the so-called 'Ploesti Express', Lt. H.H. Christensen, co-pilot of 'Blonds Away' of the 389th BG, recalled, also post-war: "*we saw two or three enemy fighters that were Bulgarian Avias. They flew outside our gun range and did nothing threatening us. We did not know that these airplanes were not equipped with radios and assumed they were announcing our location to the air defences.*" There is no report from the US side of any fire exchange, so the assumption that the *Dogan* pilots could only watch the bombers from a distance seems reasonable.

After the bombs were released on targets in Ploeşti and the vicinity from extra low level, the surviving 'Liberators' attempted to return either to their home base in Libya, or to find a safe landing ground anywhere, at any friendly or neutral location they could possibly reach. This time, the decimated bomber units did not return in one big pack, as on their way towards Rumania, but rather scattered along many miles, some limping back with their fuselage peppered with bullet or shrapnel holes, with one or even two engines knocked off, their propellers in feathered position. This time, the Bulgarians were waiting for them, prepared, refuelled and ready to 'draw blood'.

First, four *Dogans* took off in a hurry from Bozhurishte, at 15:10. Another seven of their comrades from Vrazhdebna followed minutes later.

The Dunlop-model port tyre of aircraft No. 63 of the 632nd Yato was punctured during taxiing on Marno Pole/Karlovo main air base, on 11 September 1942. Notice the yellow painted upper wingtips; however, the elevators don't appear to have received the same paintjob. The close-up photo shows the yellow painted nose and rudder, as well as the mid-fuselage band. Stara Planina Mountain range offers a majestic background décor.

Both *yata* were led again by their commanders, *Poruchik* Marin G. Petrov (612. *Yato*) and *Poruchik* Rusi I. Rusev[32] (622. *Yato*), respectively. This time, the biplanes had time to climb as high as they could, with

31 As described in 'Black Sunday', by Michael Hill, Schiffer Publishing Ltd., Atlgen, USA, 1993, page 54.

32 Former Captain Rusev – expelled post war from the air force for 'subversive anti-state activity' and harassed by the Communist authorities – was killed by Bulgarian border guards during a botched defection attempt through the Bulgarian-Turkish border on the night of 16th to 17th of August 1948. Along Rusi Rusev, two other airmen, former Maj. Nikolay Boshnakov and former Lt. Yordan Yordanov, were also killed that night. The location of their burial place is unknown even today. On 12 October 2016, a monument was erected to their memory near the village of Georgi Dobrevo, not far from the location where they were gunned down then presumably buried in secret.

Post-accident photo documenting the collision between an Avia B.534 Dogan, No. 11, and a Fw 44J Vrabche, LZ-FOS, NN 18/7021. This incident happened on 23 August 1943, when Ppor. Stefan Marinopolski ran over two parked Vrabche, LZ-FOY and LZ-FOS, while landing on Sofia (Vrazhdebna) air-field. Of special interest is the emblem painted on the front area of the trainer's fuselage. Such emblems were seen very rarely on Bulgarian aircraft.

their prospective targets in sight. However, only the *Dogans* of the 612th *Yato* could make contact with a small pack of 98th Bomb Group B-24Ds in the airspace above Vratsa, as they limped back towards the Osogovo Mountains, heading to their base in Libya. With the Americans now flying under 1,000 m, some significantly lower, the slower biplanes inched in on the straggling bombers, closer and closer, until they could dive upon them. The attack was successful in hitting several targets; however, the 7.92 mm bullets could do only minimal damage to the enormous all-metal 'Liberators'. The other *yato's* members missed the Americans and landed without firing a shot.

Due to the various top speeds of individual *Dogans*, most Bulgarian pilots could not perform a con-centrated attack; rather they attacked individually, as soon as they could reach their targets one by one. Not all of them could close in enough to fire their armament efficiently. Despite the inefficient way of attack, it appears that at least two 'Liberators' suffered damage due to the *Dogans'* bullets.

B-24D 'Daisy Mae' (s/n 41-11815) from the 415th Bomber Squadron, 98th Bomber Group, with 1st Lt. Lewis N. Ellis at the controls, was hit in the two port engines by machine gun fire, causing her airspeed to decrease rapidly. Despite the damage inflicted by Bulgarian Avias and some more by *Luftwaffe* fight-ers, 'Daisy Mae' could return to its home base at Benghazi, where it crash landed while on autopilot, but with all crew members alive, some wounded. They were up in the air for an astonishing 14 hrs. and 35 mins.[33]

B-24D 'Cornhusker' (s/n 42-40322), piloted by 1st Lt. Ned McCarty, also from the 415th Bomber Squadron, suffered multiple hits from the Avia fighters' rifle calibre machine guns. Damage was incurred to engines Nos. 3 and 4; the former's propeller had to be feathered. The same source quoted earlier[34] gives the following account: "*The Bulgarian Avias made two different attacks on the Liberators, inflicting damage on THE CORNHUSKER. The old fighters were too slow to maintain contact with the Liberators. Lt. Dwight Patch of the 98th recalled, <<I did see Ned McCarty get hit in both left engines. They streamed white smoke out past the tail, but he kept them going as we climbed over the mountains and flew towards the Adriatic.>>*" Later on, the damaged bomber was caught by *Luftwaffe* Bf 109Gs of IV./JG 27 over the Ionian Sea and finished off, with all on board being lost at sea.

To the frustration of the *Dogan* pilots, they were forced to break off their attacks after just one fir-ing pass due to the fact that even a damaged B-24D could outrun the Avia B.534[35]. Nevertheless, they still pursued the Americans in the hope that they could catch a slow flying one, which they actually did, close to Kyustendil, although this second firing pass remained ineffective. At that point, with fuel low, the *Dogans* had to break off the chase and return to their base. In the end, no victory points were awarded by the VNVV HQ to any *Dogan* pilot, meaning that even 'efficient firing upon an enemy bomber' claim was not considered as trustworthy to air force officials, most probably due to lack of witnesses or wreckage. All four USAAF bombers officially considered as shot down by Bulgarian airmen were attributed to *Strela* pilots (for details, see the relevant chapter).

---

33 The day after 'Daisy Mae' had landed, ground crewmen counted more than 150 holes all over the ship, inflicted by flak shrapnel, machine gun bullets (many of those must have been caused by the Avia B.534s) and 20 mm shells.

34 Black Sunday, by Michael Hill, Schiffer Publishing Ltd., Atlgen, USA, 1993, page 154.

35 The top speed of the B-24D was 303 mi/h (487 km/h) at 7600 m, while cruising speed 215 mi/h (346 km/h), compared to the Avia B.534's top speed of 380 km/h.

Dogan No. 40 ended up 'sampling' corn following an overly long taxiing on Daskal-Atanasovo airfield. At the edge of the maize field, the aircraft tripped on a fuel barrel (notice the number 87 painted on it, most probably identifying the fuel octane) and nosed in. The incident, involving Podofitser Petăr Bisov of the 652nd Yato, happened on 14 August 1942, and ended up with only minor damage to the airframe. The view revealing the bottom of the aircraft shows that both elevators and the rudder were painted yellow, and the serial number was repeated on the lower wingtips, in black. The rearward tapering yellow flash, ending in line with the rear cockpit window, is faintly visible on the fuselage side. Notice the glossy finish of the camouflage top covering lacquer, as well as the national markings.

While the *Dogan* fighters had damaged at least two of the B-24s, they did not escape unscathed – at least based on the American on-board gunners' accounts. At least three of the tiny biplanes were reportedly hit by the return fire of B-24 gunners. However, due to the absence of a *yato* combat diary, there is no information available if any of them were indeed damaged in combat, or during landing. The already quoted Bulgarian post-combat report mentions only briefly *"no Bulgarian aircraft was lost"*.

On 7 August, Tsar Boris III summoned to his palace in Sofia the two senior officers of 3/6. *Orlyak* who took part in the victorious air battle, *Poruchik* Stoyanov and *Podporuchik* Bochev, and decorated them with the prestigious 'Order of Bravery' 4th Grade, 2nd Class. Stoyanov mentions in his post-war memoirs that *"another officer was waiting and joined us at the Palace – the commander of the '6/12 Eskadrila'."* He does not name that officer; however, it can be safely ascertained that he was *Poruchik* Marin G. Petrov, commanding officer of the 612. *Yato*, who took also part in the epic air battle. Stoyanov does not explicitly mention if the third officer was also decorated; however, most probably he was, otherwise he would have not been summoned by the Monarch at the same time as the other two officers. Stoyanov also recalls that later *Podofitser* Yordan N. Kubadinov [1/6. *Orlyak*] was also decorated, with the less prestigious 'Order of Merit'. Being a low-ranking NCO, he was not called to the palace, and the award was presented to him elsewhere. The fact that he was singled out for an award could mean that he was one of the *Dogan* pilots who actually scored hits on one of the 'Liberators'.

The half-successful attack of the 1/6. *Orlyak Dogans* against the 'Liberators' represented the first and last time when they had the chance to fire their guns against the USAAF, even though the American warplanes would start to show up regularly over Bulgaria from later on the year. It became clear to everyone that the ageing Czech biplane was hopelessly outdated in the modern air war. Moreover, the Avia B.534s had neither on-board radios, nor oxygen supply for the pilots to fly at high altitude. Their numbers were insufficient as well. At the end of August, the entire 1/6. *Orlyak* had only 16 serviceable *Dogans* and 12 fighter pilots available, including the *yato* commanders. This was well under the theoretical strength of 9+3=12 aircraft per *yato*, plus the *orlyak* staff, amounting to a total of 40 aircraft and an identical number of pilots per *orlyak*.

Compared to the other accidents from 1942, illustrated by photos, this one appears to be the most serious. Dogan No. 35 was damaged when Bf 109E Strela No. 7/7057, flown by Podofitser Dako P. Dakov of the 672nd Yato, veered off course and crashed into it. As a consequence, the engine tore off its mount, the lower starboard wing and upper port wing were damaged, the undercarriage broke off. Both aircraft had to be written off following the violent collision. Apparently, the airframe had been repainted in places (like the outer part of the upper starboard wing, the lower fuselage area underneath and in front of the cockpit, as well as the lower starboard wing root) with a lighter shade colour, probably mid-green, covering earlier repairs.

Summing up, by August 1943, the *Dogans* were neither qualitatively nor quantitatively up to the task they were originally assigned with, i.e. interceptor fighter. They had no place any more in combating the new enemy, superior in every aspect.

The Avia B.534's future role had to be redefined, in earnest.

Reinventing the *Dogan*

The immediate aftermath of the American bomber pass-through in Bulgarian airspace on 1 August was that the relocation of the Bf 109G-equipped two half-*yata* to the two airfields around Sofia, to relieve the inept Avia B.534s, was hastened. The actual 'changing of the guard' happened on the 12th August. Following that move, the ageing biplanes were retired from Sofia to Marno Pole/Karlovo, home of their parent 1/6. *Orlyak* and the sister 2/6. *Orlyak*, until their eventual fate was to be decided.

The solution came indirectly, with the arrival from Germany of Junkers Ju 87R-2/R-4 dive bombers the very same month. The famed *Stukas* were assigned to the Graf Ignatievo-based 1/2. *Orlyak* of the 2nd Army Air *Polk*, which would be renamed *shturmovi polk* (assault regiment). The dozen German dive bombers formed a *shtuka yato* (Stuka squadron) within the *orlyak*. It has been decided that the *polk* would get a second *orlyak* as well, the 2/2., to be equipped with the Avia B.534[36]. Initially, the 2/2. *Orlyak* would also get a single squadron, called *shturmovo yato* (assault squadron), to be equipped with a dozen *Dogans*. *Kapitan* Tsviatko P. Kolev was named *orlyak* commander. He would lead the assault *Dogan* unit until the end of the war and a couple of months beyond.

The Avia B.534 was *not* a natural choice for the ground assault role. Its four vz. 30 type fuselage mounted 7.92 mm machine guns and six Pantof vz. 35 type underwing bomb racks, each designed to carry a 10 kg splinter bomb, or a 20 kg cluster bomb, as well as lack of armour protection for the pilot and engine, did not make the aircraft type ideal for ground attack. Heavier calibre guns and especially

---

36 It has to be noted that with the change in role from fighter to assault, the aircraft type did not change the *Nomenklaturen Nomer* originally assigned to it, in this case 7037, the Avia B.534 keeping the 'fighter' category throughout its service life.

While taking off from Marno Pole on 15 June, the engine of Dogan No. 44/7037 quit, compelling the pilot, Zam. of. Mihail T. Uzunov of the 632nd Yato, to belly land his powerless mount, causing 40% damage. Thanks to the different type of black/white negative film, the yellow is shown prominently in these photos. This allows the onlooker to identify the area painted in yellow: engine cowling, rearward tapering fuselage flash, rudder and elevators. This was one of the rare occasions when the aircraft's original construction number (425) was displayed on the fin.

Most post-accident photos documenting taxiing incidents look pretty much the same: broken undercarriage leg, lower wing and propeller. This series of photos, depicting Dogan No.71/7037, is no different. On 29 May 1942, Kand. podof. Georgi N. Atanasov of the 662nd Yato performed a bad landing on Marno Pole air base, slightly damaging his mount.

Another series of photos depicting the usual accident scene, with the exception that the undercarriage appears to be unbroken. This 'pilot's monument' – as such incidents, when the aircraft ended up on its nose, were informally called by airmen all over the world – was performed by 662ⁿᵈ Yato pilot, Zamestnik ofitser (Warrant Officer) Toni E. Tonev, at Marno Pole main air base, on 13 April 1942. The damage inflicted to the airframe of aircraft No. 70/7037 was minor, officially assessed at 15%. The shiny, glittering undersurface colour gives the strong impression of silver finish, which was the most common occurence. Curiously, the lower struts of the horizontal stabiliser appear to be painted half silver, half khaki, possibly testimony of repaint after a previous accident.

larger calibre bombs, along with at least some armour protection of vital areas, would have been needed. Despite the shortcomings, this was the sole role the Avia B.534 could take on, in order to stay in combat service.

Alongside the mentioned Ju 87Rs came also a new batch of Bf 109Gs in the late summer of 1943, which would complete the equipment of the 3/6. *Orlyak*. With the arrival of Dewoitine D.520 fighters from France in September the same year, it was the turn of the 2/6. *Orlyak* to transfer from the *Dogan* to the new equipment, *yato* by *yato*. The transfer was completed by the end of the year. Next to transfer from the *Dogan* to the Dewoitine was 1/6. *Orlyak*. The process was completed by January 1944. At that

point, all surviving Avias had already been transferred to their new parent unit, the 2/2. *Orlyak*, as well as to various schools and training units.

Interestingly, a German document dated 9 March 1944, describing the order of battle of the Bulgarian air units (*bulgarische Fliegerverbände*), does not list the Avia B.534 as part of "2. *Stukaregiment*" located at Graf Ignatievo, only "*Zwei Stukastaffeln, Ju 87R-4 und D-5*". However, it mentions the regiment as a "*Rahmenverband*", namely a 'frame unit', to be expanded. Indeed, it was (or rather had been) expanded with a group that included the Avia biplane, as noted above.

By the end of 1943, there was no Avia B.534 serving any more in the fighter role the aircraft type was originally intended for. The era of the 'fighting *Dogan*' was over.

With more and more *Dogans* being relieved from their original fighter duty, they were relegated to the 2/2. *Orlyak*, as well as to various schools and training units. A second *yato* was formed within the *orlyak*. The sister *Stuka* group (1/2.) would also get its second, then third *yato* with the arrival of more

Variations to the same theme. This time, Dogan No. 50/7037 ended up on its nose following a botched taxiing on Marno Pole/ Karlovo, on 20 April 1942. The pilot, Kandidat podofit-ser Stefan D. Petrov of the 642ⁿᵈ Yato escaped unhurt. This time, both the upper and the bottom wingtips were painted yellow, as were the rudder and the elevators. A yellow mid-fuselage band and a rearward tapering flash were applied as well. The aircraft's serial number was not shown on the outer lower wingtips (or was overpainted with yellow). Based on the shininess of the undersurface finish, the area appears to be covered with silver paint. Interestingly, only one bomb rack was attached to each lower wing. Another Dogan in the background, at right, taxies at high speed, as on Marno Pole it was business as usual.

aircraft. In mid-1944, the enlarged 2. *Shturmovi Polk* would consist of a staff and two *orlyatsi*, the latter made of four plus two *yata*, in total.

2. Shturmovi Polk	231. *Yato*
Shtab na Polka	*Uchebno Yato*
1/2. *Shtuka Orlyak* (Junkers Ju 87)	2/2. *Shturmovi Orlyak* (Avia B.534)
Shtabno krilo	*Shtabno krilo*
211. *Yato*	241. *Yato*
221. *Yato*	251. *Yato*

The theoretical number of aircraft to be assigned to the assault *polk* was 4 for the *polk* staff, 2 for each *orlyak* staff, 36 for the 'Shtuka' *Orlyak* and 24 for the *Dogan Orlyak*, i.e., 68 aircraft in total. In reality, only 21 *Dogans* were assigned to the 2/2. *Orlyak* by the end of 1943, though more arrived in early 1944.

Due to the surplus in *Dogans* by late 1943, those under repair were evaluated and the ones in poor condition scrapped. A document issued by the technical department of the VNVV, dated 24 December 1943, reflecting the situation extant on 23 November, lists the following nine *Dogans*, which were in this dire condition: 10, 32, 38, 40, 50, 57, 63, 66 and 69. Eventually, all of them were scrapped. Desperate attempts were made to keep the remaining Avias up in the air. The VNVV HQ contacted its German counterpart in trying to secure much needed spare parts and engines from the occupied Czech lands. Based on a German export document dated 5 February 1943, the Avia Company was requested to send spares for airframes and electrical accessories needed for the Avia Bn.534, as well as spare parts for the Avia 12 Ydrs engines. From the Bulgarian side, Major Slavomirov was in charge of completing this activity. More orders were placed by the Bulgarians later in the year. However, some orders could not be honoured due to the unavailability in the *Reich* of the requested spare parts and materials.

Many Avia B.534s ended up in various piloting schools. A casual look at the logbook of *Podporuchik* Petăr Manolev reveals that he flew the following *Dogans* in 1943: Nos. 5, 14, 27, 30, 31, 36, 41, 45, 47, 52, 54, 55, 58, 59, 62, 68, 69, 72. All these aircraft were flown at the Dolna Mitropoliya piloting school. No. 55 was also flown at Karlovo on 15 April, No. 27 at Balchik on 8 and 9 June, No. 69 also at Balchik on 11 June, while No. 72 also at Balchik, on 12 June. As noted earlier, at Balchik there was the Gunnery School, where pilots could perform live firing drills.

Earlier that year, several accidents happened to *Dogan* pilots, none of them fata. On 19 April, *Ppor.* Dimităr A. Dimitrov of the Piloting School performed a bad landing on Dolna Mitropoliya; the biplane bounced from the ground then fell from three metres. As a result of the botched landing, the undercarriage of *Dogan* No. 6/7037 broke off, the airframe suffered 50% damage, and undoubtedly the rookie pilot was reprimanded (see photo on page 190). The next incident happened only two days later, this time at Bozhurishte. While landing, the engine of *Dogan* No. 26/7037 suddenly quit. Luckily, the pilot, *Podof.* Kiril I. Kălvachev[37], could land safely his mount. Following the investigation, it turned out that the petrol was of bad quality, that's why the engine stopped. Also in April, on the 27th, *Podof.* Yordan Daskalov[38] damaged lightly his mount, *Dogan* No. 5/7037, rolling onto railway tracks during landing on Sofia airfield. In the summer, on 23 August, *Ppor.* Stefan Marinopolski collided with two *Vrabche* (code name for the Focke-Wulf Fw 44J trainer), LZ-FOY and LZ-FOS, while landing with *Dogan* No. 11/7037 also on Sofia airfield (see photo on page 177). All three aircraft were damaged. In his logbook, Marinopolski briefly mentioned only *zlopoluka*, i.e. accident. There are no more accidents recorded in the author's files, nevertheless further incidents certainly happened.

The last combat year for the Bulgarian airmen found most of the serviceable *Dogans* at Graf Ignatievo air base, within 2/2. *Shturmovi Orlyak*. Not much is known about their activity there. Presumably, training flights dominated, to customise the former fighter pilots to ground attack techniques. The training was occasionally mixed with live exercises, to learn co-operation with ground units and firing runs at ground targets.

An order of battle of the Bulgarian air force, undoubtedly originating from German sources, found in USAF archives[39], dated 17 July 1944, lists the following: "2. *Ground-Attack Regiment (Maj. Ilyev), with I. Ground-Attack Group (Ju 87) at Graf-Ignatievo, and II. Ground-Attack Group (in formation)*". This latter unit was supposed to be employing the Avia B.534s retired from the interceptor fighter role.

The first complete order of battle for 1944 coming from Bulgarian sources, available to the author, is dated 31 May. At that point, there were 11 serviceable and 45 unserviceable *Dogans* with the 2/2. *Shturm. Orlyak* (total 56 aircraft). This represented a surplus of 32 aircraft to the theoretical number needed: 24! Interestingly, this theoretically needed number of aircraft (24) was crossed out with pencil on the original document, and the number 21 written over it, as was the number of serviceable aircraft (11), which was replaced by 9.

The next complete order of battle available for this study is dated 1 August 1944, when the total number of existing *Dogans* was reduced dramatically, as follows: 10 serviceable and 9 unserviceable, amounting to only 19 aircraft, which was five units short of the theoretically needed 24 aircraft. This sharp reduction in extant *Dogans* is due to a massive write-off that was performed on 1 August. On that date, among the 73 warplanes – mostly fighters – written off were the following Avia B.534s: Nos. 4, 8, 10, 11, 16, 17, 20, 37, 39, 43, 49, 54, 55, 60, 64 and 66, i.e. 16 aircraft in total.

The last order of battle before Bulgaria's about face of 9 September is dated 1 September. At that date, the overall number of aircraft increased to 26, of which only 6 were serviceable, however. The low state of serviceability at this stage of the war is testimony to the poor condition of the worn-out airframes and their engines, as well as the lack of spare parts. The fact that the number of available *Dogans* actually grew is hard to explain, as seven more were officially written off on 23 August, as follows: Nos. 6, 7, 14, 25, 46, 62 and 65.

USAAF warplanes also contributed to the reduction of the *Dogan* inventory, at least on one occasion. On 28 June 1944, after being relieved from escort duty, the fighters escorting B-24 'Liberators' of the 304th Bomber Wing that targeted Karlovo main fighter air base strafed the nearby Graf Ignatievo airfield (located 40 km south) – home of the 2. Assault *Polk*. The bombers were covered by P-47 'Thunderbolts' of the 332nd Fighter Group, as well as P-38 'Lightnings' of the 14th Fighter Group (curiously, none of the pilots reported strafing in their after-mission debriefing). Besides seven Ju 87Ds of the 1/2. *Shtuka*

---

37 *Feldfebel* Kălvachev would die in a training accident while flying a Bf 109G on 11 April 1945.

38 Another document, issued on 11 November, gives the pilot's name as *Podofitser* Yordan M. Dimitrov, but it's probably a clerical error.

39 Microfilm rolls T-311 (295/519) and T-501 (189/21), located in the depository of the US National Archives (NARA), College Park, MD, USA.

Series of photos taken during the ceremony of 'blessing of the combat flag' on 30 January 1943. One of the aircraft displayed on the snowy ground of Marno Pole/Karlovo air base was Avia B.534, No. 16 (depicted also in the detail photo). For further photos of the same scene, see the Bf 109E chapter.

Orlyak, a number of Avia B.534s of the sister 2/2. *Shturmovi Orlyak* were reportedly damaged as well. Five *Dogans* were written off officially that very day, Nos. 30, 36, 40, 69 and 73. They could also have been destroyed on Karlovo base, among the approximately 40 aircraft that fell victim to the devastating bombing raid.

1944 was the last year when veteran pilot instructor *Ppor.* Petăr Manolev flew the *Dogan*. All his training sorties were logged from Dolna Mitropoliya. The first flight was performed on 8 March, aboard No. 40. Then, he flew the following aircraft: Nos. 10, 11, 16, 17, 26, 36, 47, 62 and 69. The last day he lifted aboard the much-flown *Dogan* was on 12 May, when he performed '*figuri*' (i.e. aerobatics) for ten minutes. At that point, the era of the Czech biplane fighter, relegated to trainer, ended for him.

Fighting Tito's Partisans

From mid-1941, Yugoslavian partisan activity in the so-called 'Vardar Macedonia' had become a thorn in the side of the Bulgarian Army, active in that volatile area recently awarded to Bulgaria. To counter the insurgent activity, close air support was requested and received.

According to the memories of Lieutenant General Ivan Popov[40], an order was issued on 30 December 1941 to move troops to pacify the newly acquired area. The transportation of Bulgarian occupation troops began on 7 January 1942 and ended on 15 January 1942. In this early period, an air support *yato* was probably assigned to the occupation troops. Certainly, throughout this time period Bulgarian warplanes were stationed on Nish (in Serbian Niš) airfield, located just north of the village of Medoševac, close to the city of Niš. One proof is the VNVV Order No. 494/23.10.1943, signed by the Assistant Commander of the Air Force, who ordered investigation in "*the circumstances and causes of the destruction of the second* [sic! more probably two] *Bulgarian aircraft, destroyed on Nish Airport by enemy aircraft on 20 October 1943*". Indeed, that day warplanes of the USAAF XII Bomber Command attacked the two marshalling yards of Nish at around 13:00. Presumably, the nearby airfield was not spared, either. Overall, 36 bombers participated in the raid against the yard lying to the west of the city. They were

---

40 Popov, Ivan: '*Deynost na Bălgarskoto Glavno Komandvane Prez Vtorata Svetovna Voyna*' ('Activity of the Bulgarian General Command during the Second World War'), Vol. 1, „St. Kliment Ohridski" Military publishing complex „St. George the Victorious", Sofia, Bulgaria, 1993, p. 115-116.

Podporuchik *Petăr Bochev – second-highest scoring Bulgarian fighter pilot – is sitting on the starboard wing of a Dogan used for training. Curiously, on the port wing undersurface number 2 can be seen; however, on the rear fuselage the bottom part of number 1 is visible. Replacement wing could be a plausible answer. The removable U-shape bottom panel of the engine cowling is a replacement part, and it's painted either in light grey camouflage colour, or wears only a coat of primer, also grey.*

covered by 16 P-38 'Lightnings'. Additionally, 24 P-38s dive bombed the other marshalling yard, lying to the north[41]. It was reported that *"escort of P-38s with bombs hit the field N of the yards and caused fires and destroyed 2 E/A [enemy aircraft] on the ground."* These must have been the Bulgarian warplanes mentioned in the VNVV report.

There is no information obtainable on the sporadic activity of this ad-hoc unit until early 1944. At this point, in May[42], a new air unit was tasked with combatting the increasing partisan activity. To fulfil this specific task, the VNVV HQ formed the Mixed Army *Yato* of units of the 1st Army Air *Polk*. There were six Letov Š.328s, six Avia B.534s and a single liaison Fieseler Fi 156 *Storch* assigned to this mixed squadron. The motley unit was then ordered under the 1st Occupation Army Corps of the Bulgarian Army (*Părvi Okupatsionen Korpus na Bălgarskata Armiya*), active in Bulgarian Macedonia and parts of occupied Serbia. Their base stayed at Niš airfield.

Pilots of the mixed squadron performed many reconnaissance and combat missions against local Communist partisans. However, as they operated in mountainous areas, covered by dense woods, the missions had only limited success. It was during one of these close air support missions when the low flying *Dogan* of Ppor. Konstantin Dimitrov Petsev was hit by ground fire and caught fire. The pilot had to bail out of his stricken mount. Luckily for him, he landed in friendly territory, at Trăn, in an area controlled by Bulgarian troops. One possible match from Yugoslav Communist partisan sources[43] describes the following event: in the region southeast of Prokuplje (although the location is far from Trăn), partisan anti-aircraft fire hit a Bulgarian reconnaissance aircraft on 27 March. The wounded pilot performed an emergency landing, after which German and Bulgarian troops guarded the wrecked airplane[44]. The 'Young Fighter' Communist newspaper states that the 6th South Moravian Brigade shot down a Bulgarian airplane en-route between Bela Voda-Donja Toponica, but on 28 March.

Another description coming from Yugoslav sources reported the following for 16 June: *"throughout the day, there were fierce battles between partisans of the 4th Serbian Brigade and Bulgarian troops, supported by aviation, which tried to lift the siege of the garrison in Blace. Bulgarian units could not penetrate the positions of the 4th Battalion at Slanište and of the 1st Battalion between Pretežana and Mala Draguša. At the same time, the 2nd and 3rd (Yugoslav) Battalions attacked Mađersko hill, where Bulgarian artillery pieces and mortars were located. At the end of the day, a Bulgarian airplane was shot down, which repeatedly bombed the partisan positions. The partisans recovered the radio station and weapons from the wreckage, before it was burned. Shortly thereafter, the Bulgarian army retreated to Beljolin."* On the last day of July, the 16th

---

41   See the Bf 109E chapter for additional details.

42   Ibid, p. 243.

43   Yugoslav partisans claimed shooting down Bulgarian warplanes from as early as mid-January 1944. [Many thanks to Boris Ciglić for providing information on Yugoslav Communist partisan activity in the discussed area].

44   Source: NAW T-501/256/371.

A Dogan, believed to be No. 68, carefully camouflaged by a net and foliage during field manoeuvres.

Serbian Brigade fought with Bulgarian units near the village Nesvrte, near Vranje. They reported that one Bulgarian airplane was shot down and another one damaged. The airplane crashed and burned in the Morava valley. The event was witnessed by the British liaison officer. The last two events in August, when Yugoslav partisans reportedly managed to shoot down Bulgarian warplanes, involved two shootdowns in each occasion. This does not match the Bulgarian description on the demise of the Avia B.534, or any other warplane, however.

By August, there were six Avias left in the anti-partisan squadron operating in Macedonia. These *Dogans* were destroyed by US bombings of Niš airfield. The first such air raid was performed by 51 B-17 'Flying Fortresses' of the 99th and 463rd Bomber Groups, escorted by 25 P-38 'Lightnings' of the 82nd Fighter Group, on 17 August 1944. The US crews reported four aircraft destroyed on the ground and eleven more damaged. The actual result of this unwanted attention by US bombers was three Bulgarian aircraft destroyed and seven damaged[45] (these could be either Avia B.534s, or Letov Š-328s, or a mix of them), along with a Bf 109G-6 of the *Luftwaffe*'s II./JG 51 and four more damaged.

The next US raid against Niš air base was performed on the 21st, this time by 117 B-24 'Liberators' of the 55th Bomber Wing, escorted by 49 P-51 'Mustangs' of the 31st Fighter Group. This second mission also ended with four aircraft destroyed on the ground and six more damaged. Of these total losses, two were *Luftwaffe* and the other two unspecified Bulgarian aircraft. The final bombing run against Niš air base was performed on 1 September by 55 unescorted B-17s of the 301st and 483rd BGs (although it is reported that 33 P-38s of the 1st FG flew a sweep in the vicinity of Niš). This time, the US crews claimed five enemy aircraft and a glider destroyed on the ground[46]. There is no information available from the German side.

---

45 This total number is an indirect figure, resulting of the difference between total losses reported (four destroyed and eleven damaged) minus actual *Luftwaffe* losses (one destroyed and four damaged). [Many thanks to Boris Ciglić for providing information and copies of pertinent German documents].

46 *Kandidat-podofitser* Racho Penchev Rikevski, born at Stefan Stambolovo, located in Veliko Tărnovo district, in 1922, of корпусно смесено ято, i.e. 'Mixed Corps Squadron', based at Niš airfield, died there on 1 September 1944. He is buried at Niš military cemetery, Strand u. 39, Op. 3, au 111, l. 211.

A similar ceremony also held in early 1943, but probably at a different location, is depicted in this photo, which features a krilo (trio) of Avia B.534s. A group of priests inside the makeshift gazebo-like structure are blessing the Bulgarian flag. Soon after these ceremonies, a new chapter in the service life of the surviving Bulgarian Avias would begin, which would see them in the markedly different role of ground attack aircraft.

This faded post-accident scene photo shows Dogan No. 6/7037 after it crashed due to the overly low landing speed while approaching Dolna Mitropoliya landing ground on 19 April 1943. The pilot, Podofitser Dimităr A. Dimitrov of the Piloting School, escaped unhurt – except for a hefty scare. The airframe, however, suffered extensive damage, evaluated at 50%. The numeral looks like an inverted 9. The light area on the rudder is a defect on the scanned print.

A notable Bulgarian source[47] puts the losses of the 'Smesenoto voyskovo yato', or 'Mixed Combat (Aviation) Squadron', attached to the 1st Bulgarian Army Corps, to six *Vranas* (reconnaissance/bomber Letov Š.328), three '*shturmovi Dogans*' (ground attack Avia B.534) and a *Drozhd* (liaison Fieseler Fi 156), destroyed on the ground at Niš air base.

These air attacks came just days before the Bulgarian mixed squadron was scheduled to return to its base on the mainland, and destroyed most of the Bulgarian assets deployed to Medoševac/Niš airfield.

With the Yugoslav 'adventure', the five-year front-line activity of the Avia B.534 on the Axis' side came to an end.

Changing Sides

In early September 1944, VNVV High Command, along with other Bulgarian political and military decision makers, sensed the "winds of change", and secretly prepared to exit the Axis camp. After the first Red Army units crossed the border from Rumania on 5 September, a coup d'état took place in Sofia. The Government was overthrown by the Communist-inspired 'Fatherland Front' (abbreviated as OF) on 9 September. Bulgaria officially declared war on the Third Reich. By then, however, Bulgarian troops, supported by aviation, had already engaged in fierce combat with retreating German forces in Macedonia, the south-western area of 'Greater Bulgaria'.

---

47 Milanov, Yordan: ‚*Văzdushnite voyski na Bălgaria prez voynite, 1912-1945 g.*', Eăr Grup 2000, Sofia, 2008, page 343.

After being relegated to the ground attack role in late 1943, a few Avia B.534s found themselves fighting Communist partisans in Macedonia. The low-level bombing and strafing sorties over the rugged mountainous terrain of Macedonia presented clear danger to any Axis aircraft, as demonstrated by the wrecks of what is believed to be a Luftwaffe Henschel Hs 126 (last two letters of its radio code 'AA'), crashed on a hillside, used by Bulgarian soldiers as décor for their souvenir shot taken in 1944.

Landing with the Avia B.534 was tricky, due to its narrow undercarriage. This design shortcoming led to numerous taxiing accidents, which usually caused minor damage to the wings and propeller. Details of the depicted accident involving Dogan No. 73 are unknown; nevertheless, it is believed that it happened sometime in 1943, which may explain the extremely worn appearance. This particular aircraft was officially written off on 28 June 1944; however, it is unlikely that this minor landing accident was the cause of its demise. Most likely, it was destroyed during the devastating USAAF raid against Karlovo air base. Notice the faded yellow upper wingtips (as well as the barely seen yellow elevators) and chipped national marking. This pair of photos could be a prime source for the seasoned modeller, who wishes to depict his/her model kit wearing heavily weathered and thoroughly chipped paintjob.

The new enemy meant a totally new task and combat environment for the embattled VNVV. From then on, Bulgarian warplanes performed tactical combat missions, particularly short- and long-range reconnaissance, close air support for the army, as well as bombing and ground attacks against German equipment and positions.

Separation between Bulgarian and German troops where they had been operating together wasn't peaceful, for obvious reasons. The Bulgarians had to retreat hastily from peripheral areas controlled by the Germans (e.g. occupied Greece, Macedonia), leaving behind sizeable amounts of matériel. One prime example was the large Aviation Repair Shop at Skopie airfield, shared with the Germans. When news of the Bulgarians' about-face reached Skopie in early September; the Germans were obviously not pleased by their allies' sudden defection. Therefore, the Bulgarian personnel had only minutes to evacuate the premises, to run away virtually only with the shirts on their backs. They left behind over two dozen warplanes under repair, including one *Dogan* (53/7037). Along with the single airframe, an "Ispano" engine was abandoned there as well (c/n 370870-12).

As listed earlier, the VNVV could rely on the following number of Avia B.534s on 1 September 1944: 6 serviceable and 20 unserviceable aircraft listed within 2/2. *Shturmovi Orlyak*. There is no information about the number of pilots assigned to this attack group, but it was certainly less than the number of aircraft.

On 4 September, the order of battle of the VNVV air attack force consisted of[48]:

2. *Shturmovi Polk* (Attack Regiment), C/O *Mahyor* Hristo Iliev
Shtab (staff and liaison) – Rechitsa airfield
1/2. *Shtuka Orlyak* – Rechitsa airfield
2/2. *Shturmovi Orlyak* – Malo Konare airfield

Next day, the Bulgarian Minister of Defence, Maj. Gen. Ivan Marinov, ordered by 'telephonogram' No. 1166 the VNVV combat units to perform close air support for the besieged 1st Bulgarian Army Corps, which had been attacked by Germans in the Niš-Kriva Palanka area, as soon as possibilities would permit. However, the Bulgarian air units were stationed far away from the new front lines, therefore they had to

---

48 Most data in this chapter were taken from a hand-written original diary of the VNVV's combat activity, covering the period September-October 1944.

deploy first to closer airfields, located around Sofia. Accordingly, the *Dogan*-equipped 2/2. *Orlyak* moved to Vrazhdebna, on the outskirts of Sofia, while the *Shtuka*-equipped 1/2. *Orlyak* moved to the other military airfield close to the capital, Bozhurishte. Aviation fuel and 7.92 mm ammunition were also moved to the new location, in preparation for the first combat missions. The relocation was completed by the 10th of September. At the time hostilities begun, there were nine serviceable *Dogans* with the 2/2. *Orlyak*, as follows: Nos. 2, 5, 19, 26, 28, 58, 63, 70 and 77. Ten others were in an unserviceable state. A single Bücker Bü 131 *Lastovitsa*, No. 14, was used by the staff of the assault group as a hack aircraft.

Even before the first combat missions against German ground targets could be logged, Bulgarian Avia B.534s clashed in the air with their erstwhile ally, now enemies, and it ended to their detriment[49]. On 10 September, in the early morning at 06:40 while en route from Graf Ignatievo main base where they had picked up bombs and bullets, two *Dogans* of 2/2. *Orlyak*. which had taken off later than scheduled, were suddenly intercepted by five *Luftwaffe* Bf 109Gs, near Verinsko, close to Ihtiman (located south-east of Sofia). The German fighters were escorting six twin-engine bombers, which targeted the VNVV main fuel depot at Verinsko. In the unequal air mêlée, the engine of aircraft No. 26, flown by *Feldfebel-shkolnik* Toncho Veselinov, was hit and knocked out. The pilot was wounded in his back and right arm, thus could not bail out. The *Dogan* eventually crash-landed, the bombs exploded, the pilot lost conscience. He ended up in the hospital in Ihtiman and his life was spared, but the aircraft was a total wreck[50]. There is no matching air victory claim filed by a *Luftwaffe* pilot for 10 September, but the records are incomplete. The four other *Dogans* that took off in time, led by *orlyak* leader *Kpt.* Tsviatko Kolev, were luckier, they avoided being spotted by the Germans, thus arrived at their destination unhurt.

The very first combat missions of the ground attack *Dogans* in the anti-German campaign took place on 11 September. Initially, they performed three reconnaissance sorties between 10:00 and 15:00 in the Kumanovo-Etno Selo-Shtip area. Then, at 18:40, five biplanes of 2/2. *Orlyak*, led by *Kapitan* Tsviatko P. Kolev, attacked enemy lorries on the road south-west of Kriva Palanka. Numerous enemy AA artillery pieces were spotted. At 18:55, a long enemy column, made up of about one hundred lorries and which included armoured vehicles but no tanks, was spotted on the road near Kriva Palanka-Deve Bair, moving towards Kyustendil. This column was not attacked, however, the *Dogans* returned home without firing a shot. Next day, 2/2. *Orlyak* reported five combat sorties, performed in the same area. During the most notable mission of the day, five *Dogans* strafed an enemy column made up of horse-drawn wagons spotted at 3 km north of Kriva Palanka at 7:40 in the morning. Flying at ultra-low height and firing very effectively, the biplanes caused havoc, scaring and killing horses and men alike, leaving great destruction behind. The surprised Germans could not fire back to any effect, so all the *Dogans* escaped unhurt.

Next time the assault *Dogans* took off in a combat mission was on 14 September. That day, between 13:30-14:15, 1/5. Bomber *Orlyak*, 2/2. Assault *Orlyak* and 3/6. Fighter *Orlyak* bombed and strafed enemy ground forces spotted in the Kriva Palanka area and on the road leading to Deve Bair. The four *Dogans* thrown into battle were piloted by *Orlyak* C/O *Kpt.* Kolev, *Por.* Kolev, *Feldf.-shkolnik* Poptolev and *Kand. podof.* Getov. *Kpt.* Kolev probably destroyed two vehicles and attacked a tank. Between 16:00-16:40, a *Dogan krilo* attacked an enemy truck column discovered on the Kriva Palanka-Gyueshevo road. Next day, between 8:35-9:05, the combat-ready *Dogans* strafed a motorised column west of Tsarevo Selo, 5-6 cars were reportedly destroyed. However, two aircraft did not return from the mission. It turned out that both *Dogans* were shot down by anti-aircraft fire. One force-landed near Kyustendil, the pilot escaped alive. The pilot of the other one, *Podof.* Slavi M. Stoyanov, had to bail out. He did so successfully, and returned to his unit. His mount, No. 63/7037, was obviously a write-off[51]. Also on the 15th, the headquarters of the 2nd Assault Regiment moved to Graf Ignatievo airfield.

Due to the significantly reduced number of combat-ready aircraft, the 2/2. *Orlyak* was not thrown into battle for a couple of days. On 18 September, a combat mission was assigned to a four-ship *Dogan krilo*, which had to attack enemy positions at 'Ostri vrăh' (i.e., Pointed Peak), located near Pirot, in a mission that started at 11:10. Unlike the *Stukas* of 1/2. *Orlyak*, enjoying air protection from a dozen D.520 fighters, the *Dogans* performed their mission unprotected, as it usually was the case. The radiator of No. 19/7037 was hit by ground fire (another document mentions engine trouble), and had to belly land west of Pirot. The pilot, *Kand. podof.* Georgi P. Getov, escaped without injuries, the aircraft was repaired.

Based on Order No. I-1332, issued by the Ministry of War, Army Staff, a new identification colour was introduced on Bulgarian warplanes instead of the so-called 'Axis yellow'. Effective 19 September,

---

49 A highly interesting entry can be found in the *Luftwaffe* air victory claim list for 2 September. On that day, *Major* Johann Gamringer, *Kommandeur* of NSGr. 4, claimed an 'Avia' in area No. 00757, at 11:50. It was his second victory, after the first one claimed in Spain, prior to the war! The veteran pilot must have been flying a Junkers Ju 87D-3, as this was the only armed aircraft of the staff unit. However, by checking the location of the air base of NSG 4 in that period, it was at Balice, which is the current airport of Kraków, Poland, making this claim irrelevant to the air war over Bulgaria.

50 This particular aircraft, 26/7037, was officially written off only a year later, almost to the day, on 11.09.1945.

51 *Dogan* No. 63/7037 (engine No. 341/841) was officially written off on 19 October 1944.

the new marking consisted of white to be applied, as follows: one meter wide on both wingtips (in this particular case the lower wingtip of the lower wing and the upper wingtip of the upper wing), propeller spinner and a half metre wide band on the fuselage. This change was necessary for easier recognition by Soviet airmen, particularly fighter pilots and anti-aircraft artillery personnel, in order to avoid 'friendly fire' incidents.

On the 20th of September, at 10:30, four *Dogans* performed a reconnaissance mission in the Kriva Palanka area, where they attacked an enemy vehicle column. This was only a target of opportunity, as the primary one, reported near Prilep, was not located. Upon return to the base airfield of Vrazhdebna, one *Dogan* had a landing accident, with no major consequences. Details of the combat mission performed on 24 September are lacking; however, what is known is that a *Dogan* was hit by anti-aircraft fire. The pilot was able to land on the home airfield of Vrazhdebna. His mount, No. 58/7037, was damaged but repairable.

As one can appreciate, the number of serviceable Avias decreased by the day, as did the number of pilots. In a document dated 25 September, seven *Dogans* are listed as combat ready, as follows: Nos. 2, 5, 19, 26, 58, 63, 70. An *Air Eskadra* strength return dated 26.9.1944 lists for 2/2. *Shturmovi Orlyak* seven airworthy (most probably the same ones listed the previous day) and 28 non-airworthy aircraft, but with only two available pilots! No wonder, the *Dogans* show up in VNVV operational documents less and less... A strength return dated 28 September mentions the 2nd Ground Assault *Polk* having a *Stuka orlyak* with three *yata*. A second *orlyak* exists, but it has only two serviceable "*Avia 534 (Dogan)*" [mentioned as such in the quoted document].

From October on, the activity of the *Dogans* diminished even further. Often the *orlyak* commander, *Kapitan* Tsviatko P. Kolev, logged tactical reconnaissance sorties alone (!), reporting his findings back to the Air *Eskadra* HQ. While performing air intelligence gathering, occasionally he also strafed targets of opportunity. Such tactical reconnaissance missions were carried out on the 6th, the 9th, the 24th and the 25th of October, the latter by two aircraft.

On 21 October, at 7:10, a *Dogan* trio attacked with bombs and machine gun fire enemy positions discovered north of Kriva Palanka. In the afternoon, No. 77/7037[52], piloted by *Podof.* Slavi Marinov Stoyanov, did not return from a reconnaissance mission performed in the region of Stratsin-Kumanovo-Boyanovche at 16:30. His eventual fate was a mystery to the Author for a while, as the documents available did not mention the outcome of this incident. However, it was solved with the help of Bulgarian researcher and author Boris Kodikov. It turned out that *Podof.* Slavi Stoyanov Marinov [his middle and last names were erroneously inverted in the document mentioning his disappearance, a common occurrence when dealing with Bulgarian names, D.B.] had to force-land due to engine trouble near the bridge over the River Ptchinya. He returned to his unit safely, and continued to fly until the end of hostilities. Marinov's *Dogan* was officially written off on 28 December 1945. His last flight was

---

52 The first digit of the serial number, as typed in document No. II-1203/21.10.1944, is very difficult to read.

recorded on 15 November 1944, when *"Podof. Slavi Marinov ferried an airplane to Karlovo for repairs."* Marinov survived the war[53], but was eventually killed in an aircraft accident on 29 April 1951[54].

A document dated 1 November lists among the units of *Văzdushnata Eskadra 2/2. Shturmovi Orlyak*, with two serviceable and one unserviceable *Dogan*, as well as one officer and three NCO pilot in its roster. On that first day of November, two *Dogans* took off for a reconnaissance mission at 12:30. They spotted several lone vehicles advancing on the Kumanovo-Skopie road. There was no traffic on either lane of the road west of the River Ptchinya. In the afternoon mission, performed between 15:00 and 15:30, a single *Dogan* reconnoîtred the Kumanovo-Sveti Nikole-Shtip-Zletovo-Kratovo area. No traffic

---

53 After the war, *Podof.* Slavi S. Marinov was attached of the 12th Assault Group (formerly 1/2. *Orlyak*), located in Plovdiv, where he transitioned to the Il-2 *Shturmovik*. After the formation of the 5th Assault Division, also in Plovdiv, Marinov – already an officer – joined this unit. In August 1950, he was transferred to the 20th Assault Regiment on Krumovo, where he converted to the Il-10 assault aircraft type. He lost his life on 29 April 1951, as detailed below.

54 On 29 April 1951, the Il-10 piloted by the commanding officer of the 5th Assault Division, *Mahyor* Dimităr Petkov, rammed by accident the Il-10 flown by *St. Leyt.* Slavi Marinov (as his name was given in the post-accident report) during the exercises for the 1 May parade, held on Vrazhdebna air base. Senior (1st) Lt. Marinov died in the incident, being crushed by the engine armour plate.

was observed on the roads. However, a scattered column of around 20 to 30 vehicles from Veles to Shtip, widely spread out, was spotted, slowly moving in the direction of Shtip. The head of the column was near the village of Krivodol. A heavy artillery battery was located at the road south of the Pushina M. marker, a second one near the "A" point at the Nagorichane marker. The following days were 'no fly' days for the 2/2. *Orlyak*. A *Dogan dvoyka* performed an afternoon reconnaissance mission on 4 November. During the 45 minute flight, the pilots reconnoîtred the Sv. Nikola-S. Orashats (11 km south of Kumanovo)-S. Katlanovo (23 km south of Skopie) area.

On 6 November, three *Dogans* performed a strafing mission against German positions at Peak 370. Three days later, an early morning reconnaissance flight is recorded in the area Sv. Nikola-Veles and Ibrishimovo, in central Macedonia. Right after that, a 'record' four-aircraft *krilo* attacked a train with 20 kg bombs. Forty minutes after noon, the same four aircraft took off to return over the battlefield, in the Pravtse area, where enemy trenches were strafed. After this date, the already low-level activity of the 2/2. *Orlyak* diminished to almost non-existence. Officially, the Avia-equipped assault group quit combat activity on 12 November and retired from first-line service. The days of the "assault *Dogan*" were now over.

On 14 November, a batch of six *Dogans* were officially scrapped. These were Nos. 9, 27, 33, 45, 52 and 57 (none of them were part of the 2/2. *Orlyak* aircraft that went to war). The order of battle of 2/2. *Shturmovi Orlyak* listed for 15 November six serviceable aircraft (and most probably no aircraft in unserviceable state). This will be pretty much the norm for the unit until the end of the year.

No. of serviceable/unserviceable Avia B.534s in 2/2. *Orlyak*, 1 August 1944–1 August 1945

Date (day.month)	1.08	1.09	17.09	26.09	1.10	4.10	7.10	15.10	1.11	15.11	1.12	1.01	1.02	1.04	1.08
Serviceable	10	6	3	1	1	1	1	2	2	6	6	6	2	2	0
Unserviceable	9	20	N/A	3	N/A	8	N/A	N/A	1	N/A	0	0	4	4	0
Total	19	26	N/A	4	N/A	9	N/A	N/A	3	N/A	6	6	6	6	0
Balance (to 24 pcs.)	-5	+2	N/A	-20	N/A	-13	N/A	N/A	-21	N/A	-18	-18	-18	-18	0

Between 10 September and 12 November 1944, during the anti-German campaign, 2/2. *Shturmovi Orlyak* logged a total of 71 combat missions that involved 140 aircraft, with a total of 252 flying hours. Incredibly, *orlyak* commander, *Kpt.* Kolev himself performed almost half of these, namely 67 combat sorties, 65 of which aboard the *Dogan* (the two others on the *Shtuka*)! The overall results of this war activity were 22 artillery pieces destroyed or damaged, 52 motor vehicles destroyed, along with 62 horse-drawn carriages, as well as four armoured vehicles knocked out. A train and a marshalling yard were also attacked with small bombs and machine gun fire. Besides damage to enemy targets, *Dogan* pilots produced more than 100 intelligence reports as well.

A general review of the achievements of Bulgarian warplanes during the anti-German campaign is given by a British intelligence file[55], dated 18 December (undoubtedly relying on official Bulgarian sources). This review gives the following info on the activity of the 2. *Orlyak* (not distinguishing between the results achieved by the Ju 87D and the Avia B.534 crews). "*The famous dive bombers and low level bombers [sic!, reference to the Avia B.534s] of Capt. Dimiter Karaivanov carried out 193 battle tasks, in 1,281 battle flights. In these missions the bombers destroyed 63 ground and anti-aircraft batteries, destroyed and damaged 562 enemy A.F.V.s, tractors and other motor transport, destroyed or heavily damaged 6 railway stations, cut 43 railway lines, destroyed 11 road and railway bridges, hit with heavy bombs 1 hangar workshop, destroyed or heavily damaged 346 wagons and destroyed 12 locomotives.*"

During the two-month-long combat service, four attack *Dogans* were shot down, crashed, or were damaged beyond repair (Nos. 26, 63, 19 and 77). The number of combat sorties performed by *Dogans* (i.e., 140) is petty when compared to the total number of sorties logged by all Bulgarian warplanes: 3,744 (up to 2 December). It represented a mere 3.7%. However, the percentage of the aircraft destroyed during the campaign was much higher, around 12%.

After the conclusion of the so-called 'Patriotic War' (i.e., the Anti-German Campaign in Macedonia and Kosovo), the 2. *Shturmovi Polk* had to vacate Graf Ignatievo air base, because it was taken over by the Soviet Air Force[56]. In the spring of 1945, the Avia B.534s relocated to Plovdiv airfield, while the Ju 87Ds went to Vrazhdebna, where the cadet air school's group (*Yunkerski Ucheben Orlyak*) and the paratrooper battalion (*Parashutnata Druzhina*) were also located. Indeed, Order of Battle dated 1 April 1945 lists 2/2. *Shturmovi Orlyak* as located at Plovdiv. Command of this assault *orlyak* was taken over by *Poruchik* Genadi G. Yanachkov, while the 2. *Văzdushen Shturmovi Polk* was already headed by *Kapitan* Dimităr Karaivanov from 20 September 1944. A document dated in December, but without the day being giv-

---

55 M.A.A.F. Intelligence, Air Section, A.C.C. Bulgaria, British Mission, Ref.: ACC/1/INT, found on MAAF Microfilm Roll 238, USAF HRA.

56 The 1/5. Bomber *Orlyak* would still share the airfield with the VVS units, at least in the spring of 1945.

en [most probably it was the first day of the month], lists among the units of *Văzdushnata Eskadra 2/2. Shturmovi Orlyak* with six serviceable *Dogans* and none unserviceable, as well as two officers and an NCO pilot in its roster.

From that point on, the destiny of the two ground attack *orlyatsi* separated. While the *Shtuka Orlyak* would receive in the summer reinforcement in form of eight Ju 87G-2 'Kanonenvogel' (i.e., 'cannon bird'), fitted with a pair of 3.7 cm cannon in under-wing gun pods, captured by the Red Army in occupied Austria, then handed over to their ally, the Bulgarians, the *Dogan Orlyak* experienced further depletion of its already meagre resources. This was not only due to attrition, but also due to accidents. One such occured on 16 January, when a *dvoyka* crashed while attempting to land in bad weather on Graf Ignatievo airfield. Both pilots, *Ofitser kandidat* Dimităr N. Dobrev and *Feldfebel-shkolnik* Marin G. Teofilakiev, members of the 2/2. *Orlyak*, were killed, and both aircraft, Nos. 68 and 21, were destroyed. They received orders to take two aircraft needing to be repaired to the Karlovo repair workshop, despite bad weather. Due to low visibility the pilots, without parachutes, flew at tree-top level for better orientation, but hit the landing ground and crashed to their deaths. Following the accident investigation, both commanding officers were punished with arrest, the *polk* commander for five days, while the *orlyak* commander for ten days. Another *Dogan*[57] pilot who perished, the last one, also lost his life in an accident. It was *Kandidat-Podofitser* (the

A pilot of 2/2. Shturmovi Orlyak presents one of the squadron's Dogans to young civilian men, during an 'open day' event at Vrazhdebna airfield, on a muddy winter day in late 1944/early 1945. One can observe that the entire engine cowling was painted wraparound in dark green, with light grey squiggles expanding until the bottom. The lower surface of the upper wing was painted in a similar fashion as well (details often left unnoticed by various profile artists and model kit makers). In the background, the camouflage pattern of another Dogan also finished in the so-called 'assault camouflage scheme' can be studied.

lowest NCO rank, equivalent to Corporal) Racho A. Kumanov of 1/2. *Shturmovi Orlyak*, who died on 11 September 1945, due to *"imperfect piloting skills and excessive virtuosity he displayed while flying at ultra-low height"* over his native village of Mătenitsa, near Plovdiv, hitting an oak tree. His mount, No. 58/7037[58], was a total wreck.

Somewhat surprisingly, 2/2. *Shturmovi Orlyak* employed not only Avia B.534s, but a couple of Arado Ar 96 *Soyka* trainers as well[59]. An accident report dated as late as 26 October 1945 describes the events leading to the damage of aircraft No. 24. During a routine training flight, the trainer flown by student pilot *Shkolnik* Angel Nachev, with instructor *Kapitan* Tsvetko Kolev, commanding officer of the *odtelenie* (unit), none other than the famous *orlyak* commander during the anti-German campaign, in the rear seat, belly landed due to unspecified reasons on Dolna Mitropoliya airfield.

The last Avia B.534s soldiered on in 2/2. *Shturmovi Orlyak* until July 1945, when they were replaced by Soviet specialised ground attack aircraft, namely the famous Ilyushin Il-2 *Shturmovik*. The *Văzdushni Voyski* [at this time already abbreviated only as VV, as the royal appellatio had disappeared] order of battle of 1 August 1945 lists 60 Il-2s with 2/2. *Orlyak*, which grew to three *yata* plus *shtab*. Even so, 20 aircraft were in excess to the theoretical strength of 40 aircraft. The sister *orlyak*, 1/2., was equipped identically, while all extant *Stukas*[60] were now grouped in a newly formed third *orlyak*, 3/2.

Once the Avia B.534 was removed from first line service, many were scrapped. A document dated 27 July 1945, listing all existing VV aircraft types in great detail, gives for the *Dogan* the following simple statement: *"extant units to be sent to relevant workshops for scrapping."* Such a mass write-off happened

---

57 The document states that the aircraft belonged to 1/2. *Orlyak*; however, this could be a typo.

58 NN based on post-accident report, dated 7.11.1945. The number is difficult to read. It could also be 53; however, that particular aircraft had already been written off on 23.10.1944.

59 Another crash report dated 08.08.1945 mentions that Ju 87D Stuka No. 12/7009 was also part of the 2/2. *Orlyak*; however, this could be a typo.

60 The air force clerk who penned the order of battle was apparently unfamiliar with the 'Stuka', as he variably identified the type as 'Ju-52', or 'Ju-57'.

For some reason, the Avia B.534s of 2/2. Shturmovi Orlyak did not wear large size serial numbers on their rear fuselage, as they did while on duty as interceptor fighter and trainer. The ID of the aircraft could be determined only by the small size serial number written in the upper part of the white triangle usually applied on mid-fin. This detail makes difficult to identify a certain aircraft depicted in a not perfect shot. Luckily, a high-resolution photo taken from 7 o'clock of the same aircraft (see master photo of the colour profile on page 210) reveals the identity of this Dogan: 31/7037. At the time anti-German hostilities begun, this particular aircraft was not among the nine serviceable Dogans with the 2/2. Shturmovi Orlyak; therefore, it must have arrived in the group later on, probably in early November, when the number of available aircraft increased from a meagre three to six. Curiously, the tail wheel is replaced by a rudimentary two-wheel cart with a handle that assisted moving the aircraft around. At right, a civilian registered Focke-Wulf Fw 58 Gäläb (Гълѫбъ), LZ-PBH (No. 8 on tail), is visible, behind the Avia's rudder a Junkers Ju 52/3m Sova is depicted, while at left, the sole Heinkel He 111H-16, LZ-XAC, VIP transport can be seen. The front view reveals two more aircraft in the background, a Bücker Bü 181 'Bestmann' and another Ju 52/3m Sova, probably No. 5 (LZ-UNM).

on 4 September 1945, when seven aircraft, Nos. 21, 24, 34, 68, 71, 74 and 75, were officially cancelled. Five days later, two more were struck off the lists, namely Nos. 19 and 72. Two days later, it was the turn of No. 26 to disappear from the annals of the VV, followed by No. 50 on 12 December. Another batch to be written off in 1945, on 28 December, was made by eleven *Dogans*, as follows: Nos. 2, 5, 22, 28, 41, 47, 58, 59, 67, 76 and 77. Nos. 13, 31 and 70 were also scrapped a few months later, as mentioned in a document dated 30.04.1946.

The few surviving still serviceable *Dogans* – from 23 August 1945, the aircraft type was officially identified with the DG code – ended up in the assault school. A document listing a number of airmen, dated 31 May 1946, records *Kapitan* Emanuil Ts. Nunev of 2. *Shturmovi Orlyak* [in fact, *Polk*] in the roster of the Fighter-Bomber School at Karlovo, while Tsanko S. Dilov and Veselin G. Tsvetkov, both *Urednik*[61] in the 22. *Shturmovi Orlyak*[62], as members of the Bomber School at Telish. However, there is no information on the aircraft types they flew with. Interestingly, there is no *Dogan* listed among the trainers assigned to the (air) assault school on 16 January 1946. A note sent to the school at Telish instructed the unit commander to transfer two *Dogans*, Nos. 19 and 72, to the 2ⁿᵈ Artillery Regiment for artillery observation missions. This order did not materialise, however; them having been written off instead, on 21 September. More Avias faced the wrecker's axe in 1946, too: Nos. 32, 38 and 48 on 15 October.

On 1 October 1946, among the 596 (!) conserved aircraft none was a B.534. Some could be part of the total of 206 stored trainers of unspecified type, though. The same document mentions that 97 aircraft were scrapped in September, no B.534 was among them.

The order of battle of the *Shturmovi Polk* – renamed *Shturmovi Royak* in February 1946 – did not list the type in its roster any more.

With this, the chapter in the history of the Bulgarian air force filled by the Avia B.534, which started its 'job' as a first-line interceptor fighter, then by the time it could prove its might it became obsolescent, then finished its combat career as ground assault aircraft with lacklustre performance, finally came to a close.

Colours and markings

Presumably, all Avia B.534s were delivered in the standard camouflage scheme used by the Czechoslovak air force in the pre-war era. This consisted of khaki green on upper surfaces and either light grey or shiny metal (silver) dope on the lower surfaces (the latter shade was more common). The khaki colour was a brownish green, with a more greenish hue. Certain Czech sources give FS 34097 [24097 is the more appropriate semi-gloss version, D.B.] as the equivalent of this camouflage colour. Others disagree, however. By looking, for example, at the colour applied on an original piece of transmitter of the radio transceiver Mk 35, held at the VHÚ Museum in Prague, that khaki colour seems to the author more like the next number in the FS scale, namely 24098, which has a more prominent brownish hue, albeit a bit lighter. A Czech researcher, author and publisher from Prague, Miroslav Bílý, a personal acquaintance of the author, discovered no fewer than 21 different shades of this controversial Czechoslovak khaki! For the sake of simplicity, the author will refer to this camouflage colour as 'Czechoslovak khaki', and leaves it to the Czech and Slovak colleagues to pinpoint the precise hue. Attention has to be drawn to the fact that the lower surface of the upper wing was also painted in khaki, and not in light grey, or silver, as it's often erroneously depicted on various colour artworks!

The lower surface of earlier produced machines (up to about s/n 387, manufactured in June 1938, possibly a few later ones as well) was painted in silver dope (sometimes called 'aluminium bronze'). After that, light grey (sometimes called 'dove grey') was used[63]. The interior of the cabin was painted in the same light grey colour.

The aforementioned Czech sources suggest FS 16376 for this light grey colour, which by default is shiny in appearance. It has to be noted that it's very hard, if not impossible, to differentiate between silver and light grey on black and white period photos, with the exception if the sun falls on the surface at a certain angle to reveal its shininess. Therefore, error in identifying the colour the lower surfaces were painted with generally cannot be avoided. The author will refer in the descriptions as 'Czechoslovak Light Grey, or Silver', in most cases. This light colour did not completely cover all the lower surfaces, as the lower wing's leading edges and sides, as well as the entire contour of the horizontal stabiliser,

---

61 *Urednik* literally means 'caretaker'. This rank was introduced post-war, in 1946. It replaced the rank of *Feldfebel*.

62 In 1946, the style of *orlyak* and *polk* numbering changed, the slash was eliminated. Thus, 2/2. *Orlyak* became 22. *Orlyak*, and so on.

63 Newer research shows that the usage of the silver/metal dope on the lower surfaces was much more widespread than originally thought. Light grey was reportedly used only rarely, at least on Czechoslovak Air Force machines.

were painted with a thin stripe of khaki (see colour rendition below, at right). The entire landing gear, the wing struts and, in most cases, the lower struts of the horizontal stabilisers were khaki as well.

Once the service life of the *Dogan* accumulated years, the survivors were gradually repainted in an un-identified medium green colour, referred to by the author as 'Bulgarian Mid-Green, or Green'. Possibly, it was very similar, or identical, to RLM 62 *Grün*. On some black and white photos showing Avia B.534s in VNVV service, one can distinguish between two slightly different shades of upper camouflage colour. The darker one is presumed to be the original Czechoslovak khaki, as it's usually depicted as background colour, where the paint peeled off on older aircraft. The slightly lighter one is presumed to be the newly applied 'Bulgarian Mid-Green', as it's usually seen around the original darker shade where the paint peeled off. One fine example is aircraft No. 40, where most of the vertical stabiliser (fin) – with the original factory emblem and construction number left intact, thus the area was still covered by the original Czechoslovak khaki paint – appears darker (except for the repainted bottom area) than the rest of the airframe, which is presumed that was repainted in Bulgaria. The same slight difference between the two paint hues can also be observed behind the fuselage marking, in spots around the white serial number (see detail photo and the artwork attempting to replicate it, at the bottom of page).

This khaki/mid-green over light grey/silver camouflage scheme lasted until late 1944, weeks after the commencement of the anti-German campaign. At one point in late October, the dark green surfaces (including the lower surface of the upper wing and occasionally the entire engine cowling) received squiggles and mottles in a light grey colour, possibly the same paint used on the under surfaces. This so-called 'assault camouflage scheme', or 'squiggle scheme', lasted most probably until the service life of the *Dogan* ended. A document dated 28 October 1944, issued to Bulgarian ground units, lists all Bulgarian warplanes active on the anti-German front zone in Macedonia and Kosovo, and the camouflage they were wearing. The "Avia 534 (*Dogan*) biplane" is also listed, as painted in 'dark green' (in original, тъмно-зелен). It is also stated that all warplanes wear the black X in white square type marking and white identification colours. This description reveals an important detail, namely that at this date the light grey squiggles were not yet applied on green painted areas, including the lower area of the upper wing, visible from below.

There are no photographs depicting the Avia B.534 in the so-called 'OF' (Republican) marking introduced in early October 1945; therefore, the camouflage colours worn at this late stage cannot be ascertained. It can be assumed that – except if a particular aircraft was subject of a major repair, which necessitated the repaint of the airframe – the so-called 'assault camouflage scheme' was retained until the last *Dogan* was scrapped.

Initially, when the first Avia B.534s were introduced in service with the 2. *Iztrebitelen Orlyak* (Fighter Group) in the spring of 1940, there was no individual number displayed on the airframe, except for the small size number written in the upper part of the triangle, applied in white on the mid-fin. Later, from about mid-1938, the individual number was displayed in black on the upper part of the tricolour-painted rudder, i.e., the white area, as per Order No. 53/14.04.1938. By early 1941, this black number disappeared from the rudder and reappeared as large size white number on the rear fuselage, aft of the VNVV marking. The serial number was occasionally repeated in black on the extremity of the lower

Even after hostilities ceased and the warplanes of Air Eskadra returned to their peacetime bases, flying incidents did occur, as depicted in this photo showing the Avia biplane in all too familiar 'nosed-on' position, which happened due to its narrow undercarriage wheel span. This particular Dogan wearing the peculiar late war squiggle camouflage scheme does not have the underside of the engine cowling painted in dark green; it kept the original light grey colour. The white triangle is on the mid-fin; however, the serial number is unfortunately illegible.

wings, outside the markings, but this was the exception rather than the rule. Based on photographic evidence, all *Dogans* depicted with black serial numbers on their lower wing surface belonged to the Marno Pole/Karlovo based 6. *Iztrebitelen Polk*, more precisely to the two *yata* that were always located there, namely Nos. 652nd and 662nd. There is a possibility that all the 'Karlovo *Dogans*' were repainted in early 1942, and it was then when they received black serial numbers on their lower wingtips, but this cannot be proven. Fact is, it is impossible to locate Bulgarian documents that clearly define certain markings and codes valid for certain units in certain time periods. Therefore, one can rely only on period photos and other circumstantial evidence, and try to deduct some sort of logic based on them, which might not always be the truth, though.

The serial number stayed on the rear fuselage (and rarely on the lower wingtips) for years, until late in the anti-German campaign in 1944, when the so-called 'assault camouflage scheme' was introduced. At that point, the individual number disappeared again from the airframe, and was retained only in the white triangle applied on the fin (seldom underneath the horizontal stabiliser), as was initially the case in early 1940. The black number was deleted from the lower wing surface, when it was applied.

The rudder was the only area of the airframe which changed colours at various times. Initially, for a very brief period, it stayed khaki, as the aircraft arrived from Germany. Very soon after start of service, the Bulgarian tricolour was applied on the fabric-covered surface. Soon after Bulgaria became a member of the Axis 'Tripartite Pact' on 1 March 1941, the rudder was repainted in so-called 'Axis yellow'. In most cases, both surfaces of the elevators also became yellow. The engine cowling also received a wraparound yellow paint job, usually ending in a tapered flash along the fuselage sides, spanning right up to the military marking, sometimes even beyond. The spinner was painted yellow as well. Later, in certain cases, the upper and lower wingtips also became yellow; however, this can only seldom be observed on period photos. The Author found no clear photographic evidence that the nose area was painted red, or that the rearward tapering flash, also in red, was applied along the fuselage sides of the *Dogans* as prescribed in Chapter V of the VNVV Order issued on 14.14.1938 (which was certainly implemented only partially).

For about two weeks in the anti-German campaign, the *Dogans* kept the pro-Axis yellow displayed on the airframe. Obviously, this led to confusion, particularly to the Bulgarians' new ally, the Soviets. Therefore, a new order was released by the VNVV HQ, which stipulated that all yellow had to be deleted, and replaced with white, the recognition colour of the Allies on the Eastern Front. This order came into effect from 19 September 1944. The pro-Allied white colour was applied on both the lower and upper wingtips, as well as in shape of a fuselage band, usually placed aft of the markings, but in rare cases on the mid-fuselage just aft the cockpit. The spinner was painted white, too. National markings remained unchanged. The white identification colour disappeared only in late 1945, after the introduction of the so-called 'OF'-marking in early October 1945. It is doubtful though that any of the obsolete Avias received this new military marking, as by then the few survivors were eyemarked for scrapping.

Additional info see:
http://mmpbooks.biz/assets/
BFC/05.pdf

Avia B.534-V Dogan, 41/7037, DSF Aviation Workshop, Bozhurishte, February 1940. Camouflage colours: Czechoslovak khaki green on upper surfaces, over light grey or shiny metal (silver dope) on under surfaces. Tsarist roundel type VNVV marking on fuselage sides and wing surfaces, in six positions.

A recently assembled Avia B.534 Series V, NN 41/7037, parked in front of the DSF Workshop at Bozhurishte, in early 1940. The roundel type military marking was freshly applied on the fuselage sides, but not yet on the wings.

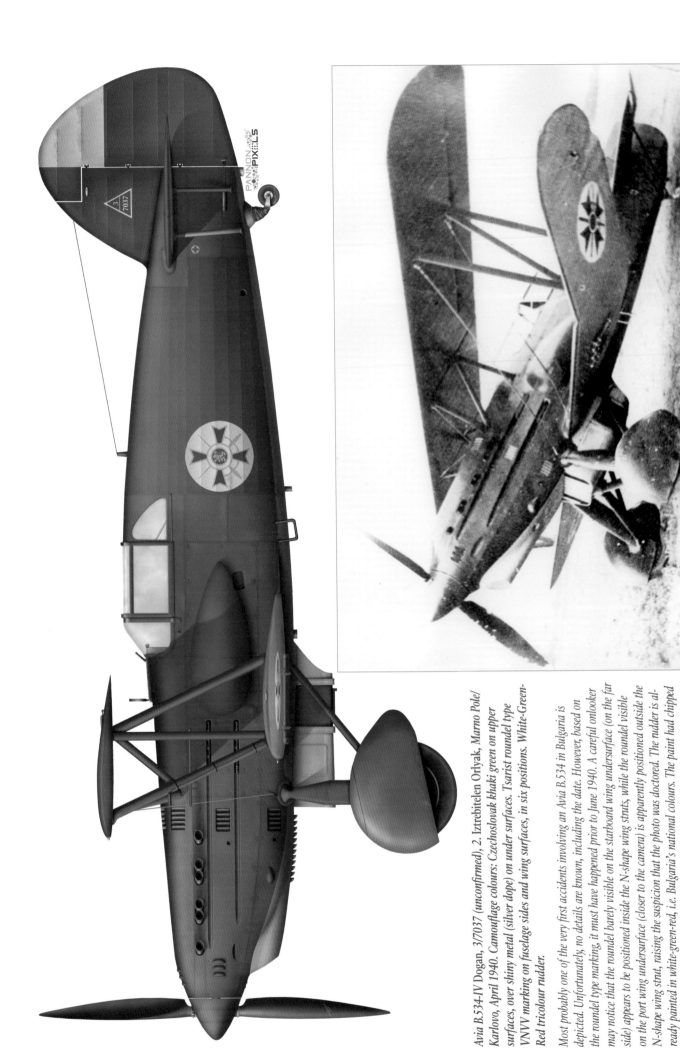

Avia B.534-IV Dogan, 3/7037 (unconfirmed), 2. Iztrebitelen Orlyak, Marno Pole/
Karlovo, April 1940. Camouflage colours: Czechoslovak khaki green on upper
surfaces, over shiny metal (silver dope) on under surfaces. Tsarist roundel type
VNVV marking on fuselage sides and wing surfaces, in six positions. White-Green-
Red tricolour rudder.

Most probably one of the very first accidents involving an Avia B.534 in Bulgaria is
depicted. Unfortunately, no details are known, including the date. However, based on
the roundel type marking, it must have happened prior to June 1940. A careful onlooker
may notice that the roundel barely visible on the starboard wing undersurface (on the far
side) appears to be positioned inside the N-shape wing struts, while the roundel visible
on the port wing undersurface (closer to the camera) is apparently positioned outside the
N-shape wing strut, raising the suspicion that the photo was doctored. The rudder is already painted in white-green-red, i.e. Bulgaria's national colours. The paint had chipped
off the propeller blades in many places.

Avia B.534-V Dogan, 4/7037, 1ˢᵗ Army Air Polk, Bozhurishte, mid-1940.
Camouflage colours: Czechoslovak khaki green on upper surfaces, over light grey, or
shiny metal (silver dope) on under surfaces. St. Andrew cross type VNVV marking
on fuselage sides and wing surfaces, in six positions. White-Green-Red tricolour
rudder. Black serial number on rudder top.

Fine in-flight study of Dogan No. 4, an Avia B.534 Series V, taken in mid-1940, with
a majestic mountain range providing picturesque background. This time, the aircraft's serial number shows up on the airframe, in this case on the rudder top, in the white segment
of the Bulgarian tricolour. Most 'old school' pilots preferred to fly with open cockpit,
reportedly 'to hear the engine's roar better'.

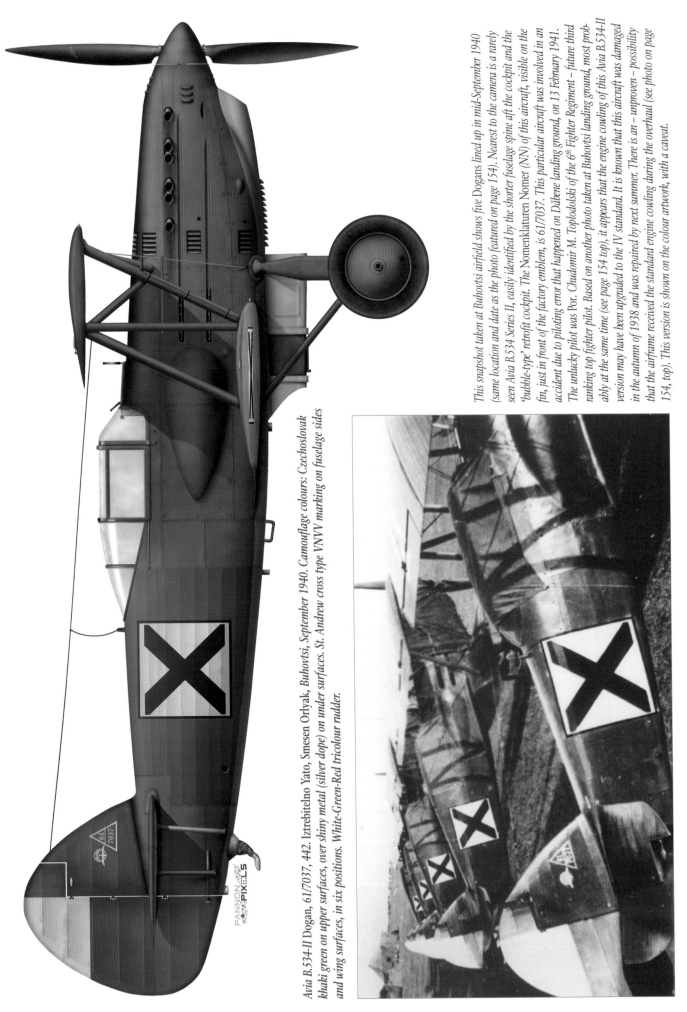

Avia B.534-II Dogan, 61/7037, 442. Iztrebitelno Yato, Smesen Orlyak, Buhovtsi, September 1940. Camouflage colours: Czechoslovak khaki green on upper surfaces, over shiny metal (silver dope) on under surfaces. St. Andrew cross type VNVV marking on fuselage sides and wing surfaces, in six positions. White-Green-Red tricolour rudder.

This snapshot taken at Buhovtsi airfield shows five Dogans lined up in mid-September 1940 (same location and date as the photo featured on page 154). Nearest to the camera is a rarely seen Avia B.534 Series II, easily identified by the shorter fuselage spine aft the cockpit and the 'bubble-type' retrofit cockpit. The Nomenklaturen Nomer (NN) of this aircraft, visible on the fin, just in front of the factory emblem, is 61/7037. This particular aircraft was involved in an accident due to piloting error that happened on Dăžene landing ground, on 13 February 1941. The unlucky pilot was Por. Chudomir M. Toplodolski of the 6th Fighter Regiment – future third ranking top fighter pilot. Based on another photo taken at Buhovtsi landing ground, most probably at the same time (see page 154 top), it appears that the engine cowling of this Avia B.534-II version may have been upgraded to the IV standard. It is known that this aircraft was damaged in the autumn of 1938 and was repaired by next summer. There is an – unproven – possibility that the airframe received the standard engine cowling during the overhaul (see photo on page 154, top). This version is shown on the colour artwork, with a caveat.

Avia B.534-IV Dogan, 74/7037 (c/n 387), 1st Army Air Polk, Bozhurishte, early 1941. Camouflage colours: Czechoslovak khaki green on upper surfaces, over light grey, or shiny metal (silver dope) on under surfaces. St. Andrew cross type VNVV marking on fuselage sides and wing surfaces, in six positions. White-Green-Red tricolour rudder. White serial number on rear fuselage.

Majestic in-flight shot of Dogan No. 74, taken in early 1941. The rudder is still adorned with the Bulgarian national colours, which would soon disappear, giving way to the Axis yellow, along with other similarly coloured identification features. The photo is not clear enough to positively determine if the rearward tapering red fuselage flash was applied or not. The serial (board) number is displayed on the rear fuselage, in large white numerals. This is the location where it would stay until shortly after Bulgaria's about-face and exit of the Axis Camp in September 1944. The apparently tall pilot would certainly had to lower his head if he wanted to close the cockpit canopy.

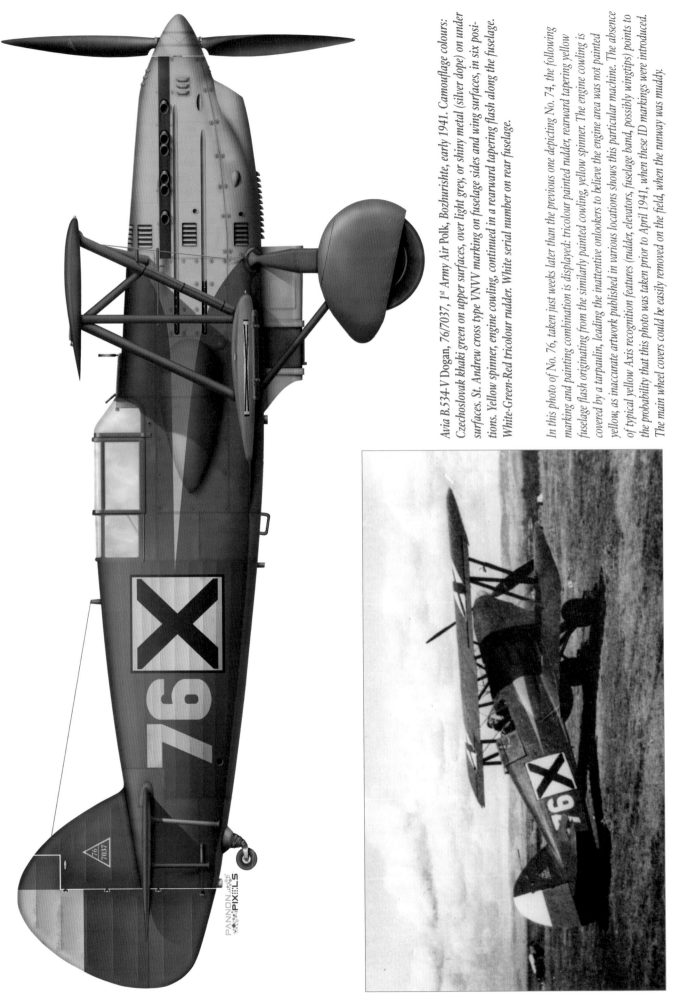

Avia B.534-V Dogan, 76/7037, 1st Army Air Polk, Bozhurishte, early 1941. Camouflage colours: Czechoslovak khaki green on upper surfaces, over light grey, or shiny metal (silver dope) on under surfaces. St. Andrew cross type VNVV marking on fuselage sides and wing surfaces, in six positions. Yellow spinner, engine cowling, continued in a rearward tapering flash along the fuselage. White-Green-Red tricolour rudder. White serial number on rear fuselage.

In this photo of No. 76, taken just weeks later than the previous one depicting No. 74, the following marking and painting combination is displayed: tricolour painted rudder, rearward tapering yellow fuselage flash originating from the similarly painted cowling, yellow spinner. The engine cowling is covered by a tarpaulin, leading the inattentive onlookers to believe the engine area was not painted yellow, as inaccurate artwork published in various locations shows this particular machine. The absence of typical yellow Axis recognition features (rudder, elevators, fuselage band, possibly wingtips) points to the probability that this photo was taken prior to April 1941, when these ID markings were introduced. The main wheel covers could be easily removed on the field, when the runway was muddy.

206

Avia B.534-IV Dogan, 63/7037, 1st Army Air Polk, Bozhurishte, May 1941. Camouflage colours: Czechoslovak khaki green on upper surfaces, over light grey, or shiny metal (silver dope) on under surfaces. St. Andrew cross type VNVV marking on fuselage sides and wing surfaces, in six positions. Yellow spinner, engine cowling, upper and lower wingtips, rudder and elevators. Narrow yellow mid-fuselage ring. White serial number on rear fuselage.

A Dogan flight made of at least six machines cruises in Bulgarian airspace – the element where the aircraft naturally belongs to. Both identifiable Avia fighters, Nos. 63 and 28, wear full Axis recognition features, consisting of yellow spinner, engine cowling, mid-fuselage band, rudder and elevators (curiously, the rearward tapering flash is missing). These identification markings were implemented shortly before the Axis' anti-Yugoslav Campaign of early April 1941.

Avia B.534-V Dogan, 40/7037 (c/n 415), Shkola za Vissh Pilotazh, Marno Pole/Karlovo, mid-1941. Camouflage colours: unidentified Bulgarian mid-green on upper surfaces, on fuselage sides and wing surfaces, except for the fin, which stayed in original Czechoslovak khaki colour, over light grey on under surfaces. St. Andrew cross type VNVV markings, in six positions. Yellow spinner, engine cowling, continued in a rearward tapering flash along the fuselage, upper and lower wingtips, rudder and elevators. White serial number on rear fuselage.

The Dogan pilot signals with his right arm prior to takeoff. The following text is written on the original photo's verso: "With the Dogan (Avia 534) in the Fighter school, Karlovo, 1941". Aircraft No. 40/7037, built in 1938, was one of the very few that displayed the original construction number on the starboard side fin, right above the factory emblem: 415. It was not written on the port side fin (or it was overpainted at a later stage), as per the photos featured on page 178.

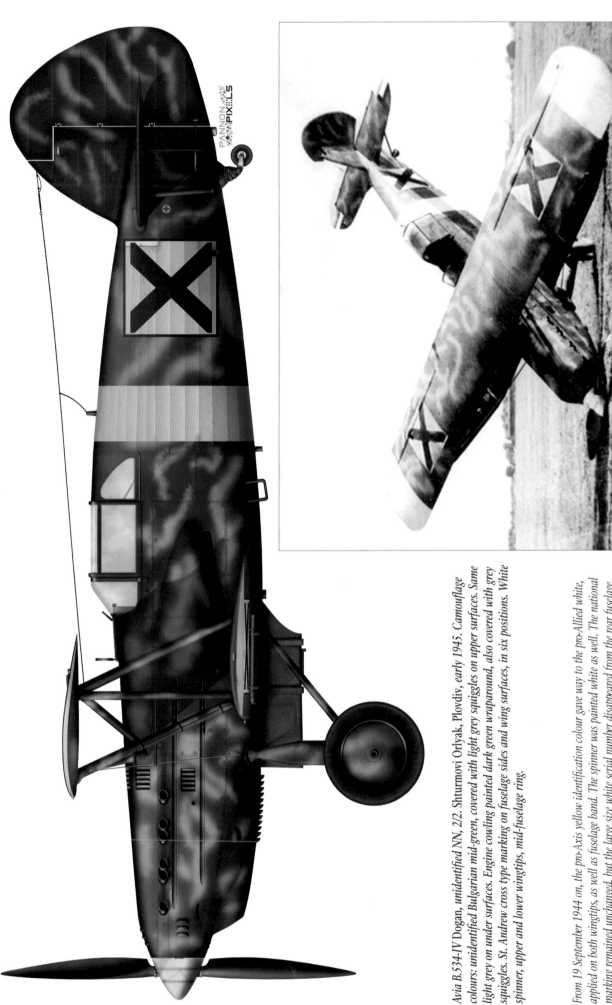

Avia B.534-IV Dogan, unidentified NN, 2/2. Shturmovi Orlyak, Plovdiv, early 1945. Camouflage colours: unidentified Bulgarian mid-green, covered with light grey squiggles on upper surfaces. Same light grey on under surfaces. Engine cowling painted dark green wraparound, also covered with grey squiggles. St. Andrew cross type marking on fuselage sides and wing surfaces, in six positions. White spinner, upper and lower wingtips, mid-fuselage ring.

From 19 September 1944 on, the pro-Axis yellow identification colour gave way to the pro-Allied white, applied on both wingtips, as well as fuselage band. The spinner was painted white as well. The national marking remained unchanged, but the large size white serial number disappeared from the rear fuselage. A further change in the appearance of the pro-Allied Dogans happened sometimes in late October, when light grey irregular squiggles were sprayed over the original dark green camouflage colour. The wide, white mid-fuselage band and the marking pushed rearwards are unusual. The triangle is missing from the fin.

Avia B.534-IV Dogan, 31/7037, 2/2. Shturmovi Orlyak, Vrazhdeb-na, November 1944. Camouflage colours: unidentified Bulgarian mid-green, covered with light grey squiggles on upper surfaces. Same light grey on under surfaces. Engine cowling painted dark green wraparound, also covered with grey squiggles. St. Andrew cross type marking on fuselage sides and wing surfaces, in six positions. White spinner, upper and lower wingtips, rear fuselage ring.

Superb two-third view of NN 31/7037, taken in late 1944, which allowed the artist to create an accurate artwork. The squiggle-style late war 'assault' camouflage scheme is prominent. There are two other shots of the same machine published on page 197.

Avia Bš.122 *Osa*
The Nimble Czech Fighter-Trainer

Part of the large deal secured by Bulgaria with Germany by an Agreement dated 19 August 1939, which comprised used ex-Czechoslovak warplanes sold at discount price, were 16 Avia Bš.122 trainer biplanes, powered by Walter 'Castor' II radial engines of 260 hp output. The airframes had the following construction numbers: 1, 2, 3, 7, 9, 12, 13, 14, 16, 20, 22, 23, 26, 35, 42 and 43. This first batch arrived in Bulgaria disassembled, by rail, in October the same year.

In the next agreement, signed on 26 February 1940, a dozen more Avia Bš.122s were included (two construction numbers. are known: 21 and 31). Ten of them arrived in Bulgaria in May, while two more units were delivered in June the same year. A final aircraft, the 29th, was a different type, a Ba.122 civilian aerobatics airplane[1], fitted with a more powerful Avia Rk-17 nine-cylinder radial engine of 355 hp and with a special carburettor allowing prolonged inverted flight. This one-off[2] was ordered by the VNVV directly from the Avia *AG Flugzeugindustrie* in Prague on 12 January 1940[3], and delivered on 28 November the same year[4], based on the *Flugbericht* issued that day for „*Avia Ba 122, Kennzeichen D-IX-WC*[5]*, Werk-Nr. 45*". Once the aircraft was taken over by the Bulgarians, the Avia Works issued invoice Nr. 677 on 05.12.1940. Minutes taken on 12 February 1941 at Marno Pole detail the handover of "*Avia BA-122 Nr. 45 and engine Rk 17 Nr. 1229*". On 18 February 1941, a permit was issued for „*AVIA 122, N.8474/39, Class B1, registration D-IXWC*". With this last aircraft, the deliveries were completed.

---

1   The information given by certain Czech sources, namely that the prototype of an improved version, called Avia B.222, No. 1, was sold to Bulgaria in 1939 cannot be proven and is improbable.

2   It is erroneously claimed that this particular aircraft had previously been in *Luftwaffe* service as RB+CL, as this one was actually constr. no. 31, and was still in service with *Flugzeugführerschule* (FFS) A/B 4 in February 1942.

3   This deal included the dozen Avia B.135s (see respective chapter for details).

4   The last Ba.122 built, construction number 45, was test flown by Avia factory pilot František Zemánek on 27 November 1940, and the acceptance flight was performed by German pilot Radtke the same day. Zemánek died in a flying accident on Letňany airfield, on 11.02.1941, while attempting to take off with Avia B.71 c/n 213 (SE+FU), but crashed in a parked Ar 96B-1, W.Nr. 4062 (KO+OJ).

5   The reusable ferry registration D-IXWC had been used before on a Henschel Hs 126K (W.Nr. 3918) transferred to Estonia during the Spring of 1940.

OK-AVI was the prototype of the Avia B.122 aerobatics biplane. The mixed construction airframe was powered by a seven-cylinder Castor II radial of 240 hp. It is depicted here at the international aerobatic competition called 'La coupe mondiale d'acrobatie aérienne', held at Paris in July 1934. The Bš.122 model was an evolution of this early prototype.

The Bš.122 was the improved military version of the single-seat advanced/aerobatics trainer type, the Ba.122[6]. The original B.122.1 prototype (OK-AVI) first flew on 12 May 1934, and the much improved Bš.122.1 on 11 August 1936, with factory test pilot Oldřich Košař at the controls. The airframe was of mixed construction. The iplane was powered by a seven-cylinder Walter 'Castor' IIA radial engine of 240 hp. In total, 45 Bš.122s were ordered by the Czechoslovak Ministry of National Defence from the Avia factory in 1936. All of them entered service with the Czechoslovak air force in the following year. The aircraft captured by German troops during the invasion of Czechoslovakia in March 1939 were impressed into *Luftwaffe* service, or placed in storage. Some were then sold to the Axis allies, Bulgaria and Slovakia.

Based on his logbook, *Feldfebel shkolnik* Georgi Stoyanov Georgiev took part in a mission to inspect and test fly ex-Czechoslovak aircraft gathered at Merseburg, Germany. During his stay at this air base between 18 August and 18 October 1939, he performed six landings aboard an *Osa*, with a total flying time of one hour. These brief test flights were performed at 300 m altitude. Unfortunately, no further details are given.

Right after the aircraft's arrival to Bulgaria, the VNVV high command took the type in inventory and assigned to it the code name *Osa* (Wasp), based on Order No. 116/16.11.1939. The *Nomenklaturen Nomer* (Register Number) allocated by the VNVV to the aircraft type – listed in Bulgarian documents simply as 'Avia 122', without any prefix – was 7013. The last digit means specialised advanced trainer, in this particular case fighter trainer, just like the Focke-Wulf Fw 56A (7003).

The first 16 aircraft were planned to be distributed among the following air force units, as per a draft Order of Battle plan, dated 18.11.1939:

- *Uchebno Yato* (Training Squadron) of the *2-i Iztrebitelen Orlyak:* 4 aircraft,
- *Uchebno Yato* (Training Squadron) of the *Yunkerski Ucheben Orlyak* (Officer Cadets Training Group): 4 aircraft,
- *Shkola za Vissh Pilotazh* (High Aerobatics Piloting School): 8 aircraft.

Once assembled at Bozhurishte main air base in late 1939, the Avia Bš.122s were assigned to the top training and school units of the VNVV, as planned. Four went to the 22. *Uchebno Yato* (22nd Training Squadron) and eight to the *Shkola za Vissh Pilotazh* (High Aerobatics Piloting School), both part of the *2-i Iztrebitelen Orlyak* (2nd Fighter Group), based at Marno Pole/Karlovo airfield. These two training units were under the same command, headed by *Kapitan* Krăstyu Antonov Atanasov, while his deputy was *Kapitan* Chudomir Milanov Toplodolski. Four instructors were assigned to this élite air school, namely *Podporuchiki* Lyuben Zahariev Kondakov, Stoyan Iliev Stoyanov, Vasil Pantev Shishkov and Dimităr Georgiev Tamahkyarov. The last four Bš.122s were taken over by the 28. *Uchebno Yato* (28th Training

---

6   In total, 60 B/Ba.122s were produced - serial numbers 1 to 45 and 101 to 115 (these 15 machines were the exported to the USSR).

This photo depicting 'Avia B.A. 122.8' (see front fuselage side, wing struts, wingtips, as well as fin-and-rudder) comes from Bulgarian sources. It's unclear if it had any connection to the Bulgarian aviation, as the construction number of the single Ba.122 in Bulgarian service was 45. Curiously, the Czechoslovak register was retouched from the rear fuselage, but was left on the wing undersurface.

Squadron) of the *Yunkerski Ucheben Orlyak* (Officer Cadets Training Group), based at Sofia-Vrazhdebna airfield. The commanding officer of the training squadron was *Poruchik* Vladimir Atanasov Hristov.

Future bomber pilot, Petăr M. Vălkovski, first boarded an *Osa*, No. 2, for a 15-min. acclimatization flight from Marno Pole air base, as early as 12 March 1940. He then flew Nos. 12 and 3 in the next couple of days.

Prominent Bulgarian instructor and fighter pilot, *Podporuchik* Petăr Manolev, registered his first flight aboard an *Osa* in his logbook on 25 March 1940. That day, he performed four short sorties aboard No. 5, flying *"figuri"* (literally, figures). Two more sorties, of 25 and 20 mins. duration, were logged aboard the same aircraft the next day. In that period, according to the handwritten note in his logbook, he was assigned to the *Shkola za Iztrebitelni Lettsi* (School for Fighter Pilots) – the informal name of *Shkola za Vissh Pilotazh* (High Aerobatics Piloting School) – located at Marno Pole/Karlovo[7].

On 2 May, he boarded aircraft No. 12 for a record long two-hour flight from Karlovo to Sofia. He returned from Sofia to Karlovo aboard the same aircraft on 8 May, this time in only 55 minutes. He flew next the *Osa* No. 19 on Bozhurishte airfield on 23 May, for a full hour. This short entry denotes that the second batch of Avia Bš.122s must have been impressed into service by then, or it was Manolev who test flew the freshly assembled aircraft.

Other *Osas* flown by *Podporuchik* Petăr Manolev at the School for Fighter Pilots in 1940 were (in chronological order) Nos. 18, 1 and 2.

Due to the intensive use of the Avia Bš.122s in training, many accidents and incidents – at least seven of them fatal – were recorded in the annals of the Bulgarian air force.

At the beginning of 1941, all 29 *Osas* were still available. Of these, nine were damaged in accidents.

Two single-seat Avia Bš.122s flank a two-seat Avia trainer at the company airfield Letňany, shortly after the Germans took over control in March 1939. The original Czechoslovak identification numbers are kept on the fuselage; however, the Nazi swastika is painted on the rudder and the Luftwaffe Balkenkreuz on the wings. Most of the requisitioned Avia Bš.122s ended up being sold to Bulgaria later the year.

---

7   Parts of the school were temporarily dispatched to Asen airfield.

The very first incident of the year was logged on 24 February, when *Poruchik* Pavel Lazarov Pavlov force landed with aircraft No. 10 on Marno Pole airfield following engine failure. The *Osa* was damaged 30%, the pilot escaped unhurt.

The first fatal accident – officially categorised as 'aviation catastrophe' – happened on 2 June 1941. That day[8], while training on how to keep formation, *Podporuchik* Ivan Georgiev Kănchev[9] collided in mid-air with another aircraft he was trying to align himself with. The aircraft became uncontrollable, and the unlucky pilot crashed to his death at the village of Hisarya, north of Plovdiv. There is another fatal accident listed for 2 June, when *Podporuchik* Marin Ivanov Marinov collided with another aircraft while training and crashed, also at Hisarya. Most probably this is the other victim of the same incident.

On 9 September, yet another fatal accident occurred to an *Osa*. This time, it was improper manoeuvres that claimed the life of the careless pilot. While performing aerobatics over Karlovo airfield, the aircraft of *Podporuchik* Kiril Georgiev Popov fell in a tailspin and crashed into the ground at full speed.

On 26 May 1941, the following *Osas* were servng within 6th Fighter *Polk* (Regiment): Nos. 4, 5, 9, 20, 22, 25, while No. 14 was serving within the Yunker (Officer Candidate) Training School. *Osa* No. 24 (powered by Walter 'Castor' engine No. 136) was recorded as extant on Yambol airfield on 27 December 1941. On the same date, *Osa* No. 5 (powered by Walter 'Castor' engine No. 35) was extant on Sarafovo airfield. Finally, *Osa* No. 18 (powered by Walter 'Castor' engine No. 134) was based on Novgradets (today called Suvorovo[10]) airfield, also on the same day.

Also in late December 1941, the following *Osas* were recorded as being based at Kazanlăk airfield: Nos. 2, 4, 7, 8, 10, 11, 17, 20, 22, 23 and 27.

The next year was better for *Osa* pilots, none of them lost his life. Only two accidents were recorded. Aircraft No. 5, flown by *Podporuchik* Petăr Vladimirov Dimov of the 662nd *Yato*, crash-landed on Karlovo airfield on 27 April 1942 with the landing gear having been already damaged before the botched landing. The aircraft was damaged 80%, but was eventually repaired, as it was scrapped only on 27.02.1947. The other accident involved aircraft No. 12, flown by *Kapitan* Nikola Stoyanov Boshnakov, of 632. *Yato*. On 2 November 1942, while returning from a night training sortie to Karlovo air base, he landed from too high an altitude, and the undercarriage subsequently broke.

Future fighter pilot, Stefan Marinopolski recorded in his logbook his first flight with an *Osa* on 19 May 1942. He logged several more training flights, performing '*figuri*', with the same aircraft on 20, 21 and 22 May, before switching to a *Siniger* (locally made DAR-9 biplane).

A letter dated 9.12.1942 asks Berlin for spare parts for the 204 existing ex-Czechoslovak aircraft from 1939. The list includes: "*Schulflugzeuge S.122-28 Stück*". One can assume that this is the number of this aircraft type still extant in the official lists at that date.

---

8 Another Bulgarian archival source gives the date of his death on 2 May 1941, which is most probably a typo.

9 2nd Lt. Kănchev, born in 1915, was *Krilo* commander in the 1st Air Regiment.

10 Its present name is in honour of Russian *Generalissimus* Alexander Suvorov, one of the most famous Russian military commanders.

A row of six Avia Bš.122s, wearing the so-called Tsarist roundel style military marking, photographed on a gloomy spring day of 1940. The aircraft nearest to the camera, 'Black11', is subject of a colour artwork.

1943 was also a bad year for *Osa* pilots. At least two of them died, while two others were wounded in various accidents and incidents. The first one involved the venerable *Poruchik* Petăr Dimitrov Manolev, experienced fighter pilot and instructor. While flying from Dolna Mitropoliya to Bozhurishte on 26 February to bring aircraft No. 2 for repair work, he had to perform an emergency landing on unfamiliar terrain, as the destination airfield could not be located in dense fog. The pilot escaped with minor scratches, but the aircraft was severely damaged, estimated at 80%. Despite the extended damage, the *Osa* was repaired and would eventually resume training duty.

Podporuchik Yanko D. Dishliev was not so lucky, though. On 15 March, he had to suddenly force-land his powerless mount from 100 m after his engine had quit in the most critical phase of the take-off from Bozhurishte airfield. The pilot was severely wounded and the aircraft, No. 3, written off, as the damage was estimated at 100%. *Podporuchik* Lyudmil D. Nakov was even lesser lucky, as he lost his life when he attempted to make a sharp turn while flying at low level over Dolna Mitropoliya airfield on 7 June 1943[11]. The slowly flying aircraft lost airlift, slid sideways and crashed to the ground in a ditch, killing its occupant and destroying the aircraft, No. 9 (see photo on page 219, top). There was another fatality listed for that day, namely *Podofitser* Vasil M. Dimitrov. Reportedly, he was killed also while flying aboard an Avia B.122 at the time of his demise at Dolna Mitropoliya; however, this cannot be confirmed[12]. There is a remote possibility that both airmen were flying in the same aircraft and both were killed in the same accident. It is unlikely, but not impossible, that two people were flying in a single-seat aircraft. Aviation history, not only Bulgarian, has seen more strange occurrences than this.

Two more accidents were recorded in the autumn of 1943. In the first one, *Podporuchik* Georgi M. Georgiev repeated the "figure" performed by his colleague, *Podporuchik* Nakov. On 14 October, after returning from an anti-partisan reconnaissance mission, *Podporuchik* Georgiev also carelessly attempted to make a turn at low speed. His mount lost critical airlift and crashed to the ground at Svezhen, southeast of Karlovo. However, Georgiev was luckier than his late colleague and survived the accident, but his aircraft, No. 11, was destroyed[13]. The other accident happened at Marno Pole air base, on 6 November. After completing a training flight, *Zamestnik ofitser* (Warrant Officer) Gencho Dimitrov Ivanov of the 692nd *Yato* hit a cow on landing and turned over, breaking the main undercarriage and propeller (see photo and colour profile on page 224). Aircraft No. 8 was repaired and resumed duty within weeks.

The final accident of the year happened on 8 December[14], and was a fatal one. *Podporuchik* Ivan T. Vălchev (or Vălchov) of 1/6. *Orlyak* lost his life during a training sortie from Vrazhdebna airfield, in unknown circumstances.

A list of trainer aircraft compiled on 24 December 1943, reflecting the situation of 23 November, lists the following *Osas* labelled 'under repair, assess the possibility to scrap them': 8, 10 and 12. None of them were actually scrapped at that time though, as their official write-off date is in 1946.

---

11 A comprehensive list of dead soldiers lists Nakov as died on 7 May 1943, but this could be a typo.

12 A comprehensive list of dead soldiers does not lists Dimitrov (although it does list Nakov).

13 Aircraft NN 11/7013 was officially written off on 11.09.1945.

14 Another source gives the date of Vălchev's death at 12 August 1945, or even on 8 December 1945, but these versions are less likely to be true.

A page from a wartime logbook of Petăr M. Vălkovski, with several entries referring to acclimatisation flights aboard the Oca (spelled Osa in Latin characters), Nos. 2, 12 and 3, based at Marno Pole airfield. The entries date as early as mid-March 1940, shortly after the type had started service with the VNVV.

Little detailed information surfaced of the type's service in 1944, although certainly it was extensively used to train would-be pilots for advanced piloting skills and aerobatics. For example, reconnaissance pilot Zhelyu Zhelev flew *Osa* No. 14 on 12 February 1944, and No. 25 on the following day, both at Dolna Mitropoliya air base. Later on the month, he performed *'figuri'* with *Osa* Nos. 21, 14, 1, 4 and 23. These sessions on the single-engine top notch trainer type were put to good use when he switched from multi-engine aircraft to single-engine fighters, namely the Dewoitine D.520, in April the same year.

It has to be noted that the last aircraft to arrive to Bulgaria, the sole Ba.122, was officially written off first of all the 29 Avias, namely on 1 August 1944, due to unknown circumstances.

On 27 July 1945, 20 *Osa* still existed, as follows:

Possibly the same row of six Avia trainers depicted on the preceding page is shown at a steeper angle. The seven-cylinder Walter 'Castor' II radial engine of 260 hp is shown prominently. Some front engine covers (behind the propeller hub) displayed holes, others not.

- 15 aircraft at *Văzdushnite Uchebni Chasti*:
  5 aircraft at *Iztrebitelna Shkola*: Nos. 4, 7, 14, 23 and 25,
  1 aircraft at *Văzdushnoto Uchilishte*: No. 15,
  8 aircraft at 2/2. *Orlyak*: Nos. 1, 2, 5, 12, 13, 18, 20 and 24,
  1 aircraft at DSF Lovech: No. 16 (to be delivered to the air force school).
- 4 aircraft in two *Kurierski Yata*:
  2 aircraft at 3/6. *Orlyak*: Nos. 22 and 27,
  2 aircraft at 2/6. *Orlyak*: Nos. 8 and 17.
- 1 aircraft at *Iztrebitelnata Shkola*: No. 10.

Training with the Avias continued in the post-war era as well. On 15 August 1945, two trainers collided in mid-air during mock combat exercises. While one of the pilots, *Podporuchik* Bogomil Părvanov Simeonov, could bail out of his stricken aircraft in time, the other one, *Podporuchik* Zdravko Milanov Toplodolski, was less fortunate, losing his life in the accident. He was the last known *Osa* pilot to be killed.

Radiogram (radio transmitted telegram) dated 23 August 1945 lists the cipher (code letter) assigned to each aircraft code name, for briefer communication. *Osa* was assigned with the letter 'O'.

After spending considerable time at piloting schools, the single Avia Ba.122, constr. no. 45, was reportedly used to tow targets for aerial gunnery purposes at Balchik air base. This unique *Osa*, carrying civilian registration LZ-TAD, is mentioned in the logbook of *Podporuchik* Petăr Manolev, who flew this particular aircraft from Marno Pole air base on 19 May 1941. According to Manolev, only pilot instructor *Kapitan* Dobri Donevski (an 'old hand', born in 1905), and himself were allowed to fly it. Later on, it was assigned to DAR at Lovech, to serve as advanced trainer for the factory's test pilots until 1944, when it was written off.

On 11 September 1945, four *Osa* were officially written off, Nos. 3, 9, 11 and 22. Along with the airframes, three aero engines were also scrapped the same day. They are identified as Walter 'Super Castor I', Nos. 35 and 48, as well as Walter 'Castor II', No. 127.

In late June 1940, a new military marking was introduced, in line with the other Axis powers' cross-shape markings. The depicted Avia Bš.122, No. 17, displays this new VNVV markings sometime in the late summer of 1940.

A detailed inventory of the VNVV aircraft park of 15 January 1946 lists 16 extant *Osa*, 12 serviceable and 4 unserviceable, all with the *Iztrebitelno-shturmova shkola* (i.e., Fighter-Ground Attack School).

On 19 June 1946, the following six serviceable *Osa* still existed: 1, 4, 13, 14, 17 and 18. The rest were either placed in storage, or scrapped. Curiously, aircraft No. 16, which probably soldiered on the longest, is not mentioned. On 19.03.1947, two *Osa* were officially written off: Nos. 1 and 7, along with their Castor II engines, Nos. 123 and 133.

Based on the testimony of his logbook, prominent airman and test pilot Major Petko Popganchev flew the *Osa* often, well after the war's end (see Annex 2, available on-line, see next page). From October 1944 to June 1947, he flew only aircraft No. 16. Curiously, his following flight with an *Osa* was performed on an aircraft called *Chayka* (i.e., Seagull). Most probably, *Osa* No. 16, based at Lovech, had been renamed as such at a certain point between 4 June and 4 December 1947. Popganchev's final flight aboard *Chayka* took place on 26 June 1948.

This is the last time the Avia Bš.122 was mentioned in the documents consulted by the Author. Certainly, the nimble Czech high-end trainer did its duty, and served well generations of Bulgarian fighter pilots in honing their skills.

A trio of Avia fighter trainer biplanes is depicted on Bozhurishte main air base in the second half of 1940. The rudder is painted in Bulgaria's national colours. Oddly, the rudder is not divided equally in one-thirds for each colour, as is the case on other aircraft types, but the white (on top) and red (on bottom) stripes are wider than the green (in centre). The aircraft at right is No. 2.

Camouflage and markings

Additional info see:
http://mmpbooks.biz/assets/
BFC/06.pdf

A row of six Avia Bš.122s
lined up in late 1941. Notice
two of the aircraft had their
rudders (and elevators)
painted in yellow, while the
other four still keep their
early standard tricolour
rudder. The aircraft's black
individual serial number dis-
appeared from the top rudder
and reappeared in white on
the fuselage, aft the military
marking. Occasionally, the
serial number was displayed,
in black, on the lower wing
surface as well.

Based on a protocol taken at Marno Pole (Karlovo) airfield on 12 February 1941, the sole Ba.122 *"had been taken over* [from the Avia Company] *in disassembled, painted state* [on 28.11.1940]*."* This document proves that this particular aircraft – most probably like the earlier ones – arrived from the factory already painted with locally available (presumably German-origin) paints and lacquers.

There is no concrete information available linking the Avia Bš.122 to any particular paint or colour shade. Judging by the fact that at the time the Germans took over the AVIA Works, the trainers were all painted in silver dope overall, one can assume that the dark green over light blue (or silver/metal) livery these aircraft arrived to Bulgaria were achieved with German origin paints. Therefore, the camouflage paints and lacquers were probably of the Herboloid family, supplied by Herbig-Haarhaus AG, detailed in the Camouflage Paints and Colours of Bulgarian Aircraft chapter.

As listed in Annex 1 of that chapter, Company Herbig-Haarhaus submitted an offer of aviation lacquers and paints to the Bulgarian air force on 25.01.1940, which included the following aircraft paints (*Flugzeugelacke*): '*grün für camouflage* BC.6954/6663' (i.e., camouflage green) and '*blau* BC.6954/6663' (i.e., blue). These two paints were *probably* used in giving camouflage livery to the Avia trainers (and other types of similar purpose supplied to the Bulgarians by the Third Reich). However, no details are available of the shades of these colours; therefore, the Author has *assumed* the standard early *Luftwaffe* hues RLM 62 Green and RLM 65 Light Blue. The lower surfaces of some aircraft may have been left in the original silver/metal finish. Obviously, these are only assumptions, which can be overruled if quality colour photos are unearthed, or more detailed information becomes available from archives.

The Bulgarian tricolour was applied on the rudder using the following Herboloid paints: '*fahnengrün*' (Flag Green), '*fahnenweiss*' (Flag White) and '*carminrot*' (Crimson Red), all of the same BC.6954/6663' type finishing paint. Colour '*schwarz*' (black) of the same paint family was used for letterings and markings. The yellow markings were brushed on using '*gelb-schwach-orange*' (Light Orange Yellow) paint. Interior surfaces may have been painted with '*grau*' (Grey) BC.9022, or '*silber*' (Silver) BC.6954/6663. The diluent (thinner) used for all these aircraft paints was identified by Herbig-Haarhaus as BC.2787. Later on, from about April 1942, the more advanced single-layer BC.12431 type of aircraft finishing paints and lacquers by the same German manufacturer were most probably used as top cover layer of the airframes that needed a new coat of paint.

After the last stocks of German aviation paints and lacquers were exhausted in about late 1944/ early 1945, the Bulgarians turned to the Soviets, their new ally. However, the author could not find any reference to Soviet paints being used by the VNVV, but the choice seems obvious.

As for markings and codes, the Avia Bš.122s followed VNVV standards of the time. For details, please consult the Markings and Codes of Bulgarian Aircraft chapter.

Podporuchik *Lyudmil D. Nakov* lost his life due to pilot error, while flying at low level over Dolna Mitropoliya airfield on 7 June 1943. The slowly flying aircraft lost sustentation, slid sideways and crashed in a ditch, killing its occupant and destroying the aircraft, No. 9, whose fuselage broke in two. There is another fatality listed for that day, namely Podofitser *Vasil M. Dimitrov*. Reportedly, he was killed also while flying aboard an Avia B.122 at Dolna Mitropoliya; however, this cannot be confirmed. There is a remote possibility that both airmen were flying in the same aircraft and both were killed in the same accident. Certainly, there is no second cockpit visible on the photo. It is unlikely, but not impossible, that two people were flying in a single-seat (!) aircraft. Aviation history, not only Bulgarian, has seen much stranger occurrences than this supposition.

Aircraft No. 2 has its serial number applied on the lower wing surface – a rare occurrence. The egg-shaped cylinder cooling holes on the engine cover plate were not always present. The curved exhaust collector pipe was also not identical on all 28 Avia Bš.122s.

*Pre-flight scene with student airmen and their instructor basking in the sun, near Avia Bš.122, No. 21.
The rudder of the biplane is painted yellow, as are the elevators.*

219

On this particular aircraft, No. 9, the cooling holes are missing from the round engine cover plate. The other photo taken at the same time reveals that No. 22, seen at left, also does not have holes in the spherical shape plate.

Another view of the same scene, revealing the serial number of the nearest Osa as being 9. Two Focke-Wulf Fw 56 Komars are visible in the background. Both types were classified by the VNVV as advanced fighter trainers, and accordingly had their four-digit Nomenklaturen Nomer (Register Number) ending in 3.

A group of Bulgarian fighter pilots have a moment of pause in front of one of the Osas. Notice the two different uniform colours and styles, one with high and stiff collar (the airmen at right), while the other with open neck and darker colour (the podofitser at cen-tre-left). This detail points to post-November 1940, after the change of uniforms in the Bulgarian Army and Air Force, from green colour & open collar (M1936) to blue-grey colour & high collar (M1940).

Osa No. 5, flown by Podporuchik *Petăr Vladimirov Dimov* of the 662*nd* Iztrebitelno Yato, 6*th* Polk, somersaulted while landing on Karlovo airfield on 27 April 1942. The aircraft was damaged 80%. The yellow rudder and elevators are visible. Notice the light colour painted engine front cover has cooling holes in it – one for each cylinder.

Osa No. 24 (powered by Walter 'Castor' II engine No. 136) was recorded as extant on Yambol airfield on 27 December 1941. It is depicted here following a minor collision with another Avia at an unspecified date.

The sturdy Avia fighter trainer, No. 17, is depicted in mid-air, sometime in 1942.

A couple of weeks after Bulgaria unilaterally jumped the Axis ship in early September 1944, the VNVV aircraft received pro-Allies identification markings, consisting of white fuselage band and wingtips. Osa No. 27 displays these white identifications, which are often erroneously depicted as yellow. See colour profile for details.

Balázs Kakuk

Avia Bš.122.22, 'Black 11', 11/7013, Shkola za Vissh Pilotazh (High Aerobatics Piloting School), Marno Pole/Karlovo, May 1940. Camouflage colours: Dark Green upper surfaces, Light Blue under surfaces. Roundel-style national marking in six positions. Rudder in Bulgarian tricolour (White, Green, Red). Black serial number on rudder top.

The Avia Bš.122s wore the so-called Tsarist roundel style military marking only for a short while, until late June 1940. Therefore, this photo was taken before that date, on what appears to be Marno Pole/Karlovo main fighter air base. The aircraft's individual number, 11, is displayed on the rudder in large, black numerals. It is applied contrary to, or as a loose interpretation of, Order No. 53/14.04.1938, which stipulated that the number should be applied on the white area of the rudder.

223

Balázs Kakuk

Avia Bš.122.14, 'White 8', 8/7013, 3/6. Iztrebitelen Orlyak, 692. Yato, Zamestnik ofitser (Warrant Officer) Gencho Dimitrov Ivanov, Marno Pole (Karlovo), 6 November 1943. Camouflage colours: Dark Green upper surfaces, Light Blue under surfaces. Cross-style national marking in six positions. Yellow rudder and elevators. White serial number on rear fuselage side and on lower wingtips, in black.

The final accident of 1943 happened on 6 November. After completing a training flight, Zamestnik ofitser (Warrant Officer) Gencho D. Ivanov of the 692ⁿᵈ Yato landed on a grazing cow and somersaulted, breaking the main undercarriage and propeller. Aircraft No. 8 was repaired and resumed duty within weeks.

224

Balázs Kakuk

Avia Bš.122, 'White 27', 27/013, Kazanlăk, December 1941.
Camouflage colours: Dark Green upper surfaces, Light Blue under
surfaces. Cross-style national marking in six positions. Yellow rudder
and elevators. White serial number on rear fuselage side and on lower
wingtips, in black.

'White 27' is parked in front of the hangars, on a grassy field covered by
a thin layer of snow, in late 1941. Notice the yellow rudder (the elevators
were yellow as well).

Balázs Kakuk

Avia Bš.122, 'White 27', 27/7013, Kuriersko Yato, 3/6. Iztrebitelen
Orlyak, Bozhurishte, February 1945. Camouflage colours: Dark
Green upper surfaces, Light Blue under surfaces. Cross-style national
marking in six positions. White mid-fuselage band, as well as upper
and lower wingtips. White serial number on rear fuselage side.

The same aircraft depicted previously, 'White 27', is shown here also
during wintertime, wearing a new coat of darker green paint. However,
this time the year is early 1945 and Bulgaria was by then firmly in the
anti-Axis camp. This new allegiance is visible by the white mid-fuselage
band and both wingtips, identification colour of the pro-Soviet Bulgarian
air force.

226

Arado Ar 96B *Soyka*
Bulgaria's Modern Versatile Trainer

With the influx of advanced German aircraft technology into Bulgaria in the late 1930s, the necessity for a modern, versatile trainer aircraft type to train hundreds of airmen needed to operate these warplanes became urgent. All trainer aircraft existing at that time in the rosters of the Bulgarian air force were representing the 'old technology', biplanes or parasol wing types, built locally, or imported, of mixed construction, having fixed undercarriage and fixed pitch propeller. Therefore, one of the aims of the Bulgarian military delegations visiting various European countries in the late 1930s was to secure a modern trainer aircraft type for the VNVV. The choice fell upon the two-seat[1], all-metal Arado Ar 96 monoplane, with retractable undercarriage and variable pitch propeller, featuring modern on-board instruments. The possibility of some sort of armament fitted to the airframe was left open.

The Bulgarians inquired at Arado *Flugzeugwerke* GmbH, headquartered in Potsdam, Germany, about the possibility to purchase a number of Ar 96s in 1938. A 'letter of intent', signed on 23 February 1939, called for the delivery of a total of 24 Ar 96s of two different types - one of them civilian (unarmed) and the other one military (armed). Both types were powered by an Argus As 410Aa-1 air-cooled, 12-cylinder inverted-V engine of 460 hp, and featured a two-blade variable pitch metal propeller.

The final contract was eventually signed on 8 May 1939, calling for four Ar 96B *Schulflugzeuge* (basic school aircraft) and twenty Ar 96B *mit Militär-Ausrüstung* (with military equipment). Delivery was scheduled from May to August 1940, as follows: four in May, six in June, seven in July and seven in August. An *Antrag Reichsbürgschaft* from June 1939 reinforces the details included in the contract for the four Ar 96B (*Schule*) and twenty Ar 96B (*Militär*).

The armed version featured a cut-out in the mid-fuselage top, just aft of the rear cockpit, which was open. In this location, a 7.92 mm calibre MG 15 machine gun was fitted onto an Arado-style mounting, type K. A fixed MG 17 machine gun, also of 7.92 mm calibre, was mounted on the starboard side of the nose section, firing through the propeller arc. Aiming of the fixed machine gun was done with a Revi C-12 reflector gunsight. Additionally, an ETC 50 bomb rack was attached to each lower wing surface.

Arado factory drawing showing the longitudinal cross section of the special version, with rear gunner, designed and built to the Bulgarian order. Several details (like the antenna mast) differ to the actual aircraft.

---

1   The Arado Ar 96 is the only two-seat aircraft discussed in the book (except for the very few Bf 109G and D.520 modified in Bulgaria into two-seaters). This is because the Ar 96 was *the* most used advanced trainer aircraft, the backbone of honing the piloting skills of the would-be Bulgarian fighter pilots.

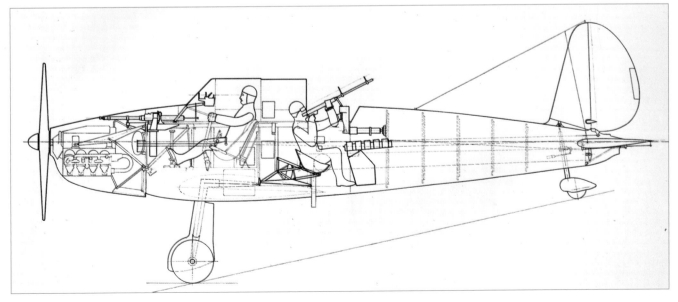

Detail factory photo of the rear gunner's stand, including the rearward firing MG 15 machine gun, mounted on a flexible lafette type K, Arado-style.

Lieferschein (Delivery Note) of one of the 20 Ar 96s (armed version) delivered to Bulgaria in 1940/1941. The document clearly spells the sub-type of the aircraft as B-1 (in this case, referring to aircraft Werknummer 96 0103, which was assigned with the Bulgarian Nomenklaturen Nomer 18/7042). Document filled in Neuendorf, Germany, on 17 June 1941. This document clarifies the mystery surrounding the precise sub-type of the Ar 96 built specifically for Bulgaria, which was not identified so far in specialised literature.

There was a receiver and transmitter radio set installed too. A visible detail related to the radio set is the belly antenna, used by the long wave length radio. When it was not used, it could be retracted into the fixed tube with a hand driven wheel by the rear gunner. The rear gunner's stand is visible on the factory detail photo (see above).

Considerable effort was made by the Author to identify the proper sub-type version of the armed variant, peculiar to the Bulgarian order, initially without success. At the outset, it appeared that there were two possibilities: 'B-1M', found in several publications, without any backing documents, and the hypothetical 'B-4', sub-type which is left empty in an overview of all Arado Ar 96B versions (which does not list the version with the rear gunner, though)[2]. Neither possibility could be confirmed, however. Even the official notice by Arado *Flugzeugwerke* sent to the Bulgarian military attaché in Germany on 28 November 1940, informing him of the actual take-off of five 'Ar 96Bs' towards Sofia, via Hungary and Rumania, with the planned arrival on 30 November, does not specify the aircraft's sub-type. The breakthrough happened when the German factory *Lieferscheine* (delivery notes) of four Arado 96s (Nos. 16, 18, 19 and 20/7042), to be delivered by rail, were found in the Bulgarian archives (see at left). The documents clearly spell the aircraft's sub-typ: B-1! No other distinctive note, or suffix is given. Therefore, the Author refers to these two sub-types as Ar 96B-1 (unarmed), or Ar 96 Series 35 (i.e., NN 7035), and as Ar 96B-1 (armed), or Ar 96 Series 42 (i.e., NN 7042).

First arriving in Bulgaria were the four unarmed Ar 96B-1s. The aircraft were built at the Arado Plant located in Brandenburg, and had *Werknummern* from 60 to 63. They were painted in light grey overall, and sported washable German civilian ferry registrations: D-IXWA, D-IXWI, D-IXWM and D-IXWN. Flight permits were issued to them for 25 May 1940. The route they had to follow was Graz-Zagreb-Belgrade-Sofia. They were followed

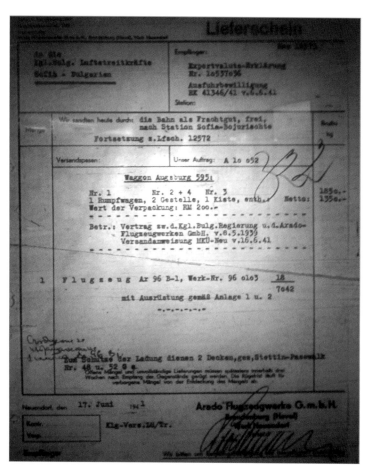

---

2 *Baureihenübersicht der Ar 96 B. Quelle: Flugzeug-Baureihenblatt Ar 96 vom 20.9.1944* (information kindly provided by Hans-Georg Dachner).

by 20 Ar 96Bs built by AGO[3] *Flugzeugwerke* GmbH in Oschersleben, which arrived from late 1940 to mid-1941. These were unique in fuselage configuration and armament, as described earlier. They had the following *Werknummer* batches: 70-75, 82-85, 92-96 and 101-105. The civilian ferry registrations ranged in the D-IXW_ and D-IYU_ and D-IYW_ series (see page 231, top, for details).

An RLM '*Schnellbrief*' (i.e., fast letter), dated 5 November 1940, details the *planned* flying route for the 20 Ar 96Bs (in batches of five aircraft, flown by German ferry pilots), as follows: Vienna-Graz-Zagreb-Belgrade-Sofia, with a scheduled stop-over at Belgrade, Yugoslavia, and a possibility to land at Zagreb, too. In the end, it seems that most aircraft arrived by rail, as proven by Bulgarian documents.

Bulgarian protocol taken at Bozhurishte, dated 17 October 1941 (thus almost one year after the scheduled arrival of the Arados to Bulgaria), refers to a single Ar 96B-1 (W.Nr. 96 0074, VNVV NN 5/7042) that had arrived by air. Sixteen more Ar 96B-1s (all NN 7042) had arrived in railway cars, as follows: 4, 6, 7, 8, 9, 10, 11, 12, 13, 14, 15, 16, 17, 18, 19 and 20. Thus, only Nos. 1, 2 and 3 are missing. Those had arrived earlier, presumably by air, like No. 5. The Arado factory *Lieferscheine* for all the aircraft that arrived by rail are dated mid-June (from 15 to 24) 1941, which represent the dates these aircraft were readied in Germany for dispatch to Bulgaria. It has to be noted that all VNVV Register Numbers (NN) were already assigned to individual aircraft in the factory.

Quite interestingly, a comprehensive list of all armed Ar 96Bs (no sub-type version is given) that arrived in Bulgaria, compiled meticulously by a Bulgarian technician, gives the following acceptance dates by the Bulgarian air force: only six at unspecified date in 1940 (Nos. 1, 2, 3, 10, 13 and 15), while the rest of fourteen in 1941, as follows:
- No. 5 on 23 May,
- Nos. 6, 9, 12 and 20 on 9 September,
- Nos. 4 and 8 on 23 September,
- Nos. 7, 16 and 18 on 26 September,
- No. 17 on 2 October,
- No. 19 on 6 October,
- No. 11 on 8 October,
- No. 14 on 17 October.

The almost one-year delay between the ferry flight and official acceptance date of the last Ar 96B-1s cannot be explained without backing documentation. However, most likely it was about some sort of warranty issues with the manufacturer, Arado, as the aircraft arrived in Bulgaria obviously in a serviceable state.

Once the the first units of the Ar 96B-1 trainer arrived in Bulgaria in late 1940, they aroused considerable interest. The type was officially called *Soyka* (Jay) by VNVV decree No. 116/16.11.1939 (one

Arado factory photo of one of the Ar 96B-1s with the open rear gunner configuration á la Bulgaria. This particular photo has been widely published, identified as Ar 96 V9. However, this identification is erroneous, as the depicted aircraft is one of the twenty armed ones built to Bulgarian request. Both the ferry registration, D-IXWZ, and the slightly visible last two digits of the construction number, 75, applied on fin top, identify this particular aircraft as Arado Ar 96B-1, W. Nr. 96 0075, which became the sixth such aircraft in Bulgarian service (6/7042). Notice the overpainted Bulgarian roundel marking on the mind-fuselage, underneath the hyphen, and on the wing outer surface. The black service writing on the rear fuselage was in Bulgarian.

---

3   AGO stands for *Apparatebau GmbH Oschersleben*.

Two views of another Ar 96 B-1 (armed version) readied to be transferred to Bulgaria in late 1940. This particular one, D-IXWP, W.Nr. 960070, was the first unit of this peculiar version, being registered in Bulgaria as NN 1/7042. See page 234 for a couple of photos of this very aircraft, registered in Bulgaria as 'White 1'.

year before the aircraft's arrival!), and assigned with two different *Nomenklaturen Nomera* (NN, i.e. Registration Numbers): the unarmed version 7035, while the armed version was 7042. In all Bulgarian documents, the Arado Ar 96B-1s were identified only with the code name, *Soyka*, and the respective NN.

At first glance, the choice of an NN category ending in 5, which meant 'transport, sports, medical, courier and utilitarian' aircraft, is surprising. One possible explanation could be that the unarmed type was probably not meant to be used as aircrew trainer, but rather as courier aircraft, or fast transport. However, this theory is confirmed by the actual distribution of the *Soykas*, as detailed below. The selection of a NN category ending in 2 for the armed version of the Arado was not surprising, as that category was reserved for advanced trainers, like the domestically-made DAR-8A, or the *Chuchuliga* ('Lark') series of KB biplane aircraft types. The KB type biplanes could be fitted with a forward and/or rearward firing machine gun, just like the armed version of the Ar 96B.

The aircraft were planned to be distributed among the following air force units, as *dopǎlnitelno* ('extra' asset), as per a draft Order of Battle plan, dated 18.11.1939:
- *Uchebno Yato* (Training Squadron) of the *1-i Lineen Orlyak* (literally 'Linear', actually Battle[4], or Close Support Group, assigned to a particular army), Bozhurishte: 6 aircraft,
- *Uchebno Yato* (Training Squadron) of the *Yunkerski Ucheben Orlyak* (Officer Cadets Training Group), Vrazhdebna: 9 aircraft,
- *Shkola za Vissh Pilotazh* (High Aerobatics Piloting School), Karlovo: 9 aircraft.

The earliest mentioning of a *Soyka* (No. 2/7035) in active service is dated February 1941. The very same aircraft is listed as serving with the *1-i Armeyski Orlyak* (1st Army Group) on 26 May 1941 (having suffered an accident previously, see below). *Soyka* No. 17/7042 is listed at Kazanlǎk on 27 December 1941, being under technical inspection.

Not much is known about the Arados' service during the war, and this should not surprise anyone. Most probably they soldiered on as trainers, reliably, without much fanfare, except for the occasional ac-

---

4   '*Lineen korab*' means 'battleship' (just like the German word *Linienschiff*).

Low quality still that shows the arrival of the first unarmed Arado Ar 96B-1s to Bozhurishte airfield, in the autumn of 1940 (see also photos on page 243). Despite the poor quality, one can observe the overpainted German ferry markings on the fuselage, still retained on the wing upper surface. The washable paint was crudely removed from the fuselage, revealing the Tsar-type military roundel on the mid-fuselage. However, by the time the first Arados arrived in Bulgaria, this military marking was already obsolete.

Table of Arado factory data and ferry registrations (1940/1941)

No.	Type	W.Nr.	Ferry registration
Unarmed version			
1.	Arado Ar 96B-1	960060	D-IXWA
2.	Arado Ar 96B-1	960061	D-IXWI
3.	Arado Ar 96B-1	960062	D-IXWM
4.	Arado Ar 96B-1	960063	D-IXWN
Armed version			
1.	Arado Ar 96B-1	960070	D-IXWP
2.	Arado Ar 96B-1	960071	D-IXWQ
3.	Arado Ar 96B-1	960072	D-IXWR
4.	Arado Ar 96B-1	960073	D-IXWU
5.	Arado Ar 96B-1	960074	D-IXWX
6.	Arado Ar 96B-1	960075	D-IXWZ
7.	Arado Ar 96B-1	960082	D-IYUE
8.	Arado Ar 96B-1	960083	D-IYUF
9.	Arado Ar 96B-1	960084	D-IYUH
10.	Arado Ar 96B-1	960085	D-IYUJ
11.	Arado Ar 96B-1	960092	D-IYUN
12.	Arado Ar 96B-1	960093	D-IYUO
13.	Arado Ar 96B-1	960094	D-IYUP
14.	Arado Ar 96B-1	960096	D-IYWB
15.	Arado Ar 96B-1	960095	D-IYWC
16.	Arado Ar 96B-1	960101	D-IYWD
17.	Arado Ar 96B-1	960102	D-IYWJ
18.	Arado Ar 96B-1	960103	D-IYWL
19.	Arado Ar 96B-1	960104	D-IYWM
20.	Arado Ar 96B-1	960105	D-IYWO

cidents (only one of them fatal, due to indiscipline). On 14 October 1941, a total of 24 Ar 96Bs existed in the VNVV aircraft roster (along with 28 Argus As 410 engines). Of these, four had been damaged in accidents, but all repairable. Those were repaired at the Plovdiv Repair Workshop of the 5th Aviation Regiment (*Parkova Rabotilnitsa Kăm 5-i Văzdushen Polk*).

Details of only a couple of accidents are known. The first one happened on 25th March 1941. The protagonist of this very first accident involving this new aircraft type was the very first aircraft impressed in service, namely 2/7035! That day, pilot *Zamestnik Ofitser* (Warrant Officer) Zahari I. Manolov crash landed No. '2/7037[5]' of the *1-i Armeyski Orlyak* (1st Army Group) on Bozhurishte airfield. The cause of the accident given in the investigation report was pilot error, but construction defects also contributed to the event. According to the report, fuel could not be pumped from the main tank. A complaint was subsequently filed with the Bulgarian representative of the Arado Works, *Dipl. Eng.* Krăstev. The other incident also happened in March, four days later. In that accident, No. 3/7042 was damaged during a hard landin,g also on Bozhurishte airfield, by *Feldfebel-shkolnik* Bogomil D. Georgiev.

Three incidents are preserved in documents for 1942, as follows:

- on 19 March, *Soyka* No. 18/7042 of the 2nd *'Lineen' Orlyak* suffered an accident on Manole airfield. The crew, *Podporuchik* Vasil S. Păev (pilot) and *Kandidat Ofitser* Georgi I. Ivanov (student), escaped unhurt.

---

5   The last number is obviously a typo, as the number was actually 2/7035.

One of the first Arado trainers to arrive, with the temporary ferry civilian registration washed off the airframe, revealing the Bulgarian military marking on the mid-fuselage (barely seen behind the heels of the Bulgarian technician peering into the cockpit).

- on 5 June, *Soyka* No. 19/7042 of the 2nd Army *Orlyak* suffered an accident on Graf Ignatievo airfield. The pilot, *Podporuchik* Mladen I. Dimitrov, escaped.
- on 9 June, *Soyka* No. 7/7042, also of the 2nd Army *Orlyak*, suffered an accident also on Graf Ignatievo airfield. The pilot, *Podporuchik* Sava S. Saratenov, escaped as well.

Another accident is recorded for 15 April 1943. On that date, following the return from a mission to take stereoscopic photographs, the pilot of Ar 96B-1 (mentioned as such in the post-accident report), No. 4/7042, *Kapitan* Yanko T. Stefanov, forgot to lower the landing flaps during the high-speed landing on Vrazhdebna airfield, the tail hit the ground and the aircraft's undercarriage collapsed. Both the pilot and his passenger, *Yunker* Ivan V. Dinchev, escaped unhurt, and the aircraft suffered 35% damage.

Podporuchik Petăr Manolev, instructor assigned to the Dolna Mitropoliya piloting school, flew *Soyka* No. 13 on the following dates in 1943: 23, 24, 30, 31 August and 8, 11, 23 September.

Argus *Motoren GmbH* technician Baumann visited Bulgaria between late August and late September 1943 upon the request of the *Luftwaffe* Mission in Bulgaria, to service Argus engines and propellers. In his report, he mentions the following: on Vrazhdebna airfield he found Ar 96B, constr. no. 12 [sic!, in fact, it was the Bulgarian serial number], which had a faulty regulator of the air/fuel mix (i.e. carburettor). The problem was solved by replacing the component. Also on Vrazhdebna, he found another unserviceable Ar 96B, constr. no. 16 [see previous note], fitted with Argus As 410 engine, constr. no. 368[6], which had piston No. 2 cracked and cylinder blocked due to a bad spark plug. On Yambol airfield, he serviced Argus As 410, constr. nos. 3341, 3330, 3441, 4654 and 4667[7]. On 21 September, he found at Dolna Mitropoliya engine As 410, constr. Nos. 223 and 444[8], in poor shape[9]. Generally, the Argus employee complained of inadequate workmanship of Bulgarian technicians, lack of proper maintenance, improper storage of matériel, etc.

In 1944, as part of "*Erweiterungsprogramm* (or 'Extension Program') 'Barbara'" (informally known as "*Barbara-Programm*"), ten unarmed Ar 96Bs were delivered by the Germans to Bulgaria, among other military aircraft. The decree calling for this delivery (along with 18 Bü 181s, 10 Fw 58s and 2 Ju 52s) was registered as 6. Abt. Nr. 1089/44 g.K.v. 21.4.1944. The delivery schedule was the following: 3 in March, 3 in April and 4 in May 1944. Interestingly, an earlier decree, calling for the delivery of 4 Ar 96s (along with 2 Gotha Go 145s), No. 6. Abt. Nr. 0436/44 g.K.v. 26.1.1944., was cancelled. Two acceptance protocols filled at Bozhurishte airfield in 1944, the first one dated 21.06, while the second one 30.06., stand proof of the delivery of 5+5 Ar 96B-7s, with the following *Werknummern*: 450006, 450007, 450008, 450009, 450010 and 450036, 450037, 450038, 450039, 450040. Based on the construction numbers, the aircraft were built at the Avia Plant in occupied Czechoslovakia, as part of a batch of 70 airframes (450001 to 450070), in 1944. The airframes were powered by Argus As 410A-2 engines of 465 hp. Once impressed in Bulgarian service, they received subsequent registration numbers (NN), in

---

6   At its official takeover on 26.9.1941, Ar 96B-1, No. 16/7042 (W.Nr. 960101), was fitted with this very As 410Aa-1 engine. This means that there was no engine replacement needed in the previous two years of service.

7   All these were replacement engines, none of them arrived together with the batch of aircraft.

8   Upon its arrival, Ar 96B-1, No. 19/7042 (W.Nr. 960104), was fitted with As 410Aa-1 engine, constr. no. 444.

9   He also mentions the following propellers, constr. nos. 614040, 613901, 612967, 611417, 611017.

the 5 to 14/7035 row. A German report dated after Bulgaria's defection from the Axis camp states that all ten latecomer Ar 96Bs were still in VNVV service in September 1944.

One of the first original Ar 96Bs to arrive in Bulgaria, No. 4/7035, crashed on Lyubenova Mahala airfield, on 17 August 1944. Upon returning from an engine test flight to Stara Zagora, the powerplant started to vibrate and emit smoke. Oil pressure fell quickly, power dropped. The pilot, *Feldfebel* Radko M. Modev, pilot instructor with 1. *Razuznavatelen Orlyak* (Reconnaissance Group), decided to land as quick as possible. However, before touching the ground, the engine quit and the propeller stopped spinning. The pilot force-landed in a meadow with lowered undercarriage, but the aircraft rolled into a ditch. Luckily, both the pilot and the passenger, *Podofitser* Nikifor Y. Simov, aircraft mechanic, escaped unhurt but the aircraft was seriously damaged.

A single *Soyka* (NN 13/7042) was abandoned at the Aircraft Repair Workshop in Skopie when Bulgarian troops hastily retreated following Sofia's about-face and exit of the Axis camp, as detailed in a report dated 3.04.1944 [sic! Probably wrong year, it must be 1945]. Besides the single airframe, two As 410 engines were lost there as well (W.Nr. 2829 and 4702).

A couple of *Soykas* took active part in the anti-German campaign of autumn 1944. An entry in the Combat Diary of the VNVV, dated 18 September 1944, notes: *"A four-aircraft courier* krilo *was formed on Vrazhdebna airfield. It consisted of two 'Uragans' (Do 17) for military postal service to army headquarters and two Soykas (Ar 96) for 'army press' transport duties."*

The first identified fatal accident involving a Bulgarian Arado 96 happened on 7 September 1944. That autumn day, after completing a routine training flight, the overconfident Lieutenant Vasil Georgiev Shahanov decided to 'show off' and performed a low-level pass. This violation of air discipline cost his life, as he crashed into the ground near Haskovo, south of Stara Zagora.

On 11 November 1944, *Soyka* NN 16/7042 of the 6th Regiment was damaged by *Podporuchik* Evgheni A. Karakanovski, in a hangar at Bozhurishte airfield. The aircraft was repairable, so it could have more flying hours recorded in its logbook.

The *Soyka* was the workhorse of the Bulgarian air force training units. Due to the intense training schedule, incident and accidents occurred at regular intervals. One such accident is registered for 6 April 1945, involving aircraft 11/7042 of 2/6. Fighter *Orlyak*, which was damaged during landing on Bozhurishte airfield by *Ppor.* Tacho Popov due to piloting error.

As detailed in the Bf 109G *Strela* chapter, in the spring/summer of 1945, a large number of ex-*Luftwaffe* and ex-MKHL (Hungarian air force) aircraft were recovered from several Austrian airfields, notably Zeltweg[10]. After summary repair by Bulgarian technicians, these were flown back to Bulgaria, with the consent of Stalin himself. In June-July, the recovered aircraft were assembled on the South-Hungarian airfield of Pécs, close to the Yugoslav border. Among them were a number of Arado Ar 96s, which were

---

10 When British forces moved in to Zeltweg airfield on 21 July 1945, recently evacuated by Soviet troops, they found, among other aircraft, eleven Ar 96s of the Hungarian air force, along with a twelfth one still wearing *Luftwaffe* codes (VE+YF, W.Nr. 650156, which was a B-7 sub-type).

In this series of three photos Bulgarian ground crew flocks around the armed version of the Arado Ar 96B-1, just delivered to Bulgaria. The German civilian ferry registration is still retained on the airframe. Only four such aircraft arrived on their wings, Nos. 1, 2, 3 and 5, the rest were delivered by rail. The crewman in the rear cockpit rests his right hand on the rearward firing machine gun's lafette, Arado-style, type K.

The first aircraft with rear gunner (White 1) was photographed on the tarmac of Bozhurishte airfield in early 1941. The civilian men are probably Arado employees. The nose mounted machine gun (as well as the rearward firing one), removed during the ferry flight over foreign countries, was not mounted yet. Interestingly, the aircraft's individual serial number on the fuselage was initially applied in white.

On the second, smaller photo, underneath the chin of the soldiers at left, a tiny surface of the white painted rudder can be seen. Some of the Bulgarian soldiers wear their ranks on the uniform's sleeves (technical officers), while others on the epau-

lettes (shoulder boards). One can differentiate the airmen from the army soldiers by the wings flanking and laurels surrounding the visor cap's oval badge, as well as the royal crown atop.

repaired at *Gl. r. r.* Plovdiv workshop, then flown to Telish main air base. The number of recovered Arados is uncertain – one source mentions 33 such aircraft – but the only reliable source available to the Author lists 19 'trophy' *Soykas*. Based on a photograph, at least one was of the A sub-version[11], but probably there were more.

An interesting incident is recorded in the post-war memoires of Yordan Pelev, former member of the long-range reconnaissance 73. *Yato* (squadron):

"In those days, we moved the booty aircraft from Austria to our airport [Pécs, Southern Hungary]. Among the 'trophies' were numerous Soyka [Ar 96], but also some biplanes. They all had Hungarian markings – wide, regular crosses, complete with the colours of the Hungarian flag.

These aircraft drew the attention of the local population – mainly women from the city [Pécs]. These women apparently were great patriots, as every day they came to the airfield to protest against us who took away 'their' aircraft. They did not know the rules of war, namely the winner captures and takes away the defeated side's weapons and other materials.

To handle this unpleasant and long-running situation, and to calm the spirits on the airfield, we sent a message to Gen. [Zahari] Zahariev, who then turned to the Russian [Soviet] commander of the city for assistance. At the end, the Russians [Soviets] removed forcibly the local population from the airfield and forbade every kind of protest."

An unusual incident happened to one of these 'trophy' Arados, which had international effects. On 25 July 1945, pilot *Podporuchik* Viktor Topliyski of 2/6. Fighter *Orlyak* was ordered to transfer an unspecified 'trophy *Soyka*' [sic! mentioned like this in the original document] from Bozhurishte to Plovdiv repair shop. Two other identical 'trophies' were ferried as well. However, unlike his colleagues (*Kpt.* Boris Teofilov and *Ppor.* Veselin Tenev), who arrived safely at the destination, Topliyski landed in Drama, Greece, reportedly due to navigation error (the pilot overshot the target by about 125 km, in clear weather). The Greeks promptly protested at the 'hostile aerial reconnaissance flight'. Initially, the Bulgarians officially denied the landing in Greece happened, based on miscommunication with Plovdiv. A diplomatic scandal between the two unfriendly states followed suit. At the end, Command of the VV received internal confirmation of the incident only on 16 August, thus 22 days later! They had to officially admit

---

11 Most of these captures were possibly ex-Hungarian Air Force aircraft, as the Magyars were known to employ a large number of Ar 96As, the largest outside Germany.

guilt and apologise, which quite understandably was a huge embarrassment for the air force and the country. All this is detailed in a lengthy document of the *Kommandir na Narodnite Văzdushni Voyski*, or Commander of the People's Air Force (notice the 'People' appellation in the title of the air force, sure sign of the growing Communist influence), signed by the head of VV, Maj.-Gen. Gancho Manchev, dated 31 October 1945.

Another of these 'trophy' Ar 96Bs was involved in an accident that happened on 26 October 1945. The aircraft, No. 24[12], belonging to the 2/2. *Shturmovi Orlyak*, was damaged during a bad landing on Dolna Mitropoliya airfield, when the instructor pilot, *Kapitan* Tsvetko P. Kolev, forgot to lower the main undercarriage, bellying the trainer. The crew, which also included *Urednik-shkolnik* Anghel I. Nachev, escaped unhurt. Interestingly, No. 24 is not listed among the aircraft extant on 27 June 1945 (see below). Quite probably, this aircraft, with a high serial number, was actually an ex-*Luftwaffe*, or ex-MKHL 'booty' machine brought to Bulgaria only a couple of months earlier.

Radiogram dated 23 August 1945 lists the cipher (code letter) assigned to each aircraft code name, for briefer communication. *Soyka* was assigned with the letter 'A'.

A Bulgarian Air Force Command (*Komandir na VV*) document (No. 65/27 June 1945) lists all aircraft types available at that date. Among them was the *Soyka*.

This somewhat dark photo shows the MG 17 machine gun mounted on the starboard side of the engine cowling to advantage.

A total of 36 such aircraft were extant:

I, At *Văzdushnite Uchebni Chasti*: 26 aircraft, as follows:

A, *Yunkerskiya Ucheben Orlyak*: 4 aircraft (will stay there).

No. 5 (series 42),

No. 15 (series 45 [sic!]),

Nos. 3 and 18 (series 35).

B, *Văzdushnata Shkola*, Telish: 2 aircraft (will stay there).

Nos. 13 and 14 (series 42).

C, 2. *Rem. Rabotilnitsa*: 1 aircraft (to be handed over to the air force school).

No. 17 (series 42).

D, 2/2. *Shtuka Orlyak*: 16 aircraft.

Nos. 16, 18, 19, 20 (series 42),

Nos. 1, 6, 7, 8, 9, 10, 11, 12, 14, 15, 16 and 17 (series 35).

E, 6. *Polk* at Karlovo: 3 aircraft.

No. 9 (series 42),

Nos. 13 and 15 (series 35)[13].

II, *Iztrebitelniya Polk*: 5 aircraft.

2/2. *Orlyak*: No. 1 (series 42) and No. 4 (series 35), to be handed over to 2/6. *Orlyak*,

2/6. *Orlyak*: Nos. 2 and 11 (series 42), to stay there,

6. *Polk*, Karlovo: No. 7 (series 42), to stay there.

III, *Shtumoviya Polk*: 5 aircraft.

2/2. *Shtuka Orlyak*: Nos. 4, 6, 8, 10 and 12 (series 42), to stay there.

One can notice reference to three 'series': 35, 42 and 45.

So far, it's known that the original four unarmed Ar 96Bs received the NN 7035 – the 'series 35' is most probably referring to these. Ten more such unarmed aircraft arrived in 1944 from Germany, while many more were transferred from Soviet captures taken in Austria in mid-1945, as detailed earlier.

The 20 armed Ar 96Bs, with rear gunner, which arrived in late 1940 received the NN 7042, so the 'series 42' is most probably referring to these. There was no further shipment of this peculiar sub-type.

---

12 no NN number is mentioned in the original accident report; however, it could not be the version with the rear gunner, but was most likely of a regular production B sub-type, or the old 'A' sub-type from captured stocks.

13 No. 15 (series 35) is repeated twice, while no No. 15 in 'series 42' is mentioned in the document. The sole 'series 45' mentioned is also recorded as No. 15. Therefore, most probably it's a clerical error, so one of the No. 15s actually belonged to the armed 'series 42' version.

Finally, one can speculate on the aircraft sub-type 'series 45' is referring to, thus the NN would be 7045[14]. However, this NN was already assigned to the Junkers Ju 52/3m transport, so it could be a typo. Or, the more banal solution is that the person who typed the list simply typed 4 instead of 3.

The Author believes that most probably it refers to the A sub-type (taken as war booty from Austria, as detailed earlier). The existence of this sub-type is documented by a photograph taken in the 1950s, where the Ar 96A (clearly identified by the exhaust pipe) sports the Communist-style red star type of air force marking. The Author found no write-off protocol for any the *Soykas* with the NN 7045 (or 7095). More research in the archives is needed to clarify this minor 'mystery'.

Soyka No. 26 (certainly a 'trophy' aircraft) was flown by fighter pilot Stefan Marinopolski on Balchik airfield on 2, 6 and 8 November 1945, in preparation of transferring to the Yak-9 fighter.

The Order of Battle of the restructured *Văzdushni Voyski* of 1 November 1945 lists ten *Soykas* with *Iztrebit. Shturmova Shkola* (Fighter and Ground Attack School), of which seven were serviceable. Next month, the number grew with another unserviceable one.

The 15 January 1946 Order of Battle lists the following units where the *Soyka* was still operating:
- 2nd Ground Attack (*Shturm.*) *Royak*, 21st *Orlyak*: 11 Ar 96 (4 serviceable and 7 unserviceable),
- 6th Fighter *Royak*, 26th *Orlyak*: 5 Ar 96 (3 serviceable and 2 unserviceable),
- Flying School: 8 Ar 96 (6 serviceable and 2 unserviceable),
- Blind Flying Academy: 2 Ar 96 (1 serviceable and 1 unserviceable),
- Fighter and Assault Aviation Academy: 10 Ar 96 (6 serviceable and 4 unserviceable).
- The total number of listed Ar 96s thus was a whopping 36 aircraft (20 serviceable and 16 unserviceable)!

One of these, No. 9, was flown by *Por.* Petăr Manolev at Karlovo School, on 21 May 1946.

On 1 October 1946, eight *Soyka* were listed with the *Văzdushni Uchebni Chasti (*Air Training Units). Ten *Soykas* had been scrapped. Other Ar 96s were among the 203 'conserved' school and trainer aircraft, stored in a used state of up to 60%. One of the Telish-based Arados, No. 27/7035, was involved in an accident that happened on 18 October 1946. That day, Ivan Aleksandrov, student pilot at the fighter and ground attack school, performed a heavy landing and broke off the main undercarriage.

On 9 July 1947, *Soyka* No. 6/7035 from the Air School, with pilot Captain Konstantin Konstantinov at the controls, landed outside the landing strip of Telish airfield. The aircraft was damaged 45%. The aircraft with the highest known serial number, 32/7035, was officially written off on 4 April 1947. On the same date, an Argus As 10C-3 (No. 4455598) engine was also scrapped. It can be safely assumed that the engine belonged to the scrapped airframe. Therefore, this particular *Soyka* was an 'A' sub-type, certainly a 'trophy' aircraft (hence the high board number). Two further similar occurrences were locat-

---

14 A comprehensive VNVV document, dated 18 December 1945, that lists all NNs and code names existing at that time, identifies 7045 as the NN for the Junkers Ju 52 'Sova' (the Ar 96A was not listed). Therefore, one can speculate that the NN for the Ar 96A was actually the unassigned 7095 (all other numbers ending in 5 were taken by 1945), and the 7045 listed in this document was a clerical error. To make thing more complicated, 7045 was originally assigned to the Fi 156 'Storch' (as noted in a document dated February 1941), which eventually received the NN 7065. Or, simply, the 7045 is correct, and it is a duplication situation (which is known to have occurred in at least one other case). Therefore, the Author uses the NN 7045 in this book, as found in the aforementioned document.

ed by the Author, *Soyka* Nos. 26 and 29, both scrapped along with the weaker Argus engine, thus 'A' model, both officially written off on 10 April 1947.

A list of aircraft types and their engines in repair, dated 18 March 1948, lists the Ar 96 fitted with Argus As 410A engine (i.e., Ar 96B) being repaired at Plovdiv, while the Ar 96s fitted with Argus As 10C engines (i.e., Ar 96A) being repaired at Yambol and Telish. This is yet another proof of the Ar 96As being used in Bulgaria.

The logbook of *Podporuchik* Spas Todorov Minchev contains a note about the sole aircraft accident in his career. It involved an unidentified *Soyka*, that was damaged 15% in a bad landing on Telish airfield, due to piloting error, on 25 March 1948. As a consequence, the landing gear broke and the propeller bent. The crew was unhurt. The air force unit Minchev was attached to is identified as the Telish-based Fighter-Bomber School, where he served as *Podporuchik* student pilot[15].

An interesting side story connected to the topic refers to the two Czech Avia C-2B1s (copy of the Ar 96B, manufactured in Czechoslovakia post war), transferred to Bulgaria in 1948.

Bulgarian Communist leader, Georgi Dimitrov, visited the Avia factory in Prague, in 1948. To honour this high-level visit by a fellow Communist top dignitary, the factory took the official name of '*AZNP, Závod Avia – J. Dimitrova*' (AZNP, Plant Avia – G. Dimitrov). Also, two aircraft produced at the plant at that time weres offered as a gift. The two C-2 aircraft were delivered from the Avia Factory to Bulgaria

---

15   Student pilot Minchev was assigned to the following air force units: 10 January 1945-23 April 1946: *ShZO*, at Kazan-lăk airfield, *Shkolnik-letets* (student pilot), 1 May 1946-31 July 1946: *Shturmovo-Iztrebitelna Shkola* (Ground Attack-Fighter School), at Karlovo airfield, *Urednik Shkolnik-letets* (First Sergeant student pilot), 1 July [sic!] 1946-11 October 1946: Fighter-Bomber School, at Telish airfield, *Urednik Shkolnik-letets* (First Sergeant student pilot), 12 October 1946-15 September 1947: the People's Military Air School „Georgi Benkovski", at Sofia airfield, *Urednik Portupei-Yunker* (First Sergeant student). From 1 October 1947: Fighter-Bomber School, at Telish airfield, *Podporuchik Shkolnik-letets* (2nd Lt. student pilot).

Another view of a Soyka, taken from about the same angle, as the one on page 233 top, shows 'Black 8', parked in front of a hangar. The bomb rack is well visible underneath the starboard wing. The lower wingtips appear to be painted in yellow, as was about 2/3rd of the engine cowling and possibly the rudder and elevators as well. The aircraft's individual number is applied on the fuselage, in black, as is on the lower wing surface. A rarely seen detail, typical to the Bulgarian version of the Ar 96B-1 with rear gunner, is the rectangle glass panel under the mid-fuselage, adjacent to the underbelly antenna mast. The number 83 chalked in white on the propeller cone and spinner represents the last two digits of the aircraft's construction number, W.Nr. 960083. Notice the 7.92 mm calibre MG 17 machine gun, mounted on the starboard side of the nose section, firing through the propeller arc.

by air, on 5 May 1948. The aircraft were marked with temporary ferry markings OK-CRA (C-2B1.598) and OK-CRB (C-2B1.599). They were flown by Czech pilots Lt. Col. Kremla and Staff Captain Smolík[16]. The Bulgarians returned the favour, and donated the single Heinkel He 111H-16 VIP transport (originally, a personal gift of Göring to Tsar Boris III) to the Czechs[17]. These two Czech-made Arados ended up serving with the Air Force Academy at Dolna Mitropoliya. Presumably there was no differentiation made in documents between these copies and the original Ar 96s.

The second and last fatal accident involving a Bulgarian Ar 96 happened as late as 26 May 1950. That day, during a regular training flight, the worn engine of Ar 96B-7, No. 21, stopped in mid-flight, at 150 m altitude. The aircraft then stalled and crashed near Rakita. Unfortunately, both crewmembers, *Uchenik letets mladshi kursant* (Student airman junior cadet) Hristo T. Gramatikov and instructor *Podpor.* (2nd Lt.) Slavcho S. Slavchev, were killed. The doomed *Soyka*, impressed in Bulgarian service on 17.08.1945 (thus a 'trophy' aircraft), was a total write-off (see photo and artwork on page 250).

A detailed register including all aircraft in service with the air force, compiled at an unknown date post war, lists only *Soykas* with the NN 7035, i.e., unarmed trainers. The register includes the following serial numbers, without giving any further details, however: 2, 3, 4, 5, 8, 9, 11, 12, 13, 15, 16, 17, 18, 20, 22, 23, 24, 25, 26, 27, 28, 29, 30, 31, 32, 33, 34, 35. We know that *Soyka* No. 21/7035 was destroyed on 26 May 1950, therefore, this list must have been compiled at a later date. There is an apparent conflict between some write-off dates from the mid-1950s; however, there is a strong possibility the surviving aircraft were renumbered at one point, just like the *Strelas* were.

The last Arado 96s of the 58[18] units (minimum) in Bulgarian service soldiered on until the mid-1950s. They were operated off Telish airfield[19], where a military piloting school was based. The survivors already sported the Communist-style markings, quite unusual for a German wartime design, branded by then as 'fascist technology' in Communist terminology. Despite this epithet, the Arados flew until the mid-1950, as the longest serving German-made, thus 'fascist', airplane type.

---

16 Cpt. Smolík was an ex-RAF fighter pilot, DFC holder. Shortly after this ferry flight, he was fired from the Czechoslovak Air Force as 'reactionary'. He then emigrated to the UK, where he rejoined the RAF.

17 This He 111 was used by VLÚ (*Vědecký letecký ústav* – Scientific Aviation Institute) located in Prague-Letňany, where it served as VIP transport.

18 4 unarmed+20 armed+10 unarmed+~22 trophy+2 Czechoslovak=~58 pcs.

19 Based on his logbook, prominent airman Petko Popganchev flew aboard an unidentified *Soyka* at Telish three times, on 13 April 1951.

Camouflage and markings

The Arado Ar 96 Bs arrived from Germany in light grey overall. There were three theoretical possibilities for this colour, namely the early DKH L40/52, RLM 63 (three shades[20]), or RLM 02. The author and the collaborating artists considered several paint sample versions of these light grey shades, and compared them to the available photos. Also specialised literature was consulted. In the end, the most probably paint worn by these Arados was determined to be RLM 02, and the shade is shown in the profiles of the early Bulgarian Arados (*Grüngrau*, or Greenish Grey). Most probably, the airframes were painted with Ikarol 133 RLM-*Grau* (02) top cover (finishing) paint – a Warnecke& Böhm product.

The aircraft wore black temporary German civilian ferry markings on the fuselage sides and wing upper and lower surfaces, and Germany's national symbols on the tail surface, all applied with washable paint. The early style round Bulgarian military markings, applied at the factory on the mid-fuselage and wings, were covered by mid-grey, also a washable paint. The rudder was in Bulgaria's tricolour [White (top), mid-Green (middle) and blood-Red (bottom)], also covered for the ferry flight by removable light grey paint. The area around the exhaust pipes was heat resisting matt black. The propeller spinner and blades appear to be painted in RLM 70 Black Green.

The early style, roundel type military marking was already *passé* by the time the Arados eventually arrived in late 1940. Therefore, it was immediately replaced with the current, Axis-style black cross in white square type marking. The black VNVV serial numbers were applied in Bulgaria, initially on the rudder top and on wing under surfaces. Later on, the serial number was moved to the rear fuselage, aft of the military marking, applied briefly in white, then in black.

Finally, the identification was completed with the typical VNVV triangle on mid fin, identifying each aircraft individually [on the top of the 'fraction', the aircraft's serial number, while on the bottom, the aircraft type's *Nomenklaturen Nomer* (NN), or Register Number]. The NN assigned to the unarmed version was 7035, while the armed ones, with rear gunner were assigned with 7042. It's unclear if the 'war trophy' Ar 96As were assigned a separate NN.

Based on an order issued by VNVV HQ on 14 April 1938, in an effort to standardise the identification colours used on aircraft, based on their role, all trainer aircraft had to be painted in yellow. However, it is highly improbable that the Arados received such a yellow coat of paint while in Bulgaria. There are several photos where the Axis yellow markings on wingtips and engine cowling are clearly different to the lighter colour airframe, which the Author believes kept its original factory light grey.

The only other known Soyka displaying crocodile mouth nose art is 'Black 20', the last of the batch of armed Ar 96B-1 trainers. The officer in the rear cockpit is Polk. Racho Stanimirov, while in the front seat Kpt. Dimităr 'Karacha' Karaivanov, future Stuka pilot, is seated. Notice the barely seen yellow on the upper wingtip. The elevators and rudder are yellow as well.

---

20   There were three different RLM 63 shades: *Hellgrau* (=RAL 7040), *Lichtgrau* (=RAL 7042) and *Grüngrau* (=RAL 7003), the latter identical to RLM 02 (source: *Gegenüberstellung der RLM-Farben mit den heutigen RAL-Farben*, by Siegfried Fricke, Scale magazine No. 3/96).

Additional info see: http://mmpbooks.biz/assets/BFC/07.pdf

During the invasion of Yugoslavia by German troops in April 1941, a thin yellow band appeared on the mid-fuselage, often combined with a solid yellow engine cowling (either fully covered, or only the front 2/3rd area). Later, possibly from 1943 on, both surfaces of the wingtips became yellow as well, alongside the rudder and elevators. About ten days following Bulgaria's about-face and defection from the Axis camp on 9 September 1944, all 'Axis-yellow' paint was removed, and replaced with a white rear fuselage band, the same colour covering both surfaces of the wingtips.

In contrast to the initially delivered 4+20 all-grey B-1 aircraft, the ten Ar 96B-7s received in mid-1944 arrived in green/blue camouflage colours. Based on photographic evidence, some were painted in a single-tone green, most probably RLM 71 Dark Green on the upper surfaces and RLM 65 Light Blue on the under surfaces. Others show a regular two-tone green upper camouflage scheme (RLM 70/71), over RLM 65. After the war, the surviving aircraft were repainted on the upper surfaces in what appears to be a single-shade dark green colour, possibly of Soviet origin.

It is interesting to note that the Arado Ar 96 is the only aircraft type discussed in this book that wore all versions of the military markings of the Bulgarian air force, namely the early royal roundel type, the pro-Axis black-cross-in-white-square type, the immediate post-war OF roundel and, finally, the Communist-style red star with the Bulgarian cockade in centre.

In this particular case, the Ar 96B-1 wears yellow wraparound engine cowling and both the lower and upper surfaces of the wing-tips are yellow. Presumably, the rudder and elevators are yellow as well. The airmen, identifiable by the wings on their visor cap and by the wings embroidered over the right pocket of their uniforms, are busy reading the newspaper, and only the kneeling army man pays attention to the photographer. This 'civil-ian' (i.e. unarmed) trainer was photographed on Karlovo airfield, in October 1943.

The photo of 'Black 11' was undoubtedly taken after Bulgaria's early September 1944 about-face, as identified by the white fuselage band, upper wingtips and spinner. The Nomenklaturen Nomer (NN, i.e. Register Number) of this variant with rear gunner, 7042, is clearly visible in the bottom row of the triangle applied on mid-fin, while the aircraft's individual serial number, 11, was written in the top row. Due to dark appearance of the greenish-grey variant of the RLM 02, most artists have mistaken this colour to dark green, and drew their profiles accordingly – erroneously. Often, the rear fu-selage band and wingtips are depicted yellow, which again is an error.

Two photos depicting derelict Soykas in 1947, photographed by one of the soldiers assigned to guard the airfield. Worth noticing how the yellow coat of paint faded away on the rudder of the engineless No. 5. This phenomenon reveals the Bulgarian tricolour, which, in turn, also faded, revealing the original German marking underneath, consisting of a red horizontal band with a white dot in centre and a black swastika inscribed in it.

On 4 October 1945, the Axis style 'Black X in White Square' type military marking gave way to a new one, closely connected to the ruling pro-Communist party, the Otechestven Front, or Fatherland Front (abbreviated OF). This particular incident happened long after that marking change, namely on 26 May 1950. It involved Soyka No. 21/7035, of the Telish based piloting school. Luckily, the aircraft's original construction number is given in the post-accident report, W.Nr. 55 0448 (formerly GM+VN). This identifies the aircraft as a Letov-built B-7, produced sometimes in late Summer of 1944, which was then captured by Soviet troops at Zeltweg airfield in Austria, and subsequently handed over to the Bulgarians in mid-1945, being part of the official figure of 19 such 'trophy' Ar 96s. Unfortunately, both crewmembers died in this accident, which most probably represented only the second deadly incident that involved an Arado Ar 96 during the approximately fifteen years of service in the Bulgarian air force – an enviable record by any standards.

Judging by the identical paint chip-off seen on the exhaust pipe, both photos (top and left) show the same aircraft. Highly interestingly, this is not a 'regular 'Berta', but an early 'Anton' Bulgaria officially never received from Germany! Therefore, it can be assumed that it is one of the so-called 'trophy' aircraft recovered in Austria immediately after the war's end with the Soviets' consent. It could very well be an ex-Hungarian air force machine, which retreated to Austria in early 1945, then was abandoned there, just to be recovered by Bulgarian technicians. Also uniquely among surviving photographic images of Bulgarian Arado 96s, the aircraft sports the Communist style red star on the fuselage. This is explained by the date written on the bottom of one of the photos, August 1953.

These photos were taken immediately after the batch of four unarmed, all-grey Ar 96B-1s had landed on Bozhurishte main airfield in September 1940. Notice the black German civilian ferry markings visible on the starboard wing (...WA), which identifies this particular ship as the first Ar 96B-1, D-IXWA, W.Nr. 96 0060 (future NN 1/7035 in Bulgarian service). Also note the overpainted Bulgarian air force roundel close to the wingtip. The washable paint covering the military marking had already been removed from the fuselage. Notice the Bulgarian airplane seen in the background, at left, already sports on its wing the new 'black-St. Andrew-cross-in-white-square' type marking!

Arado Ar 96B-1, unarmed (W.Nr. 96 0060, ferry registration D-IXWA), 1/7035, Bozhurishte, September 1940. Camouflage colours: RLM-Grey (RLM 02) overall. Spinner and propeller blades black. Roundel style national marking in six positions (partially covered). Rudder in Bulgarian tricolour (White, Green, Red).

Depicted are the first unarmed Arado Ar 96B-1 trainers to arrive to Bulgaria in September 1940. The temporary civilian ferry registration was washed of the fuselage, revealing the Bulgarian military marking. The German registration was left untouched on the wing undersurface (...WA). This identifies the aircraft in the foreground as the first Ar 96B-1, D-IXWA, W.Nr. 96 0060 (future NN 1/7035 in Bulgarian service).

*Arado Ar 96B-1, unarmed (W.Nr. 96 0060), 1/7035, 'Black 1',
Bozhurishte, October 1940. Camouflage colours: RLM-Grey (RLM 02)
overall. Spinner and propeller blades black. Axis style national marking
in six positions. Rudder in Bulgarian tricolour (White, Green, Red).*

*The factory applied roundel type Bulgarian military markings the aircraft
arrived with from Arado Flugzeugwerke lasted only a couple of days,
at most. They were replaced by the square type, valid at the time of the
aircraft's arrival to Bulgaria. The aircraft's black individual serial number
was applied first on the rudder top, over the white national colour segment,
as per Order No. 53/14.04.1938. This practice also did not last too long, as
soon after, the serial number was moved to the fuselage, where it stayed for
the rest of the aircraft type's wartime service.*

245

Arado Ar 96B-1, armed (W.Nr. 96 0085), 10/7042, 'Black 10', 1ˢᵗ Armeyski Orlyak, April 1941. Camouflage colours: RLM-Grey (RLM 02) overall. Thin yellow rear fuselage band. Propeller blades black. Axis style national marking in six positions.

'Black 10' stopped on its nose following a botched landing sometime in 1941. This undated post-accident photo allows the onlooker to study many details of the armed version of the Ar 96B-1. Notice the narrow yellow mid-fuselage band applied in early April 1941, just prior to the invasion of Yugoslavia, to all Axis aircraft flying in the area, Bulgarians included. By that time, the vivid Bulgarian tricolour had disappeared from the rudder.

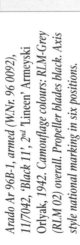

Arado Ar 96B-1, armed (W.Nr. 96 0092),
11/7042, 'Black 11', 2nd 'Lineen' Armeyski
Orlyak, 1942. Camouflage colours: RLM-Grey
(RLM 02) overall. Propeller blades black. Axis
style national marking in six positions.

The Soyka in the rear appears to sport
a spectacular marking in form of a crocodile
mouth painted on the engine cowling. The
aircraft's individual serial number is believed to be
'Black 11'.

Arado Ar 96B-7, armed (W.Nr. 450006), 5/7035,
'White 5', mid-1944. Camouflage colours: Black Green
(RLM 70) and Dark Green (RLM 71), over Light Blue
(RLM 65). Propeller spinner yellow, blades black. Axis
style national marking in six positions.

During the spring of 1944, ten Ar 96Bs were transferred
to Bulgaria as part of the so-called 'Barbara-Programm'.
This particular aircraft was most probably part of this
delivery. The fuselage number 'White 5' denotes that this
was the first such aircraft, as four unarmed B-1s had
arrived much earlier, in late 1940 (Nos. 1-4). The barrel of
the nose mounted MG 17 machine gun protrudes over the
starboard side of the engine cowling. This detail points to
the sub-version possibly being a B-3 (the similarly armed
B-8 appeared only later on), in contrast to the German
delivery documents, which state the sub-type of these ten
aircraft delivered in 1944 as the unarmed B-7. Notice the
black curtains in the rear cabin, consistent with blind
flying training. Despite the indifferent quality of the photo,
the standard Luftwaffe style segment camouflage pattern
is recognisable.

Arado Ar 96B, unarmed, 15/7035, 'White 15', mid-1945. Camouflage colours: unidentified Dark Green, over Light Blue. White rear fuselage band and wingtips. Propeller blades black. Axis style national marking in six positions.

Judging by its serial number, 15, this Ar 96B was the first aircraft coming from the captures in Austria, impressed in Bulgarian service in mid-1945 (the first four arrived from Germany in 1940, the next ten in 1944). The white wingtips and fuselage band date the photo as post-September 1944, when these pro-Soviet marking have been introduced – consistent to the aforementioned theory. The aircraft appears to be painted on the upper surfaces in a uniform dark green colour, over light blue, or grey. The dividing line of these two colours runs unusually high on the fuselage side, pointing to a paint job performed in Bulgaria. The woman in the rear seat apparently enjoys the ride with the open cockpit. This may hint to warmer temperatures, thus placing the time of this snapshot sometime in the summer of 1945.

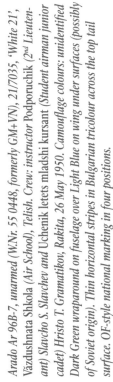

Arado Ar 96B-7, unarmed (W.Nr. 55 0448, formerly GM+VN), 21/7035, 'White 21', Vâzdushnata Shkola (Air School), Telish. Crew: instructor Podporuchik (2ⁿᵈ Lieutenant) Slavcho S. Slavchev and Uchenik letets mladshi kursant (Student airman junior cadet) Hristo T. Gramatikov, Rakita, 26 May 1950. Camouflage colours: unidentified Dark Green wraparound on fuselage over Light Blue on wing under surfaces (possibly of Soviet origin). Thin horizontal stripes in Bulgarian tricolour across the top tail surface. OF-style national marking in four positions.

This deadly accident involving a Soyka happened on 26 May 1950. It concerned a 'trophy' Ar 96B-7, No. 21/7035, of the Telish based piloting school. Both crewmembers died in this accident that happened near Rakita, 35 km west of Sofia. The aircraft was in Bulgarian service since 17.08.1945. See page 242 top for another photo depicting the same catastrophe. Curiously, the white serial (board) number is applied on the rear fuselage, aft the military marking, and not in front of it, as per official regulations. The ubiquitous triangle most probably ended up underneath the horizontal stabiliser (tailplane).

250

Messerschmitt Bf 109E *Strela*
Bulgaria's Top-Notch Arrow

With the acquisition of second-rate Czechoslovak, Polish and German fighters in 1937-1939, the fledgling Bulgarian fighter air arm received a much needed numerical boost in aircraft. However, within a couple of years it became clear that this was only a stop-gap measure, as the era of the agile but slow biplanes or gull-wing fighters had passed. The rapid pace of aircraft technology advances and the combat events of the recently erupted war all pointed to the rise of fast all-metal monoplane fighters, which accelerated and climbed well, and were armed with rapid-fire machine guns and cannon.

The decision makers of the Bulgarian armed forces obviously took notice of this fact. Therefore, Sofia looked at avenues to modernise its fighter force with state-of-the-art models, taking its limited financial resources into account. Since Bulgaria was increasingly turning toward the resurgent Germany and Italy[1], the choices were pretty much limited to what these leading Axis countries had to offer. The other conjectural possibility, the Soviet Union, proved to be a dead end[2]. As Italy herself was in desperate need of modern monoplane fighters, only Germany was left as a viable source. Indeed, Germany was one of the leaders in modern aviation technology. In the domain of fighter aircraft, it was Messerschmitt *Flugzeugwerke* AG and its top model, the famous Bf 109, which was making the headlines of the new air war.

However, Hitler needed all available warplanes for the *Luftwaffe*, heavily engaged in the war. Nevertheless, in order to persuade the Balkan state to firmly anchor itself to the Axis camp, Berlin reluctantly gave the seal of approval to Messerschmitt AG for a limited export to Bulgaria. Once the green light was secured, talks that had been lingering with the potential Bulgarian customers since 1939 sped up.

---

1   The wife of Tsar Boris, *Tsaritsa* Yoanna (Giovanna), was the daughter of King Victor Emmanuel III of Italy.

2   Little known fact is that in the autumn of 1940, the Bulgarians secretly negotiated with the Soviets – at that time the Germans' allies – the purchase of a substantial number of fighter aircraft (believed to amount to 120 units), mainly various models of the Polikarpov I-16. The planned deal did not materialise, however.

Bulgarian military delegation in visit to Germany, 'shopping around' for armament, including aircraft. The high-ranking officer in centre, with red greatcoat lapel, is believed to be Major General Dimităr V. Ayryanov. One of the best purchases secured was ten brand new Messerschmitt Bf 109E-3s, the top-of-the-line fighter aircraft type coveted by all of Germany's smaller allies.

In order to master the modern German aircraft technology, six selected Bulgarian lieutenant pilots were sent to the flying school at Werneuchen, in Germany, in 1938. Over there, they were not only taught how to bring out the best of the aircraft, but also how to lead and teach other pilots. Depicted is the graduation ceremony held at Werneuchen, in March 1939. The six Bulgarian graduates are lined up beside their German instructors (at left). They are (from left to right): Lt. Vasil Shishkov, Lt. Dimităr Lazarov, Lt. Stoyan Stoyanov, Lt. Asen Kovachev, Lt. Aleksandăr Gunchev and Lt. Nikolay Yordanov.

The Bulgarian Government informed DRT by a letter dated 20.7.1939 that it wished to purchase ten 'Me 109s'. In early March 1940, a Bulgarian delegation, led by Lieutenant General Rusi H. Rusev[3], Inspector General of Armaments, visited Messerschmitt *Flugzeugwerke* AG's headquarters in Augsburg. The Bulgarians' aim was to secure the purchase of the Bf 109, enough to equip a fighter squadron. At the end, a draft contract was signed on 4 April 1940 which stipulated the sale of ten Bf 109E-3 fighters and six Bf 108B-1 *Taifun*, *i.e.* Typhoon (the latter intended to be used as conversion trainers to the Bf 109). The '109 airframe was to be powered by a DB 601Aa engine of 1,100 hp (at 2,400 rpm and 3,700 m altitude), fitted with a three-blade VDM propeller. Interestingly, the aircraft was to be equipped only with a pair of MG 17 machine guns mounted over the engine and no armament in the wings, standard to the E series. The cockpit canopy was the later production squared one, typical for aircraft from the E-4 series onwards[4]. The unit price set was 185,000 *Reichsmarks*, considerably higher than the regular price Messerschmitt received for a similar aircraft sold to the *Luftwaffe*, thus the Bulgarian deal secured a hefty profit for the company. The ten commissioned aircraft were brand new ones, built at *Wiener Neustädter Flugzeugwerke* (WNF) in Wiener Neustadt, Austria (part of the so-called 'Greater German Reich').

Correspondence between the Bulgarian Ministry of War and Messerschmitt AG, dated 11 April 1940, referring to contracts from 4 and 6 April 1940, calling for "*six training aircraft, type number 108 and 10 fighter aircraft, type number 109*", mentions that the shipment had transited through Yugoslavia. Indeed, the transport arrived by train to its destination station, Dragoman, on 17 April 1940. After the delivery was completed and countersigned by the Bulgarian party, Messerschmitt AG issued Invoice No. 60-01921, dated 9.08.1940, stating the delivery completion of "10 *Jagdeinsitzer* Me 109 E *Werk-Nr. 5221-5230 nach Bestimmungsstation Dragoman*"[5].

The crates were downloaded from the rail cars later that month and transported to the main military airport of Bozhurishte, where they arrived in early May, as proven by a Protocol signed on 6.05.1940. Once there, the airframes were assembled at the local DSF (*Dărzhavna Samoletna Fabrika*, or State Airplane Factory), under the supervision of Messerschmitt technicians. After the test flights, performed first

---

3   General Rusev was executed by the Communist authorities in Sofia, on 1 February 1945, following a mock trial. As a curiosity, Brazil's president at the time of writing, Dilma Rousseff, is related to him through her father, Bulgarian-born Petăr Rusev.

4   This detail often lead various authors and enthusiasts to the erroneous conclusion that the Bulgarian 'Emils' were of the E-4 (or, even the E-7) sub-type.

5   Curiously, individual *Übernahmebestätigung* (Confirmation of receipt) issued for the ten Bf 109E-3s are dated earlier than the draft contract's signing date, namely on 03.04.1940 (while the certificates for the six Bf 109B-1s to even earlier, on 29.03.1940).

This photo originating from Bulgaria depicts a neat row of ten Messerschmitt Bf 109D fighter aircraft, used by Bulgarian pilots for conversion training, lined up on Werneuchen airfield. The nearest aircraft wears on its rear fuselage the S2+M58 code, while the one behind it S2+M53 (outlined in white).

by factory pilot Waneck[6], then by his Bulgarian counterpart, *Podpor.* Stoyan I. Stoyanov[7], the aircraft were handed over to the would-be independent 6th *Iztrebitelen Polk* (Fighter Regiment) headquartered in Karlovo. This élite fighter unit, officially formed on 1 July 1940, was subordinated directly to the Bulgarian Army's General Headquarters. Based on his logbook, Stoyanov flew the 'Me 109 *Strela*' for the first time in Bulgaria on 14 June 1940, on Bozhurishte airfield (see below). The maiden flight, categorised as преМинаване (basically, transition), lasted 55 minutes. The second flight, performed later on the same day, was a bit shorter, 45 minutes. Since there is no individual number of the *Strela* mentioned in the logbook, one can assume that at that time it actually had none, only the so-called 'Tsarist roundel' type military marking may have been applied on the airframe.

The takeover procedure is mentioned in the memoirs of the top scoring Bulgarian fighter pilot, General (ret.) Stoyan Stoyanov, called 'We defended you, Sofia' (page 42)[8]: *"In [early, D.B.] June 1940, I was called to Sofia, to the air force headquarters. There, I was told a new fighter aircraft is going to be delivered soon – the Me 109 Emil, which was already fighting on the fronts in Europe, over England and Africa. As*

---

6   Other Bulgarian sources give the German test pilot's name as 'Wacker'.

7   Stoyan Iliev Stoyanov (12 March 1913 – 13 March 1997), future top scoring Bulgarian fighter ace.

8   Edition published by Eăr Grup 2000, Sofia, Bulgaria, in 2011.

№ по редъ	№ от лет. дневникъ	Дата 1940	Пилотъ Наученикъ съ който е изпълнена задачата	Самолетъ	Кратко изложение на задачата
133	5179	8. VI.	е -а-м-ъ	Оса 21	Влачене ръкавъ
134	1885	11. VI.	Wанеск	лебедъ	опознавателно
135	1886	–"–	в. а - м-ъ	–"–	кацане
136	1893	–"–	съ ученикъ	–"–	–"–
137	1915	12. VI.	–"–	–"–	–"–
138	1916	–"–	–"–	–"–	–"–
139	1919	13. VI.	–"–	–"–	–"–
140	1923	–"–	–"–	–"–	–"–
141	1928	–"–	–"–	–"–	–"–
142	2003	14. VI.	е-а-м-ъ	Ме 109 „Стрела"	преминаване
143	2019	–"–	–"–	–"–	–"–
144	2020	15. VI.	съ ученикъ	Ме 108 „Тайфунъ"	Навигационна и кацане на чуждо летище

This page from test pilot Ppor. Stoyanov's logbook lists his first flight aboard the Bf 109E Strela, performed from Bozhurishte airfield, on 14 June 1940. The morning flight lasted for 55 mins., while the second one in the afternoon for 45 mins.

After passing acceptance tests, the aircraft were applied the roundel-type Bulgarian military marking, in six positions, and serial numbers running from 1 to 10. This scheme was very short lived; however, as a new, 'Black-X-in-White-Square' style military marking was introduced in late June 1940, to better conform to the Axis standards. Depicted along a freshly marked Bf 109E, which lacks an identification number, is the confidently smiling Podporuchik Stoyanov, one of the first Bulgarian pilots to master the Emil. *This and the photo on page 257 that show a Bulgarian Bf 109E wearing the so-called 'Tsarist roundel' contradict statements that the Bulgarian* Emils *carried no such marking.*

I was known to be an expert of this aircraft [he had been at a training course in Germany, see below, D.B.], *I was ordered to accept them for the Bulgarian side, by test flying each of them after the German factory test pilot. My next task after this was to train the first five pilots*[9], *who would become the kernel of a new fighter unit that was going to be armed with these aircraft. The airplanes, 10 combat Me 109Es and 4* [actually 6, D.B.] *trainer Me 108s, arrived to Bozhurishte by train. Here they were assembled by German technicians. According to the practice and the international trade rules, these had to be tested in flight by the chief pilot of the Messerschmitt factory and by me after him. Only after that were the handover protocols signed."* After the work had been completed, Messerschmitt AG issued to its Bulgarian customer Invoice No. 60-04949, dated 02.04.1941, for *"Zum zusammenbau sowie zum Einfliegen der von uns gelieferten 10 Jagdflugzeuge Me 109 E"* (*i.e.* "for assembly and test flight of the 10 Me 109 E fighter aircraft delivered by us").

Even before the Bf 109E actually entered service, the type officially received a typical Bulgarian code name, *Strela*, or Arrow, by an air force decree dated 15 May 1940. This was a departure from the norm, as by then all aircraft types received mainly birds' names. The bright yellow engine cowling, followed by a rearward tapered yellow flash along the fuselage, indeed gave the sensation of an arrow to the onlooker. The Bf 109E was assigned the military register number 7047 (*i.e.* the fifth fighter aircraft type in VNVV service). The VNVV serial numbers ran from 1 to 10, and coincided with the last digit of the original German construction number (W.Nr. 5221 to 5230)[10].

In order to master the new German aircraft technology, the seven best Bulgarian fighter pilots[11] were sent to the *Luftwaffe* fighter pilot training school at Werneuchen, Germany, in June 1938 (see photo in the He 51 chapter, page 82). They were trained by German instructors not only to be skilled fighter pilots, but also as flight leaders and instructors, who would subsequently train their comrades once back in Bulgaria. In March 1939, another batch of five pilots[12] arrived to Werneuchen for training. The courses did not go on smoothly, however. Two of the latecomer student pilots perished in air accidents[13].

Transition to the new, superior German fighter type did not progress smoothly in Bulgaria, either. Despite using the docile 'smaller sister', the Bf 108 *Taifun*, to introduce the Messerschmitt technology, including the usage of retractable landing gear, conversion to the powerful Bf 109E occasionally

---

9   The new ‚Strela' trainees were: *Ppor.* Lyuben Z. Kondakov, *Ppor.* Stoyan I. Stoyanov [sic!], *Kand. of.* Gencho D. Ivanov, *Podof.* Yordan S. Todorov and *Podof.* Aleksandăr A. Petkovski [based on document issued by the C/O of 2. *Iztr. Orlyak* on 14.06.1940].

10   Intriguingly, secondary sources mention that the Bf 109E series in the W.Nr. 5227-5252 range received *Stammkennzeichen* (radio call codes) from RB+ZA to RB+ZZ row. However, it's unlikely that aircraft manufactured for export were assigned such codes.

11   Lt. Aleksandăr Gunchev, Lt. Nikolay Yordanov, Lt. Asen Kovachev, Lt. Dimităr Lazarov, Lt. Stoyan Stoyanov, Lt. Dimităr Tamahkiarov and Lt. Vasil Shishkov.

12   Lt. Chudomir Toplodolski, Lt. Georgi Genchev, Lt. Bogdan Iliev, Lt. Matey Todorov and Lt. Dimităr Spisarevski.

13   Lt. Georgi G. Genchev and Lt. Matey P. Todorov, both died on 2 May 1939 while flying *Luftwaffe* Arado Ar 68 fighters. In a training flight, the Ar 68 trio encountered dense fog and the two Bulgarian student pilots crashed into a hill near Werneuchen.

Austrian workers prepare the fuselage of an Emil to be loaded upon a flatbed railway carriage prior to shipment to Bulgaria. Notice the typical Bulgarian camouflage scheme on rear fuselage and the lack of military markings. The propeller is painted in a light colour, definitely not black green, as it should have been according to Luftwaffe standards.

The ten commissioned Bf 109E-3s were delivered from the WNF aircraft factory at Wiener Neustadt, in Austria, to Bulgaria in late April 1940. They arrived already painted in camouflage colours, but devoid of any serial numbers or national markings (except for the rudder, which was painted in Bulgaria's tricolour). They also lacked the 20mm wing cannon, which were purchased and fitted only later on. This detail is visible on this head-on photo, taken shortly after assembly at DSF-Bozhurishte. For the side view of the same aircraft, see page 282, top.

ended up in accidents. It was often the narrow track undercarriage that bent, or broke, during take-offs and landings. However, the damage could be fairly easily repaired, or the damaged wing/landing gear replaced, thus the aircraft could be back in the air within weeks. A German document notes that in October 1940 two such accidents occurred, to W. Nr. 5222 and 5224 (VNVV Nos. 2 and 4, respectively). Both *Strelas* were repaired and eventually resumed duty. Next year, six accidents were recorded involving Bf 109Es, none of them ending up in a write-off, however, and no lives were lost, either.

Order of battle, dated 1 July 1940, the date the would-be famous 6. *Iztrebitelen Polk* was officially formed, does not list the Bf 109Es, as probably they were not combat ready yet. When they eventually entered active service in August, the ten Bf 109Es were assigned first to an unnumbered *Yato Strela*, then to 682. *Yato* of 1/6. *Iztrebitelen Orlyak*, based at Marno-Pole airfield, near Karlovo. When 692. *Yato* was formed in October, the ten '109s were split in two, and assigned in equal numbers to both squadrons.

Once officially in service, the *Emils* completed to the Bulgarian order showed their shortcomings in equipment. The armament, consisting of only a pair of 7.62 mm MG 17 machine guns, proved insufficient for the latest requirements of air combat. Also, they could not fly higher than 5,000 m, as the aircraft were not equipped with oxygen bottles. These deficiencies were soon rectified. Powerful, rapid-fire 20 mm MG-FF cannon (by Ikaria), were eventually fitted to each wing (standard to all

Header of the Bulgarian Certificate of Acceptance (удостовѣрение за приемане) of the first Bf 109E. It lists the model of the aircraft (Bf 109 E 3), the construction number (5221), the manufacturer (literally, Veener Noyshteter Flugzoygverke G.m.b.H., which of course means Wiener Neustädter Flugzeugwerke G.m.b.H.), the type of the engine (DB 601A), constr. number (11453), the model of the airscrew (V.D.M.), constr. number (134485) and the weights.

Bf 109Es from the E-3 version), and oxygen systems were purchased and retrofitted to all *Emils*.

The first real combat activity of the *Strelas* happened during Operation 'Marita', the *Wehrmacht* drive against Yugoslavia and Greece. In April 1941, the two Bf 109E-equipped *yata* were deployed to Asĕn landing ground, near Kazanlăk air base, not far from the country's southern borders with Greece, where the threat was deemed the greatest by the Army Headquarters. The VNVV order of battle of 5 April 1941 lists all ten Bf 109Es at Asĕn. Although eventually the *Strelas* did not fire their armament in anger, they performed the task of covering the volatile southern border with success.

After the singing of the Tripartite Pact on 1 March 1941, which allied Bulgaria to the resurgent Germany, Italy and Japan, *i.e.* the Axis, Berlin was more eager to export weapons to its newest ally, knowing they would be put to the advantage of the Axis' cause. One of the first deals struck was the delivery of nine additional Bf 109Es, which would complement the existing ten *Strelas*. The contract, calling for the sale of nine used but refurbished[14] Bf 109E-3a (where the 'a' suffix denoted 'export' aircraft), was signed on 17 July 1941. It included, among other smaller details, additional armour attached to the pilot's seat. The engine to be fitted to the airframe was the same that powered the first batch, too (DB 601Aa). Curiously, the armament remained only the two cowling mounted machine guns, with no cannon fitted to the wings. A welcomed improvement was the automatically set propeller pitch (the first batch of aircraft featured manually set pitch mechanisms). Despite the improvements, the unit price was lower than the previous deal, set at 149,783 *Reichsmarks*, while the total value of the contract, which included two spare engines, was 1,355,520 *Reichsmarks*. This was because, in contrast to the first batch, the aircraft of the second batch were not new, but rather previously used then refurbished ones. They were manufactured by different factories in different timeframes, and had suffered various degree of damage prior to general overhaul and upgrade to E-3a standard.

The individual pedigree of this second batch was reconstructed by the author, as follows:
- Airframe *Werknummern* (corroborated by several sources. In brackets, the available history):
- **1231** (manufactured as Bf 109E-3 by Erla, recorded as 100% loss on 20.12.1939, while in service with II./JG 186, collided over Nordholz with another Bf 109E, W.Nr. 3646, of same unit. Pilot bailed out. Possible typo in accident record).
- **1644** (manufactured as Bf 109E-3 by Erla, in service with II./JG 53 in Sept. 1940, recorded as Bf 109E-4. Lightly damaged during combat on 17.09.1940, then force landed following another air combat ten days later at Wissant, France, 15% damage).
- **4832** (manufactured as Bf 109E-1 by Arado, in service with 6./JG 53, force landed following engine trouble at Berck-sur-Mer, France, on 10.10.1940, 30% damage) .
- **5212** (manufactured as Bf 109E-3 by WNF, in service with 5./JG 53, recorded as Bf 109E-4. Lost in air combat over the English Channel on 23.11.1940, pilot Fw. Josef Wurmheller escaped. Possible typo in loss record).
- **5589** (manufactured as Bf 109E-4 by WNF, KB+HZ, in service with 4./JG 54 in Oct. 1940).
- **5903** (manufactured as Bf 109E-4/B by WNF, originally fitted with DB 601N engine. In service with 4./JG 53, recorded as Bf 109E-7. Lightly damaged in air combat over the English Channel on 11.10.1940).
- **5908** (manufactured as Bf 109E-4/B by WNF, originally fitted with DB 601N engine. In service with 1./JG 77, recorded as Bf 109E-1. Lost in air combat over the English Channel on 31.08.1940. Pilot Fw. Adolf Borchers rescued. Possible typo in loss record).
- **5932** (manufactured as Bf 109E-7 by WNF. In service with II./JG 53. Crashed at St.-Inglevert, France, after engine damage, on 13.10.1940, 80% damage. Pilot unhurt. Possible typo in loss record).
- **6012** (manufactured as Bf 109E-1 by Fieseler. Damaged in France around 07.05.1940. Scheduled to be sent for repairs to Erla in Leipzig, but reportedly did not arrive there. No further info).
- DB 601A-1 powerplants, *Werknummern*: 10055, 10155, 10261, 10239, 60620, 61482, 62841, 62688.
- VDM propellers, *Werknummern*: 15258, 231222, 30519, 27460, 30242, 31785, 12148, 30393, 90404.

---

14 In original: „*gebrauchte, jedoch grundüberholte*".

Further on, the construction number of the 18 Rheinmetall MG 15 machine guns, the 18 20 mm Ikaria cannon, the 9 Telefunken FuG 7 radio sets and the 9 Schröder type parachutes are listed as well. The total amount of the contract is set at 1,355,520 RM. Document signed by the Bulgarians on 4 September 1941.

The nine refurbished aircraft were loaded onto a flatbed train at the railway station closest to the airfield of Grossenhain, and left for Karlovo station on 7 August 1941[15]. The '109s arrived on 23 August[16], and were subsequently assembled, assisted by factory technicians. After the fighters were declared fit for service, they were assigned to the same main unit, the independent 6th *Iztrebitelen Polk*, headquartered at Karlovo airfield. They received Bulgarian serial numbers in the 11–19 range.

A Messerschmitt AG invoice to the Bulgarian War Ministry in Sofia, dated 24 January 1942, details the hourly wages of Messerschmitt employees sent to Bulgaria to assist with the placing in service of *"9 gebrauchte Jagdeinsitzer Me 109 E3A"* (9 used Me 109 E3A single-seat fighters). This assistance was based on the contract signed on 17 July 1941. The invoice listed the following people: *Chefpilot* (chief pilot) [Otto] Brindlinger (in Bulgaria between 10-21 September), *Waffeningenieur* (armament engineer) Bayer (10-29 September) and *Monteur* (assembly technicians) Keitler and Grandtner (10-29 September).

With the influx of the additional nine Bf 109Es, the first the two Bf 109E-operating squadrons (682. and 692. *Yata*) of the 3/6. *Orlyak* (officially formed in early 1942, probably April) were beefed up to the theoretical strength of nine aircraft per squadron. Later on, however, all three *yata* could be equipped uniformly with Messerschmitts (the Avia B.534s of the 672. *Yato* being reassigned to a training unit).

The new fighter group structure was, as follows:
- 3/6. *Iztrebitelno Orlyak*, including *Shtab* (Staff), commanding officer *Kapitan* Krăstyo Atanasov,
- 672. *Iztrebitelno Yato*, commanding officer *Poruchik* Nikolay Yordanov,
- 682. *Iztrebitelno Yato*, commanding officer *Poruchik* Ivan Rusev (died on 15 April 1943 in a flying accident, replaced by *Por.* Stoyan Stoyanov),
- 692. *Iztrebitelno Yato*, commanding officer *Poruchik* Dimităr Lazarov.

Following Germany's attack against the Soviet Union in June 1941, air incursions into Bulgarian airspace by VVS warplanes intensified. Even a few minor bombings on Bulgarian soil by Soviet aircraft occurred, most probably by accident, as Bulgaria and the Soviet Union were not officially at war. As a consequence, the air defence of the Bulgarian coast had to be strengthened, under the Black Sea Air

Superb, rare view of an early Strela wearing the so-called 'Tsarist roundel'. Leaning against the prized new weapon is Feldfebel Yordan S. Todorov, 'the Pirate'. On the verso of this original print Todorov's dedication can be read to "Bai Georgi" (i.e., Old George). He dated the photo taken on Bozhurishte airfield in July 1940. Clearly, the same lighter shade camouflage colour (mid-green) was applied on the fuselage side and on certain areas of the wing surface as well. Notice the golden lion in centre of the marking looking backward, not forward as it should.

---

15 The individual *Übernahmebestätigung* (Confirmation of receipt) issued for the 9 Bf 109E-3a's are dated earlier than their delivery date, namely on 31.07.1941.

16 Minutes taken at Marno Pole, dated 3.09.1941, referring to invoice No. 60 02577, issued by Messerschmitt AG on 8.08.1941, confirms that nine Me 109 E-3a's, with construction numbers 1231, 1644, 4832, 5212, 5589, 5903, 5908, 5932, 6012, arrived there in dismantled state on 23.08.1941.

Defence Command. For this task, an *orlyak* with three half-strength *yata* was established under the code name 'Galata' (Order No. I-2733/1.10.1941), effective 10 October. Two half-*yata* were equipped with the modern Bf 109E monoplane, while the third one had the obsolescent Avia B.534 biplane. Accordingly, ten Bf 109Es relocated to airfields close to the Black Sea shores, five at Balchik (from the 682nd *Yato*), covering the northern area, and five to Sarafovo (from the 692nd *Yato*) covering the southern area. The six Avia B.534s of the 442nd *Yato* went to Novgradets.

Each fighter unit of the 'Galata' *Orlyak* had two aircraft on alert at all times, fully armed, capable of take-off three minutes after warning arrived from either coastal spotters, or the German radar station south of Varna. Another pair was to be ready for take-off within half an hour. Patrol areas were assigned and two-way contact protocol with the anti-aircraft defence system located in the area was established. Usually, a two-aircraft '*dvoyka*' (pair) patrolled the area over Bulgarian waters, and beyond, often venturing over 100 km distance from the shores. A comprehensive list of aircraft in service with the VNVV on 27 December 1941 lists four Bf 109Es at Balchik (Nos. 2, 3, 5 and 9) and five Bf 109Es at Sarafovo (Nos. 12, 13, 14, 15 and 16). The tenth aircraft was most probably under repair.

On a few occasions, Bulgarian airmen spotted Soviet aircraft, usually seaplanes, but no shooting down actually occurred. The Bulgarians probably wanted to avoid raising the ire of their neighbour across the Black Sea. Also many were fond to their Slavic 'big brothers', being covertly or openly Russophiles. Unconfirmed sources mention that many times no ammunition was loaded into the patrolling aircraft, precisely to avoid any unwanted incidents.

One such encounter with a VVS intruder happened on 26 October 1941. That Sunday morning, the Bf 109E patrol of the 692nd *Yato*, manned by *Zamestnik ofitser* Gencho Dimitrov Ivanov and *Podporuchik* Ivan Todorov Stefanov, intercepted a 'Catalina'[17] seaplane in Soviet markings over the Black Sea, near Cape Emine, about 54 km south of Varna, and approached it at close range. However, no shots were fired, officially due to the armament jamming. When news of the unsuccessful interception reached Sarafovo base, another pair took off immediately. However, the two pilots, *Feldfebel* Aleksandăr Aleksandrov Petkovski and his *vodach* (leader), *Podporuchik* Mihail Grigorov Georgiev, could not spot the intruder and returned home empty handed.

While the ten Bf 109Es were on patrol duty at the Black Sea coastline, the remaining nine aircraft were used for training purposes at Marno Pole/Karlovo airfield. There, with the help of the *Strelas*, along with the Bf 108 *Lebeds*, a significant number of airmen honed their skills in the art of being a real fighter pilot, flying a state-of-the-art aircraft type, a potent war machine. However, the intense training claimed its toll, luckily only in matériel and not in lives. As noted earlier, six accidents involving Bf 109Es occurred in 1941, none fatal though. The following year the number of accidents increased further.

---

17 Probably a licensed early PBY 'Catalina' variant, known as ГСТ (GST, abbreviated from *Gidro Samolyot Tyazheliy*, or Heavy Hydroplane, in Russian), known to serve within the VVS Black Sea Fleet (ChF) in 1941.

On 14 October 1941, with the arrival of the 'winter season', the existing nineteen *Strelas* and 21 DB 601 engines are listed to be maintained by *Glavni Remontni Rabotilnitsi* (Main Repair Workshop) Karlovo, where 340 workers were assigned to the airframe and 140 workers to the engine repair section.

Not only training activity was to blame for the accidents, but also active service, too. One such 'combat' event happened on 20 May 1942, when *Strela* No. 10, flown by *Zamestnik ofitser* (Jr. Warrant Officer) Ivan N. Bonev of the 682nd *Yato*, based at Balchik airfield and on alert, took off hurriedly to intercept an unidentified target spotted close to Bulgarian airspace. While rolling on uneven terrain, the tyre punctured and the aircraft crashed to a halt, leaning onto its starboard wing. Another incident happened only ten days later, on the other airfield located on the Black Sea shores, Sarafovo. That day, after completing a training flight with two of his comrades, *Ofitserski kandidat* (Chief Warrant Officer) Georgi R. Kyumyurdzhiev of the 692nd *Yato*, landed his aircraft, No. 11, in the shallow waters of Lake Vayakyoisko, near Burgas. The pilot could swim ashore, and the half-submerged aircraft was salvaged and eventually returned to service, despite sustaining 80% damage (see pages 276–277).

The next string of accidents happened in August. On the 2nd day of the month, *Kpt.* Doncho N. Dimitrov of the 672nd *Yato* veered off to the left while landing on Marno-Pole airfield and broke the port undercarriage of aircraft No. 6. Twelve days later, it was the turn of *Podofitser* (Serg.) Dako P. Dakov of the same squadron to crash his mount, No. 7, also due to the same shortcoming of the Messerschmitt design (i.e. narrow main wheel track), which coupled with insufficient training and inadequate piloting skills could easily end up in an accident. During take-off from Daskal Atanasovo airfield, the aircraft suddenly turned to the left due to the engine torque. The pilot could not stop the speeding machine, which crashed into a parked Avia B.534 *Dogan* biplane, No. 35. Following the violent collision, both aircraft had to be written off.

The autumn months of September, October and November were marred by further incidents, as follows: on the 6th September, *Strela* No. 3, piloted by *Kapitan* Nikola Videnov from the Marno Pole air base command, was involved in a minor accident when it veered off the runway during taxi and its port undercarriage leg collapsed. On the 14th, a parked aircraft, the same unlucky No. 3, in the hangar at Balchik was damaged when an out-of-control Letov Š.328 *Vrana* reconnaissance biplane rammed it. On the last day of October, *Zamestnik ofitser* Ivan N. Bonev had to force-land his mount, No. 10, after the engine quit in mid-flight. Luckily, he reached Balchik airfield, so both he and his machine escaped. Finally, the last accident of the year involving a *Strela* was also a result of engine malfunction. During take-off from Marno Pole, the DB 601A powerplant of the freshly repaired, but apparently very unlucky, No. 3 suddenly stopped at 50 m altitude, compelling the pilot, *Kapitan* Nikola M. Videnov[18], to belly land his aircraft, which sustained 20% damage. This incident reportedly happened on 06.11.1942[19].

Not only the Bf 109Es, but also the Bf 108B trainers assigned to the 6th *Iztrebitelen Polk* were involved in accidents during training of fighter pilots. One such accident happened on 12 March 1942 to a *Lebed* assigned to the 682nd *Yato* based on Balchik airfield. Aircraft No. 2 force landed in the hands of *Podofitser* Anton B. Atanasov called "Schwarz" (Black). Another *Lebed*, this time No. 1 of the 692nd *Yato*, had to belly land on Marno-Pole airfield following engine trouble on 24 February 1943. The pilot, *Podporuchik* Georgi R. Kyumyurdzhiev, escaped the incident unhurt.

The first part of the New Year saw little activity by the Bf 109Es. Indeed, by 1943, after a couple of years of continuous service, the aircraft were worn-out and started to become obsolescent. The expected arrival of the superior 'Gustav' version of the Bf 109 gradually placed the *Strelas* in the second line of fighters. Nevertheless, they remained excellent for training and enhancing the fighter pilots' skills. Continued training meant continued accidents, however. The first recorded one happened on 22 March, when *Feldfebel* Tsvetan D. Gruev of the 692nd *Yato* made a basic pilot's error in forgetting to lower the main undercarriage while landing on Marno-Pole/Karlovo airfield. The subsequent belly landing resulted in 40% damage, and rendered the aircraft, No. 14, unserviceable for a couple of weeks. The next en-

A happy Bulgarian officer, believed to be the venerable Cpt. Petko N. Popganchev, links arms with an equally happy civilian man, most probably a disguised German pilot, in front of one of the recently assembled Strelas. *The 'St. Andrew's Cross' type marking is faintly visible on the starboard wing's under surface. The engine cowling was not yet painted yellow. Concomitantly, the yellow "arrow" is missing as well from the fuselage side.*

---

18   At this time, Cpt. Videnov was a test pilot of the Karlovo Repair Works and performed a test flight with this *Strela*, following a scheduled maintenance.

19   The similarity of the circumstances with the accident that happened on 6 September, as well as the same pilot, and the fact that the day was the same only the month different, may lead to the probability that it's the same accident reported twice, only the month being erroneously typed.

Men and their machine. The airmen are: Podporuchik Stoyan Stoyanov (on top) and Poruchik Lyuben Kondakov (underneath him). On ground, from left to right: Feldfebel Pelovski, Poruchik Dimităr Lazarov, Kapitan Petko Popganchev, Kapitan Krăstyo Atanasov (Commanding Officer of 1/6. Orlyak), unidentified German pilot (in civilian clothes), two unknown airmen and Feldfebel Yordan Todorov. Notice the Emil does not yet have the yellow wraparound paint job on the cowling and the yellow flash on the fuselage. Also, the 2-cm wing cannon is not mounted either. The aircraft is already identified with the 'black-X-in-white-square' type markings. The date of this souvenir shot is probably autumn of 1940.

Another shot taken probably at the same location and time. From left to right: Poruchik Lyuben Kondakov, Poruchik Dimităr Lazarov, unidentified German pilot (in civilian clothes), Kapitan Krăstyo Atanasov, two unknowns and Podporuchik Stoyan Stoyanov. Photo reportedly taken in a hangar at Balchik airfield. Notice how the early roundel shape military marking was covered by the new square shape marking, as seen on the wing undersurface.

try in the accident log is dated a week later. That day, the propeller adjusting mechanism malfunctioned, which resulted in a botched emergency landing at Vedrare, south-east of Karlovo. The aircraft, No. 13, hit a wall and was wrecked and the pilot, Ppor. Georgi M. Georgiev, was wounded.

The 7th April was a black day for the airmen flying the *Emil*. That day, the first recorded fatal accident happened. After the engine of No. 14 caught fire in mid-flight, the stranded pilot, *Podofitser* Penyo D. Malev of the 692nd *Yato*, bailed out of the burning aircraft, which was now flying out of control at over 600 km/h. His Schroeder type parachute shredded to pieces due to the high speed, and the unlucky pilot fell to his death at Voynyagovo, south-west of Karlovo. Only eight days later another fatal accident happened. This time, the rudder of No. 15 detached while the pilot was making a loop during aerobatics. The uncontrollable aircraft fell to the ground near Balchik, taking its pilot, *Por.* Ivan I. Rusev, to his death. Obviously, the double deaths, both apparently caused by aircraft failures, shook the morale of the Messerschmitt pilots. In only 18 days, three Bf 109Es were lost, all from the second batch, by coincidence Nos. 13, 14 and 15[20]. Nevertheless, after the investigations concluded, flights had to continue.

The Germans replaced the lost three *Strelas* with three refurbished 'Gustavs'. Air Force Command letter dated 11 June 1943 had the following subject: *"aircraft replacements for the three lost 'B.F.109s' with three fully repaired 'B.F.109.G.2s', with construction numbers 13517, 13491 and 10365."* Indeed,

---

20 This series of sombre events was vividly recalled by veteran fighter pilot Petăr Manolev, during an interview with the author in Sofia, on 22 May 2004 (at that time he was 88, suffering from Parkinson's disease, but displayed excellent memory).

this was confirmed by a letter of *DLM Bulgarien, Gruppe Technik*, dated the same day, which lists the same three Bf 109G-2s as *'Reparaturflugzeuge'*. Except for the first one, No. 36, it is unclear what VNVV serial numbers the other two replacement fighters received once in active service (see master list of all Bf 109Gs handed over to the Bulgaria air force in vol. 2).

Despite no more fatal accidents happening in 1943, smaller incidents were recorded. Among them were the 'usual' bad landings, one of them occurring on 10 May, when *Podporuchik* Marin A. Tsvetkov of the 672nd *Yato* bent the starboard undercarriage of No. 1 while landing on Marno-Pole airfield, causing 10% damage. More minor damage was suffered by aircraft No. 5, whose propeller was damaged by a Letov Š.328 *Vrana* taxiing on Balchik airfield on 4 July.

All minor accidents (damage up to 40%) were handled by local workshops, but major ones, or general overhauls, had to be done in specialised workshops. The closest one was located in neighbouring Rumania, where the A.S.A.M.[21] at Pipera, near Bucharest, specialised in repairing Bf 109s of the *Luftwaffe*, ARR (Rumanian air force) and VNVV. An undated document (probably issued in 1943) lists Bf 109Es Nos. 1, 3 to 6 and 9 (complete with engines), being transported to Pipera, Rumania. Seven DB 601A-1 engines (W.Nr. 11486, 11449, 11453, 67141, 11457, 11440 and 62841) were heading to *Wiener Flugmotorenwerk* GmbH, located in Hamersdorf-Herenholz in Austria, for repair.

An interesting technical detail was revealed to the author by retired veteran flying instructor and test pilot Petǎr Manolev, dean of the surviving wartime Bulgarian fighter pilots in the early 2000s, during an interview in Sofia, on 22 May 2004. Mr. Manolev recalled that at the end of April 1943, bomb racks were experimentally fitted to an *Emil*, suitable for 50 kg bombs. The bombs could be released electrically. Each *yato* received 10 such bomb racks. However, the project to transform the *Strelas* into fighter bombers did not go beyond experiments and test flights.

The first US air raid of the autumn of 1943 campaign against wartime Bulgarian territory was performed against Skopie[22] marshalling yard – listed as 'Yugoslavia' in US documents – by XII Bomber Command B-25s, escorted by P-38s, on 18 October. As there were no Axis fighter units stationed in the area, the bombing raid was performed unopposed in air, but met with anti-aircraft fire[23].

As a consequence of this raid, two Bf 109Es belonging to the 672nd *Yato* of the 3/6th *Orlyak*, along with three pilots, were dispatched to the airfield of Petrovats, near Skopie, located in the south-western corner of the so-called 'Greater Bulgaria', as 'gate guards'. The pilots on alarm had to look for any incoming enemy aircraft formations. If such intruders appeared in great number, the fighters had the task to take off, gain height and follow the enemy at a safe distance, sending through radio information about their number, type, height and course.

The alarm *dvoyka* saw action the very next day. On 20 October, being alerted that a large enemy formation was heading towards Sofia [actually, the Americans targeted Niš – see B.534 chapter], the pair took off at 12:30, but did not discover the enemy, so it landed at 13:10. Upon being informed about the real target, located at about 140 km north, the two '109s took off again at 13:20, but it was already too late, the enemy was gone. The combat mission was made even more difficult because of bad radio communication with the ground control.

Soon after the military marking change, an eye-catching feature was also applied to the Bulgarian Emils. It consisted of a yellow wraparound engine cowling, followed by a rearward tapering flash along the fuselage sides. This artwork gave the impression to the aircraft of a flying arrow, which by coincidence (or not) was also the code name the type was identified with within the VNVV: Strela (arrow). The rudder was also painted yellow, which covered the Bulgarian national colours, adding to the overall appearance of an Axis aircraft (chrome yellow being the overall recognition colour of an Axis aircraft flying in Central or Eastern European airspace). No. 4 was often flown by Podporuchik *Stoyan I. Stoyanov*

---

21   ASAM=*Administraţia Stabilimentelor Aeronauticei şi Marinei*, or Administration of the Aeronautical and Naval Establishments (Workshops).

22   Today known as Skopje, capital of the Republic of Macedonia, or FYROM.

23   On 18 October, a P-38G (s/n 43-2552) of 97th Fighter Squadron, 82nd Fighter Group, was lost at Skopie while bombing a train and an ammunition dump. The pilot, 2nd Lt. John Homan Jr., was buried in a park in Skopie. It is uncertain what caused his demise; but most probably it was ground fire.

The next day, the 21st, Bulgarian fighter pilots were to have their first recorded encounter with USAAF fighters, which in the coming months would be their most common and deadly opponents. On that Thursday, the two Skopie-based *Strelas* took off four times because of information relayed about incoming enemy aircraft. The first two missions performed in the morning were without incident. The third take-off happened at 12:40, simultaneously with a couple of Italian aircraft landing. Despite two earlier alarms being proven false, the pilots on duty, *Podporuchik* Mihail G. Grigorov and *Podofitser* Yoto P. Kamenov, immediately took off this time as well. Minutes later, they spotted a number of unidentified aircraft flying towards Skopie. Based on the combat diary of 3/6. *Orlyak*, *Podof.* Kamenov's attention was distracted by the appearance in the airspace of a number of Italian fighters, identified as Macchi MC.200s and MC.202s. After positively identifying them as 'friendly', and probably thinking the reported other ones are also allies, Kamenov returned to Skopie airfield. However, he did not inform his *vodach* (leader) about his intention, a major breach of protocol, leaving him alone facing the enemy.

Unlike his inattentive *voden* (wingman), *Ppor.* Grigorov's attention was not distracted by the Italian allies, and he carried on with the patrol mission, flying alone. He spotted about 20 USAAF P-38 'Lightning' fighter-bombers as they attacked the railway station of Skopie[24]. Instead of following idly the enemy as mere onlooker, as ordered, the Bulgarian decided to engage them. On singling out one of the P-38s and attacking it from the rear, Grigorov was able to strike the starboard wing and engine of the aircraft flown by 1st Lt. Douglas A. Neilson with cannon and machine gun fire. The American warplane reportedly started to burn and descend. Ground observers reported that the aircraft eventually crashed, thus *Ppor.* Grigorov officially earned an air victory, the first one after the famous Operation 'Tidal Wave'. However, the P-38 of 1st Lt. Neilson[25] of the 95th Fighter Squadron, damaged in the tail section, was actually able to return to Italy.

---

24 USAAF war chronology lists P-38s of the XII Bomber Command attacking the marshalling yard at "Skoplje, Yugoslavia". Another US source mentions twelve P-38s of the 95th Fighter Squadron and twelve P-38s of the 97th Fighter Squadron, both assigned to the 82nd USAAF Fighter Group, made their way across the Adriatic Sea. Each P-38 had been armed with a single 500-lb. bomb, with the marshalling yards at Skopie being the intended target.

25 1st Lt. Neilson is first recorded flying a sortie on 18 September 1943, during a strafing mission of airfields around Foggia, Italy, by the 82nd F.G. His P-38 was shot down by flak, but he evaded capture and returned to his unit on 5 October. He completed his 50-mission tour of duty on 4 April 1944.

The last aircraft of the first batch (No. 10) is flanking others on Marno Pole (Karlovo) airfield, located in a mountainous region. When 692. *Yato* was formed in October 1940, the ten extant '109s were split in two, and assigned in equal number to both squadrons (yata), namely 682nd and 692nd.

This photo has no explanation to date. It was certainly taken in Bulgaria (the original photo comes from there), there is a Bulgarian soldier standing at the port wing. The Emil sports the typical yellow decoration adorning Bulgarian fighters; however, it displays Luftwaffe crosses, but no individual serial number. Unfortunately, there is nothing written on the reverse of the original photo; therefore, the Author could not find a plausible explanation.

Pilots of one of the two Bf 109E-equipped squadrons of 1/6. *Orlyak* discuss the daily tasks in front of aircraft No. 5, flanked by No. 2.

Upon returning to Lecce air base, 2nd Lieutenants Bert Lutz and James Rogers the 97th Fighter Squadron submitted claims for a 'Me-109' each, damaged in this mission[26]. The Bulgarian pilot, Grigorov, also reported two American aircraft shot down. However, eventually one of the victories was assigned to anti-aircraft artillery, the other to *Ppor*. Mihail G. Grigorov. According to the memoires of Grigorov, the second aircraft was also shot down by him; however, the victory was taken away from him by the decision of the commander of the German aviation unit stationed on the airfield, *Hauptmann* [Joachim] Kirschner [*Gruppenkommandeur* of IV./JG 27]. While neither side actually lost any aircraft, the fight over Skopie was a première for both parties, being the first USAAF-VNVV fighter duel in a long series – much bloodier than this initial one – that would last until Bulgaria's unilateral exit from the Axis camp in the following September.

Based on the combat diary of 3/6. *Orlyak*, the 'alarm *dvoyka*' was recalled from Skopie on 3 November, but returned there on the 13th. Just in time, as another USAAF raid, this time clearly targeting the Bulgarian Kingdom, was about to take place.

The next enemy incursion in Bulgarian airspace was the first actual air attack planned and executed against Bulgaria[27]. On 14 November 1943, 96 B-25 'Mitchell' bombers of the 12th AAF (48 of the 321st Bomb Group and 48 of the 340th Bomb Group), escorted by 46 P-38 'Lightning' fighters of the 82nd Fighter Group (this time subordinated to the 15th AAF), targeted the marshalling yard of Sofia. The USAAF combat report mentions the following: *"Eighteen Axis fighters attack the bombers over the target, but they are driven off by the P-38s, whose pilots down three Bf-109s and two FW-190s[28] against the loss of one P-38."* The sole P-38 loss was inflicted by the alarm Bf 109E pair based at Skopie. 2nd Lieutenant Roy R. Hurst of the 95th Fighter Squadron lost an engine over Sofia during the battle with Bulgarian fighters and was forced to retire early from the fight. On the return flight over what is described as 'Yugoslavian airspace', 2nd Lieutenant Hurst and his P-38G (s/n 42-13238), called 'Hallock', became separated from the rest of the pack. Reportedly, the 'Lightning' crashed into mountains south-west of Skopie, at 13:30 hours. 2nd Lt. Hurst actually fell victim to the guns of *Podporuchik* Mihail G. Grigorov, who scrambled upon receiving news of the returning American formation. Grigorov and his wingman had taken off during the incoming leg of the raid, too, but were too late and could not catch the intruders. This time, they managed to intercept the lone 'Lightning' on the return leg and Grigorov reportedly downed it near Debăr (about 100 km south-west of Skopie). However, his claim was not officially confirmed, so Grigorov received no victory point.

The American warplanes returned to Bulgaria ten days later. This time, instead of the two-engine 'Mitchell' medium bombers, four-engine 'Liberator' heavy bombers were tasked to give a lethal blow to the same target. In total, 36 B-24s of the 98th and 376th Bomber Groups, with an escort of 48 P-38s of the 82nd Fighter Group, were sent to raid, for the second time, the marshalling yard at Sofia. Eventually, however, about one-third of the warplanes had to return early. By the time the rest reached the

---

26   2nd Lt. Bert W. Lutz of the 97th Fighter Squadron claimed a Me 109 damaged over Skiplje (sic!), while 2nd Lt. John C. Rogers of the 95th Fighter Squadron a Me 109 damaged 10 min. (sic!) off Skiplje, both at 10:05 a.m.

27   The previous air raid against Skopie was regarded by the Americans as carried out against Yugoslavia, even though that country ceased to exist in April 1941. However, during the war, the American strategists did not take into consideration the realities on the ground, and used pre-war maps that often showed state borders that had long changed, to plan the combat missions over Europe.

28   In fact, US fighter pilots were credited with more enemy fighters, as follows: 3 Bf 109s confirmed, 1 Bf 109 probable and 4 Bf 109s damaged (all by 97th Fighter Squadron), along with 2 Fw 190s (by 95th Fighter Squadron), all claimed over Sofia, all at 12:30 p.m.

target area, the Bulgarian interceptors – including the Bf 109E pair scrambled from Skopie – were already waiting for them. This time, the defenders were better organised, and claimed several 'kills', of which two B-24s and a P-38 are listed as losses in USAAF annals. In the ensuing mêlée, the Americans fighter pilots were credited with two destroyed and one probable Bf 109, all over Sofia. One of their victims was *Podporuchik* Mihail G. Grigorov, whose *Strela* was hit in the engine. With thick oil film covering the windshield, Grigorov had to belly-land his *Emil* almost blind, wheels up. Before being hit, he had managed to damage a 'Liberator', though, which was credited to him (2 points). *Podporuchik* Mihail G. Grigorov became the only Bulgarian fighter pilot to be credited with an air victory scored aboard a Bf 109E. This was the last known air victory scored by a pilot of an *Emil* flying in Bulgarian colours.

The final piece of the Bulgarian Bf 109E's combat activity comes from an interview the Author made with *Kapitan* (ret.) Dimităr S. Lazarov in his Sofia home on 22 May 2004. The veteran airman, who had just turned 90 eight days earlier, vividly recalled how he scrambled in his Bf 109E from Karlovo air base, where he was an instructor, upon sighting the enemy bomber formation on 30 March 1944. Earlier, on 10 January, he had also taken off to intercept the enemy, but could not find them due to thick clouds and bad weather. This time; however, upon penetrating the clouds, he suddenly found himself in the middle of a bomber box. He had no choice but fly with them at close range, at less than 100 m distance. He was so close to them, he remembers, that the gunners could not fire at him, as they would have hit fellow bombers. Therefore, they flew for a while in tight formation, until Lazarov decided it was time to take his chances and try to escape from this nasty situation. Suddenly, he put his *Emil* in a steep dive and made himself as small as possible in the pilot's seat. Luckily, no bullet found him, although he saw tracers flying very close to the cockpit, so he could safely land. A colleague of his, *Kapitan* Ivan Boyadzhiev, flying a Dewoitine D.520, who ended up being also alone, initially teamed with him for a while. However, he wasn't so lucky, as was shot down by US gunners.

The front view of the same No. 5 is seen here, in company of Kapitan Krăstyo Atanasov *(foreground), commanding officer of 3/6. Orlyak. The biplane in the background, at right, is a* Vrana *(Letov Š.328).*

When asked his opinion about the Bf 109E, Cpt. Lazarov – who had flown virtually all fighter types the VNVV had in service during the war – stated: "*My opinion about the Emil is very good! It was fast and powerful. The cabin's width was ideal, the controls handy, the instrument panel well structured. The armament, consisting of two machine guns and two cannon, was enough. When we performed live firing exercises at the Karlovo gunnery range, myself and most of the student pilots scored very good results. I did not manage to shoot down any aircraft, though. I scrambled twice against the Americans, but had no chance to fire upon them. Overall, it was an excellent machine.*" When asked to compare it to the Dewoitine D.520 he also flew, Cpt. Lazarov firmly stated that the two models could not be compared, the German model was far superior to the French one.

This event was the last one where the author could identify the combat use of Bf 109Es in active duty with the VNVV. Although combat or training flights certainly happened later on, the available documents do not distinguish between the sub-types, usually referring to all Bf 109s by the code-name *Strela*, valid for both the E and G sub-types[29]. Therefore, it could very well be that the 'Arrows' listed in various reports were actually '*Gustavs*', and thus are dealt with in the appropriate chapter.

Following the arrival of the first '*Gustavs*' in late February 1943, all serviceable *Strelas* were concentrated into one squadron, the 672nd *Yato*. By then the number of serviceable Bf 109Es had dwindled due to accidents and usual wear. On 1 August 1944, for example, nine Bf 109Es were written off (Nos. 3, 4, 6, 8, 9, 10, 16, 17 and 19), leaving only five extant *Strelas* within VNVV.

The German side of the Messerschmitt repair workshop at Pipera-Bucharest, Rumania (called A.S.A.M.), reported the following six Bf 109Es and their engines repaired over there during 1943/1944: airframe W.Nr. 5221, 5223, 5224, 5225, 5226 and 5229; engine W.Nr. 30813, 22426, 21034, 11470, 10066 and 11297. Judged by their *Werknummern*, all these aircraft were part of the first batch (Nos. 1, 3, 4, 5, 6 and 9).

---

29 Except the cases when the NN is given, which were different for the two sub-types.

These three photos depicting No. 10 and ground personnel were taken on Asĕn landing ground. The wing cannon are already installed.

One comprehensive record of extant aircraft, dated 27 July 1945, lists only four *Strelas*[30], in service with 3/6. *Orlyak*, namely Nos. 2, 11, 12 and 18[31]. This is the last date any Bf 109E appears in the VNVV annals available to the author. Based on his logbook, famed top 'ace' pilot *Mahyor* Stoyan I. Stoyanov flew the Bf 109E as late as June 1946! Soon after this date, the last surviving Bf 109Es (Nos. 1, 2 and 12) were scrapped, closing an important chapter in Bulgarian fighter aviation.

An interesting side story, hitherto unreported, is the existence of several early production Bf 109 airframes in Bulgaria, delivered by the Germans as training matériel for technicians and other ground personnel. A German letter issued in Sofia by *DLM Bulgarien, Gruppe Technik*, dated 14 March 1944[32], lists the following such non-flyable 'demo' aircraft:

Another Emil, *quite possibly identical to the one depicted earlier, is seen during preparation for a drill on Asĕn landing ground. The wing retrofitted with the powerful, rapid-fire 20 mm MG-FF cannon, can be observed.*

Fahrbarer Prüfstand (Mobile Test Bench) Bf 109 E-1, W.-Nr. 6175 (with engine DB 605 A-1, W.-Nr. 64285)
Exerzierflugzeug (Training Aircraft) Bf 109 (E) V22, W.-Nr. 1800
Exerzierflugzeug (Training Aircraft) Bf 109 E-1, W.-Nr. 1575
Exerzierflugzeug (Training Aircraft) Bf 109 D, W.-Nr. 3099

These *Lehrflugzeuge* (teaching aid aircraft) were delivered in December 1943, and lasted only until 30 March 1944, when they were destroyed during the bombing of Sofia airfield

Colours and markings

The first batch of ten brand-new Bf 109E-3s arrived from WNF to Bulgaria in a special 'Bulgarian' camouflage scheme applied at the factory. It consisted of two distinct tones of greens on the upper surfaces and light blue on the under surfaces. The precise shade of colours is unfortunately not confirmed, despite the (sole) existing colour photo of a Bulgarian fighter aircraft (see page 273), as well as the actual camouflage paint types found by the Author in Bulgarian archives.

Offer No. 601/29.01.1941 by Messerschmitt AG, listing the spare parts and accessories for the batch of Bf 108Bs and Bf 109Es delivered the previous year, includes the following paints and lacquers: 84 kg

---

30 From 23 August 1945, the aircraft type was officially identified with the ST code, thus still considered in service.

31 Interestingly, Nos. 1 and 5 are omitted, probably lying somewhere in unserviceable status, waiting to be repaired.

32 Many thanks to Jaroslav Kreč for kindly forwarding the document to the Author.

A Strela (possibly No. 10) is being refuelled on Asĕn landing ground by a Mercedes-Benz Lo 2000 fuel tanker. The military licence plate, B 80041, identifies it as 'special purpose vehicle', as per military control number allocation order of 15 July 1938. At that time, vehicles of the air force were not yet separated from army vehicles, hence the B prefix (read: V, as Voenen, i.e., Military), as opposite to BB (read VV, Văzdushni Voyski, i.e. Air Force), introduced later.

Beautiful scenic shot of Strela E, No. 10, possibly made by the photographer standing on the fuel tanker depicted in the previous photo. It was most probably also taken at Asĕn landing ground. Notice the absence of the 20 mm cannon from the wing, the port being covered by sheet metal. Apparently, the worn areas of the leading edge were patched with some sort of dark green colour.

The first Strela, No. 1, is depicted during manoeuvres, probably on Asěn airfield. The wing cannon are already installed.

Feldfebel *Atanas A. Matev* – depicted in front of a Bf 109E-3 without wing cannon – was probably the last survivor of the Bulgarian wartime fighter pilots' community. He died on 18 September 2013, at the age of 99.

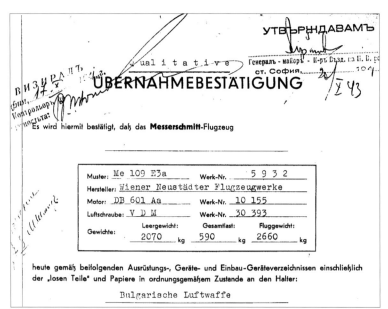

Header of the German Certificate of Acceptance (Übernahmebestätigung) of one of the Bf 109Es of the second batch handed over to the Bulgarian air force. The document was issued at Großenhain on 31 August 1941, counter-signed on 17, then 20 October 1941, at Sofia. It lists the model of the aircraft (Me 109 E3a), the construction number (5932), the manufacturer (Wiener Neustädter Flugzeugwerke), the type of the engine (DB 601 Aa), constr. number (10155), the model of the airscrew (VDM), constr. number (30393) and the weights.

Line-up of a mixture of Bf 109Es from the first batch (Nos. 8 and possibly 1, at the far end) and the second batch (Nos. 13 and 16). Although of poor quality, this photo proves that at least a few aircraft of the second batch arrived in the camouflage scheme identical to the first batch, i.e. Dark Green (L 40/70) fuselage spine and upper engine cowling and mid-Green (L 40/62) fuselage and engine cowling sides, over Light Blue (L 40/65), although the wing upper surface was most probably in mono colour (Dark Green, L 40/70). Notice the second batch aircraft sport smaller size serial numbers. The military marking on the fuselage was also of smaller size (as it did not have to cover the early cockade marking, as the previously applied square type marking had to on the first batch of aircraft). The small dots all over the aircraft are spots on the photograph.

Other aircraft of the second batch arrived in mono colour upper surfaces of Dark Green (possibly RLM 71), over Light Blue (RLM 65), as seen on bellied No. 14. This particular aircraft was damaged 40% when the careless Feldfebel *Tsvetan D. Gruev* of 692. *Yato* forgot to lower the undercarriage while landing on Marno-Pole airfield on 22 March 1943. Only nine days later, this very aircraft was lost in a fatal in-flight accident, which claimed the life of Podofitser *Penyo D. Malev* of the same squadron.

Eight Strelas are lined up on Marno Pole air base. Curiously, the line-up includes an aircraft with apparent Luftwaffe Balkenkreuz on its fuselage, but sporting the peculiar Bulgarian rearward tapering fuselage flash (the second one from the far side). This particular aircraft is also depicted on another photo (see page 263).

Most of the accidents were not fatal, and the aircraft could be subsequently recovered. Such a minor accident happened to No. 1 on 10.05.1943, when Pod-poruchik *Marin A. Tsvetkov* of 672. Yato performed a hard landing on Mar-no-Pole airfield, damaging the aircraft 10%.

A similarly light accident was suffered by No. 17 at an unknown date, this time to the port undercarriage. Typically, following such a taxiing accident, the unlucky aircraft could be rendered serviceable again within a week's repair work.

No. 19 (W.Nr. 6012) was the last Emil to see service with the VNVV. This particular aircraft was flown by top pilot Stoyan Stoyanov at Karlovo on 10 and 14 October 1941. Little else is known of its service life, except that it was eventually struck off charge on 1 August 1944.

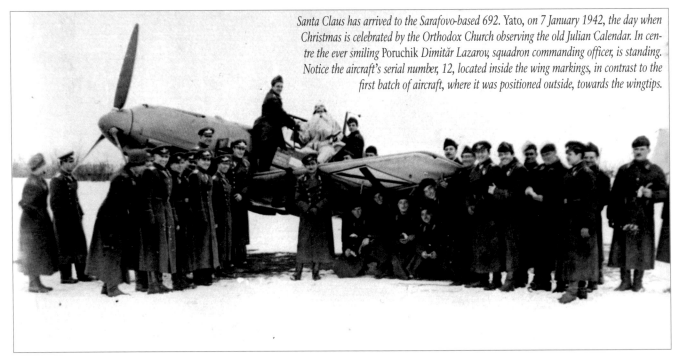

Santa Claus has arrived to the Sarafovo-based 692. Yato, on 7 January 1942, the day when Christmas is celebrated by the Orthodox Church observing the old Julian Calendar. In centre the ever smiling Poruchik Dimităr Lazarov, squadron commanding officer, is standing. Notice the aircraft's serial number, 12, located inside the wing markings, in contrast to the first batch of aircraft, where it was positioned outside, towards the wingtips.

This is the only known colour photo depicting a Bf 109E (or any fighter aircraft, for that matter) in Bulgarian markings and colours. It shows the same Strela pair, patrolling the Black Sea coastline depicted below. This unique photo must have been taken from either an ultra-low flying aircraft, or from a ship, rather. Thanks to the (somewhat faded) colours, the difference between the three camouflage paints can be clearly observed: dark green on top surfaces, mid-green on fuselage sides (the narrow stripe underneath the fuselage marking of No. 9 is the closest to the true hue, as it is reflecting less the sunlight) and light blue on lower surfaces.

Sarafovo was the airbase of the Bf 109E-equipped half-squadron-strong unit of 692. Yato charged with the defence of the southern sector of the Black Sea, while the other half-squadron-strong Bf 109E unit of 682. Yato was based at Balchik and charged with the defence of the northern sector of the Black Sea. These two units formed the so-called 'Galata' Orlyak, together with an Avia B.534-equipped third fighter unit. Based on a report dated 27 December 1941, it appears that the Bf 109Es assigned to Sarafovo were from the second batch, while those based on Balchik of the first batch. If so, this dvoyka, or pair (Nos. 3 and 9) patrolling the scenic seacoast were from the Balchik-based 682. Yato. The first shot was taken above the cliffs of Cape Kaliakra, while the other one in the area of today's famous tourist resort of Albena.

Any time spent over the waters meant the pilots had to wear life vest in case of ditching. This was the case of this meditative pilot leaning against No. 9, depicted in the previous photos. Most likely, he was part of the so-called 'Galata' Orlyak. The life vest appears to be a 'Kapokvest' of German manufacture. The stain left on the fuselage side by spilled fuel is a detail noteworthy to the modellers.

A similarly bulky life vest is worn by Poruchik Stoyan I. Stoyanov seated in the cockpit of one of the alarm '109E parked on the concrete runway of Balchik airfield. Notice the lack of back armour, peculiar to the Emils of the first batch.

Group photo in front of the Strela from the first batch, photographed at Balchik. The sitting man, at left, is Feldfebel Yordan S. Todorov, 'The Pirate'.

Poruchik Stoyan I. Stoyanov (left), commanding officer of 682. Yato, is seen in the company of Kapitan Krăstyo A. Atanasov (right), commanding officer of 3/6. Orlyak, on Balchik airfield. Photo taken at the ceremony of handover of command by Atanasov to Stoyanov. To the left, Bf 109E No. 9 is parked.

Strela No. 3 of the 682. Yato, piloted by Kpt. Nikola M. Videnov, was involved in a minor accident on 6 September (or November) 1942, when it veered off the runway during taxi and its port undercarriage leg collapsed on the rough terrain of Marno Pole (Karlovo) air base, causing 20% damage. The front view reveals a strange detail, namely that only the port wing cannon was installed! As noted in the main text, the 2 cm (20 mm) MG-FF (Ikaria) wing cannon were retrofitted after the aircraft's arrival, as they were shipped separately. Notice the patchwork around the cannon barrel root.

In contrast to the armour-less version depicted earlier, this particular aircraft has the extra armour attached to the rear of the pilot's seat. Sitting in the cockpit is Podporuchik Stefan N. Marinopolski.

One of the few original war-time prints in the Author's personal collection that depict a Bf 109E shows a pilot wearing life vest, most likely assigned to the Sarafovo based fighter unit (692. Yato) of the 'Galata' Orlyak. This theory is backed by the serial numbers of the Emil in the background, No. 14.

Emergency ditchings not necessarily happened in the Black Sea. This incident, depicted in this series of four photographs, involved aircraft No. 11, which landed in the shallow waters of Lake Vayakyoisko, near Burgas on 30 May 1943. The pilot, Podporuchik Georgi R. Kyumyurdzhiev of 692. Yato, could swim ashore, and the half-submerged aircraft salvaged, despite the seriously twisted airframe.

Bulgarian military men gather in front of two Messerschmitts (a '109, at left, and a '108, at right) on Karlovo airfield, on 15 August 1942.

This and next page, top: The airfield of Marno Pole/ Karlovo was the scene of an elaborate ceremony held almost half a year later after the previous summer shot, at the so-called 'blessing of the combat flag'. This ceremony is depicted in a series of photos, featuring two Bf 109E-3s (Nos. 8 and 14) and an Avia B.534 (No. 16), taken on 30 January 1943. Notice the mid-wing position of the markings on aircraft No. 8 and the lack of serial number painted on the wing, in contrast to No. 14, which has the markings applied more to the extremities of the wings and the serial number. The double-peak mountain seen in the background was colloquially called by the soldiers garrisoned in Karlovo 'Young woman's tits' (Момини гърди).

Below: A series of three accidents (two deadly) that incidentally happened to subsequently marked aircraft (Nos. 13, 14 and 15) in the span of only 18 days in the spring of 1943 left a deep mark in the memories of Emil pilots. These incidents were vividly recalled to the Author by one of the very few surviving witnesses, Petăr Manolev, over 60 years later. Depicted is No. 13, destroyed in a botched landing at Vedrare, on 29 March 1943. Luckily, the pilot, Ppor. Georgi M. Georgiev, escaped alive, although wounded. The pilots of the other two aircraft (Nos. 14 and 15) were not that lucky, both perishing in the catastrophes. Notice the barely visible rearward tapering yellow flash along the fuselage and also the barely visible nr. 13 on the port wing inner surface (the crack runs between 1 and 3).

Depicted is pilot Ppor. Pavel E. Pavlov, called 'Pavleto', casually sitting on the wing root of one of the Emils of the Sarafovo-based alarm 692. Yato of the 'Galata' Orlyak. Notice the 'Devil' (Дявол, Dyavol) emblem adorning the yellow engine cowling, which is equally described as Ppor. Mihail Grigorov's personal sign, or as used on Strelas dispatched to Sarafovo (the most likely version).

Something is unusual with this Emil depicted in Bulgaria. The spinner looks odd, and there is no trace of any marking on wing undersurface, or fuselage side. Also, the camouflage colour on the lower fuselage side looks way too dark, and the wavy demarcation line is also weird. The usual rearward tapering flash along the fuselage is also missing. One possible explanation is that this airframe is unserviceable, and was photographed after the war, parked on a forgotten corner of an airfield.

Not much useful information can be drawn from this photo showing a Bf 109E covered with protective canvas. However, the spinner is well visible, and the light grey mottles sprayed over it are quite unusual. This photo could have also been taken in the immediate post-war period.

aircraft paint L 40/62 DKH, 84 kg aircraft paint L 40/65 DKH and 84 kg aircraft paint L 40/70 DKH[33], all delivered in 28 kg cans, a barrel of 100 kg paint thinner, and 2 kg black insignia/markings paint. Contrary to some published sources, the L40/xx coding does *not* identify a specific colour paint, but rather a category of paint, and usually was completed with the colour description. However, in the aforementioned offer no specific colour shades were given, therefore, no particular colours can be positively identified. That's why one can rely only on an educated guess while attempting to identify the shades of camouflage colours. With this pragmatic approach, the Author *believes* the camouflage scheme worn by Bulgarian '109Es consisted of Dark Green (similar to RLM 71, *not* RLM 70 Black Green) fuselage spine and upper engine cowling, while the fuselage and engine cowling sides were Mid-Green (a bit lighter than RLM 62). The upper surfaces of the wings were a combination of these two green colours, applied in so-called 'splinter' scheme. All under surfaces were in Light Blue (similar to RLM 65).

It has to be mentioned that the application of standard *Luftwaffe* 'splinter' type camouflage scheme on the wings of export fighter aircraft is unique to the Bulgarian machines, and cannot be readily explained, as officially this was forbidden, in connection with the standard RLM 70/71 colours (for details, see Camouflage paints and colours chapter). All other fighter and fighter trainer aircraft, exported to an allied, or neutral, country, before and shortly after the start of the war, wore different camouflage schemes, mostly consisting of a single green on the upper surfaces, over light blue, or in overall light grey.

As it was the case with standard *Luftwaffe* Bf 109Es, the propeller spinner is believed to be Black Green (RLM 70), while the blades were Dark Green (RLM 71). The rudder was divided horizontally into three equal areas, White (top), vivid Green (middle) and blood Red (bottom) – Bulgaria's national colours. At delivery, the aircraft did not have any Bulgarian military markings, or codes applied. The inside surface of the main undercarriage leg panel appears to be very dark, possibly matt Black. A detail unnoticed so far by aircraft profile makers or modellers is that the aircraft's type ('Messerschmitt Me 109') and the construction number (e.g., 'W. Nr. 5221') were applied at the factory on both sides of the fin root, in Black, over what appears to be a Black Green background.

Once acceptance flights were completed, the aircraft received the early-style military markings of the VNVV, the so-called 'Tsarist Roundel', in six positions (fuselage sides and both wing surfaces) (see photo on page 257). This was completed by a serial number running from 1 to 10, applied in White on fuselage sides, aft of the military marking, and in Black on the wing under surfaces, outside the military marking. Finally, the identification was completed with the typical VNVV triangle on mid-fin, in White, identifying each aircraft individually (on the top of the 'fraction', the aircraft's serial number, while on the bottom, the aircraft type's *Nomenklaturen Nomer*, or Registration Number, i.e. 7047, was written).

Following the change of the Bulgarian air force's military markings in late June 1940, thus only a couple of weeks after the first batch of Bf 109Es had entered service, the previous roundels were covered with large size black bordered white squares, featuring a diagonal black cross in the centre. However, the square could not be applied in large enough size to completely cover the roundel; therefore, small circle slices were left out, visible on good quality period photos to the attentive onlooker (see photo on

---

33   The abbreviation DKH is reference to the paint supplier Dr. Kurt Herberts & Co., based in Wuppertal.

Side view of one of the first Bf 109E-3s following the assembly at DSF-Bozhurishte in late April 1940. The camouflage – consisting of Dark Green (L 40/70 DKH) top surfaces, mid-Green (L 40/62 DKH) on fuselage sides and Light Blue (L 40/65 DKH) on the under surfaces – was painted on at the WNF, as was the Bulgarian tricolour on the rudder. All other markings were applied in Bulgaria. Photo taken on 'Sofia' (actually Bozhurishte) airport, also used by civilian air traffic.

next page, top). In at least one documented case, the new marking was applied in much smaller size on the fuselage sides. In this case, the previous large roundel was overpainted before the new, smaller size marking was applied (see photo on next page, bottom).

Shortly after the military marking change, the Bf 109Es also received an 'arrow' (hence *Strela*) style yellow decoration, typical for Bulgarian warplanes. This consisted in a wraparound engine cowling, followed by a rearward tapering flash, running along the fuselage sides up to the tail. The colour of the Bulgarian Messerschmitts' fancy paint job was bright yellow (possibly RLM 04). On the detail photo of No. 7 (see next page, top), it can be observed that the yellow flash is painted *over* the left-out circle slice of the previous roundel, aft of the new square markings. This minor detail, coupled with another photo showing aircraft No. 5 (see photo on page 287) with new square-type marking, but *without* the yellow flash, reinforces the fact that this arrow-like flash was applied *after* the marking change. The propeller spinner was either painted yellow, or it kept its original Black Green colour. At one point, possibly in the spring of 1941, prior to the invasion of Yugoslavia and Greece by the *Wehrmacht*, the tricolour on the rudder was covered with a layer of bright yellow (RLM 04) paint.

The second batch of Bf 109Es that arrived in late August 1941 wore two distinct camouflage schemes.

This photo of No. 3 reveals a minor, nevertheless important detail unnoticed so far the aircraft's type ('Messerschmitt Me 109') and the construction number (here 'W. Nr. 5223') were applied in the factory on both sides of the fin root, in Black, over what appears to be Black Green background. The pilot nearby the aircraft is Feldfebel Yordan S. Todorov 'The Pirate'. He became the first Bulgarian fighter pilot victim of the all-out air war with the USAAF. Todorov died in action on 14 November 1943, in a botched belly landing after suffering combat wounds in a dogfight with P-38 'Lightnings'. Notice how faded the L 40/62 Dark Green appears on this photo.

Some of them retained a scheme identical to the first batch, i.e. Dark Green fuselage spine and upper engine cowling and mid-Green fuselage and engine cowling sides, over Light Blue (see photo on page 270, centre). However, photographs show that this time the upper wing surfaces were uniform Dark Green. The second camouflage scheme was simpler, consisting of only Dark Green (possibly RLM 71) over Light Blue (possibly RLM 65). The rudder was initially painted in the Bulgarian tricolour; however, this gave way very soon to 'Axis' yellow, just like the aircraft from the first batch. Latecomers also received the typical yellow wraparound engine cowling and fuselage flash.

Based on photographic evidence, the aircraft of the second batch sported smaller size serial numbers. The military marking on the fuselage was also of smaller size (as they did not have to cover the early cockade-type marking). Another notable difference in markings and codes of the second batch was the position of the wing marking and serial numbers.

This time, the square type marking was painted more towards the tip of the wing, and in smaller size. The serial number was applied on the lower wing surface inside, towards the fuselage. On a couple of aircraft the serial number was applied, in White, on the upper wing surface as well. The serial numbers ran in continuation of the first batch, *i.e.* from 11 to 19.

Unit or personal emblems were rare on Bulgarian aircraft. Luckily for modellers, the Bf 109E was an exception. Two distinct emblems are known. Both are linked to the so-called '*Galata*' Orlyak, based on the Black Sea coast from October 1941. Both emblems represent the Devil (Дявол, *Dyavol*). The former shows a devil figure as a red sketch, with no background colour (see photo and artwork on page 290), inspired by a drawing published in a wartime Bulgarian comics magazine. The latter shows also a red devil, this time in full colours, emerging from clouds, getting after his prey [undoubtedly inspired by the *Gruppe* emblem of the *Luftwaffe*'s 2./JGr. 101 (ex-5./ZG 1), later IV./JG 1, even later I./JG 1; only the colours being slightly different, because a black/white photo published in a German magazine was the inspiration]. For detail photos and artwork, see page 292.

A significant change in colours and markings happened in October 1945. At that point, the square-style 'pro-Axis' marking was replaced with roundel-style one, the so-called 'Fatherland Front' or OF-style marking, as detailed in the markings and codes chapter. Parallel to, or about the same time as this change, the camouflage colours also changed radically. The previous Dark Green over Light Blue scheme gave way to a new scheme, typical for Bulgarian single-engine fighters and bombers of the immediate post-war era. There are only a couple of photos known of a Bf 109E wearing this camouflage scheme and marking. Based on them, it is believed the camouflage colours consisted of an Olive Green basecoat with Light Grey squiggles over it, applied on upper surfaces, while the under surfaces were probably Light Blue. Quite possibly these paints were of Soviet origin, in the A-x, AGT-x or AMT-x series[34], but there is no proof for this theory. Along with changing the markings, the fighters' serial (board) numbers also restarted with 1. Therefore, the sole identifiable Bf109E in OF-marking, White 1, was not

In the case of aircraft No. 4, the fuselage marking is much smaller than the one seen on other Emils. This occurrence can be explained that this particular aircraft – often flown by top pilot Podporuchik Stoyan I. Stoyanov – did not have the previous roundel type of markings applied, as no sign of any overpainted area around the fuselage markings is visible. Notice the cannon were not installed in the wing yet.

---

34 AGT paints were glossy equivalent of AMT nitro-lacquers for mixed metal-wood construction aircraft, while A-xx-g paints were glossy equivalents of A-xx-m oil paints for all-metal aircraft.

Close-up of a Bf 109E sporting the 'Red Devil walking on clouds, looking for its prey' emblem (clearly inspired by a Luftwaffe unit emblem). Ppor. Mihail Grigorov is crouching, at left, while Ppor. Pavel Pavlov is sitting, at right.

Additional info see:
http://mmpbooks.biz/assets/BFC/08.pdf

necessarily the first *Emil* that entered VNVV service (since only four *Strelas* were still airworthy at that point, Nos. 1, 2, 5, 12, chances for a match are 25%).

In late September 1944, all distinctive yellow identification marks – linked to the Axis period – disappeared (except for the propeller cone). It has to be noted that the afore-mentioned new OF-style marking was applied on the fuselage sides and lower wing surfaces only. The Bulgarian tricolour appeared again on the tail surface, this time in form of three narrow bands applied horizontally on the entire tail surface. The Bulgarian air force triangle moved under the tailplane (horizontal stabiliser). The aircraft's individual number stayed the same style, but on fuselage sides only, now placed in front of the marking. This was the last type of identification the surviving Bulgarian *Strelas* wore. None of them soldiered long enough to receive the Communist inspired five-point red star type marking.

Excerpt from the technical manual of the Bf 109C/D, detailing various colours (including the camouflage ones) recommended to be used and the (preferred) paint manufacturer. Under 'Fertiganstrich (außen)' [Finish (outside)], the 'Sichtschutzfarbe' (literally, colour against sighting, i.e., camouflage colour) of paint producer Dr. Kurt Herberts (DKH) are listed. The same type of paints by the same company were imported by Bulgaria, for their Bf 109Es. Notice the colour shade of each paint type is spelled out in writing, and do not match those known from the RLM standard (for example, RLM 70 was black green, in contrast to the DKH L 40/70, which apparently was dark green, a lighter shade).

Flugzeug Teilbezeichnung	Baustoff	Anzahl des An-striche	Musterbezeichnung des Anstrichmittels	An-wendung	Trocken-Zeit in Stunden Luft		Bemerkung
Fertiganstrich (außen)		1×	DKH-Ölgrund L 40/41	spritzen	8	—	Nach Schablone
Führerraumaufbau (außen)		1×	DKH-Fugenkitt	ziehen			
		1×	DKH-Nitrodecklack grau L 40/51	spritzen	3	—	Beim Sichtschutz-
Fertiganstrich (außen)		1×	DKH-Sichtschutzfarbe grün L 40/71	spritzen	4	—	anstrich Farbübergang nicht scharf abgesetzt,
		1×	DKH-Sichtschutzfarbe dkl. grün L 40/70	spritzen	4	—	sondern Farbe in ca.
		1×	DKH-Sichtschutzfarbe blau L 40/65	Kreuzgang spritzen	4	—	50 mm ineinander verlaufen.
Sporn:							
Gußteile	Stahlguß	1×	DKH-Einschichtmetall 432	spritzen	4	—	
Fahrwerk:							
Gußteile	Stahlguß	1×	DKH-Einschichtmetall 432	spritzen	4	—	
Schweißteile	Stahl	1×	DKH-Einschichtmetall 432	spritzen	4	—	
Radverkleidungsgerüst		1×	DKH-Einschichtmetall 432	spritzen	4	—	
Verkleidung (innen)	Dural pl.	1×	DKH-Einschichtmetall 432	spritzen	4	—	
Verkleidung (außen)	Dural pl.	1×	DKH-Ölgrund L 40/41	spritzen	8	—	Vor dem ersten An-
		1×	DKH-Nitrodecklack grau L 40/51	Kreuzgang spritzen	3	—	strich sandstrahlen Berührungsstellen
Leitwerk:							innen sowohl wie
Querruder, Höhenruder Seitenruder, Klappen		1×	DKH-Sichtschutzfarbe blau L 40/65	Kreuzgang spritzen	4	—	außen mit Einschicht- metall vorstreichen
Einzelteile u. Bleche	Dural pl.	1×	DKH-Einschichtmetall 432	spritzen	4	—	bzw. spritzen.

IX 94

135

The first aircraft of the second batch of Bf 109Es, No. 11 – with No. 13 in the background – is photographed at "Burgas airfield, on 19 August 1942". In fact, the airfield was Sarafovo, located about 10 km north-northeast of Burgas (currently an international airport), home of the 692nd Fighter Yato of the so-called 'Galata' Orlyak.

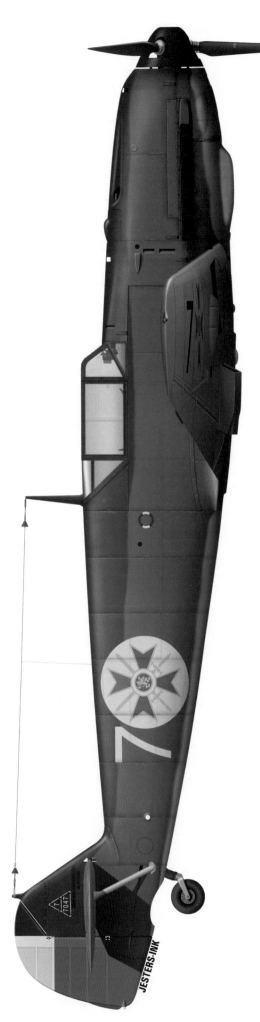

JESTERS-INK

Messerschmitt Bf 7/7047 Strela (W.Nr. 5227), No. 7/7047, 2. Iztrebitelen Orlyak, Bozhurishte airfield, June 1940. Camouflage colours: Dark Green (L 40/70 DKH) engine cowling upper area, fuselage spine and fin, mid-Green (L 40/62 DKH) fuselage sides. Wing upper surfaces the same Dark Green and mid-Green, applied in so-called 'splinter' scheme. All under surfaces Light Blue (L 40/65 DKH). White-Green-Red rudder. Propeller spinner Black Green (RLM 70), propeller blades Dark Green (RLM 71). Serial number in White on fuselage sides and Black on wing under surfaces.

This photo of 'White 7' is a good example of how the early roundel-type military marking was covered with the new, square-like marking introduced in late June 1940. Circle slices still protrude from underneath the square, faintly visible on both the fuselage (see blow-up on page 283, top) and wing under surface. The retrofitted 2 cm Ikaria wing cannon, with circular patchwork around it on the wing leading edge, is noteworthy. The depicted muscular airman is 'Pavleto', i.e. Poruchik Pavel Evstatiev Pavlov. On the back of the photo he wrote the following: "To 'Tedi' (nick name of Todor Valkov), as remembrance from Pavlov. Karlovo airfield, 29 June 1943."

Messerschmitt Bf 109E-3 Strela (WNr. 5225), No. 5/7047, 6th Iztrebitelen Polk, 1/6. Iztrebitelen Orlyak, Marno-Pole airfield, July 1940. Camouflage colours: Dark Green (L 40/70 DKH) engine cowling upper area, fuselage spine and fin, mid-Green (L 40/62 DKH) fuselage sides. Wing upper surfaces the same Dark Green and mid-Green, applied in so-called 'splinter' scheme. All under surfaces Light Blue (L 40/65 DKH). White-Green-Red rudder. Propeller spinner Black Green (RLM 70), propeller blades Dark Green (RLM 71). Serial number in White on fuselage sides and in Black on wing under surfaces.

'White 5' received its new style 'pro-Axis' markings very recently, most probably in late June 1940. The previous, roundel-type markings can faintly be seen underneath the black bordered white square. This time, the square was large enough to entirely cover the roundel. The typical Bulgarian yellow 'arrow' flash, wrapping the engine cowling and running along the fuselage sides, is yet missing. Notice the two-tone Green camouflage colours on the wings, applied in 'splinter' scheme. No. 5 suffered an accident sometime in the early summer of 1943, and was subsequently sent for repair to ASAM-Pipera workshop, located near Bucharest, Rumania, where all '109s in service with the Luftwaffe and its local allies, in need of major repair, were taken care of.

JESTERS-INK

Messerschmitt Bf 109E-3 Strela (W.Nr. 5224), No. 4/7047, 1/6. Iztrebitelen Orlyak, pilot Poruchik Stoyan I. Stoyanov, Karlovo airfield, April 1941. Camouflage colours: Dark Green (L 40/70 DKH) engine cowling upper area, fuselage spine and fin, mid-Green (L 40/62 DKH) fuselage sides. Wing upper surfaces the same Dark Green and mid-Green, applied in so-called 'splinter' scheme. All under surfaces Light Blue (L 40/65 DKH). Yellow (RLM 04) wraparound engine cowling and rearward tapering flash along the fuselage sides, as well as rudder and elevators. Propeller spinner Black Green (RLM 70) with Light Grey tip, propeller blades Dark Green (RLM 71). Serial number in White on fuselage sides and in Black on wing under surfaces.

Reportedly, No. 4 was the personal mount of Poruchik Stoyan I. Stoyanov (seen at right) in 1940/1942. Notice the unusually small fuselage marking and the two-tone wing camouflage scheme. 'White 4' was the protagonist of one of the very first accidents that happened to an Emil while in Bulgarian service, when it crashed sometime in October 1940. It was repaired and resumed duty, being eventually scrapped on 1 August 1944.

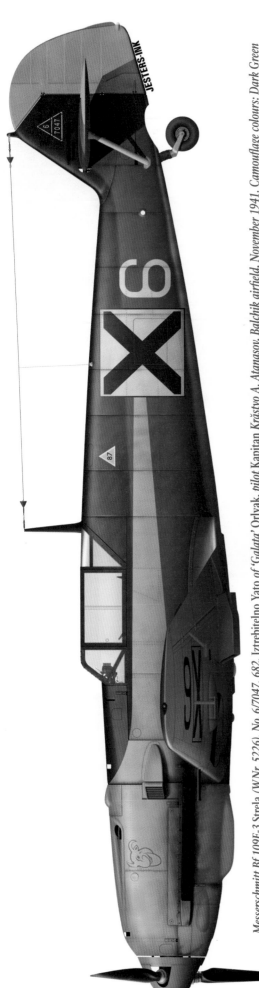

Messerschmitt Bf 109E-3 Strela (W.Nr. 5226), No. 6/7047, 682. Iztrebitelno Yato of 'Galata' Orlyak, pilot Kapitan Krăstyo A. Atanasov, Balchik airfield, November 1941. Camouflage colours: Dark Green (L 40/70 DKH) engine cowling upper area, fuselage spine and fin, mid-Green (L 40/62 DKH) fuselage sides. Wing upper surfaces the same Dark Green and mid-Green, applied in so-called 'splinter' scheme. All under surfaces Light Blue (L 40/65 DKH). Yellow (RLM 04) wraparound engine cowling and rearward tapering flash, as well as rudder and elevators. Propeller spinner Yellow (RLM 04) with Black Green (RLM 70) tip, propeller blades Dark Green (RLM 71). Serial number in White on fuselage sides and in Black on wing under surfaces. Yato emblem on engine cowling sides, in Red.

'White 6' was one of the aircraft assigned to the so-called 'Galata' Orlyak, defending the Black Sea coastline against Soviet intruders. While dispatched to the seaside airfield of Balchik, reportedly it wore an emblem, depicting a devilish figure out-lined in red. The emblem was reportedly painted on Strelas based at Balchik (682. Yato). The accident shown in this photo happened on 2 August 1942, when the aircraft piloted by Kpt. Doncho N. Dimitrov veered to the left while landing on Marno-Pole airfield, and broke the port undercarriage.

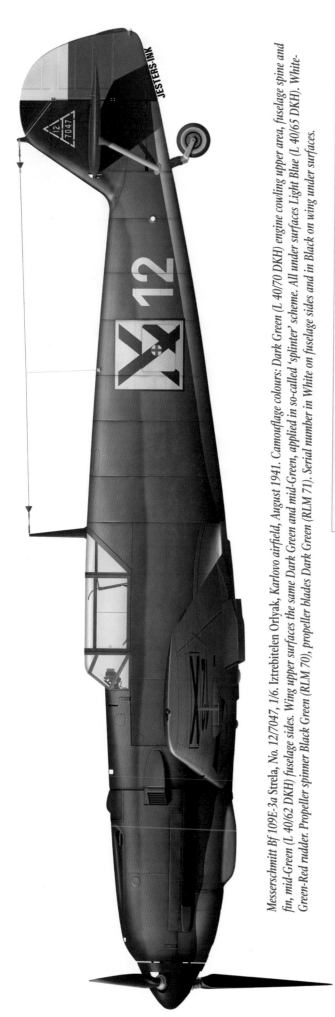

Messerschmitt Bf 109E-3a Strela, No. 12/7047, 1/6. Iztrebitelen Orlyak, Karlovo airfield, August 1941. Camouflage colours: Dark Green (L 40/70 DKH) engine cowling upper area, fuselage spine and fin, mid-Green (L 40/62 DKH) fuselage sides. Wing upper surfaces the same Dark Green and mid-Green, applied in so-called 'splinter' scheme. All under surfaces Light Blue (L 40/65 DKH). White-Green-Red rudder. Propeller spinner Black Green (RLM 70), propeller blades Dark Green (RLM 71). Serial number in White on fuselage sides and in Black on under surfaces.

This snapshot taken at Karlovo airfield in August 1941 shows the assembly of the aircraft of the second batch that had been delivered by train. Notice how the port wing is about to be lifted in position, as the light grey painted area on the lower fuselage, where the wing will be fastened to, appears to be white. Interestingly, the cockpit canopy is of earlier, rounded design, peculiar to the Bf 109E-1s and E-3s. The people in the foreground are top Bulgarian pilot Stoyan Stoyanov (at left, in uniform), who would test fly the aircraft to be handed over by the Germans to the VNVV, and two German airmen (centre and right), said to be flying instructors. The rudder was painted in Bulgarian colours at the workshop in Germany, and would very soon be overpainted with 'Axis yellow.' The wheel bay for the tail wheel was faired over with a thin plate, thus the lower tail contour appears to be straight. The camouflage scheme worn by this particular aircraft caused considerable headache to the Author. Although throughout the years he has instructed several artists on how to paint dozens and dozens of aircraft profiles based on black/white photographs, this time he could draw no firm conclusion. The camouflage scheme of aircraft No. 12 worn on the fuselage could have been either the original two-tone style (L 40/70 and L 40/62) used on the first batch of Emils, with dark green wavy stripes applied on certain areas, or plain monotone Dark Green (possibly RLM 71), and only the sunlight reflecting off the uneven surface of the stressed metal skin playing tricks on the onlooker. The first version is strengthened by the fact that the dividing line between two camouflage colours can be clearly seen on the upper area of the engine cowling on the aircraft in the background. In the end, after much debate, the balance tipped in favour of the standard Bulgarian two-tone green upper camouflage scheme.

291

Messerschmitt Bf 109E-3a Strela, No. 14/7047, 692. Iztrebitelno Yato of 'Galata' Orlyak, pilot Podporuchik Mihail G. Grigorov, Sarafovo airfield, November 1941. Camouflage colours: Dark Green (L 40/70 DKH) fuselage and fin, as well as wing upper surfaces. All under surfaces Light Blue (L 40/65 DKH). Yellow (RLM 04) wraparound engine cowling and rearward tapering flash along the fuselage sides, as well as spinner, rudder and elevators. Propeller blades Dark Green (RLM 71). Serial number in White on fuselage sides and upper wing surfaces, while in Black on wing under surfaces. Yato emblem on engine cowling sides.

No. 14 was the personal mount of Podporuchik Mihail Grigorov, identified in the archives as such (and not No. 11, as often depicted). Aboard it, Grigorov jumped on a formation of P-38 Lightnings that dive bombed Skopje railway station on 21 October 1943, claiming one of them. Strela No. 14 is depicted on Karlovo airfield, during a ceremony held on 30 January 1943. Notice the aircraft's serial number painted in white on the all-green upper wing – typical feature of the Emils of the second batch painted in monotone green. The 'Red Devil' walking on clouds, looking for its prey' emblem (clearly inspired by the Staffel emblem of the Luftwaffe's 2.JGr. 101, or later by the Gruppe emblem of IV./JG 1, only the colours being slightly different) is equally reported as Grigorov's personal sign, or as used on Strelas dispatched to Sarafovo (692. Yato), as part of the coastal defence 'Galata' Orlyak (the most likely version). The Luftwaffe Bf 109E depicted at top left was part of 2.JGr. 101 in late 1939, as identified by the Staffel emblem. The background of the shield here was yellow, opposite to the more realistic light blue, as used in the Bulgarian version (see detail photo from Bulgarian sources at top right).

292

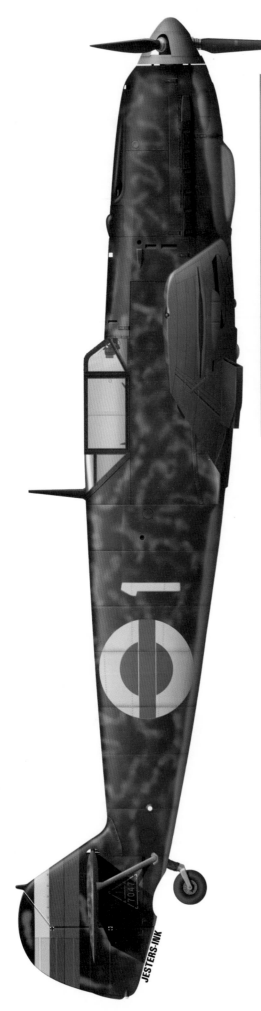

Messerschmitt Bf 109E-3 'Strela', No. 1/7047, 3/6. Iztrebitelen Orlyak, Karlovo airfield, winter of 1945/1946. Unidentified Dark Green basecoat on the upper surfaces, with equally unidentified Light Grey squiggles all over. Light Blue on lower surfaces (possibly Soviet-origin aviation paints were used). Bulgarian tricolour applied as horizontal bands across the tail surface. Yellow propeller spinner. Serial number in White on fuselage side. OF-type military marking in four positions.

This is one of the only two known photos (plus one still from a period movie, at top right) that show a Bf 109E with the so-called 'Fatherland's Front (OF)' markings, introduced immediately post war. The colours worn by the aircraft are unidentified, and left to the reader to ascertain. The Author believes the camouflage scheme was very similar to the so-called 'assault camouflage', worn by Avia B.534s and D.520s, consisting of Dark Green over Light Blue, with Light Grey squiggles all over the upper surfaces. The origin of the paints is also unclear, could be of Soviet manufacture. This original photo (which was made on 'raster' type photopaper) has been signed on the back by the top-scoring Bulgarian pilot, Cpt. Stoyan Stoyanov, and was addressed to Col. Donevski.

Appendices

List of Approximate Rank Equivalents

VNVV	Luftwaffe	USAAF
Generals		
General-polkovnik*	Generaloberst	Colonel-General
General-leytenant	Generalleutnant	Lieutenant-General
General-mahyor	Generalmajor	Major-General
Senior Officers		
Polkovnik	Oberst	Colonel
Podpolkovnik	Oberstleutnant	Lieutenant-Colonel
Mahyor******	Major	Major
Junior Officers		
Kapitan	Hauptmann	Captain
Poruchik	Oberleutnant	1st Lieutenant
Podporuchik	Leutnant	2nd Lieutenant
Kandidat-Ofitser/Ofitserski Kandidat	Oberfährnich	Chief Warrant Officer
Warrant Officers		
Zamestnik-Ofitser 1 kl.	N/A	Jr. Warrant Officer 1st Class
Zamestnik-Ofitser 2 kl.	N/A	Jr. Warrant Officer 2nd Class
Zamestnik-Ofitser 3 kl.	N/A	Jr. Warrant Officer 3rd Class
Zamestnik Kandidat-Podporuchik**	Stabsfeldwebel	Master Sergeant
NCOs		
Feldfebel/Urednik***	Hauptfeldwebel	First Sergeant
Podfeldfebel**	Oberfeldwebel	Technical Sergeant
Feldfebel-shkolnik/Urednik-shkolnik****	Feldwebel	Staff Sergeant
Podofitser	Unterfeldwebel	Sergeant
Kandidat-Podofitser	Unteroffizier	Corporal
Enlisted Men (not flying personnel, used in school)		
Efreytor/Otbornik*****	Gefreiter	Private 1st Class
Rednik	Flieger	Private

Notes:

* rank introduced in 1946, based on Soviet model (did not exist before 1946)

** rank not used

*** rank introduced in 1946, replaced *Feldfebel*

**** rank introduced in 1946, replaced *Feldfebel-shkolnik*

***** rank introduced in 1946, replaced *Efreytor*

****** The Author opted for this transliteration of the Cyrillic word майор, as it's closer to the original Bulgarian pronunciation (Mah-yor) than how the word Major is pronounced in English (Ma-dzhor).

Post-war changes of royal uniforms and the introduction of several new names for existing ranks were officially sanctioned by three orders, from 1 April, 14 May and 6 August 1947. However, these new rank names were already in use in 1946, possibly based on a preliminary order.

The Bulgarian Army has been preparing the introduction of the rank of Marshal to honour the anniversary of the ascending to the throne of Tsar Boris. Marshal uniform and paraphernalia were prepared; however, due to the tsar's death, they were not issued. Some authors mention this rank as real; however, in fact, there was no official order issued.

After an airman's rank the word '*letets*' (i.e., airman) was very often added in official documents.

Bulgarian Air Force Unit Structure

Dvoyka = Pair (2 aircraft)
Troyka = Trio (3 aircraft)
Chetvorka = Foursome (4 aircraft)
Krilo = Flight/Squad (3–4 aircraft)
Shtab = Staff (4–6 aircraft)
Vodach = unit leader
Voden = wingman (in case of a *dvoyka*)
Iztrebitelen = Fighter
Yato (pl. *yata*) = Squadron (12–16 aircraft)
Orlyak (pl. *orlyatsi*) = Group (40–54 aircraft)
Polk = Regiment/Wing (124–168 aircraft)
Văzdushna Eskadra = Air Division (included a Staff, 2nd Linear, 5th Bomber and 6th Fighter Regiments)

Examples of Unit Numbering System

1/6. *Orlyak* = 1st *Orlyak* of the 6th *Polk*
682. *Yato*, 6 = *polk* number, 8 = number of *yato* within *polk* (1 to 9), 2 = type of *yato* (2 = fighter unit)

First Actual Order of Battle of (the Still Secret) VNVV*

"With the arrival of aircraft newly delivered from abroad and their takeover by the acceptance commissions, they have to be handed over to the main storages of the V.V., after which they have to be distributed, as follows: (…) All other aircraft to be assigned to the 1st *Armeyski Orlyak*, from where to be distributed to the 1st and 3rd *Orlyaki*, as written below: (…)

3rd *Iztrebitelen Orlyak* (Fighter Group)
1st *Iztrebitelno Yato* (Fighter Squadron)
    4 Heinkel He-51, No. 5, 6, 7, 8 and number 11
    2 Fw-56, No. 9, 10 and number 11
    4 P.Z.L. P.24, No. 1, 2, 3, 4 and number 11
2nd *Iztrebitelno Yato* (Fighter Squadron)
    4 Heinkel He-51, No. 5, 6, 7, 8 and number 22
    2 Fw-56, No. 9, 10 and number 22
    4 P.Z.L. P.24, No. 1, 2, 3, 4 and number 22
3rd *Iztrebitelno Yato* (Fighter Squadron)
    4 Heinkel He-51, No. 5, 6, 7, 8 and number 33
    2 Fw-56, No. 9, 10 and number 33
    4 P.Z.L. P.24, No. 1, 2, 3, 4 and number 33
Uchebniya Orlyak (School Group) (…)

Note: The aircraft P.Z.L. P-23 and P-24, as well as the [similarly] not yet delivered aircraft Heinkel 45 and 78 [sic! most probably 51], will be added according to the afore-described distribution when they will arrive in Bulgaria."

*Issued at an uncertain date, probably in late 1936 (a reference to "11 January next year" is mentioned in the text).